NIXON'S GAMBLE

NIXON'S GAMBLE

How a President's Own Secret Government
Destroyed His Administration

RAY LOCKER

Guilford, Connecticut

An imprint of Rowman & Littlefield

Distributed by NATIONAL BOOK NETWORK

British Library Cataloguing in Publication Information Available

Library of Congress Cataloging-in-Publication Data Available

ISBN 978-1-4930-0931-2 (hardcover : alk. paper)
ISBN 978-1-4930-1945-8 (electronic)

♾™ The paper used in this publication meets the minimum requirements of American National Standard for Information Sciences—Permanence of Paper for Printed Library Materials, ANSI/ NISO Z39.48-1992.

To Maggie and Abbey,
the lights of my life

Contents

Contents

Prologue

BITTER AND COMBATIVE, RICHARD NIXON SAT FACING MEMBERS OF A Washington grand jury who had flown to California to hear him, on June 25, 1975, testify on behalf of his former director of the Federal Bureau of Investigation, L. Patrick Gray. Nixon had resisted testifying since he resigned the previous August, claiming his health, including blood clots in his legs that required surgery the previous fall, kept him from traveling. So the grand jury came to the makeshift courtroom at the Coast Guard station in San Clemente, California, where Nixon was living out his exile.

Prosecutors wanted to know if Gray had lied under oath when he testified that he did not know of several wiretaps the FBI had placed on the telephones of a navy enlisted man, Yeoman Charles Radford, who was suspected of leaking White House secrets to the press. Nixon knew Gray had not lied because he had never told Gray about the wiretaps or much of anything else, for that matter. His entire White House, Nixon testified, was based on secrecy and the need to know. His Secretaries of Defense and State often learned what Nixon was doing through the newspaper or by accident. Few knew that he had a secret team of investigators, nicknamed the Plumbers, who spied on those suspected of leaking secrets. Gray had no need to know of the wiretaps, so Nixon felt no need to tell him.

You and the prosecutors, Nixon said, can "kick the hell out of us for wiretapping and for the Plumbers and the rest," but because of secrecy "we have changed the world." Secrecy shortened the Vietnam War, and "the secret Cambodian bombings saved at least ten thousand lives." Secrecy enabled him to reach an arms control deal with the Soviet Union. If he had to negotiate in public, Nixon said, "with no security whatever, then the United States is finished as a great power. Maybe a lot of people don't care, but I care a great deal. I think all of you care a great deal.

"That is what Yeoman Radford is about, and I would strongly urge the Special Prosecutor don't open that can of worms, because there is even more."[1]

There were *many* more. All presidents keep secrets. It has been impossible to run a government without them. Franklin Roosevelt developed the atomic bomb without ever telling his vice president, Harry Truman, who only learned of it after Roosevelt died and Truman became president. Nixon, however, sat scorned and humiliated in the witness chair because he had raised secrecy to an art form, gambled with history and lost.

Nixon's secrecy helped him reach audacious goals that reshaped US foreign policy and created an enduring personal legacy. Reaching those goals, however, cost him the presidency.

Nixon wanted to restore the relations with China that the United States cut off in 1949, when Mao Tse-tung's Communists overwhelmed the feeble, pro-US government of Chiang Kai-shek. Twenty years of isolation had left eight hundred million people on the fringe of world affairs, a mystery to all but a few westerners allowed to travel there. Antipathy toward China, much of it drummed up by Nixon and his fellow members of the pro-Chiang China Lobby, rose even more after China intervened in the Korean War. US policymakers since then had been paralyzed by the fear of another Chinese horde, particularly in Vietnam. If he won the China gamble, Nixon knew, his other plans would fall into place.

He wanted to thaw the Cold War with the Soviet Union and slow down the costly arms race, which had the world on edge. Both sides' deep nuclear arsenals could destroy the world many times over. Fear of mutual destruction was no substitute for real détente, Nixon believed, and he sought a world where the rivals could talk without bluster or histrionics.

In Southeast Asia, Nixon wanted to end the war in Vietnam that he knew could not be won on the battlefield. More than thirty thousand US troops had already died there, and the American people lacked the patience for more fighting. But Nixon needed the leverage the war gave him with both the Soviets and Chinese, because a unilateral withdrawal would show weakness. So Nixon had to bleed the United States out of Vietnam while simultaneously appearing to be so unpredictable that China and the Soviet Union could not take him for granted. His national security adviser, Henry Kissinger, would spend three years in secret talks with the North Vietnamese while the rest of Nixon's government, as well as South Vietnam, remained in the dark.

Each of those goals had committed and well-connected opponents. The Pentagon believed any concessions to the distrusted Chinese and Soviets weakened America. Nixon and the China Lobby had sold an entire generation of Americans that Mao could still be driven from power and Chiang restored. They would see any deal with the Chinese communists as a betrayal. The Soviets were even more dangerous, as they imprisoned Eastern Europe behind an Iron Curtain of repression. In Vietnam, a unilateral withdrawal would only embolden America's enemies by showing a "provocative weakness."

Twenty years in Washington, a city of multilayered intrigues and calcified interest groups, showed Nixon that frontal attacks failed, so he gambled that he could reach these three huge goals in secret. If they knew Nixon's true plans, the bureaucracy and interests would try to stop him. Bureaucracies, Nixon believed, inevitably assumed the shapes and colors of the constituencies they served. State Department diplomats swirled in a global cocktail circuit that prized cosmopolitan wit and urbanity over the patriotism and values of heartland Americans. The military too often believed it could solve every problem by force. Nixon knew the military would consider his plans to be appeasement; they could scuttle diplomacy with a well-timed whisper in the ear of an easily alarmed senator. He believed the CIA had cost him the 1960 election, so Nixon distrusted them and could not have their "facts" ruin his plans. They, too, had powerful friends in Congress and had to be kept in the dark.

He planned to use a revived National Security Council modeled on what he had observed as Dwight Eisenhower's vice president. Ike's NSC assembled information from various government agencies and then sifted it for the president's decision. Nixon wanted more. He, unlike, Eisenhower, had no intention of letting the Secretary of State or the CIA director guide his policies. Nixon would do that himself and shield his decisions from the bureaucracy, and, by extension, Congress.

Nixon, Kissinger wrote, "had an extraordinary instinct for the jugular." He realized conditions were changing, and he exploited them. "If the [National Security Council] system of elaborating options interested him for anything, it was for the intelligence it supplied him about the views of a bureaucracy he distrusted and for the opportunity it provided to camouflage his own aims."[2]

That put Nixon in a race against powerful institutions that often bowed to no one, not even a president. He had mastered Washington as a young congressman and would not let it beat him. His early scheming, however, created resentments and distrust, which further fueled his paranoia. His secrecy meant he had to rely too heavily on the men around him, but not all of them shared Nixon's agenda. When their interests inevitably collided, they dumped Nixon to save themselves.

Before the collapse, Nixon restarted US relations with China, toasted Mao, and walked atop the Great Wall of China. He reached a nuclear arms deal with the Russians, which enabled the eventual collapse of the Soviet Union in 1991. He fashioned a peaceful end to the Vietnam War that created at least a smokescreen behind which US troops could finally leave while the South Vietnamese government remained standing, however shakily. Nixon created the template for the modern national security state by consolidating power in the White House and reducing the influence of the Departments of Defense and State. He subordinated the intelligence community, and he pushed plans that anticipated the intelligence fusion that followed the 9/11 attacks. Much of today's federal government bears the enduring stamp of Richard Nixon as much as anyone, including President Barack Obama, is loath to admit it.

Those victories came with a tremendous personal cost. Nixon never inspired great fervor, and he lacked Lyndon Johnson's powers of persuasion. No one did anything because Dick Nixon wanted something; they often did so in spite of it. Nixon had to fight for everything he earned, and he knew what he had to do to win. That fervor and determination inspired some life-long loyalties as well as created a cadre determined to destroy him. When he stumbled, they set upon him, and they never gave him the benefit of the doubt, which he had never given to others. By August 9, 1974, when his marine helicopter lifted off the south lawn of the White House to carry Nixon to exile in California, his humiliation obscured his successes, perhaps forever.

Those were the circumstances that led the ailing and beleaguered ex-president to the witness stand in San Clemente, where he tried to spare Gray, an almost slavishly loyal subordinate crushed by Nixon's methods, from going to trial on federal perjury charges. Nixon was also trying to spare himself long enough to show that his gamble was worth it to himself and the American people.

Part I: Taking the Gamble

CHAPTER ONE

Origins

NIXON RESORTED TO SECRECY, BECAUSE WHAT HE PLANNED BORE LITTLE resemblance to the Richard Nixon so many Americans thought they knew. His was the classic American story of rising above humble means to make it to the top. Nixon was born January 9, 1913, in Yorba Linda, California, about thirty miles east of Los Angeles in rural Orange County. His father, Frank, was a failed citrus rancher who spent the day of his son's birth trying to save a freezing grove. The family, Nixon would later write, lived a "hard but happy" life, and eventually they had enough money to send young Richard to nearby Whittier College and to fight unsuccessfully to save two of their children— oldest son Harold and youngest son Arthur—from dying from tuberculosis.[1] It was a life marked by faith, hard work, suspicion of elites, suffering, and sadness. His mother, Hannah, raised the five Nixon boys and tried to navigate the stormy moods of her husband, who cultivated the standard resentments of an unseen Establishment preying on hard-working Americans. "My father had an Irish quickness both to anger and to mirth," Nixon wrote, and he learned not to cross him. "Perhaps my own aversion to personal confrontations dates back to these early recollections."[2]

After Whittier, Nixon received a scholarship to the new Duke University law school, where he studied diligently and earned high marks but failed to land a job with law firms in New York or Los Angeles. His trips to the elite law firms, such as New York's Sullivan & Cromwell, stirred Nixon's resentment of the Eastern Establishment that he thought condescended to him. His application to join J. Edgar Hoover's FBI was rejected because he was deemed "lacking in aggressiveness."[3] Nixon returned home to handle commercial litigation for local oil companies at a Whittier firm. While performing in a local theater production, he met fellow cast member Thelma "Pat" Ryan. He pursued her avidly, and after a few unsuccessful proposals, she agreed to marry him in 1940. Shortly after the Japanese attack on Pearl Harbor, the couple moved to Washington, where Nixon handled tire rationing at the federal Office of Price Administration. The work bored him, and like millions of other young American men, Nixon entered the navy in August 1942.

No one would mistake Nixon's war service for that of his longtime rival, John F. Kennedy, who rescued his crewmembers after the Japanese sank his boat, the PT-109, in action near the Solomon Islands. Nixon also served in the Pacific, but he handled logistics on Guadalcanal and other islands. Mustered out of the navy on New Year's Day 1946, Nixon faced a crossroads. He could either return home to practice law or find another path. That path found him.

Local business leaders in Orange County had spent ten years lamenting their inability to oust their local congressman, Democrat Jerry Voorhis, an avid New Dealer first swept into office in 1936 with Franklin Roosevelt's second-term landslide. GOP leaders considered 1946 as potentially another lost opportunity until banker Herman Perry, who had served with Nixon on the Whittier College board of trustees, remembered his former associate. He found Nixon, then still in Baltimore finishing out his military service, and asked if he wanted to run for Congress. Nixon said yes, and the local Republican leaders anointed him to challenge Voorhis. His backers soon realized they had found a dogged candidate, who would soon earn an enduring reputation as an aggressive campaigner willing to do anything to win.

Nixon called Voorhis a pawn of organized labor and its political action committee, an accusation that drew perilously close to calling Voorhis a socialist at a time when the Red Scare was gaining strength and the Iron Curtain had fallen across much of Eastern Europe. Nixon caught Voorhis flat-footed; the gentlemanly incumbent had never faced someone this driven. Nixon's attacks were engineered by one of the masters of the new age of political consulting—Murray Chotiner, who would serve Nixon's baser political needs for the rest of his career. Nixon won by fifteen thousand votes, as dozens of Republicans swept into office and took control of Congress for the first time since the early 1930s. The thirty-three-year-old Nixon was going to Washington with the reputation as a politician willing to do anything to win. "Of course I knew Jerry Voorhis wasn't a communist," Nixon told a young associate. "I had to win. That's the thing you don't understand. The important thing is to win."[4]

Freshman representatives were expected to be seen but not heard, and voters often used their first chance to wash out those swept into office by a national wave. Nixon vowed to not let that happen. He found the issue he needed in early 1948 as a member of the House Un-American Activities Committee (HUAC). First created in 1938, the committee had lost much of its appeal by 1946, when the Republicans hoping to retake the White House in 1948 used it as a weapon to attack Truman and the Democrats as soft on communism. Nixon seized the platform with gusto. In the summer of 1948, hearings on communists in the Roosevelt and Truman administrations focused on Alger Hiss, a diplomat who had advised Roosevelt at the 1945 Yalta Peace Conference and the creation of the United Nations. A former associate, *Time* magazine writer Whittaker Chambers, claimed he and Hiss had been members of the Communist Party in the 1930s and that Hiss had resisted when Chambers begged him to leave the party. It was not a completely new accusation; a 1945 report by ardent anticommunist priest John Cronin, who had received leaked files from the FBI, had called Hiss "the most influential Communist" in the State Department.[5] Hiss, now the president of the Carnegie Endowment for International Peace, angrily denied Chambers's accusations. Nixon believed otherwise and enlisted the help of FBI director J. Edgar Hoover, who also suspected Hiss was a Communist and Soviet spy. Hoover sent confidential FBI files to Nixon, often using young agent William C. Sullivan, a future head of the Bureau's intelligence division. Nixon never stopped seeking new ways to damage Hiss, even as the liberal elites rallied behind him.

Nixon knew Hiss was lying, but he needed to test his evidence, lest he reach too far and end up empty-handed. He called Michigan Republican Homer Ferguson, whose Senate subcommittee was also investigating suspected communists. Ferguson deputized his staff counsel, William Rogers, to help Nixon, which kindled a decades-long relationship between the two men. The handsome and friendly Rogers had the social ease that Nixon never gained. He reviewed Nixon's evidence and told the congressman, who was just six months his senior, that Chambers was telling the truth.[6] More work remained, however. Hiss also had influential Republican friends, including John Foster Dulles, the prominent Sullivan & Cromwell partner and Republican Thomas Dewey's likely Secretary of State if he beat Truman that November. At the time, a Dewey victory seemed inevitable, which forced Nixon to tread carefully. Nixon and a House colleague went to New York on August 11 to meet Dulles and his brother, Allen, at the Roosevelt Hotel, the Dewey campaign headquarters.[7] Nixon showed the brothers the evidence, and Foster Dulles was convinced. "It's almost impossible to believe," he said, "but Chambers knows Hiss."

Blessed with Dulles's imprimatur, Nixon kept hammering at Hiss. Nixon's fortunes depended heavily on Chambers, "one of the most disheveled persons I had ever seen," Nixon wrote later. So much of the deck seemed stacked against Nixon. Hiss represented the elite, highly educated, and credentialed America, while Nixon, and certainly Chambers, were outsiders who had to fight for acceptance. But they won. Hiss was eventually convicted of perjury in January 1951 and sent to prison, while Nixon, flush with success, learned the benefits of fighting political battles in the media. The case, Nixon realized, had turned him "into one of the most controversial figures in Washington, bitterly opposed by the most respected and influential liberal journalists and opinion leaders of the time." He professed not to care, but the rejection gnawed at him, and the lessons from the Hiss case were those to which he turned throughout the rest of his career.

By 1950, the thirty-seven-year-old Nixon was a Republican rising star and the party's best choice to challenge two-term Democrat Sheridan Downey, who suddenly retired. In his place rose Representative Helen Gahagan Douglas of Los Angeles, a former actress and liberal activist married to actor Melvyn Douglas. She never had a chance. Downey endorsed Nixon, who relied on Chotiner and his negative campaign playbook to make sure Douglas was pigeonholed as a naïve liberal out of step with ordinary Californians. Chotiner printed campaign flyers on pink papers to highlight her record, and Gahagan Douglas was dubbed the "Pink Lady." Nixon won by almost twenty percentage points but also locked in his reputation as a dirty campaigner.

Nixon kept a low profile in the Senate, but the 1952 presidential election created a new opportunity. Truman, the polls showed, had virtually no chance to win a second full term. Republican Dwight Eisenhower, the general who had led Allied forces in Europe during World War II, seemed almost certain to win the presidency. If elected, Eisenhower would be sixty-two when he took office. He needed a young running mate willing to do negative campaigning for someone who appeared above politics. Nixon, thirty-nine, knew he could do that job. He outmaneuvered his rivals at the Republican National Convention, and Eisenhower asked Nixon to join him on the ticket.

Then Nixon's rise hit a potentially fatal snag. In September, various publications had reported that a group of rich Californians had contributed to a special fund that subsidized Nixon's travel around California and the country. His enemies, angered by his 1946 and 1950 campaigns and the Hiss case, gleefully seized on the fund issue. A nervous Eisenhower did not immediately jump to his running mate's defense. Aided by Chotiner and William Rogers, Nixon decided to save his spot on the ticket by delivering a nationally televised speech to defend himself. He entered the El Capitan Theater in Los Angeles on September 23, to face the cameras.[8] What followed was a display of earnest pleading and bravado, as Nixon laid out his finances for the entire nation and issued a steel-plated challenge wrapped in profamily velvet. One of the gifts from the fund was a package that a donor said the Nixons needed to pick up at the Baltimore train station, Nixon said. "It was a little cocker spaniel dog in a crate that he sent all the way from Texas. Black-and-white-spotted. And our little girl—Tricia, the six-year-old, named it Checkers. And you know the kids love the dog and I just want to say this right now, that regardless of what they say about it, we're gonna keep it."[9]

The address, immortalized as the "Checkers Speech," received almost universal acclaim. Eisenhower, relieved by the speech, greeted Nixon at the airport in Wheeling, West Virginia, and delivered his blessing. "You're my boy!" he told Nixon.[10] Granted his reprieve, Nixon gladly performed Eisenhower's campaign dirty work. He called Truman soft on communism and Secretary of State Dean Acheson an appeaser of the Soviet Union. They won easily in November. He maintained that role as vice president. Eisenhower gave him little of consequence to do, so Nixon dogged Democrats for the next eight years and built political support from Republicans around the country. As a member of the National Security Council, Nixon mostly watched as the Dulles brothers—John and Allen, the Secretary of State and CIA director—dominated policymaking. Nixon won praise for his composure during a 1958 trip to South America, which was marred by protests. Students in Peru threw objects at him while protesters in Caracas, Venezuela, attacked the car in which he was riding with his interpreter, an army colonel named Vernon Walters. They survived the terrifying experience, which bonded Nixon and Walters for the next fifteen years. Nixon returned home as a hero. A year later, Eisenhower sent Nixon to Moscow, where he engaged in an impromptu debate with Soviet leader Nikita Khrushchev over the relative merits of capitalism and communism. While press coverage was mixed, Nixon's fellow Republicans loved it. By 1960, when term limits forced Eisenhower to leave office, Nixon had no credible challengers for the Republican nomination for president.

From a crowded Democratic field emerged John F. Kennedy, who matched Nixon's strength with more of his own. While Nixon was young, Kennedy was younger. Nixon served in the war; Kennedy was a war hero. Nixon, as he showed with the Checkers Speech, was good on television; Kennedy was a TV star blessed with great hair, charm, and a beautiful wife. And after eight years of an aging Eisenhower, the first president to turn seventy while in office, Kennedy provided the sharper contrast Americans wanted. Nixon faced another challenge. After fourteen years as an unrivaled Cold Warrior, Nixon found himself being crowded on the right. The Soviet Union, Kennedy claimed, had opened a "missile gap" that left United States vulnerable to Russian nuclear weapons. On Cuba, where leader Fidel Castro had dashed into the arms of the Soviet Union, Kennedy said the Eisenhower administration was too soft. Kennedy, who had been briefed by the administration, knew there was no missile gap and that the Central Intelligence Agency was training an army of Cuban exiles to topple Castro. Nixon was prevented from saying anything because doing so would violate secrecy. Kennedy continued to press his advantage, and, boosted by his appearance in the four nationally televised debates, won a narrow victory. Nixon resented what he considered the Kennedys' unfair campaign tactics and the favorable treatment the Democratic candidate received from the campaign press. Although his supporters wanted him to challenge suspected vote fraud in Illinois and Texas that could have stolen the election, Nixon took the loss gracefully in public, but he believed he had been robbed of his best, if not only, chance at the White House. That feeling was magnified again two years later after he lost an ill-conceived race for governor of California that ended with a rambling, drunken election-night news conference.

Nixon seemed finished, but his fortunes were unexpectedly revived when Kennedy was killed in Dallas on November 22, 1963. That made Lyndon Johnson, the larger-than-life Texan, president. He used his considerable wiles and Kennedy's memory to pass the Civil Rights Act and to roll to a huge election victory in 1964 over conservative Republican Senator Barry Goldwater of Arizona. The following year, Johnson created the Great Society, the largest expansion of progressive policies since the New Deal. But the growing war in Vietnam soon turned into a perpetual crisis for Johnson. Southern whites soured on national Democrats after the Civil Rights Act and urban riots that scarred black neighborhoods in cities across the country. Nixon, who was then the one viable Republican with a national reputation, moved to exploit the growing discontent. He spent 1966 campaigning everywhere for Republicans, rebuilding his national base as Democrats suffered huge losses. By 1968, Nixon aimed at another shot at the Republican nomination, and many Americans braced for a return of Tricky Dick Nixon.

Eight years out of office had changed Nixon. He began to see a world with different shades of red and signaled that a future Nixon presidency would not resemble his old rhetoric. In July 1967, Nixon called for more trade and contact with the Soviet Union, while still recognizing the Soviets' ultimate aim of spreading communism around the world. A *Foreign Affairs* article in October 1967 found Nixon ruminating on relations with the Soviet Union and Communist China.[11] He laid out the benefits of stronger relationships with communist powers while remaining vigilant. China, he wrote, could not remain "forever outside the family of nations, there to nurture its fantasies, cherish its hates and threaten its neighbors."[12] His acceptance speech at the

Republican National Convention in August 1968 left even more clues, as he extended "the hand of friendship to all people, to the Russian people, to the Chinese people."[13] The *New York Times* editorialized about this new direction and wondered about its authenticity: "Mr. Nixon's real task in the campaign will be to persuade skeptics that his positions reflect conviction, not expediency."[14] But in a race against Vice President Hubert Humphrey, an exuberant liberal, Nixon would always be the more conservative choice. Most pundits viewed the "new Nixon" of 1968 as mostly a triumph of packaging over substance and not the opening moves of a future president planning to reshape the global political order.

To put his plans into motion, Nixon first needed to get elected. That seemed assured after the disastrous Democratic Convention in Chicago marred by clashes between police and antiwar protesters. Democrats appeared divided and chaotic. Third-party candidate George Wallace, the Democratic former governor of Alabama, was peeling away votes in the once-solid Democratic South. By Labor Day, Nixon had opened a twelve-point lead over Humphrey in the latest Gallup poll.

Then, instead of a coronation procession for Nixon, the campaign turned into an actual race. Humphrey and Wallace drew closer in the polls. Humphrey moved left and urged a halt in the massive bombing raids on North Vietnam. Nixon had seen this happen before. Eight years earlier, Kennedy had turned final-month developments into the narrow win that sent him to the White House. The last-minute boost that threatened to put Humphrey in the White House could come from only one place—Paris, where American negotiators were making progress in peace talks with the North Vietnamese. A break there, coupled with an end to the bombing of the North, might provide enough progress to show voters that the beleaguered Johnson administration could finally end a war most Americans wanted to end. Nixon said he had a secret plan to end the war, which would be trumped if Johnson, and by extension Humphrey, could actually show they could end the war.

Nixon could not let that happen.

He and his campaign had no one at the table in Paris, and Nixon vowed not to interfere publicly. "We all hope in this room that there's a chance that current negotiations may bring an honorable end to that war," Nixon said in his convention acceptance speech, "and we will say nothing during this campaign that might destroy that chance."[15] Nixon had other means to exert his will. His allies in the old China Lobby had contacts with the South Vietnamese government. John Mitchell, Nixon's law partner and campaign manager, reached out to one of the lobby's most prominent members—Anna Chennault, the exotically beautiful wife of former US general Claire Chennault, whose Flying Tigers air squadron had dueled Japanese Zeros over China in World War II. Head of Women for Nixon, Mrs. Chennault contacted the South Vietnamese ambassador to the United States, Bui Diem, to relay Nixon's message to South Vietnamese president Nguyen Van Thieu: Johnson will sell out South Vietnam in Paris just to get a peace deal. Nixon, Chennault's argument went, would not abandon South Vietnam as the Democrats abandoned Chiang in 1949.

Perhaps failure in Paris was inevitable. Although they had been battered after the Tet Offensive earlier in the year, the North and Viet Cong knew American morale had taken a beating. They also knew the 565,000 US troops in South Vietnam were the main thing keeping Thieu's government afloat, that the American people were growing tired of the war, and anything that reduced the US commitment would also hurt the South Vietnamese government. Thieu knew that, too. US pressure alone not would force Thieu to take an agreement he knew would destroy his country.

Still, a deal seemed possible. Johnson had set three conditions to stop bombing North Vietnam: the North Vietnamese had to respect the demilitarized zone separating the two countries, allow the South Vietnamese to join the Paris talks, and stop the artillery barrages on southern cities. The North had resisted those conditions for months, but they had finally agreed if the United States would stop bombing North Vietnam. On October 7, Johnson told Nixon about the three conditions and the chance for a stop in the bombing. He also said that any move by the South Vietnamese to bail out on the talks would risk the deal.[16] Nixon knew this raised the chance for a bombing halt and possible peace deal and tried to scuttle it, even as his campaign accused Johnson of making cynical maneuvers in Paris to gain political capital. Nixon mentioned rumors of a bombing halt but said he doubted that Johnson had played any part in such trickery.[17] Johnson had tricked no one; the North had agreed to his terms, so he stopped bombing North Vietnam. Nixon knew all of that, but he pretended otherwise. He was doing what Kennedy did eight years earlier with the missile gap and Cuba.

Johnson knew what Nixon was doing. Johnson told an audience in New York on October 27 that Nixon was making "ugly and unfair charges" about the administration's conduct of the peace talks.[18] "There's not a man in all this world that wants progress [in Paris] as much as I do, and there's not anybody that's doing more about it, either." Meanwhile, Johnson knew how far Nixon was going to sabotage the peace talks, which was a potential violation of one of the nation's oldest laws—the Logan Act of 1799, which said any interference by a US citizen in the negotiations of the government was treason.

During an October 30 telephone call, Johnson told his longtime mentor, Senator Richard Russell of Georgia, that Nixon was telling the South Vietnamese that Johnson was selling them out.[19] On the Nixon campaign plane, Johnson said, Representative Melvin Laird of Wisconsin, a longtime Republican member of the Appropriations Committee, was also spinning the campaign press corps about a possible last-minute bombing halt to boost Humphrey. That gave Nixon the advantage of floating the rumor while then refuting it to seem above the fray.

The Paris talks were scheduled for November 6, the day after the election, and Johnson still believed Thieu's representatives would attend. Johnson wanted the North and South to negotiate as equals, so he refused to have the United States negotiate directly with the North. In Saigon, US ambassador Ellsworth Bunker continued to lobby Thieu to send his negotiators to Paris, while Johnson told General Creighton Abrams, the top US commander in Vietnam, that the bombing halt was just part of the overall negotiations. The commanders agreed with the halt. They knew that stopping the bombing in the fall would have little effect on the ground war, and if they needed to resume bombing, they could do so easily. Thieu, his ear turned by Nixon's temptations, still refused to budge.

Johnson knew what Chennault and Bui Diem were telling Thieu, because the FBI, CIA, and National Security Agency were spying on them and the South Vietnamese government. NSA intercepts detailed Bui Diem's messages to his superiors in Saigon. The FBI was also monitoring Nixon's campaign, including tracking, but not bugging, their phone calls. As the chance for any progress in Paris slipped away, a frustrated Johnson on November 2 called Everett Dirksen of Illinois, the Republican leader in the Senate and Johnson's old friend.

"Now I'm reading their hand," Johnson told Dirksen. "I don't want this to get in the campaign. And they oughtn't to be doing this. This is treason."[20]

Dirksen agreed. Nixon had to stop.

"I think it would shock America if a principal candidate was playing with a source like this on a matter this important," Johnson said. "I don't want to do that. But if they're going to put this kind of stuff out, they ought to know that we know what they're doing. I know who they're talking to and I know what they're saying. And my judgment is that Nixon ought to play it just like he has all along, that it's not going to affect the election one way or another."

Dirksen said he would call Nixon directly to tell him Johnson's concerns and then have Nixon call Johnson.

"I know this," Johnson said, "that they're contacting a foreign power in the middle of a war."

"That's a mistake," Dirksen told his old friend.

Dirksen reached Nixon and the Republican candidate called Johnson, who was at his Texas ranch, from the campaign in Los Angeles the following day. Nixon did what Johnson expected; he lied.

"I just want you to know that I'm not trying to interfere with your conduct of it," Nixon told Johnson. "I'll only do what you want and [Secretary of State Dean] Rusk want me to do. But I'll do anything."

"Well, that's good, Dick," Johnson replied, who knew Nixon was lying.[21]

Nixon would continue his denials in his memoirs, published in 1978, five years after Johnson's death. He wrote that Johnson was furious about comments made by Robert Finch, the California lieutenant governor and Nixon campaign aide. "Bryce Harlow urged me to call Johnson to calm him down—and I did so Sunday morning. . . . He calmed down, and the rest of our conversation was relatively cordial."[22] Nixon did not know Johnson had recorded the call.

On November 4, Johnson and his team had to shoot down a developing story by the *Christian Science Monitor*, then a newspaper with a wide readership in Washington, that sources in Saigon were saying that Thieu would boycott the talks because of assurances from the Nixon campaign. Johnson wanted the story killed to protect his sources of information, most importantly the CIA, FBI, and NSA, and keep his knowledge out of the press.[23] A telegram from Walt Rostow, Johnson's national security adviser, to the president in Texas summed up his position as well as those of Rusk and Secretary of Defense Clark Clifford. "So far as the information based on such sources is considered, all three of us agreed: (A) Even if the story breaks, it was judged too late to have a significant impact on the election. (B) The viability of the man elected as President was involved as well as subsequent relations between him and Johnson. (C) Therefore, the common recommendations was that we should not encourage such stories and hold tight the data we have." Rostow then appended more proof of Chennault's collusion with Nixon's campaign, reporting the details of surveillance that showed that shortly after being contacted by the *Monitor* reporter, Chennault left her home for the Vietnamese embassy. After thirty minutes there, she then traveled to an unmarked office on Pennsylvania Avenue that housed a Nixon campaign office. She then went back to the Vietnamese embassy for another meeting, Rostow's report said.

Johnson's hopes died by November 5. Thieu said his government's representatives would not go to Paris. Nixon would end the day the next president. He won with 43.4 percent of the vote, about five hundred thousand more than Humphrey's total. Johnson sent Nixon a congratulatory telegram and another to Humphrey to boost his spirits. On November 6, Johnson announced the talks in Paris were dead.

In 1991, Nixon wrote British politician Jonathan Aitken, who was writing what would be a very positive biography of him, that the claims of the Chennault affair were a "canard." Thieu, Nixon wrote, would never have agreed to what Johnson wanted, so any overture to him from anyone would have made no difference. Chennault, he wrote, "used to bend John Mitchell's ear as to what was going on in Vietnam and what our position should be." Mitchell would listen, puff his pipe, and say little to Nixon about "this massive information and misinformation which came to his attention." "I did not and I am confident Mitchell did not ever considered [sic] using Chennault as a channel to get to Thieu."[24] Coming at the end of his life but before the availability of records and telephone calls that showed the extent of his campaign's involvement with Chennault, Nixon's claims to Aitken are hard to square with the record. Nixon knew the extent of the negotiations for the bombing halt and the potential damage it could have on his chances for the presidency. He could not afford to leave anything to chance, and he would spend his entire presidency trying to cover the tracks he left with the Chennault affair.

Nixon had played a secret, high-stakes game of backchannel diplomacy and won; he would not forget the lesson. His success came at a price higher than he imagined at the time. Enough of Nixon's rivals and allies knew what he had done. The "New Nixon" was a sham. "If this thing ever got out, this war is over, as far as the American people are concerned," Rusk told Johnson on November 9. "Yes, yes, I think so," the president replied.[25] Nixon's allies and future members of his administration also realized their future boss was someone whose every word had to be verified before it could be trusted.

CHAPTER TWO

Nixon Takes Charge (1969)

HUDDLED IN THEIR DARK OVERCOATS TO BEAT THE WIND AND COLD DRIZZLE, the leaders of official Washington gathered on the platform on the East Front of the Capitol facing the National Mall on January 20, 1969, to witness Richard Milhous Nixon sworn in as the nation's thirty-seventh president. Nixon had long imagined this moment, believing it should have happened eight years earlier. With his wife, Pat, holding the two Milhous family Bibles, each open to Isaiah 2:4, Nixon took the oath of office from his fellow Californian, Chief Justice Earl Warren, and then turned to address the crowd of 250,000 Americans gathered below him. Nixon spoke to a tired nation seeking direction and vowed to provide it. His "government will listen," Nixon said. "We will strive to listen in new ways—to the voice of quiet anguish, the voices that speak without words, the voices of the heart—to the injured voices, the anxious voices, the voices that have despaired of being heard. Those who have been left out, we will try to bring in. Those left behind, we will help to catch up." "It was as if he had rays coming out of his eyes," said Nixon's new chief of staff, H. R. Haldeman.[1] Gone, as influential columnist James Reston would write in the next day's *New York Times*, was "the hawkish, political, combative, anti-Communist, anti-Democratic Nixon of the past."[2] In his place stood an assured fifty-six-year-old man trying to distance himself from his earlier image. "As we learn to go forward together at home, let us also seek to go forward together with all mankind," Nixon continued. "Let us take as our goal: where peace is unknown, make it welcome; where peace is fragile, make it strong, where peace is temporary, make it permanent. After a period of confrontation, we are entering an era of negotiation."[3]

Perhaps Nixon actually meant the words when he said them. After two consecutive summers of riots burning the heart of American cities, and a president, Lyndon Johnson, whose lack of candor spawned the term *credibility gap*, the two hundred million people Nixon now led wanted to believe him. But on the inaugural platform behind Nixon sat members of his new team who already suspected his words were only for show. They, particularly the incoming Secretaries of Defense and State—Melvin Laird and William Rogers—sat straight-faced and passive, knowing that Nixon had approved a plan stripping their departments of much of the autonomy and influence they had enjoyed during the Johnson administration and replacing it with a centralized foreign policy run out of the White House by Nixon himself. The pomp and ceremony at the Capitol belied the turmoil already bubbling within Nixon's administration.

Nixon wiped away the uplifting words of his inaugural speech that afternoon, when he issued National Security Decision Memorandum 2, which locked in what Laird, Rogers, and others had spent the previous weeks trying to prevent or water down. Instead of open communication with the president, the new directive forced the nation's security apparatus to funnel its ideas, intelligence, and proposals to Nixon through his new national security adviser, former Harvard professor Henry Kissinger. Nixon would then decide what he wanted to do, and Kissinger would issue the edicts to the Pentagon, State, the Central Intelligence Agency and elsewhere. It was the heart of Nixon's gamble to reach his audacious goals as president and to do much of it in secret.

Nixon set this plan in motion almost immediately after winning the election. Working out of the venerable Hotel Pierre, Nixon first announced his new chief of staff, Los Angeles–based advertising executive Haldeman, a former Nixon advance man and manager of his 1962 campaign for governor of California. Nixon also put out the word that cabinet officials would enjoy more autonomy than Johnson's and that his personal staff would not "dominate the functions or control the direction of the major agencies and bureaus of the Government," a November 14, 1968, *New York Times* report said.[4] That was the message for public consumption. Meanwhile, Nixon and his team focused on the forty-five-year-old Kissinger, who had advised New York governor Nelson Rockefeller's unsuccessful bid for the Republican nomination. After Rockefeller dropped out, Kissinger quietly fed Nixon's campaign inside information he learned from consulting with the American peace negotiators in Paris. Kissinger's closed-door support, coupled with his growing reputation as a foreign policy expert, led Nixon's advisers, such as Richard Allen, to recommend Kissinger join the new administration. Nixon and Kissinger met three times at the Pierre in November, and by the end of the month, press reports said Kissinger would either head the State's Policy Planning Council or become Nixon's special assistant for national security, Walt Rostow's job for Johnson. Rostow mostly balanced the competing ideas flying during Johnson's freewheeling policy lunches, where decisions were made on the fly, often too spontaneously and without detailed information. Nixon envisioned a different role for Kissinger, upon which he elaborated when he announced Kissinger's selection on December 2. His new national security adviser, Nixon said, would focus on long-term planning and help reorganize the National Security Council. Nixon also explicitly said what Kissinger would not do—come between Nixon and the Secretaries of State and Defense. "I intend to have a very strong Secretary of State," Nixon said.[5]

Nixon, who never trusted career diplomats, had no intention of letting the State Department determine his foreign policy. Instead, he wanted to return to Eisenhower's NSC, a centralized and militarily structured group that controlled policy from the White House. The major difference would be at the State Department. Eisenhower's Secretary of State was John Foster Dulles, who had spent more than twenty years as the Republicans' top foreign policy mind before taking the job. Nixon had resented what he considered Dulles's high-handed role under Eisenhower and planned to be his own Secretary of State. The last thing he wanted was another Dulles trying to push him around, so he picked his old friend William Rogers to run State. Rogers had been Eisenhower's second-term attorney general and then a well-connected New York corporate attorney. Rogers was not a foreign policy expert, but Nixon did not want one; he needed someone who looked the part of a ceremonial diplomat. In Nixon's cabinet, Rogers would have limited access to his old friend, the president, and would never be the strong Secretary of State Nixon professed publicly to want.

Although Nixon had only met Kissinger once before the election, he knew enough from a speech earlier in 1968 that Kissinger shared his belief in secrecy, which Kissinger called essential for a successful foreign policy. Nixon wanted Kissinger to design a National Security Council structure that would minimize the public exposure that accompanied cabinet agencies and congressional oversight. Kissinger, a secret Nixon campaign aide during the peace talks, would be Nixon's partner in secrecy in the White House. To succeed, Nixon had to keep his plans hidden from a hostile Congress and the media. Their policy would be secret, which was "just the way we wanted it," Haldeman would later say.

In Kissinger, Nixon had found another outsider who had fought his way to power. Born in Furth, Germany, in 1923, Kissinger fled the country with his parents in 1938 as it became increasingly obvious what Adolf Hitler had in mind for his nation's Jews. They moved to New York, where by 1943, Kissinger was attending night classes in accounting on the way to a seemingly pedestrian middle-class life. Then he was drafted into the army and sent a year later to Camp Claiborne, Louisiana, the training base for the 84th Infantry Division, which was ready to deploy to Europe and join the fight to liberate Germany. Kissinger might have become just another German-speaking American soldier slated to help in the race to capture as much German territory before the Russians, but he instead caught the notice of another German expatriate working for the army, Fritz G. A. Kraemer, a monocle-wearing eccentric and policy analyst. Fifteen years Kissinger's senior, Kraemer was also a private, but he carried far more gravitas. He took on Kissinger as his private project. "My role was not discovering Kissinger," Kraemer would say later. "My role was getting Kissinger to discover himself."[6] Kraemer guided Kissinger to Harvard after the war and helped choose the topics of Kissinger's master's and doctoral theses.

By 1957, Kissinger was a member of the Harvard faculty and the author of a new book, *Nuclear Weapons and Foreign Policy*, which made the thirty-four-year-old professor a sought-after voice in policy circles. He began advising Eisenhower, Kennedy, and then Johnson on military and nuclear missile planning. By the time of the 1968 campaign, the demand for his services had grown to the point at which he could have served in either a Humphrey or Nixon administration. When Nixon offered Kissinger the NSC job, Kissinger went to Kraemer, who was then a policy analyst working in Johnson's Pentagon. "I told him that in his personal interest, he should not take the job," Kraemer said. "It was too hard, too thankless, and he would be worn to pieces. Then I told him that he must put his personal interest aside, and take it for the country because he was the most qualified man for it. It was his duty."[7] Kissinger took his advice.

Kissinger enlisted Morton Halperin, a young Harvard protégé who had served in Johnson's Pentagon, to help draft the NSC plan. Halperin wrote most of it with Kissinger's input, but both worked from Nixon's vision. "Nixon was always the teacher," campaign adviser Richard Allen said. "Kissinger always the student."[8] For extra support, they consulted General Andrew Goodpaster, the soldier-scholar who had been one of Eisenhower's principal military advisers. It was no surprise Goodpaster supported a plan that he believed would repeat what he knew had worked before. Goodpaster's seal of approval gave the concept political cover. The plan, which Kissinger sent Nixon on

December 27, called for regular NSC meetings and a dedicated staff that would collect and analyze incoming options from the various agencies. Gone were Johnson's Tuesday lunches, which often had no real follow through. Under the Kissinger-Halperin plan, the council would meet on specific topics, and each participant would arrive armed with detailed policy options prepared by their agencies. The State Department would no longer coordinate policies between departments. The NSC staff would do that, and only one person, Kissinger, would steer options to Nixon. "From within the Pierre they promptly conceived and began what would become a seizure of power unprecedented in modern American foreign policy," wrote Roger Morris, a holdover from Johnson's NSC who would remain with Kissinger.[9]

The next day, Kissinger, Laird, and Rogers joined Nixon at his home in Key Biscayne, Florida, to discuss Kissinger's proposal. The session, as all the participants would learn quickly enough, was just a formality. Nixon had already approved the plan. Neither Laird nor Rogers had much to say, since they had neither anticipated Nixon's early decision nor the details of Kissinger's blueprint. They also got off easy. Nixon made one change in Kissinger's draft. He removed the director of the Central Intelligence Agency from the NSC completely. Nixon wanted the CIA to report to the NSC through the Defense Secretary. Not only would CIA director Richard Helms, whom Nixon had surprisingly agreed to keep on because of Johnson's recommendation, lose his regular access to the president, he would be denied a seat at the NSC table.

Laird quickly regained his bearings after Nixon's surprise announcement on December 28. The genial but wily eight-term representative from Wisconsin had risen to become the top Republican on the Appropriations Subcommittee that controlled the Defense budget. Few could better navigate the complexities of congressional politics or work the press. Nixon had hoped Laird would use those skills on the Hill for his benefit, which, at times, actually happened. Just as often, however, Laird would fend for himself, his department, and his prerogatives. Cutting Helms and the CIA out of the NSC loop struck Laird as more than foolish. It was suicidal. Nixon's impetuous decision, Laird continued, meant the NSC meetings would become a "'closed loop' in which all intelligence inputs would be channeled through a single source, the Assistant and his NSC staff."[10] Better for the CIA director to attend the meetings and participate directly than to communicate through him, Laird argued. Kissinger agreed and said he would take it up with Nixon. That gave Laird at least a small victory.

At State, however, Rogers may not have realized his old friend Nixon had isolated him, but Rogers's newly minted lieutenants surely did. U. Alexis Johnson, the incoming undersecretary for political affairs, figured out the meaning of Kissinger's plan in just a two-minute meeting with him at the Hotel Pierre in early January. Along with Elliot Richardson, the attorney general for Massachusetts who would be the number two at State, Johnson was named as the department's number three officer on January 4, 1969. A canny career diplomat who was just ending a three-year stint as ambassador to Japan, Johnson knew State would no longer coordinate interagency policy; it would be lucky to participate at all. "Some rough roads lay ahead," Johnson wrote.[11] On his flight back to Tokyo, Johnson wrote a backchannel message to Richardson, warning him of the consequences of Kissinger's plan. Richardson responded quickly, writing a counter-proposal that restored many of State's lost powers.[12]

Kissinger had anticipated State's move and warned Nixon it was coming. Kissinger's aides saw Johnson and his State allies as dinosaurs grown thick by too many dinners at diplomatic receptions. Kissinger wanted Nixon to stick with the plan, which was never in doubt. A Boston Brahmin like Richardson would never sway Nixon; Richardson represented almost everything Nixon thought was wrong about State. His mind was made up, Nixon told Kissinger on January 13, and he ordered him to tell Laird and Rogers. Nixon made one exception. He acceded to Laird's wish that the CIA remain part of the NSC, but he added one condition. Helms or his representative would only be allowed to brief the council at the start of discussions of key issues. They would then have to leave the room while specific policies were discussed.[13] Nixon would not give Dick Helms the chance to be the next Allen Dulles.

By inauguration day, Kissinger had assembled most of his NSC staff. Richard Allen, the Nixon foreign policy adviser during the campaign, was named as the nominal deputy, although Allen did not want the job and Kissinger seemed ill disposed to give him much authority. Halperin would join the staff, and many considered him Kissinger's logical deputy. Morris would stay, as would Helmut Sonnenfeldt, a longtime State official, friend of Kissinger, fellow German refugee, and protégé of Fritz Kraemer. Kissinger needed a military aide, but he lacked the intimate knowledge of the Pentagon or any candidates for the job. He reached out again to Kraemer and to Joseph Califano, another army official and longtime Johnson aide; Goodpaster; and former Defense Secretary Robert McNamara. All came back with one name: Alexander Haig, a colonel who had worked closely in the Pentagon with all of them. Kraemer's recommendation sealed it for Kissinger, who hired Haig.

CHAPTER THREE

First Moves (1969)

NIXON'S RUSH TO REACH HIS GOALS—OPENING A RELATIONSHIP WITH China, ending the war in Vietnam, and easing tensions with the Soviet Union—began when he entered the White House. Kissinger's brief was clear: assemble the NSC staff and bring Nixon the options he needed to make decisions. The meaning of that became clearer after Nixon signed National Security Decision Memorandum 2, which locked in the NSC reorganization. The agencies would have to give Nixon what he needed or they would suffer the consequences. By the afternoon of January 21, Kissinger, at Nixon's direction, issued memoranda seeking information on policies for Vietnam, the Middle East, foreign aid, international monetary issues, NATO, Japan, and overall US military posture. Nixon then reiterated his desires in his first full NSC meeting that afternoon.[1] By 2 p.m., Nixon and eleven aides took their seats around the oval table in the White House Cabinet Room. Some were there because of their constitutional duties, such as Vice President Spiro Agnew, whom Nixon viewed as a necessary evil and nothing more. Others, such as Secretary of State Rogers and Secretary of Defense Laird, would carefully monitor signs of their boss's duplicity. This would be strictly Nixon's show, as Kissinger and Haig, who rapidly became Kissinger's de facto deputy, moved the scenery and props.

Nixon quickly set the tone, saying the NSC meetings had to be tightly limited to only those legally required to be there. He extended that to include the chairman of the Joint Chiefs of Staff, Army General Earle "Bus" Wheeler, and the Undersecretary of State Elliot Richardson. Then Nixon put the CIA and its director, Richard Helms, firmly in their places. Helms would open the meetings with an intelligence briefing and then leave, because, as Nixon said, he wanted the CIA director to provide intelligence but not shape policy. In an awkward performance, Helms gave his briefing and left quietly.[2] Nixon continued by mentioning the need to maintain secrecy and cited Johnson's fear of leaks. I don't have such a fear, Nixon said, but we need to maintain discipline, because the meetings were meant for participants to speak freely. The NSC, he emphasized, was not a democracy. He would have no open votes over which policy to follow. "I will make the decisions," Nixon said, after he received all viewpoints and deliberated in private.[3]

The meeting was remarkable for many reasons. Not only did Nixon firmly display his control over the process—Kissinger was certainly no puppet master—he deliberately misled his own team. He blamed Johnson for the obsession with leaks, which Nixon would make an art form, and promised an open door that he would quickly close.

At the Pentagon, Laird knew Nixon too well to be fooled. The following day, Laird sent Kissinger a memo saying it would be best "if all official communications between DOD and your office were to come through the Secretary of Defense." That would let him know what the White House wanted and how to satisfy the president, Laird said.[4] Also, Laird made the first of what would be several recommendations that Kissinger close the liaison office between the NSC and Joint Chiefs of Staff, which Laird saw as a way for the White House to bypass him and go straight to the Chiefs. Using the office only invites trouble, Laird said, and Kissinger would eventually wish it were gone. Kissinger declined to follow Laird's advice, much to his chagrin later. Kissinger promised Laird he would keep him informed of communications between the White House and Pentagon. Laird knew better than to believe him.

Nixon claimed in his memoirs that leaks forced him to narrow his circle of foreign policy advisers. "It is an ironic consequence of leaking that instead of producing more open government, it invariably forces the government to operate in more confined and secret ways."[5] That was a convenient fiction written in hindsight and to explain away his obsession with secrecy.

During the transition, Nixon had said he would not let his White House aides push around his cabinet. Nixon and Kissinger quickly disproved that claim. Haldeman staked out their territory with State, telling Rogers in a February 1 memo that anything related to State and Nixon had to be cleared through Haldeman first.[6] Rogers got the message.

Meanwhile, Kissinger was facing management challenges with the diverse group of personalities colliding at the National Security Council. Many, starting with Halperin and Helmut Sonnenfeldt, had exaggerated views of their own influence. Others, such as Richard Allen, were rapidly neutralized. Rising rapidly was Haig, who worked harder and read more incoming documents or cable traffic than anyone else. His experience as a diligent and thorough staffer to General Douglas MacArthur, the overlord of US troops in the Pacific and Korea, and to top Pentagon officials in the

Johnson administration showed him the importance of speed and follow through. Haig was also a protégé of hardliner Fritz Kraemer, with whom he worked in Johnson's Pentagon. "Kraemer was seen as one of the ultimate wise men, an energetic thinker who had a wide knowledge of history and warfighting and how civilizations rise and fall," said Joseph Califano, a top aide in the Kennedy and Johnson Defense departments and a key Johnson adviser in the White House. "He had a lot of fans among the Army colonels and lieutenant colonels at the time," which included Haig.[7] Haig quickly took the measure of the NSC and his colleagues and warned Kissinger in a February 7 memo of a growing chaos inside the council. "The NSC staff," Haig wrote, "is not properly organized and that the functions of the components of the staff ... have not been sufficiently delineated and formalized to insure the kind of smooth staff work that is essential." Haig showed his ambition by claiming to have none. Kissinger needed a deputy, Haig told his boss, if the NSC was going to function as Nixon desired.[8] Kissinger would not make Haig the official number two at the NSC until June 1970, although he became Kissinger's de facto deputy shortly after sending the memo. By April 15, as he wrote Laird a note supporting Haig's promotion to brigadier general, Kissinger was calling Haig "the finest officer I have known. . . . In short, I could not operate without him."[9]

At the heart of Nixon's new policy lay his desire to resume relations with mainland China, which would then unlock his plans elsewhere. It was a change of direction for Nixon, who built his career on his support for Chiang Kai-shek through the China Lobby, a group of hardliners who blustered for the overthrow of Mao Tse-tung's government and anyone who "let" it happen.

China, as Nixon wrote in his 1967 *Foreign Affairs* article, needed to be engaged and brought into the family of nations.[10] Relations with China would then force the Soviet Union to reach its own deal, because it could no longer rely on China against the United States. North Vietnam would also lose the blind support of China and be encouraged to end the war. Nixon also knew that Chiang had no chance to regain power. It was either deal with Mao or ignore the Chinese government. Nixon chose Mao. He just could not make that decision public, at least not yet.

The China initiative gained more urgency as China's problems with the Soviet Union worsened. Nixon wanted to exploit those tensions to draw the Chinese closer and away from Moscow. Nixon mentioned China prominently in meetings he conducted on his first days in office, noting that there would not be a short-term change, but in the long term the Chinese could not be "living in angry isolation."[11] By January 31, he was moving more quickly. That day, he received a CIA report that cited a Polish source who said his government believed the "Americans 'know the Chinese are now more anti-Soviet than anti-American' and are exploring the possibilities of rapprochement with the Chinese."[12] Nixon told Kissinger the next day that they should encourage the attitude the administration is "exploring possibilities of rapprochement with the Chinese." But, Nixon cautioned, they needed to send that signal privately.[13] Fewer than two weeks into his administration, Nixon had opened another backchannel with Kissinger, who followed up with National Security Study Memorandum 14 seeking more policy options for China.

❦

Along with the China opening, Nixon knew he needed to fix the troubled relationship with the Soviet Union that had lingered since the end of the 1962 Cuban missile crisis. No progress had been made on arms control, and the arms race between the two nations saw each seeking a new type of missile or larger warhead. Israel's rapid victory in the Six-Day War of 1967 left the US-backed nation with huge swaths of new territory and a newly embittered group of neighboring Soviet-backed Arab nations spoiling for another fight. The Soviets' 1968 invasion of Czechoslovakia that crushed the reformist "Prague spring" stopped a nascent move toward arms control. Meanwhile, the Soviets had done little to push their client, North Vietnam, to reach a deal at the Paris Peace Talks, which continued to drift aimlessly. The two nations had much to discuss.

Since his time as vice president, Nixon fancied himself a Soviet expert, especially after his "kitchen debate" with Soviet leader Nikita Khrushchev in 1959. Nixon "got" the Soviets, he believed, and with Kissinger at his side Nixon knew he could bend the US-Soviet relationship to his advantage. At the core of Nixon's plan was a concept that quickly became known as "linkage": relations between the United States and Soviet Union would be determined holistically. Movement on any issue—arms control, for example—had to be accompanied by progress on all other issues, such as Vietnam or the Middle East. The great issues are connected, Nixon wrote Rogers on February 4, and they cannot sustain "a crisis or confrontation in one place and real cooperation" in another.[14] On his third day in office, Nixon had Kissinger send National Security Study Memorandum 9, which directed the Departments of Defense, State, and Treasury and the CIA to research the military, political, and economic issues regarding the Soviet Union and report back to the NSC by February 20.[15] These were the matters Nixon would link; he needed as much intelligence as he could get in order to exploit that linkage.

There was only one logical contact with the Soviet Union—Anatoly Dobrynin, the veteran ambassador to the United States. Dobrynin knew the United States well and spoke and understood English like a native, and, most importantly, talking to him was like talking to Leonid Brezhnev and the Politburo. Dobrynin had played this role before, working with Attorney General Robert Kennedy to find a way to end the Cuban missile crisis, and meeting secretly with Secretary of State Dean Rusk on Vietnam and other issues for Johnson. Dobrynin also realized the new benefits for his country with the new Nixon administration.

Kissinger would work directly with Dobrynin, because there was no need to delegate the Dobrynin talks to anyone else who would have to report back to Kissinger anyway. Kissinger knew only he could present Nixon's true feelings to the Soviets through Dobrynin.

Nixon wanted to keep the Dobrynin meetings secret, but too many in the bureaucracy considered themselves Soviet experts. State had coordinated Johnson's secret meetings with Dobrynin. Rogers, who was slowly realizing that his old friend was cutting him out of the loop, had already met officially with Dobrynin, about which he reported back to Nixon on February 13.[16] Two days later, Nixon told Haldeman to call Rogers and tell him that Nixon and Dobrynin would meet alone. Haldeman relayed the message, and Rogers predictably objected. The White House placated Rogers by including a State representative—Soviet expert and future US ambassador Malcolm Toon—in the meeting with Nixon and Kissinger.

Toon's presence meant little, since Nixon dismissed both Kissinger and Toon at the end of the meeting and told Dobrynin that anything important needed to be discussed with Kissinger first. But before the Nixon-Dobrynin meeting, Kissinger had made sure Nixon had as much information as he could handle. "You should be aware that Dobrynin is a friendly and outgoing individual who has long enjoyed close personal contact with leading American officials," Kissinger wrote Nixon on February 15.[17] On Vietnam, Kissinger recommended that Nixon emphasize that "we seek an honorable peace for all concerned; we have no wish to humiliate Hanoi and do not intend to see Saigon or ourselves humiliated." Nixon, Kissinger urged, should tell Dobrynin that he "will not be the first president to lose a war; therefore you intend to end the war one way or the other (This is deliberately ambiguous.)."[18]

Nixon kept to Kissinger's script, and Dobrynin said the Soviet government liked Nixon's statement about looking forward to negotiations, not confrontation.[19] Nixon thanked Dobrynin and the Soviets for their willing-ness to talk and laid out his embrace of linkage. They needed to tie strategic arms talks with the Middle East and Vietnam, Nixon said, and "progress in [one] area is bound to have an influence on progress [in] all other areas." The official parts of the meeting went smoothly, all recorded, but the real busi-ness occurred in the eleven minutes Nixon spent alone with Dobrynin before Toon and Kissinger entered the Oval Office.

Nixon told Dobrynin that he and Kissinger needed to have a confiden-tial channel that Dobrynin would later describe as "unprecedented in my experience and perhaps in the annals of diplomacy."[20] Nixon had "every con-fidence in his secretary of State," he told Dobrynin, but Kissinger had to do the real work, because they could not let anyone know beyond Kissinger and Nixon. So not only did a growing circle of officials inside the new Nixon administration gradually realize they were out of the loop of making policy, but the ambassador to the Soviet Union realized it as well.

Just as Nixon fancied himself a Soviet expert, he also considered him-self a blunt practitioner of *realpolitik*. While Dobrynin recounted that Nixon "was friendly and raised no controversial issues," Kissinger thought Nixon was both insecure about his performance with Dobrynin and convinced he had pushed a hard bargain. Nixon called Kissinger into his office four times that day, Kissinger would write later, seeking praise for the "tough" way he handled Dobrynin. Kissinger provided the routine assurances, although he believed that Nixon had been conciliatory to the Soviet ambassador.[21] Nixon's official diaries show, however, that he met with Kissinger only *twice* that day after the Dobrynin meeting, an indication that Kissinger, too, felt compelled to exaggerate his own importance.

Nevertheless, Nixon had laid the foundation for Kissinger's secret chan-nel with Dobrynin and the Soviets. Their first meeting came four days later in the White House's Map Room, where rhododendron bushes obscured the windows. Dobrynin entered the White House secretly through an entrance in the East Wing, away from most staff members and the press. While Nixon brushed out the bold strokes of his policy toward the Soviet Union in the February 17 meeting, Kissinger got into greater detail in his first meeting with Dobrynin. Unlike the earlier meeting, no US official, not Kissinger or a secretary, kept notes, and Kissinger did not include the details in his memoirs. But Dobrynin did.[22] The message he conveyed to his superiors in the Krem-lin about Vietnam and the US plans there were anything but "ambiguous," as Kissinger had described to Nixon in his earlier talking points. Dobrynin told Kissinger that he and Nixon should disregard the forces in the United States who thought a military victory in Vietnam was still possible and that the new administration would seek a genuine peace "based on sober consideration of the actual situation in Vietnam." Kissinger said the United States had no ultimatums for the Soviets on Vietnam but that "they favor a peaceful settlement" to the war, Dobrynin recorded in a memorandum he sent to Moscow the following day.[23] Any settlement, however, must not look like a US surrender or "outright military defeat," Dobrynin wrote. "Second, the Nixon Administration cannot accept a settlement that would be followed immediately (Kissinger stressed the word *immediately*) by a replacement of the South Vietnamese Government." That would look like a "backroom deal by Nixon—the United States 'handing over' the Saigon Government to the tender mercies of its enemy. However, the United States would have no objections if, after an agreement is reached, events in Vietnam were to take their own 'purely Vietnamese' course and develop 'in keeping with the historical conditions and experience of the Vietnamese people.'"[24]

Dobrynin's conclusion was clear: "In general . . . Nixon is primarily concerned about his own political reputation and how the settlement in Vietnam might affect his political future. In all likelihood, that will be the main yardstick he will use in his approach to matters of war and peace in Vietnam." Twenty-five years later in his memoirs, Dobrynin's impressions of that meeting remained the same. Nixon would not accept "an abrupt shift in policy" in Vietnam but had "no objection to a gradual evolution."[25] In other words, unlike his top commanders who believed they could actually win the Vietnam War on the ground, Nixon did not. The war could only end at the negotiating table, preferably with the Soviets' help, and then South Vietnam was on its own. While Kissinger professed that the United States would not abandon its South Vietnamese allies and wanted the Soviets to push their communist client in North Vietnam, he and Nixon essentially told Dobrynin and, by extension, the top Soviet leadership that they would accept an end to the war that would also mean an eventual end to South Vietnam. Kissinger and Nixon, however, did not tell their own Secretaries of State or Defense or their military leaders what they told Dobrynin, who took away the lesson that it did not really matter what the Russians did or did not do with North Vietnam, because the United States was not in it to win. If that was not Kissinger's intent, neither he nor Nixon left any contemporaneous account of the meeting to contradict the impression that Dobrynin quickly reported back to the Kremlin. One month after taking office, Nixon had established a secret channel with the Soviet Union that only he and Kissinger knew about and signed off on telling the Soviets that the Vietnam War would eventually be a losing proposition. Nixon and Kissinger did not broadcast that news, but others in the administration eventually figured it out for themselves.

US commanders welcomed Nixon's election, because they believed he would let them fight the war they wanted. No longer would Johnson micromanage the war from the Oval Office. Many Americans may have been demoralized by the 1968 Tet Offensive, thinking the North Vietnamese and Viet Cong had won a great moral victory, but General Creighton Abrams, the top US commander in Vietnam, and Ellsworth Bunker, the US ambassador to South Vietnam, considered Tet a huge communist defeat. An administration able to start fresh would give the Pentagon the ability to finish the war the commanders believed they were winning. While many in Vietnam and Washington had ridiculed Abrams's predecessor, General William Westmoreland, for his optimistic pronouncements that he could see a "light at the end of the tunnel" in Vietnam, enough top military leaders believed Abrams had actually turned on that light. Abrams had begun to train the South Vietnamese military to fight on its own, and he believed US forces and the South Vietnamese could keep eroding the Viet Cong and North Vietnamese enough to give South Vietnam a chance to survive. No one leading the US war effort realized that Nixon and Kissinger were telling North Vietnam's prime sponsor, the Soviet Union, that the United States was not in the fight to win.

Nor would the Pentagon realize it at first, because Nixon's first moves were strong. Two days into his administration, Nixon approved a Joint Chiefs request to mount an offensive in northern South Vietnam, just below the Demilitarized Zone and slightly to the east of the border with Laos, where the CIA was supporting a secret army of Meo tribesmen as a check on the communists. While the CIA backed General Vang Pao's army, the military had never sent its own forces there. That changed with Operation Dewey Canyon, in which more than two thousand marines poured into the area to cut North Vietnamese supply lines.[26] The marines surged into the A Shau Valley, capturing large arms and munitions caches and killing about 1,400 enemy troops. At some point, marine units captured hilltops inside of Laos, a violation of the country's neutrality, as they tried to protect the offensive's right flank. By the time the offensive ended in March, it had captured about four hundred tons of enemy arms and ammunition. About 125 marines died. It was the kind of aggressive action the Chiefs wanted in Vietnam; they soon realized it would not happen more often.

Five days after Nixon authorized Dewey Canyon, he and Kissinger visited the Pentagon for lunch with Laird and some of his top officers.[27] Laird sought greater clarity from Nixon about his plans for Vietnam and to pitch some of the Chiefs' ideas for the war. Although he doubted the value of maintaining a deep commitment in Vietnam, Laird knew he had to win over the top brass, since they were his most powerful constituency and had great influence in Congress. At lunch, Kissinger asked Laird for potential military actions in Vietnam, but he emphasized that they would either be real or "feigned."[28] The Chiefs did not want decoy maneuvers, but real action. They now heard Nixon ask for the same kind of play acting they had seen with Johnson. Nixon and Kissinger's request was aimed more at sending signals to North Vietnam for failing to agree to anything at Paris. Five weeks later, Kissinger received from Laird and the Chiefs a list of options that Haig called "more extensive than the type you and the President visualized as acceptable signals of US intent to escalate military operations in Vietnam in the face of continued enemy intransigence in Paris."[29] The Chiefs' plans included "actual or feigned" airborne and amphibious operations in North Vietnam; airborne or airmobile strikes at enemy posts in Laos and Cambodia (both were still neutral); air and naval operations against North Vietnam; subversion of the population and preparation for "active resistance by the people against the Hanoi regime"; and a plan for escalating the war against North Vietnam. While Nixon was willing to send two thousand marines into a remote corner of South Vietnam, he was not willing to commit to a much wider escalation of the war. Haig's recommendation to Kissinger was simple and prophetic—thank Laird for the ideas and ask for "lower level actions."[30]

Laird and the chiefs never learned during Nixon's presidency what he had allowed Kissinger to tell Dobrynin about the future US commitment in Vietnam. Instead, as they saw what Nixon and Kissinger considered more important when dealing with the North Vietnamese—symbolic actions meant to prove a point rather than to win a war—they started to wonder if Nixon was the president they thought he would be.

The success of Dewey Canyon encouraged Abrams, whose clear-and-hold strategy had recaptured vast swaths of territory across South Vietnam. He and his team believed they could win the war on the ground, although Laird had serious doubts. Abrams's reputation as a military leader, forged in the snow of the Battle of the Bulge, influenced those at the highest levels of the Pentagon. If Abrams believed the United States could win on the ground, they did too, and their optimism could not be ignored easily, if at all.

Less than three weeks after Nixon arrived took office, Abrams and Wheeler presented a plan to knock out what military leaders called the Central Office for South Vietnam (COSVN), essentially the North Vietnamese version of the Pentagon hidden in the Cambodian jungle and a clear violation of Cambodia's neutrality.[31] Abrams wanted to destroy COSVN with B-52 strikes, and he and Wheeler felt confident Nixon would agree, since he had already signed off on Dewey Canyon. Abrams made his proposal February 9, and Bunker agreed, telling Rogers on February 12 that Cambodian prince Norodom Sihanouk had known of COSVN's location for years but had done nothing about it.[32]

Two days later, Kissinger told Nixon that Rogers should tell Bunker to drop the bombing request because of Nixon's upcoming trip to Europe. Kissinger and Nixon then opened a new secret backchannel to Abrams that excluded Rogers. Kissinger told Nixon in a February 19 memo that Abrams was asked to keep planning for airstrikes "strictly within military channels" and to send a team to Washington to brief the White House.[33] This meant that Nixon had, in short order, cut Rogers out of the Dobrynin channel and the plan to widen the war to Cambodia. And Abrams knew that his president was running a secret channel around Rogers and Bunker. On February 18, a two-officer briefing team from Abrams's command arrived at the White House for a meeting with Kissinger, Laird, Deputy Defense Secretary David Packard, Wheeler, Haig, and Col. Robert Pursley, Laird's military aide. The officers laid out the details of the planned raid, COSVN's location, their intelligence, and the details of the planned raid. Kissinger told Nixon their intelligence seemed accurate and their "strike plans sound. There is every reason to believe there would be no Cambodians in the target area."[34]

Kissinger laid out several options for the attacks. They included an overt and deliberate bombing raid in response to a Viet Cong or North Vietnamese attack, a covert strike US forces would call a mistake, and a covert strike that would be called a mistake in response to a major enemy attack against a South Vietnamese city. Kissinger concluded the White House could not call an attack accidental because of the communication between Rogers and Bunker, which showed the proposed bombings were clearly planned and sent through proper channels. Covert or overt attacks against COSVN, Kissinger wrote, were not acceptable, because they would draw criticism as unwarranted escalations of the conflict. But bombers could make a "covert 'accidental' strike against COSVN Headquarters" that would show the Soviets they were serious about the war without forcing the Soviets to say anything publicly. Abrams, Kissinger wrote, should keep planning for an attack right up to the Cambodian border and that if anything happened in the region near the Fishhook area of Cambodia, it could be used "as a pretext to strike COSVN Headquarters."[35] If nothing happens in the area, then the NSC should consider the bombing proposal again in March. Nixon agreed.

Bombing Cambodia, Kissinger told Nixon, would show the Soviets they were serious about the war, but he and Nixon already knew that Kissinger would send Dobrynin the opposite message—that Nixon would accept a peace treaty as long as it did not look like a US defeat on the battlefield. Then if the South Vietnamese government fell after a decent interval, Nixon would accept that as an unfortunate reality. In Nixon and Kissinger's double game, they used one secret channel to encourage Abrams to escalate the war into Cambodia while they also sent a far different message to the Kremlin via Dobrynin. Abrams never learned what Kissinger told Dobrynin, so the Soviets knew more about long-term US intentions than Nixon's own commanders.

Kissinger told Laird on February 22 that Nixon had approved the bombing.[36] He also alerted Laird about the secret backchannel to Abrams for the planning of the airstrikes. Laird already suspected Nixon's secrecy and motives, and he now watched Nixon and Kissinger's end run around Rogers, Bunker, and the rest of the bureaucracy. Laird was ambivalent about the bombing, which he supported to placate his top commanders in the hope of trading his backing of the bombing for their support of his plan to start removing US troops from Vietnam. Laird also realized it was impossible to keep a B-52 carpet-bombing campaign on a neutral country secret. On February 25, Laird wrote Nixon to say he and Wheeler had "no doubt that the proposed strikes can be executed effectively," but the secrecy bothered him.[37] Too many people already know about the planned mission, Laird wrote, in part because of Bunker's February 12 message to Rogers. "It is reasonable to assume some of the people who saw the Bunker message would not look with favor upon this mission. . . . By virtue of the presumed widespread knowledge of this possible mission, it would be difficult to claim, and make credible, an operational error."

The secret bombings also meant Nixon could avoid any congressional scrutiny, because if the American people wanted the United States to get out of Vietnam, they also did not want troops or aircraft going into neutral Cambodia. If Nixon admitted that he had ordered B-52 raids in Cambodia, he would have to seek congressional approval and oversight, which he had reorganized the NSC specifically to avoid. If Congress did not approve, and given the desire to leave Southeast Asia, it seemed likely it would not, then Congress would take the money away. "Who are we hiding the raids from?" an air force pilot asked early in the raids. "Well, I guess the Foreign Relations Committee," he was told.[38]

Nixon believed the secret nature of the bombing matched the North Vietnamese lies about their presence in Cambodia. North Vietnam, Nixon reasoned, could hardly object to being attacked where they said its troops were not. Still, Kissinger and Nixon wavered on whether to go ahead, until a combined North Vietnamese and Viet Cong offensive pushed Nixon to act. On March 9, as the enemy offensive continued, Nixon issued another order for the bombing, but he delayed action because Laird was in Vietnam and unable to discuss the issue in person.[39] One week later, Kissinger urged Nixon to start bombing, because the administration would look weak to Hanoi if it did not respond to the latest offensive.[40] Also, Kissinger continued, "retaliatory action, if combined with a proposal for private talks, will serve as a signal to the Soviets of the Administration's determination to end the war. It would be a signal that things may get out of hand." Nixon then summoned Laird, Kissinger, Rogers, and Wheeler to tell them he would authorize the strikes. The meeting, Kissinger wrote in his memoirs, "led to hours of the very discussion that he found so distasteful and reinforced his tendency to exclude the recalcitrants from further deliberations."[41] Nixon endured the meeting, and the bombing would start in the early morning hours of March 18.

At the White House, Nixon and his NSC team nervously awaited the results. That afternoon, early in the morning in Cambodia, Kissinger sat in his office with aide Morton Halperin when Haig broke in with a cable from Vietnam.[42] The strikes had worked; the air crews said they had spotted seventy-three secondary explosions, presumably from US bombs detonating enemy ammunition stores. Kissinger, elated, turned to Halperin, who had not known about the raids, and warned him to keep quiet. Later that evening, Wheeler gave Kissinger more details. The secondary explosions, the chairman of the Joint Chiefs said, were "about 4 to 7 times the normal bomb burst," and "this was significant," Kissinger told Nixon. The North Vietnamese were "in a high state of alarm."[43]

Kissinger and Nixon initially thought their bold leadership had enabled them to gain a quick advantage over the North Vietnamese. They soon realized that COSVN was only a loose assortment of people and equipment hidden deep in the Cambodia jungles, just like the Ho Chi Minh Trail was a series of footpaths and tiny roads that evaded easy detection and destruction. No single bombing mission could eliminate COSVN, not even a B-52 strike capable of laying bare a patch of jungle one thousand feet wide and four miles long. Soon, Breakfast evolved into a series of airstrikes called Menu with code names based on various meals, such as Dinner, Snack, or Dessert. Abrams would pick bombing targets in Cambodia and send a message through a classified navy communication channel to the Joint Chiefs in the Pentagon, who would pass the request to Laird for his approval. Then, Abrams and his commanders would submit two strike plans, one for the

Cambodian site and another for a nearby location in South Vietnam. Both would be approved, but only the Cambodian target would be attacked.[44] The B-52s, flying at night and directed by ground radar, would pass over the fake target in South Vietnam and continue onward to Cambodia where they would drop their payload on the real target. When the bombers returned, their crews filed reports as if they had dropped their bombs in South Vietnam, while the reports for the real attacks in Cambodia were transmitted via a secret channel back to Washington. It was an elaborate way to falsify the record of a major expansion of the Vietnam War that neither Congress nor the American people would learn about for four years. When they did, amid Nixon's growing political problems, it would build into a growing outrage over Nixon's secret government.

⌒

Along with the concerns at the Pentagon created by Nixon's real or "feigned" request for Vietnam, another early sign for the military that Nixon was not who they thought he was came in late March with his desire to return control of the island of Okinawa to Japan. The scene of an 82-day battle in 1945 that left more than 12,500 US troops killed or missing, Okinawa had been under US control since 1945. Unlike bases in Japan, where US forces could not station nuclear weapons, no such restrictions hindered operations in Okinawa. But Japanese protests kept building, and by late 1968, the State Department was calling for the island to be returned to Japanese control. "The overwhelming impression I have after ten days in Japan and Okinawa is that we have reached the point of no return on the reversion issue," wrote Richard Sneider, the State Department's head of the Japan desk in a December 24, 1968, memo. "The pressures have built up in both Japan and Okinawa to the point where I can see virtually no hope of stalling off beyond the end of next year a decision on the timing of reversion, although the actual return would take place later."[45]

Sneider had moved from State to the NSC under Kissinger, and he kept up his call for returning Okinawa to the Japanese. Wheeler and the Joint Chiefs feared Nixon would give in to the political pressure. "While there may be a political necessity of settling the Okinawa problem as quickly as possible, the US government, in its desire to attain an early and amicable solution of this issue, should recognize fully the adverse consequences of Okinawa's reversion under conditions which fail to provide adequate safeguards for our military requirements," Wheeler wrote Laird in a March 29, 1969, memorandum that was not made public until May 2015.[46] At the NSC, Haig agreed, urging Kissinger not to follow Sneider's recommendations. "I must emphasize that the price we would pay for (redacted) Okinawa, even after a settlement of the Vietnam war, would be extremely heavy," Haig wrote, adding that Sneider's memorandum was more "forthcoming than we need be in our initial dealings with the Japanese."[47]

The military was bound to be disappointed. Nixon wanted to keep Japanese prime minister Eisaku Sato, a strong US ally, happy. Someone in the Pentagon must have realized Nixon's ultimate aims, because elements of the Wheeler memo appeared the next day in a *New York Times* article by reporter Hedrick Smith.[48] It was an early example of the growing number of leaks from Nixon's secret government that set him on edge.

Early on the morning of April 14, 1969, a slow-moving, four-engine EC-121 electronic surveillance plane rose from its base in Japan to a flight path sixty miles off the coast of North Korea.[49] Its mission was to collect radio communications from the border areas of China, North Korea, and the Soviet Union. Suddenly, two North Korean MiG fighters appeared behind the aircraft, and one fired a missile without warning. The aircraft exploded and crashed immediately in the international waters, killing all thirty-one crewmen aboard. Shooting down the EC-121 was another in a long series of provocations from the North Koreans since they invaded South Korea in June 1950. Even after the ceasefire that ended the Korean War in 1953, Kim Il Sung's government had staged dozens of cross-border raids and attacks that kept the South on edge. In January 1968, a team of North Korean commandos had crossed the border and tried to assassinate South Korean president Park Chung Hee.[50] A few weeks later, a North Korean navy flotilla captured the American spy ship *Pueblo* in international waters and held the crew hostage for a year before releasing them in December. Nixon, who had criticized Johnson's response to the *Pueblo* incident, now faced his own North Korean crisis.

Kissinger woke Nixon at 7:09 a.m. on April 15 to tell him about the incident. It was the first of twelve calls or meetings that consumed almost two-and-a-half hours of the day.[51] Nixon and Kissinger wanted to respond harshly to the attack and show they would not tolerate such aggression. Kissinger dispatched Haig to get military options from the Pentagon, and by midday the Joint Chiefs had sent Kissinger a list including demands for redress, continued reconnaissance operations over North Korea, requests to the Soviet Union to ask them to ask North Korea to make amends, and airstrikes to destroy North Korean aircraft off that country's coast.[52] Five options, the chiefs said, were possible immediately.[53] Another four would have to wait days or weeks for the proper equipment to get in place. Those options included more air strikes, a feint against North Korean air defenses, and a naval blockade of North Korean ports. Most of those options could have been determined by looking at the available resources and by examining the response to the capture of the *Pueblo* a year earlier. Nixon wanted more. By late afternoon, Kissinger presented his impatient boss with another option: A Dutch fish factory ship was sailing from the Netherlands for delivery to North Korea carrying a mostly Dutch crew. "It's almost impossible to seize that," Kissinger told Nixon, who disagreed. Capturing the *Pueblo* was impossible, Nixon said, but the North Koreans did it anyway. "I think we should just pick the darn thing up," Nixon said, and worry about the Dutch later.[54] Doing nothing is not an option, said Nixon, who then made a dig at Kissinger's staff. That's even if the peaceniks on your staff disagree, Nixon said.[55] Kissinger, who was already self-conscious about the perception that his staff was laced with liberals, said he had no peaceniks on his staff. Sitting with Nixon was John Mitchell, the attorney general who was Nixon's closest adviser.[56] Nixon put him on the phone with Kissinger to repeat the same questions about the Dutch ship. When Nixon got back on the call, he kept pushing Kissinger. Don't you have anything good to tell me? No, Kissinger responded. Throughout the EC-121 crisis, Nixon constantly badgered Kissinger, who reacted like a nervous junior lawyer under pressure from a senior partner. It belied Kissinger's claims to his friends and supportive journalists that he held Nixon in his sway. No sooner had they ended their call then Nixon called Kissinger back to tell him to call Lloyd's of London, the international insurance company, to find out how much coverage the Dutch had on the ship he wanted to capture.[57]

Nixon wanted to project power and decisiveness to make the North Koreans, and perhaps more importantly, their Chinese and Soviet allies, realize the new American president would not be pushed around. In his final call with Kissinger on April 15, they pondered another option—a naval blockade. The only problem, Kissinger said, was that most North Korean ports had little traffic.[58] A blockade, technically an act of war, might send the proper signal, but it would mean next to nothing because it would not affect the North Korean economy. On Nixon's demand, Kissinger asked Laird for more detailed options.

Nixon's desire for a bold response received another blow the following day, when CIA director Richard Helms presented an analysis that gave little evidence to support doing much of anything.[59] Kim Il Sung, the review concluded, did not react to Chinese or Soviet pressure, because North Korea "has mutual defense treaties with both the USSR and Communist

China" that could draw those two nations into any US military action against North Korea.

Haig then sent Kissinger an unsolicited memo that urged action.[60] Unlike the *Pueblo* incident, which involved the safety of the crew held hostage in North Korea, responding to the EC-121 shootdown did not involve any Americans in harm's way. "All factors considered," Haig continued, "a military retaliatory strike is called for," but Nixon needed to understand and prepare for the potential North Korean responses, which could be dire. Bombing the MiGs' air base could provoke a North Korean artillery barrage on Seoul or South Korean positions along the DMZ or even another invasion. Nixon, Haig continued, had to move the proper US and South Korean resources into place to show the North Koreans he realized the scope of their reactions. If Nixon isn't willing to do that, Haig concluded, he should not launch a retaliatory strike.

Each moment eroded the chances Nixon would make a quick response, and the more pragmatic members of the NSC began to win over the president. Virtually any military action risked provoking a greater and more devastating response from the North. With Seoul just thirty miles south of the DMZ, any attack would destroy much of the city's growing economy and population. North Korea held its southern neighbor hostage by its belligerence and unpredictability. Everyone wanted to act, but no one wanted to risk destroying South Korea or have a repeat of another war. An April 17 CIA review reinforced those fears, saying that any US actions "would have any decisive or lasting effects, either in achieving stated US objectives or in inducing Pyongyang to modify its long-term policies."[61] The North Koreans would view any US show of force as simply a replay of the tepid response to the *Pueblo* seizure, the agency said. In essence, the North Koreans knew they had the advantage and acted accordingly as long as they did not provoke another ground war.

Nixon knew it, too. By the end of the night on April 17, he complained to Kissinger that he was just sitting idly after the North Koreans killed thirty-one Americans.[62] Everyone knew the plane was not in North Korean airspace, Nixon groused, but no one cared about the facts. Kissinger reminded him that if the United States retaliated, Nixon had to be prepared for a wider war, a tough call to make early in his administration. It was possible, Kissinger continued, that the United States might have to resort to the use of tactical nuclear weapons. All hell will break loose for two months, Kissinger continued, but at the end there will be peace in Asia. Even Nixon did not seem inclined to go that far, instead ruminating on the nation's declining moral fiber and the problems of doing anything militarily as long as the Vietnam War continued.

By April 18, Nixon had lost his chance to respond. The American public would back a retaliation at first, an NSC analysis showed, but then quickly lose interest.[63] The public will not "give sustained support for the Korean action because too many will conclude that US vital national interests were not engaged, as they were in the Cuban missile crisis, sufficiently to justify the risks of renewed hostilities in Korea," Sneider wrote.[64] Laird presented his own review that the best option was to launch airstrikes against two North Korean airfields. Even that, Laird continued, was not worth it, because they lacked the reconnaissance to know if the attack worked, and it could cost the United States support where it needed it more. Also, Laird added, while most Americans would also support the secret bombings of Cambodia, they would not if the Cambodia bombings were seen as part of a global US bombing offensive.

So Nixon did virtually nothing beyond ordering fighter escorts for the surveillance and intelligence-gathering missions near North Korea. The White House tried to put the best face on their move, but Nixon had disappointed the hardliners who favored action and alarmed the realists who believed from the beginning that the United States had few decent options, just like a year earlier with the *Pueblo*. Particularly alarmed was Fritz Kraemer, who still had great influence with Kissinger and Haig, who thought Nixon had lost a key opportunity to project strength and that the tepid response would only invite more attacks.[65]

Laird knew that National Security Agency intercepts had shown that the shootdown was an accident; the North Korean MiG pilot was confused and acted without orders. He considered Nixon's bluster poorly advised. So did NSC aide Lawrence Eagleburger, one of Kissinger's closest associates and a future Secretary of State. He told a friend of Nixon's alarming conduct during the heart of the crisis when the president was "ranting and raving—drunk in the middle of the crisis."[66] Haig thought Nixon had lost his nerve and let Laird get the better of him. Nixon's response was that they "cut the moral ground from beneath our own feet and [they] missed an opportunity to save lives in Vietnam by shortening the war."[67]

The EC-121 incident notwithstanding, Nixon's plans moved forward with little difficulty, mostly because few people knew the specifics. Kissinger had hidden the secret Dobrynin channel from the State Department. Reporting on the US attempts to rekindle relations with China was virtually nonexistent.

Approval of the Dewey Canyon mission and the bombing of the North Vietnamese sanctuaries in Cambodia had given Nixon enough good will with the military to minimize overt resistance to his policies. He still benefited from not being Lyndon Johnson.

The pace with which Nixon wanted to move, and the sheer amount of directives coming from Kissinger and the NSC—forty-three by April 1—provided his internal opponents with more signs of where Nixon wanted to go and tangible examples to show the press.[68] Kissinger sent out thirty-four National Security Study Memoranda, and his questions in the memoranda provided enough hints of future policies that opponents or those who wanted to inflate their importance leaked to the press, sometimes with speed that alarmed and angered Nixon.[69] Most of the leaks went to the newspaper that epitomized to Nixon the Eastern Establishment he deeply distrusted—the *New York Times*.

The torrent began almost immediately and escalated into the spring. Details of Wheeler's Okinawa memorandum were in the *Times* on March 30. On April 4, the *Times* printed a story about possible US troop withdrawals from South Vietnam.[70] Two days later, White House reporter Max Frankel reported on the administration's development of alternative policies on Vietnam.[71] It was based on the conclusions found in National Security Decision Memorandum 8, which had been distributed only five days earlier. "The Nixon Administration has set in motion an essentially secret program of diplomatic and military measures designed to extricate the United States from Vietnam," Frankel wrote in a piece that seemed copied directly from NSDM 8, which spelled out the term of any deescalation of the war effort.[72] "There will be no de-escalation except as an outgrowth of mutual troop withdrawal," the memorandum said.[73] "If they can get substantial negotiations, Administration officials would want to arrange for a schedule of mutual troop withdrawals by North Vietnam and the United States," Frankel wrote. His story showed just how much of the internal NSC deliberations, the key to Nixon's secret policies, had leaked and how quickly. The Joint Chiefs opposed many of the items, a sign of the leak's possible source. Sixteen days later, the *Times* published another story rooted deeply in another NSC memorandum, a directive about nuclear disarmament negotiations.[74] On April 24, the *Times* reported about the administration's deliberations about sending a navy electronic surveillance ship off the coast of North Korea again, just days after the end of the EC-121 crisis.[75] An April 25 story about the decision to resume selling F-104 fighters to the Middle Eastern nation of Jordan sparked Nixon to do more than just complain privately.[76] By later April, Nixon was meeting and talking on the phone with Attorney General John Mitchell and FBI director J. Edgar Hoover about how to find those who were leaking the administration's biggest secrets.[77]

CHAPTER FOUR

The Secret Wiretaps (1969)

Kissinger and Haldeman were eating breakfast at the Key Biscayne Hotel in Florida when Kissinger first saw William Beecher's May 9 story in the *New York Times*.[1] Headlined "Raids in Cambodia By US Unprotested," the story said "American B-52 bombers in recent weeks have raided several Vietcong and North Vietnamese supply dumps and base camps in Cambodia for the first time, according to Nixon Administration sources, but Cambodia has not made any protest." The Cambodia bombings were secret no more. "Outrageous!" Kissinger shouted as he waved the story at Haldeman.[2] Beecher had been particularly aggravating for Kissinger that week; this was his third story in May that featured internal NSC deliberations. On May 1, he reported on the administration's global nuclear weapons strategy, based on a secret memo issued on Nixon's second day in office,[3] and on May 6 he showed how Nixon and Kissinger had sought to retaliate against North Korea for the EC-121 shootdown.[4] The second story contradicted Nixon and Kissinger's claims they had reacted calmly to the EC-121 incident when they actually wanted to attack North Korea.

Two impulses drove Kissinger. He wanted to keep the secrecy he and Nixon cherished, but he also realized that Nixon suspected his NSC staff of leaking. During the EC-121 crisis, he had chided Kissinger for hiring "peaceniks." Kissinger knew that others, primarily FBI director J. Edgar Hoover, doubted the loyalty of some NSC staff members. He had to do something.

Kissinger first located and called Defense Secretary Melvin Laird, who was playing golf at the exclusive Burning Tree Country Club in suburban Maryland. An attendant found Laird on the course and brought him to the clubhouse, where Kissinger awaited on an open telephone line. Call Nixon, Kissinger told Laird. "He's mad as hell that you leaked that story to the *New York Times*."[5] "Go to hell," Laird responded. Kissinger had no real idea of how mad Nixon was that morning. He did not talk to Nixon until that evening, after Nixon and his best friend, Charles "Bebe" Rebozo, had spent hours sailing on Biscayne Bay.

Kissinger, however, was definitely outraged. After calling Laird, Kissinger made the first of four fateful calls that day to Hoover at 10:35 a.m. Beecher's story, he told Hoover, was "extraordinarily damaging" and they needed to find the source.[6] Hoover said he would do what he could. Kissinger called again thirty minutes later to mention Beecher's stories on May 1 and 6. Kissinger called Hoover a third time at 1:05 p.m., to stress that any leak investigation needed to be kept secret. Hoover agreed. Finally, at 5:05 p.m., Hoover called Kissinger to tell him the preliminary inquiries had revealed that Beecher may have gotten information from the press desk of the Pentagon's Southeast Asian Desk, which Hoover said was stocked with anti-Nixon loyalists of John F. Kennedy and former Defense Secretary Robert McNamara.[7]

Such sketchy earlier findings did not stop Hoover from starting the first of what would become seventeen wiretaps on government officials and reporters. Somehow Hoover's suspicion focused on someone who knew nothing about the planning of the Cambodia bombings or their execution— Morton Halperin.[8] That made the man who helped create Nixon's secret government the first person spied on because of it. It did not matter that no one could prove that Halperin leaked. Hoover had never liked Halperin, and Kissinger's priority was to save himself, find the leaker, and "destroy" him. By 7 p.m., an FBI agent went to the telephone company that served Halperin's Bethesda, Maryland, home to launch a tap that would remain for twenty-one months, long after Halperin resigned from the NSC that September.[9] The wiretaps never showed Halperin leaked anything, and what little he knew about the Cambodia bombings came from Kissinger. Cambodia was just a pretext for Hoover, who considered Halperin a dangerous dove whom Kissinger should never have hired. Joint Chiefs Chairman Wheeler also resented how the thirty-year-old Halperin had bested him a year earlier when Halperin successfully pushed for the North Vietnamese bombing halt, which Wheeler opposed. In the Senate, Barry Goldwater of Arizona, the Republicans' 1964 nominee for president, had also complained that Halperin had hurt the war effort. Kissinger heard their complaints, but he knew how vital Halperin was to him and the NSC. After all, Halperin had drafted most of what became NSDM 2. But now perception trumped reality, and Kissinger could not protect Halperin. Perhaps more importantly, Halperin's rivals knew he had talked to his previous boss, former Defense Secretary Clark Clifford, about an article on the bombing halt Clifford planned to write. Clifford knew about Nixon's interference with the Paris Peace Talks and could have exposed Nixon.

Years later, when the wiretaps surfaced as part of the Watergate scandal, Nixon, Kissinger, and Haig blamed them on Hoover, who was conveniently dead and unable to defend himself.[10] Only wiretaps can catch leakers, Nixon said Hoover told him. Haig said Kissinger had been summoned into an April 25 meeting with Nixon, Hoover, and Attorney General John Mitchell in which Kissinger was given the files of three suspected leakers on the NSC staff who needed to be tapped.[11] When he testified in a lawsuit Halperin filed against him, Nixon also said the wiretaps were discussed in that meeting.[12] But there was no meeting. Nixon's own diaries show that while he met with Mitchell that day, he only talked to Hoover for two minutes on the telephone and never had him in the White House.[13] Hoover's own calendar shows the same thing.[14] Hoover and Mitchell joined Nixon for dinner that night at the presidential retreat at Camp David, Maryland, but Kissinger was not there. The dinner conversation, Haldeman noted, "centered around all the bad guys 'they' have infiltrated into everywhere, especially State. Hoover full of hair-raising reports about all this, plus terrible problems in the courts, etc. He is a real lobbyist, and never quits. And never hesitates to chop everyone else in the process."[15]

Kissinger met with Hoover alone on May 5, FBI records show. While the FBI analysts could not cite the details of the meeting, because neither Hoover nor Kissinger left any record, the April 25 dinner, the May 5 meeting, and a May 2 call between Nixon and Hoover "tend to support the theory that Mr. Hoover had possibly discussed the very serious matter of White House leaks with the President, the Attorney General and Dr. Kissinger," the FBI concluded.[16] Nixon's daily diaries show he repeatedly spoke with Kissinger and Mitchell between May 2, when Nixon spoke to Hoover, and May 5, when Kissinger met with Hoover. While the documents do not contain the details of their discussions, it seems clear that Halperin's status as a wiretap target was sealed days before Kissinger's May 9 eruption in Key Biscayne.

Haig followed up with the FBI on May 10, and met with Hoover's deputy, William C. Sullivan, to discuss how the taps would work.[17] Sullivan controlled most of the Bureau's sensitive and secret investigations, and Haig's meeting with Sullivan was one between friends. When Haig was a junior officer serving in the Pentagon for army secretary Cyrus Vance and his top aide, Joseph Califano, Haig collaborated with Sullivan on the delicate issue of repatriating Cubans who participated in the disastrous 1961 Bay of Pigs invasion of Cuba.[18] As the FBI's intelligence chief, Sullivan investigated the returning Cubans for any security problems before they could be brought into the US military.[19] He had also shared information about suspected "Fabian socialists" in the Kennedy administration with Fritz Kraemer,

Haig's mentor at the Pentagon.[20] Sullivan, Haig would later write, "had the weary air of a man who has been sifting through other people's secrets all his life and finding them not particularly interesting."[21] The requested wiretaps, Haig said, came from "the highest authority." The names of those tapped must remain secret, and only a few officials in the White House and FBI could know the details. Wiretaps were the best way to stop the leaks that were incredibly damaging to overall foreign policy, Haig continued, and if their hunches were correct, they could stop tapping after "a few days." The list of suspects included four names—Halperin, Daniel Davidson, and Helmut Sonnenfeldt of the NSC staff and Col. Robert Pursley, Laird's military aide at the Pentagon.[22]

Davidson, another Johnson holdover, had suspiciously close ties with some journalists, including Hedrick Smith at the *New York Times*. A lawyer, Davidson had worked in Paris in 1968 and for longtime Democratic heavyweight and former ambassador W. Averell Harriman, who had served four Democratic presidents. Davidson had also been caught leaking early in his tenure in Paris. He had been warned and stopped. But that and his Democratic pedigree made him suspect. Davidson had also been Kissinger's conduit for information from the Paris talks in 1968 when Kissinger was sending reports to the Nixon campaign, so Kissinger had firsthand experience with Davidson's capacity for leaks.[23]

Sonnenfeldt had spent twenty years in the State Department before joining the NSC and had also been suspected of leaking classified information to "unauthorized sources" in the 1950s and 1960s, although a thorough investigation had found nothing and his career continued without incident. In his few months at the NSC, however, other concerns about Sonnenfeldt had surfaced. He and Kissinger may have shared the same mentor, Kraemer, but their paths had diverged over the years before they joined again at the NSC.[24] Sonnenfeldt worried about his status at the NSC, and he complained often to Kissinger that too many obstacles stood in the way of his advancement, starting with Haig, whom Sonnenfeldt suspected of leaking to the Pentagon. Roger Morris, another NSC aide, said a memo Sonnenfeldt had written for Kissinger had mysteriously found its way to the Joint Chiefs of Staff, and Sonnenfeldt was confronted with it in an interagency meeting.[25] Sonnenfeldt immediately suspected Haig. By May 10, Kissinger and Haig knew Sonnenfeldt was still close to the State Department, which was steadily being cut out of the flow of information, and was not happy. Those were enough reasons for him to be wiretapped.

At least credible reasons existed for the taps on Halperin, Davidson, and Sonnenfeldt. They worked in the NSC, knew of its secret deliberations, and had attracted powerful opponents. Not Pursley, whose file, Hoover noted, contained no "derogatory information."[26] But he came under suspicion because he worked for Laird, who had recently fought Nixon's initial impulse to retaliate against North Korea after the EC-121 shootdown.[27] Laird opposed keeping the Cambodia bombings secret, because he knew the news would eventually break, as it did in Beecher's story. Laird had also returned from a March trip to Vietnam with a detailed and skeptical assessment of US chances there. All topics—the NSC restructuring, US options in Vietnam, the planned EC-121 retaliation, and the secret bombing—had appeared in *New York Times* articles since February, including three by Beecher. Nixon and Kissinger could not seriously consider wiretapping the Secretary of Defense, but perhaps a tap on Pursley would pick up something on Laird. Haig also did not like Pursley, which seemed motive enough for him to be added as the fourth name on the list.[28]

Sullivan now had the names of the people Haig wanted to tap, but one further hurdle remained—Hoover. While Hoover had enthusiastically started the Halperin tap on May 9, he resisted doing more until he had written authorization from his nominal boss, Attorney General John Mitchell.[29] While Hoover had presided over decades' worth of wiretaps and surreptitious break-ins, he started to back away from those tactics by the mid 1960s, as public opinion had started to shift against some of the FBI's methods. In 1966, he prohibited the use of "black bag" jobs, illegal break-ins by FBI agents in which documents were photographed, rooms bugged, and telephones tapped.[30] Sullivan had protested at the time, telling Hoover the change would limit the Bureau's ability to catch potential spies and lawbreakers. Hoover would only stick his neck out on the taps if Nixon did it first. Mitchell agreed. He signed the first four wiretap authorizations and all that followed.

On May 20, Haig gave Sullivan the names of two more NSC aides—Richard Sneider and Richard Moose—who had actually done some of the planning for the Cambodia bombing.[31] Sneider, an Asia expert and former State official, had participated frequently in NSC deliberations on Okinawa and Vietnam. Sneider also had made the unfortunate mistake of disagreeing with Kissinger on key issues, including twice in April. He had recommended against a contemplated retaliation against the North Vietnamese for an attack in the South,[32] and also opposed Kissinger's desire to conduct an internal history of NSC deliberations on Vietnam, saying it would raise too many questions that could lead to leaks that Nixon was preparing to attack the Johnson administration's Vietnam policies.[33] "My judgment is that we have enough problems without this additional one," Sneider told Kissinger.

Now the aide concerned about leaks was targeted as a possible leaker. Moose played a far lesser role in the debates about Cambodia. He was, however, another Johnson holdover, and worse than that, he had already had difficulties with Haig, who was compiling the list of suspects.[34]

Seven days later, the FBI delivered some startling news—the taps on Davidson and Halperin had turned up what Sullivan called "extremely sensitive material."[35] Haig then told Kissinger, but they determined that nothing would be sent to the White House. The evidence would stay at the FBI, and Haig would read it in Sullivan's office. Sullivan recommended to Hoover that he and Nixon decide how to handle future wiretaps, but Hoover declined. He and Nixon did not talk about the taps, and Sullivan remained in control and relayed the findings to Kissinger and Haig.

Davidson resigned from the NSC on May 29. Kissinger did not want to confront his one-time source, so he delegated it to Haig, who called Davidson into his office, told him he had been caught leaking to a journalist over his home telephone, and that he had to go. Davidson admitted nothing.[36] Neither Haig nor Kissinger would ever specify what Davidson had allegedly done. Perhaps Haig's conversation only confirmed what Davidson realized earlier; as a Johnson holdover, he was an increasingly bad fit in Nixon's NSC and would have no more effectiveness after being accused as a leaker.

By July, Sullivan was urging Hoover to call off the wiretaps.[37] They had revealed nothing, Davidson's departure notwithstanding. Hoover would not budge. The White House ordered the wiretaps, he told Sullivan, and only they could stop them. The taps remained active after some of the subjects had left the White House. Davidson, who resigned in May, remained tapped until September. Halperin left the administration in September, but his telephone remained tapped. An August tap picked up an anguished call between Halperin and Kissinger in which Kissinger pleaded with his younger associate to not resign. For some reason, Hoover and Sullivan never passed the details of that conversation to the White House.[38] That was good for Kissinger, because he would later boast to Nixon that he had fired Halperin in July.[39] Throughout the rest of 1969 and into 1970, more White House aides, including speechwriter William Safire, and more reporters were tapped, starting with Henry Brandon on May 29, Hedrick Smith of the *Times* in June, and then Beecher in 1970. Sonnenfeldt's tap was removed and then reinstated in 1970 after another bout of leaks and paranoia.[40] The taps proved little other than Nixon's suspicions and the division within his government.

Eventually, the Church Committee of the mid-1970s found at least ten cases in which information from the taps was used for political, not national security, purposes.[41] After their discovery, the wiretaps remained politically toxic. Everyone involved tried to distance themselves. Mitchell lied to the FBI about approving them, and Sullivan would go so far as to claim in his memoirs that he had never met Haig before the colonel appeared in his office to start the wiretaps.[42] That was a lie, and not the first one Sullivan would tell. Kissinger would lie under oath several times about what he knew about the wiretaps and when, and the wiretap program would become one of the articles of Nixon's eventual impeachment.

Richard Nixon was the last president Hoover would serve as FBI director, although the FBI had so much information on so many people that Hoover really had no boss. By January 1969, Hoover, at seventy-four, was older than virtually anyone else in government service. He sat atop a Bureau teeming with ambitious men who had tried to stay in his good graces while they waited for him to retire or die. Any politician with secrets to keep had reason to believe Hoover knew them and would use that knowledge to keep them in line. Nixon learned that early in his career with the Hiss case, and he knew Hoover would turn on him if Hoover felt it necessary.

Hoover had already signaled to Nixon that he knew about the Nixon campaign's interference with the Paris Peace Talks. Shortly after Nixon took office, Hoover lied to Nixon and told him the FBI had bugged his campaign plane.[43] The FBI had tracked Anna Chennault, Nixon's secret channel with the South Vietnamese, and the Bureau had collected telephone records. It never bugged the campaign's plane, said Cartha "Deke" DeLoach, Hoover's deputy at the time. But it benefited Hoover to have Nixon, who knew exactly what he had done to subvert the Paris talks, believe that Hoover knew more than he actually did. Nixon had ordered Kissinger to find out more about the bombing halt, a search that Kissinger told Nixon on April 25 was fruitless and would eventually leak. Nixon temporarily dropped the idea.[44]

Sullivan, the man on whose shoulders rested the responsibility for the wiretaps, was known to friends and enemies alike as Crazy Billy. The taps would become a few more extra secrets for a man immersed in them. Sullivan looked little like the crisply dressed, white-shirted agents with neatly combed hair who dominated Hoover's inner circle. Short and pugnacious, Sullivan's clothes were often rumpled and baggy, a fashion statement his superiors often noted in his annual reviews. His office overflowed with papers, and while Sullivan looked like an absent-minded professor, he sounded like a raspy-voiced Boston street cop. He had grown up on a farm in Bolton, Massachusetts, thirty-five miles west of Boston, gone to American University in Washington, and then returned home to work as a high school teacher and principal. After four years as an Internal Revenue Service agent, he joined the FBI in 1941 shortly before the Japanese attack on Pearl Harbor.[45] His superiors quickly saw promise behind his atypical appearance. He tracked suspected subversives in Milwaukee and then moved to El Paso, where he was mentored by Charlie Winstead, the agent who had gunned down notorious bank robber John Dillinger. By 1944, Sullivan had returned to Washington as an intelligence division supervisor.[46] Hoover put him on his most sensitive investigations; in late 1945, Sullivan fed Bureau files about State Department official Alger Hiss to Father John Cronin, a fervent anticommunist.[47] Three years later the information Sullivan passed to Cronin would end up in Nixon's hands as led the case against Hiss.[48]

Sullivan spent the coldest years of the Cold War spying on suspected Soviet agents and tracking Americans helping the Soviet Union. Communists were Hoover's obsession. The Bureau developed its own counterintelligence program spying on Soviet and other agents in the United States. As deputy to Assistant Director Alan Belmont, who led the Bureau's Domestic Intelligence unit, Sullivan started his first operation against suspected communists inside the United States in 1956.[49] His performance reviews noted his avid study of communism. President Eisenhower and other officials desperately wanted to know more information about Soviet intentions. Their ardor only increased when the Soviets launched their *Sputnik* satellite in 1957 and scared Americans about their head start in the space race.[50] In some years, Sullivan gave more than sixty lectures around the country on the threat of communism, earning plaudits from civic and law enforcement groups.

Sullivan's counterintelligence agents used the same techniques on suspected communists that they used during the war on Nazi and Axis operatives. They broke into homes and offices, tapped telephones, and mailed threatening letters to the wives and colleagues of members of groups agents wanted to destabilize.[51] They created suspicions about disloyalty or infidelity by posing as cops who called targeted organizations to make them suspect each other was an informant. They sought less to build criminal cases but to destabilize and weaken their targets until they no longer posed a threat. Eventually, however, their focus changed from known communist groups to those with rather ephemeral connections to communism, such as the NAACP or local Boy Scout troops. It was, as Sullivan would tell a Senate committee almost twenty years later, a "rough, tough, dirty business and dangerous," but one Hoover, his agents, and their clients thought they were winning. They had few, if any, regrets. These programs, operating under the designation COINTELPRO, were some of the FBI's biggest secrets.

By 1961, Sullivan had become director of the Domestic Intelligence division and the FBI's representative to the US Intelligence Board, a joint panel whose members included the heads of the CIA, Defense Intelligence Agency, and the National Security Agency.[52] That put him at the heart of deliberations for national intelligence estimates ranging from the Soviet Union to China to nuclear proliferation. Hoover cared little about these meetings, which enabled Sullivan to build relationships with other intelligence chiefs, including CIA directors John McCone and Richard Helms.[53] Eventually Sullivan concluded the United States needed a more integrated intelligence system in which agencies collaborated instead of fighting each other. Helms, in particular, agreed. He and Sullivan cooperated behind Hoover's back often, including during the 1965 US occupation of the Dominican Republic, when Hoover sent FBI agents into what Helms considered a CIA operation.[54] Sullivan knew Hoover would have fired him if he had learned what he and Helms were doing. Sullivan did it anyway.

Sullivan developed a band of eclectic friends beyond those of the typical FBI agent from Hoover's closed circle. He became close to those at the heart of the Kennedy and Johnson Pentagon, particularly Haig.[55] He got to know Kraemer on the anticommunist lecturing circuit, and they had a relationship in which the Pentagon strategist felt comfortable enough to drop into Sullivan's office and accuse McGeorge Bundy, John Kennedy's national security adviser, of being a "Fabian Socialist" who viewed nuclear war as "unthinkable."[56] He traded suspicions of domestic intelligence threats with James Angleton, the CIA's counterintelligence chief who grew increasingly paranoid after he was burned by his friendship with British spy and traitor Kim Philby. Vernon Walters, Nixon's former translator and later the deputy director of the CIA, was another with whom Sullivan would discuss how to improve the nation's domestic intelligence network. Sullivan also befriended and influenced a generation of young reporters who would mature to become some of the nation's most influential, such as columnists Robert Novak and Jack Anderson and a former navy lieutenant turned *Washington Post* reporter named Bob Woodward. Starting in 1969, Novak said, Sullivan provided him with a steady stream of tips about subversive groups operating in the United States.[57]

The Bureau's counterintelligence operations expanded greatly during Sullivan's tenure as FBI intelligence chief, and fell under the umbrella known as COINTELPRO. First, because Hoover suspected communist manipulation of the civil rights movement, Sullivan started a program against Martin Luther King Jr. and other movement leaders. Despite the lack of evidence, Hoover believed that King would emerge from his cloak of nonviolence and suddenly embrace an angry, violent brand of Black Nationalism.[58] Agents tapped King's home telephone and the many hotel rooms in which he stayed while on the road. Eventually they gathered enough recordings to create a "sex tape" of King with other women. Sullivan authorized sending the tape to King's home with a letter calling King an "evil beast."[59] The FBI's intimidation never worked with King, who only fought harder. Although it never uncovered anything remotely close to communist manipulation of King, the Bureau continued spying on King until his assassination in April 1968. No matter what Sullivan said or what the evidence showed, Hoover never stopped trying to destroy King. After King's death, the Bureau spied on his widow, Coretta Scott King, and kept on digging up what it considered incriminating information on King's successor at the Southern Christian Leadership Conference, the Rev. Ralph David Abernathy, until the COINTELPROs were stopped in 1971.[60]

Sullivan was an equal opportunity secret policeman. While he hounded King and the civil rights movement—at Hoover's insistence, Sullivan would later claim—he also led the Bureau's successful penetration of the racist Ku Klux Klan in 1964.[61] FBI agents and informants destabilized the white hate group at the peak of its fight against the civil rights movement. They created bogus Klan chapters run by informants and sent anonymous letters to Klan family members, much as they did to King, aimed at breaking up their marriages.[62] By the end of the 1960s, they had broken the Klan, Sullivan bragged.

From the Klan, the FBI's COINTELPROs moved to more aggressive black groups, such as the Black Panthers, and then to what the FBI called the New Left, a grab bag of student groups focused mainly on their opposition to the Vietnam War.[63] Sullivan knew they posed no real threat. Most of them just wanted the United States to get out of Vietnam, particularly if it meant they would be drafted and sent there to fight. Sullivan still gave COINTELPRO all he had and held little back. His FBI record teems with his memos to Hoover and other officials about the aggressiveness of intelligence and counterintelligence activities at home and abroad. He vigorously carried out Hoover's paranoid vision. There was a reason Sullivan was the one subordinate Hoover addressed by his first name.

Throughout it all, Sullivan developed a reputation as the FBI's liberal house intellectual with his dark, horn-rimmed glasses and Democratic leanings. Sullivan had also mastered the Bureau's Byzantine politics. He burned, as former associate and rival Cartha DeLoach said, with "more ambition than sense."[64] His rivals and friends considered Sullivan passionate and unpredictable. His subordinates adored him, because he favored action against the enemy within, be they Soviet spies, civil rights leaders, Klansmen, or student radicals. Those instincts brought Sullivan into greater conflict with Hoover, as Sullivan thought Hoover had lost his nerve and wanted to do too little, especially when it came to cooperating with other agencies. Hoover wanted to preserve an FBI monopoly on intelligence; he bitterly fought the creation of the CIA and its predecessor, the Office of Strategic Services.[65] He punished those who cooperated with anyone.

Hemmed in at the FBI, Sullivan turned increasingly to his friends at the CIA. Angleton's doubts about FBI intelligence assets infected Sullivan.[66] He, too, began to wonder if Soviet bloc operatives were playing the FBI. If Hoover would not allow a stronger FBI, Sullivan believed, he would have to find a way to bring the FBI, CIA, and other intelligence agencies closer together. The US intelligence community was not reaching its potential, Sullivan told Helms in October 1968.[67] They needed to find a better way to move "ahead of the winds of change instead of being blown by them later on willy-nilly." Nixon's call for wiretaps and a crackdown on leaks could not have found a more willing collaborator.

CHAPTER FIVE

The Military's Harsh Awakening (1969)

EVERY ADMINISTRATION HAS DIFFERENCES AND RIVALRIES. KISSINGER'S nominal predecessor as national security adviser, Walt Rostow, often crowded out those around LBJ who wanted to slow or stop the American military commitment in Southeast Asia. At Defense, Mel Laird had different concerns. He knew he and his officers often had little chance to present their views directly to Nixon, because the president routinely went over his head to generals such as Abrams in Vietnam or Admiral Thomas Moorer, the chief of naval operations and the next chairman of the Joint Chiefs. General Vernon Walters, the military attaché in Paris, met with Kissinger and North Vietnamese negotiators there without Laird's knowledge. Often, it was only because Walters told his old friend and military strategist Fritz Kraemer what he was doing that Laird learned anything at all.[1] Laird realized he could survive only if he played Nixon's game better than the man himself.

Laird had some peculiar advantages. He oversaw the super-secret National Security Agency, which collected communications from around the world.[2] Laird received intercepts from the North Vietnamese delegation in Paris to Hanoi, so he knew what they were telling Hanoi about their secret meetings with Kissinger and Walters, his translator. Laird then passed the reports to Nixon at the White House, who read them but never told Kissinger.[3] That meant Nixon knew that Laird knew that he and Kissinger were bypassing him, but Nixon kept on doing it and never told Kissinger that they had been exposed. Laird also knew from the military pilots who flew Kissinger on his secret missions where Kissinger was going and when, negating that secret.[4]

Laird knew from the EC-121 crisis that Nixon talked tough at first and then settled for something less. The same thing happened with the Cambodia bombings. Nixon gave generals Abrams and Wheeler much of the brutal bombing campaign they wanted, but his insistence on secrecy fooled few and would eventually embarrass the administration. Laird was not alone in coming to that realization. While Nixon and the FBI never determined who made the leaks to the *New York Times* about the Cambodia bombing or his deliberations on the EC-121 crisis, the paper's Pentagon correspondent had written both stories. It is not difficult to imagine those leaks came from somewhere in the military, as did those for two stories by reporter Hedrick Smith on June 3 and 4 about US plans for the island of Okinawa and troop withdrawals from Vietnam.[5] Those stories got Smith wiretapped, but the leaks continued.

Nixon veered between the desire for a peace deal to end the Vietnam War and the impulse to look too tough to care about peace. The Soviets, however, knew from the secret Dobrynin channel that Nixon did not believe the war was winnable. That rendered much of his war strategy strictly for show and undermined Nixon's so-called madman theory, which he thought made him formidable and unpredictable. Instead, Nixon unsettled his own team, who came to distrust him, suspect his motives, and believe he was leading the nation down a dangerous road that was not what Nixon had advertised.

A key early tension point was the internal debate over when and how much of the fighting in Vietnam to turn over to the South Vietnamese. Individual units of the Army of the Republic of Vietnam (ARVN) fought nobly, and most American officers respected some of the Vietnamese counterparts. But most US commanders considered the South Vietnamese military unreliable, which was why American troops were there in the first place. The South Vietnamese lacked the ability or will to save their country from the communists, who believed they were fighting a war of liberation. Laird traveled to Vietnam in March and returned with a mixed assessment dominated by the belief that United States had to start withdrawing from Vietnam.[6] The first, Laird wrote Nixon on March 13, would be to remove "50–70 thousand US troops from South Vietnam this year." In future years, Laird continued, more South Vietnamese troops should replace more departing Americans. His commanders, however, resisted. They did not want to suddenly hand over the war to a force they knew could not hold their hard-won gains and favored a much smaller reduction of troops, perhaps twenty-five thousand in 1969.[7] They considered Vietnamization, the replacement of US troops with the Vietnamese, far more dangerous than the politicians worried about the next election.

By May, it was increasingly clear that Nixon also favored Vietnamization. He and Kissinger began work on a speech that Nixon hoped would prod Hanoi into doing something more specific. Kissinger sent him a draft on April 24, and urged Nixon to make a clear-cut position on peace by recalling that North Vietnamese negotiator Xuan Thuy had goaded Nixon by saying

"If the Nixon Administration has a great peace program, as it makes believe, why doesn't it make it public?"[8] Such was Nixon's fear of leaks that he hesitated, because he feared Secretary of State Rogers would object because it was too strong, while State bureaucrats would leak the details to portray Nixon as a hardliner. Rogers did object, as Nixon thought, but his objections were assuaged, particularly after Laird agreed with the key elements. "Mel thinks we are doing the right thing," Nixon told Kissinger in a call on May 13.[9] "What really pleases me is that Rogers thinks it is fine." He did not realize that Rogers's support was because they had sought and considered his counsel.

Although Nixon's May 14 speech was aimed at showing conditions for a Vietnam peace deal and troop withdrawals, he hinted that "the time is approaching" for a unilateral withdrawal in that departing US troops would be replaced by South Vietnamese forces "able to take over some of the fighting fronts." Nixon had hoped the speech would split the difference between his desire to appear tough and to get troops out of Vietnam. The initial reaction was encouraging, although the *New York Times* would note that "the speech sounded to some observers as if it had been written in two parts and by two hands. Observers found the flexibility of Mr. Nixon's specific proposals in contrast to his rather stern rhetoric."[10] That schizophrenia was felt in the administration as well. Military leaders wanted Nixon to do more on the ground and less in Paris.

During the next day's cabinet meeting, Kissinger called the speech "the most comprehensive statement made by an American President about Vietnam," which showed just how willing Nixon was to make peace.[11] In a bit of irony that went unnoticed by most of those in the room, Nixon exulted that the South Vietnamese government had agreed to it.[12] Six months ago, he said, no one would have predicted that South Vietnamese president Thieu would have agreed to its substance. Most of those in the meeting knew nothing about Nixon's insistence to Thieu through Anna Chennault that Nixon would give them a better deal than Johnson would. Now that Thieu had seen Nixon's better deal, he had little choice but to live with it.

The North Vietnamese, however, did little beyond continuing to attack the South from their sanctuaries in Cambodia or Laos. Very little progress came in the public or secret talks in Paris. The communists, perhaps bolstered by the knowledge that Nixon was never truly committed to staying and fighting, gave little ground. By September, Nixon and company were pondering new moves to provoke the change that would let them remove more troops while not putting the war at risk.[13]

Kissinger gave Nixon four options—maintaining the current strategy across the board, accelerating negotiations while keeping Vietnamization, accelerating Vietnamization while maintaining the current negotiating posture, and escalating the war while maintaining negotiations and stopping Vietnamization. Those options NSC first debated in a September 12 meeting with Abrams and Admiral John McCain present for a rare visit.[14] Nixon's frustrations were palpable. He wanted to make progress with the negotiations, but he called the need to pull out more troops "a political necessity."[15] But Nixon also realized what appeared to be a lull in the actions of the North Vietnamese was a trick that Abrams and Ellsworth Bunker, the US ambassador to Saigon, said was aimed to get the United States to withdraw more troops.[16]

Abrams, who had led the military's comeback from the dire days of the 1968 Tet Offensive, said they were only able to discuss withdrawals because of "the application of raw power." Stop that, he said, and "you have got an entirely new ball game."[17]

Wheeler, the chairman of the Joint Chiefs, agreed, saying that a cease fire and then negotiations would be disastrous.[18]

That fall, administration debates over war policy focused on a planned offensive against North Vietnam called Duck Hook.[19] The strikes on North Vietnam were aimed at shocking its leaders into realizing they could no longer keep stalling in Paris. In July, Kissinger had assigned three NSC aides—Haig, Anthony Lake, and Roger Morris—to develop the plan with Rear Admiral Rembrandt Robinson, the leader of the Joint Chiefs of Staff's liaison office to the NSC. They also worked with the office of the Chief of Naval Operations.[20] Laird had wanted Nixon to close the liaison office, because he knew the White House would use it to hide deliberations from him, and he was right again with Duck Hook. Robinson sent information back to his boss, Moorer, who often filled in for the ailing Wheeler.[21] Robinson and Haig, who had become close friends, embraced the Duck Hook planning enthusiastically. Lake and Morris rejected Robinson's first plan in September as too tepid and asked for another take that had to give Nixon two "operational concepts." "The action must be brutal and sustainable," they wrote, because the North Vietnamese had "proven tenacity" against attacks that did not pose an existential threat and could just wait out the attacks. Finally, the plan had to be self-contained, because "the President would have to decide beforehand, the fateful question of how far we will go. He cannot, for example, confront the issue of using tactical nuclear weapons in the midst of the exercise. He must be prepared to play out whatever string necessary in this case."[22] It was the second time nuclear weapons had been discussed in the White House that year as a possible US action. Kissinger had mentioned them in April during the EC-121 crisis. An option publicly deemed unacceptable continued to be something that those close to Nixon were willing to consider, even casually.

Kissinger, who was still following Kraemer's harder-line inclinations, liked the Duck Hook plan and sent Nixon a memo that laid out the stakes: Attempting, but failing, with Duck Hook "would be a catastrophe."[23] Failure to do anything but go all in would lead to its inevitable collapse. "It must be based on a firm resolve to do whatever is necessary to achieve success." Kissinger knew his boss well, having witnessed Nixon tip toe to the brink, talk tough, and then back down. He knew the United States could launch the attacks and then become skittish after the barrage of the inevitable worldwide and domestic criticism. Kissinger blamed the North Vietnamese for dragging out the Paris negotiations, but that would not matter to the rest of the world, which would consider Duck Hook a unilateral escalation of the war. Domestic reaction would be no better; each day, a larger percentage of Americans wanted out of Vietnam. Nixon, Kissinger reasoned, had to accept the criticism and remain firm. If he did not, the North Vietnamese would simply endure the attacks and again wait for the Americans to lose interest. "Hanoi will heavily base its decisions on its view of the seriousness of our intention to see it through," Kissinger continued.[24] "We (including the whole bureaucracy) must therefore demonstrate that domestic and foreign criticism will not deter us." The "action must be brutal," he continued. "Each action must therefore be short and compact. Once embarked on this course, we should not allow ourselves to be deterred by vague, conciliatory gestures by Hanoi."[25]

The plan called for four days of major strikes on North Vietnamese targets, including air defenses, the mining of six deep-water ports, the interdiction of the Northeast Rail Line, and attacks against a variety of selected, critical targets.[26] "Such operations would be designed to attain maximum political, military and psychological shock, while reducing North Vietnam's over-all economic capacity and war-making capacity to the extent feasible," the plan read.

Nixon liked Duck Hook, which he considered the kind of bold move that would rattle the North Vietnamese and would reinforce his self-image as a man of action. Again, however, his methods undermined him. Laird and Rogers, who had been excluded from the planning, learned what Nixon had done behind their backs. Laird knew Nixon had used the Chiefs liaison office to evade him. They told Nixon that Duck Hook would cause more problems than it would solve and ultimately weaken the US position. North Vietnam would withstand Duck Hook as it had all of the previous attacks, Laird and Rogers argued, and they threatened to quit if Nixon went ahead.[27] Nixon may have wanted them gone, but the political costs of two high-profile cabinet resignations in the first year of his presidency were too great. Nixon, Kissinger, chief of staff Haldeman and counsel John Ehrlichman hashed out the plans during a contentious meeting at the Florida retreat in Key Biscayne. Kissinger, Haldeman noted, "is of course very concerned, feels we only have two alternatives, bug out or accelerate, and that we must escalate or P (the President) is lost. He is lost anyway if that fails, which it well may. K still feels main question is whether P can hold the government and the people together for the six months it will take. His contingency plans don't include the domestic factor."[28] That factor, combined with the threat of losing two of his top cabinet officials, led Nixon to scrap Duck Hook in favor of continuing the current strategy of talks, responding to attacks, and making the occasional feint.

Kissinger's deliberations of Duck Hook were no doubt influenced by a memo he received September 29 from Kraemer, who continued to exert influence over Kissinger and Haig through a series of telephone calls and memos.[29] His five-thousand-word memo titled "The Modern World, A Single 'Strategic Theater'" raised his concerns about the United States' "deteriorating strategic position" in the world and the need to convey a much stronger global image. The world, he wrote, was focused on US actions in Vietnam, so if all signs pointed to an "ultimate pull-out, a radical reduction of military commitments, a withdrawal of US military power not simply in hotly contested Vietnam but on a worldwide scale." These words coming from the man who discovered him were clearly in Kissinger's head as he lobbied for Duck Hook. Kraemer's memo had a compelling logic and a dire outlook. The United States, Kraemer argued, was essential, but it looked like "a reluctant giant: seeking peace and reconciliation almost feverishly, withdrawing forces not in one but in many parts of the world, tired of using its physical power and firmly resolved to cut existing commitments and keep out, for a very long time to come, of any confrontation that might lead to any military involvement."

Kissinger kept Kraemer's warning to himself until after Nixon killed Duck Hook. He took the memo, attached a cover note, and sent it to Nixon on October 7 without identifying its author.[30] "Attached is a memorandum written by an acquaintance of mine which provides a rather comprehensive assessment of the United States' position in the world," Kissinger wrote Nixon. "Although I do not agree with its every last word, it does define the problem we face—the generally deteriorating strategic position of the United

States during the past decade." Nixon, Kissinger concluded, did not create the conditions they faced but "foreign policy depends on an accumulation of nuances, and no opponent of ours can have much reason to believe that we will stick to our position on the issues which divide us. When Hanoi compares our negotiating position on Vietnam now with that of 18 months ago, it must conclude that it can achieve its goals simply by waiting. Moscow must reach the same conclusion. These are dangerous conclusions for an enemy to draw, and I believe that we therefore face the prospect of major confrontations." Nixon read the memo avidly, writing notes in the margins wherever he found something that piqued his interest.[31] A week after he received the memo from Kissinger, Nixon forwarded it to Helms at the CIA, Laird, Rogers, and Attorney General John Mitchell, asking them to read it and send their comments. There is no record any of them actually followed through, a good enough measure of their feelings. Kissinger was clearly torn. Kraemer had discovered him and influenced his thinking, but now Kissinger served Nixon, who had dramatically different ideas. Nixon had confounded the military again by teasing them with the possibility of Duck Hook and then pulling the rug from under them, which left the Chiefs and their allies feeling cheap and used.

After rejecting Duck Hook, Nixon veered on a maneuver that confused his staff and the military and triggered concerns about his stability. Nixon devised a feint that he thought would show the communist world that he remained unpredictable enough that they needed to placate him. He ordered Laird to engineer an exercise that would create the impression that the United States had increased its defense condition (DEFCON) status to test the responses of the Soviet Union, China, and other rivals.[32] Participants called it the "Madman Nuclear Alert." Kissinger, Haig, and Nixon needed the exercise to seem as real as possible, a message they did not believe Laird and Defense fully understood. World leaders had to believe Nixon was crazy enough to do anything, including launch a nuclear first strike. Laird resisted at first, but Nixon eventually brought him around,[33] and Joint Chiefs Chairman Wheeler told commanders that he had been ordered "by higher authority" to raise military readiness "to respond to possible confrontation by the Soviet Union." The moves started October 13, including strategic pauses that any rival would see as a prelude to a possible attack.[34] Naval activity worldwide increased, and nuclear-armed B-52 bombers took off to circle Alaska. In a different environment and with another president, such maneuvers might have driven a different reaction from the Soviets, such as pressuring the North Vietnamese to do more at the peace talks. Instead, the Soviets did nothing. Nixon anticipated that Soviet ambassador Dobrynin would mention the alert during their planned October 20 meeting with Kissinger.[35] He did not. The alert's "Hail Mary" produced nothing except uncertainty inside Nixon's White House.

Once again, the Pentagon saw how Nixon talked tough but did not deliver. They were disappointed that he backed away from Duck Hook, because they believed it would have worked. With the nuclear alert, they felt mostly relief. Nixon's Madman Theory did not unsettle his rivals as much as it did the military leaders, who concluded they worked for a dangerous man who intentionally kept them in the dark. The Chiefs, particularly Moorer, concluded they needed more information to determine what Nixon and Kissinger were doing and thinking. Moorer told Robinson to gather more intelligence at the White House. One of Robinson's main sources was someone at the heart of Nixon's deliberations—Haig, the newly minted brigadier general who was also tipping off the army about much of what Nixon believed was secret.

—◆—

Richard Allen, the Nixon campaign aide who had recommended Kissinger as the national security adviser, had been shunted to the margins of the NSC by the fall.[36] He had little to do, felt discouraged, and planned to quit. One of his final tasks was to monitor a study of the nation's worldwide bases and defense treaties that cost billions of dollars a year. Those commitments, Allen concluded, posed a significant vulnerability for the administration, even if most of the agreements preceded Nixon. The study, conducted in late 1968, showed the United States supported 429 major military installations around the world and another 2,972 minor bases with at least one million people stationed there.[37] A subcommittee of the Senate Foreign Relations Committee was created specifically to study overseas commitments, and Democratic Senator Stuart Symington of Missouri was named its chairman. Allen knew the subcommittee would create problems, particularly if the Pentagon allowed the panel access to the study and its details.

Symington was a difficult adversary. The successful CEO of a St. Louis defense contractor became the nation's first secretary of the air force under Harry Truman. He parlayed that into a successful run for the Senate in 1952. Symington had seen the military from the inside, and his work on behalf of this state's aviation industry gave him consistent exposure to the Pentagon. In the late 1950s, Symington's collaboration with the missile industry led him to trump up the alleged "missile gap" that had undermined Nixon's 1960 presidential race. He was also close to the intelligence community and routinely recommended job candidates to the Agency directors.

He picked two able investigators, Roland Paul and former *Washington Post* reporter Walter Pincus, and set them loose on the Pentagon. Allen spent his remaining months on the NSC warning Kissinger and Haldeman about the potential for disaster. "It's our watch, and if Symington attacks, the public is not going to make a distinction between commitments that were made back then," Allen said.[38] "They exist right now, and so Nixon would get the blame." He was right. By October, Symington's investigation had exposed questionable US commitments, especially the CIA-run secret army in Laos. Symington had moved from being a dependable Cold Warrior to a dove and a persistent problem for Nixon.

Those closest to Nixon soon realized he had a potentially debilitating drinking problem that often appeared in nighttime calls to Kissinger in which Nixon's speech was slurred and his thinking erratic.[39] Many Americans had witnessed Nixon's televised news conference after he had lost the 1962 California race for governor and seen a man who had clearly had too much to drink tell reporters that they would not have Nixon to kick around anymore. John Ehrlichman, who worked with Nixon on that campaign, told Nixon he would only join his 1968 campaign if he controlled his drinking.[40] Particularly problematic, Ehrlichman said, were Nixon's trips to Key Biscayne with his longtime friend Charles "Bebe" Rebozo. "He'd go down to Key Biscayne and we wouldn't see him all weekend," Ehrlichman said. "And it was very clear that, that he got smashed."

NSC staffers, such as Roger Morris, were tasked each night with assembling a record of Kissinger's activities, including transcribing his taped telephone conversations with Nixon and others. At times, Kissinger and Haig would refer to the president as "our drunken friend."[41] By the fall of 1969, Nixon's closest security aides had reason to question his stability and sobriety, and members of the national security establishments at the CIA, Defense, and State knew they could not really trust him.

Into this environment arrived a young navy lieutenant in the summer of 1969 assigned with handling the military's most secret communications from the Pentagon to installations and locations around the world. The communications shop handled multiple secret channels, which carried the highest security clearances. Those who handled these secret messages possessed a rare window into decision making at the highest level. That lieutenant's name was Robert U. Woodward. A graduate of Yale University's Navy ROTC program,

Woodward joined the navy as a cryptologist with a top secret clearance. His first posting was on the USS *Wright*, a ship built to serve as a remote command post for the president in a time of crisis.[42] Woodward then served on the USS *Fox*, where he coordinated communications between the fleet and various navy aircraft flying missions over or near Vietnam. His commander from the *Fox*, Rear Admiral Robert Welander, recommended Woodward for a commendation and the Pentagon duty, which he accepted.

Woodward's new Pentagon posting exposed the twenty-six-year-old lieutenant to some of the nation's most powerful men. Moorer personally sent Woodward to deliver messages from the Pentagon to the White House. Many of those messages, Moorer said later, were meant for Haig, who was already Kissinger's de facto deputy. Woodward worked for Moorer as his office was developing Duck Hook with the NSC. It was no ordinary time and no ordinary job. Not only was Woodward to deliver messages to Haig, but Moorer said Woodward briefed Haig as well on developments at the Pentagon.

It was an experience Woodward was extremely reluctant to discuss. Both Haig and Woodward would deny that Woodward ever met Haig at the NSC, although Woodward would later say he met Mark Felt, the FBI official who became one of his best sources as a reporter, while waiting outside Haig's office in the White House basement.[43] While there is little evidence to suggest that Woodward and Felt met there, there is far more that shows that Woodward met William Sullivan, who coordinated the FBI wiretaps with Haig. Woodward and Haig could also not agree when they first met each other. Woodward said it was in 1973, while Haig said it was a year later in an awkward meeting outside Haig's home. Moorer was not alone in putting Woodward in Haig's presence in 1969. Laird and his press aide, Jerry Friedheim, would tell interviewers of the Haig-Woodward connection from that time, as would Roger Morris.[44] It was a propitious time and place for the two men to meet; their connection would be one of the main reasons Nixon would be forced to resign.

CHAPTER SIX

Cooking Intelligence with
SALT (1969–1970)

Nixon knew he could succeed where Kennedy and Johnson failed and broker a nuclear arms agreement with the Soviet Union. But he quickly learned the wide lead in nuclear weapons the United States had maintained for years over the Soviet Union had disappeared by 1969. The Soviets had as many nuclear weapons as the United States, which still had more accurate and modern weapons. Both sides had reasons for a deal. The United States wanted to slow the Soviet surge while the Russians wanted to avoid bankrupting themselves. Talks that started with Johnson in 1967 had fallen apart after the Russians invaded Czechoslovakia in 1968. The Soviets believed they could pass the United States in overall missile quality and warhead strength, but the costs would wreck their economy. Neither side wanted to use nuclear weapons or contemplate a postnuclear world. Neither trusted the other, and they struggled to find reliable negotiators. The secret Kissinger-Dobrynin channel bridged some of the gap but also created confusion about who really spoke for the United States.

Longtime diplomat Gerard Smith, the director of the Arms Control and Disarmament Agency, led Nixon's negotiation team. A former deputy to John Foster Dulles, Smith had the gravitas that won him the respect and deference of many, even if Nixon and Kissinger would eventually tune him out, run around him, and blame him for leaking.

On his second day in the White House, Nixon issued National Security Study Memorandum 3, which directed the CIA, Pentagon, State Department, and arms control experts to review "our military posture and the balance of power" and analyze the nation's forces, including nuclear weapons.[1] It also was leaked to the media almost immediately, which angered Nixon.

Nixon had multiple goals for the Strategic Arms Limitation Talks (SALT) that would start in earnest in 1970. He needed to preserve US advantages in submarine-based missiles and overall technology and stop the Soviets' gains in warheads capable of annihilating any American city or hard-target missile silos. The biggest US worry was the Soviets' newest ICBM, the hulking SS-9, which could carry a warhead of up to thirty megatons, more than a thousand times more powerful than the bombs that destroyed Hiroshima and Nagasaki in 1945. Large warheads limited the missile's range, but it would obliterate many times anything within its reach, including the Minuteman missile silos arrayed at sites in the northern United States. Nixon soon learned that a big enough Soviet attack could overwhelm the US ability to retaliate against Soviet cities and military targets. The Johnson administration considered the SS-9 enough of a threat to push ahead with plans for a massive antiballistic missile (ABM) system called Sentinel, but its development stalled in 1968. Nixon had to decide to push ahead with Sentinel or try something new.

The initial challenge was finding what each side was prepared to give up. One early proposal was dubbed Stop Where We Are, essentially a mutual freeze in nuclear development.[2] Nixon never took it seriously, because he thought the Russians considered themselves too far behind to honor it. For example, they knew the Americans could put multiple independent reentry vehicles (MIRVs) on their missiles while they could not. A MIRV was a warhead that broke off from its booster in space and then reentered the Earth's atmosphere on its own. A Minuteman with four MIRVs was like having four missiles in one, which quadrupled American striking power. Armed with MIRVs the Soviets lacked, US missiles were easier to target and far more accurate than the Soviet's more cumbersome weapons. Nixon also never seriously considered a freeze in MIRV testing, and neither did the Soviets. On ABM, however, Nixon saw an opening. The Soviets had an ABM system near Moscow. The United States had nothing that complete. If the United States also built an ABM system that matched the Soviets', then Nixon would gain some leverage in SALT. He wanted ABM not to use but to trade it away.

He faced two challenges: He had to show the Soviet threat dangerous enough to warrant an ABM system, which then would actually work. Then he had to get the deal through Congress. He needed more than the SS-9's size and range to make the case, because congressional experts already knew the ICBM could deliver a warhead big enough to wipe out any target. So would virtually any other Russian missile. The more important point was whether the SS-9 could deliver enough warheads to render the United States unable to respond. A single warhead atop the SS-9 would not accomplish that mission, intelligence experts believed, but an SS-9 with MIRVs could.

The debate over warheads went deep into the minutiae of nuclear policy. US intelligence believed the Soviets had the capacity to deliver multiple reentry vehicles or MRVs. An MRV could detach from the launcher while in flight and then land separately. US intelligence had monitored Soviet tests and knew they had tested SS-9s that had three MRVs that could hit three different targets with varying degrees of accuracy. Equipped with large enough warheads, that could triple the SS-9 threat but not guarantee first-strike capability. The three MRVs would land together in a close enough pattern that they would not hit enough targets, because MRV warheads could not move independently once they detached from the missile. They just fell toward Earth. What alarmed Pentagon planners was the potential that the Soviets were testing MIRVs.

Nixon and his team knew they lacked the evidence to persuade Congress to approve an ABM system. Nixon could not prove the Soviets had even tested a MIRV or that the United States had the ability to make an ABM system that could knock out an incoming ICBM. But he needed to have ABM, and the fight inside the administration to get it pitted the president, Kissinger, Laird, and the Pentagon against the CIA. It would give Nixon the short-term victory he needed but would devastate his relationship with the intelligence community.

The first meetings of the National Security Council and the committees created to analyze SALT and US nuclear posture exposed the administration's lack of consensus. Laird and the Pentagon claimed the Soviets had already tested SS-9s with MIRVs. Helms and CIA analysts disagreed, saying the Soviets' warheads lacked the typical "roll" exhibited when a MIRV detached and started its independent maneuvering.[3] That did not matter, Laird and company said, because if the Soviets did not have MIRVs now they would eventually. Rogers and State officials said developing an ABM would show the Soviets that the United States was not prepared to bargain in good faith. Nixon sided with the Pentagon. He needled Helms about the quality of their intelligence, to which Helms responded on February 12 by saying, "Our statements of Soviet accuracy are based on the real world, not estimates."[4] Nixon claimed the CIA "tended to underestimate" Soviet capabilities, which rendered their estimates meaningless. Helms disagreed, saying intelligence tended to do both. Nixon pushed again two days later, saying the United States was behind in the nuclear arms race and had to do something. Laird and the uniformed members of the military in the room agreed, but others did not. Deputy Defense Secretary David Packard, founder of computing and technology giant Hewlett-Packard, said that while the Soviets had more missiles, they were not as accurate as the Americans', and large but numbers of unreliable missiles posed less of a threat.[5] While Packard and Kissinger said neither side could launch a crippling first strike, Nixon looked "back to *Sputnik*," the 1957 Soviet satellite that launched the space race and caused a panic among US leaders.[6] The United States, Nixon told the group, is frozen in place technologically. "Are we moving forward adequately?"[7]

Smith, the arms control chief, tried to downplay the growing fear of Soviet dominance, saying, "We have led in MIRVs, [submarine-launched missiles], photo-reconnaissance."[8] Nixon wasn't listening. "They are one jump ahead of us," he said.[9] Smith, along with his allies at State, did not back down. On February 18, Rogers told the Senate Foreign Relations Committee led by Senator J. William Fulbright, an Arkansas Democrat, that he believed the nation should wait to deploy an ABM system until arms control talks with the Russians were done.[10] A day later at another NSC meeting on the issue, Smith continued his resistance to ABM and favored announcing that the United States will limit any ABM development to the same number the Soviets have and not "deploy them on first strike mode."[11] That drew immediate opposition from General Wheeler, the chairman of the Joint Chiefs, who said if he thought he had the ability to develop an ABM that gave him "first-strike capability, I would advocate it, destabilizing or not. It wouldn't bother me."[12] Nixon agreed.[13] ABM opponents, he said, were only winning the propaganda war because of their claims that the ABM would cost $100 billion and needlessly threaten the Soviets. "We can't be apologetic" about going ahead with ABM, Nixon said. "It would be a mistake to indicate we will delay a modest program until we see results" in SALT. "We shouldn't tie them together."

Laird followed Nixon's lead and told Fulbright's committee the following day about the "very rapid" progress the Soviets had made in the arms race, which made ABM essential.[14] A Wheeler memo to Laird a week later said "we want to deter Soviet nuclear attack on the United States," and if that failed, they wanted to end any conflict "with the United States in a position of relative advantage." Wheeler called for fewer missile sites than the now-dead Sentinel plan but more radar and to place ABM near the Minuteman sites. The proposal would also provide some protection to land-based bombers at certain air bases.[15] Laird presented Wheeler's plan to the White House, where Kissinger urged Nixon on March 5 to accept it.[16]

In a meeting that day in the NSC, Nixon gave Smith latitude to tell Congress that Nixon was not planning to push another full version of Sentinel, what they called the "thick" option.[17] Nixon's preference, as it was so often in the ABM debate, was to fudge the truth. "Leave the thick system hanging out there a bit and let's come down from it," Nixon told Smith. "You could say you strongly oppose it. . . . But say the matter is still up for consideration."[18] Smith's colleagues at State believed they could still sway Nixon, a sign they did not understand how Nixon and Kissinger had limited their influence. Deputy Secretary of State Elliot Richardson urged for a delay in ABM, saying it would give negotiators more leeway with the Soviets.[19] Smith and Alexis Johnson, the Undersecretary of State for political affairs, also wondered why they had to act now, since congressional opponents would pick apart the administration's plan, which lacked definition and reason.[20]

That was already happening, according to Bryce Harlow, Nixon's chief liaison to Congress, who gave Nixon a dire warning on March 10 that he would lose if he did not fight hard for ABM. Sentinel "has no chance whatsoever," Harlow said, and "even a modified system can now be passed only with maximum effort, including all-out Presidential participation." At the moment, the modified ABM would lose in the Senate by a 58–42 vote, Harlow said, because opponents "have had a field day." The White House could win but it had to fight back hard. Only forty senators were firmly opposed; Nixon could sway the remaining eighteen if he aggressively lobbed them with a campaign that presented "this system . . . as imperative for national security." If Nixon was not committed to the fight, he should avoid it. "But if the decision is to go full tilt, I think you would win."[21]

Nixon doubled down on his efforts to pass ABM, but he did it in the face of the facts. The Pentagon's science advisers thought ABM was too expensive and "can't really do the job," Nixon's chief science adviser, Lee DuBridge, told him on March 11. They were better off waiting a year for more research and development and then determining if it was worth moving ahead, DuBridge said.[22]

Nixon did not wait. He called for a "counter-offensive" that featured a bipartisan group of members of Congress at the White House on March 14.[23] Nixon found a mixed crowd of political supporters and hardened skeptics, such as Fulbright of Arkansas, who asked if it would it be better for the United States to just add more Polaris submarine-launched missiles. Nixon said the Soviets would consider that too provocative and just build more of their own missile-carrying submarines. Fulbright countered by saying the Soviets would not consider ABM provocative only because they did not think it would work. Nixon disagreed and then claimed ABM would have "no first-strike implications." But will it work? Senator John Pastore of Rhode Island asked Packard. Sort of, Packard responded. "My view is that the system in its basic concept will work," Packard answered in a less-than-ringing endorsement.[24]

Nixon followed that meeting with a news conference in which he announced the new ABM plan, called Safeguard.[25] He claimed it would be defensive only and would protect the United States from a Soviet first strike, a hypothetical attack from China, and ward off accidental attacks from any source. Perhaps he could negotiate the future of Safeguard in SALT, Nixon said, but he doubted the Soviets would be interested, since they had already invested so much in their system around Moscow. Nixon did not elaborate on his prime motivation—building Safeguard so as to trade it away. "We had to have it in order to be able to agree to forgo it," Nixon wrote in his memoirs.[26] He was also getting help from the secret FBI wiretaps meant to stop security leaks. One of the officials tapped was overheard telling someone about the ABM's prospects on Capitol Hill.

Laird worked feverishly to deliver ABM. He persuaded Nixon to declassify parts of the intelligence reports about the SS-9s, which could overwhelm US defenses, as Laird told the Senate Armed Services Committee on March 19. He repeated the claim two days later before Fulbright's committee.[27] There was "no question," Laird said, that the Soviets wanted a first-strike capability. Senate opponents remained unconvinced. Their in-house expert, Dr. Ralph Lapp, released a report in early April claiming SS-9 would not give the Soviets first-strike power. That report, the *New York Times* reported, "challenged the basic premise for its Safeguard antiballistic missile system, namely, that steps are necessary to protect Minuteman missiles against the growing number of the SS-9 intercontinental ballistic missiles."[28] The administration's argument, Lapp continued, simply did not make sense.

Less than three months into Nixon's administration, leaks from those excluded from his secret government were threatening to take down Nixon's plan for Safeguard and much of his strategy for SALT. On April 14, he sent a memo to Laird, Rogers, Kissinger, ambassador to South Vietnam Ellsworth Bunker, and ambassador to Germany Henry Cabot Lodge Jr., in which he lamented that "everyone seems to be going off in different directions. There must be a consistent line with no deviation whatever."[29] On Safeguard, he wrote, they had to focus on what the Soviets are doing, not on what they might do. Without Safeguard, the Soviet Union would increase its advantage in conventional weapons and close the gap in nuclear arms, rendering the United States as "basically a second-class [nuclear] power." The Russians already have an ABM system, Nixon said, so it is irrelevant if Safeguard will work. The United States had to match the Soviets in technological innovations in missile defense, and it cannot go into the SALT talks with an

ABM system only on the drawing board while the Soviets had an active one manned and encircling Moscow.

Nixon, for some reason, did not aim his memo at perhaps the people who needed to see it the most—Helms and his team of CIA analysts. Agency officials fought attempts to include a claim in the upcoming national intelligence estimate that the Soviets had tested a MIRV on their SS-9 missiles. The Agency clearly believed they had not. The NIE would be the product of the US Intelligence Board, which included the top officials from the CIA, FBI, Pentagon, Defense Intelligence Agency, National Security Agency, State Department, and elsewhere to provide the analysis of the full intelligence community. They remained deadlocked on the SS-9, which Helms told Kissinger in a May 26 memo.[30] While Defense officials believed it was not necessary to prove the Soviets tested an SS-9 with a MIRV, Helms said, "We cannot agree . . . since the Soviets have always tended to conduct very complete weapon systems tests. It would be a radical departure from normal practice if they were to deploy a weapon with the potential importance of MIRVs without complete testing." Pentagon analysis reached the same conclusion, Packard told Kissinger two days later, but it did not matter, since it was enough to know the possibility for a MIRV existed and they needed to plan accordingly.[31] Again, those who knew the evidence best dared not contradict the CIA on the essential fact that the Soviets had not tested a MIRV. They just wanted to wave away the inconvenient truth of the Agency's analysis.

Haig told Kissinger on May 28 they had to shut down the CIA and not allow the issue "to gather any more emotional momentum which will work to the disservice of the Administration." He urged Kissinger to get Helms to back off, so they could "minimize differences" between the CIA's analysis and the administration's claims about SS-9 and prevent congressional critics from using the divisions against them.[32] There was also opposition inside the White House. Arms control chief Smith raised the issues again on May 29 when he pushed Kissinger to reopen the issue of Safeguard. Kissinger refused.[33]

The Safeguard dissenters resorted to another leak to the press, this time a June 1 *New York Times* report that detailed how "the Pentagon is exaggerating the Soviet threat by distorting intelligence estimates."[34] Laird, the report said, had "contended that Pentagon projections of Soviet SS-9 strength were based on 'new evidence,' not available to the Johnson Administration. In secret briefings, the CIA has reportedly said it has no new intelligence information justifying Mr. Laird's extrapolation." Laird, the story continued, had called the SS-9 a first-strike weapon. "No such judgment has reportedly been reached by the intelligence community," wrote reporter John Finney, who also cited senators as reluctant to do anything to endanger Helms, who one senator called "the only one under present conditions who tells it as he sees it."

Nixon, who had only weeks earlier approved FBI wiretaps on the telephones of NSC staff members and one reporter, erupted when he saw the *Times* report. Nixon sent Kissinger a handwritten note demanding that he "Give Helms unshirted hell for this! (2) We know it is part true (his Georgetown underlings). (3) Tell him to crack down. (4) Also—tell Cushman."[35] That referred to marine general Robert Cushman, Helms's deputy at the CIA and Nixon's national security adviser while he was vice president.

Kissinger met with Helms on June 2 and discussed "in considerable detail" how the CIA's analysis would affect the ABM bill, Kissinger wrote Nixon.[36] "You may rest assured that Helms is aware of the President's views on this matter." Nixon never trusted Helms or the CIA, and he thought he had another reason for that distrust. It was possible, perhaps probable, that someone at the CIA had leaked out the intelligence details to the *Times* and friendly senators. Kissinger knew the CIA's estimates were correct, but he still carried Nixon's water and told the president on June 5 that he would ask the CIA to alter its intelligence.[37] "I have asked the CIA to have the United States Intelligence Board reassess certain aspects of the Soviet ICBM program, especially the SS-9 and multiple reentry programs." Included in the note, Kissinger wrote Nixon, was an updated position paper on Safeguard, "principally by amplifying the statement of the Soviet threat." Kissinger was putting more chips down on what he, Nixon, and the CIA knew was already a false position.

By June 12, the intelligence board had the latest version of the estimate on the SS-9 and Soviet weapons.[38] Nixon told Kissinger to "call Helms and tell him he has fifteen minutes to decide which side he is on." Kissinger called Helms and then told Nixon that Helms was "telling the truth to everyone" because there was "no evidence that [the SS-9 warheads] can be individually targeted."[39] Kissinger told Nixon he thought Helms was "on the ball."

He was not. The intelligence board approved the NIE on June 12 with the CIA's language that noted the differences between the Agency and the Pentagon on the SS-9s' guidance.[40] Kissinger was scheduled to meet with Cushman the following day to review the continued lack of unanimity that Nixon desired. Notes Haig prepared for Kissinger for the meeting said the White House was still worried that any estimate "which avoids any reasoned predictions based on the synthesis of known and probable facts, raises the question of whether an intelligence analysis is needed in the first place." The

CIA still had not been brought to heel. Abbot Smith, the CIA's director of national estimates, moved on June 16 for the board to approve the revised estimate, which contained more Agency analysis questioning the Soviets' testing of a MIRVed SS-9.

Neither Helms nor Nixon backed down. Nixon could not simply order the Agency to alter its intelligence, but he hoped to force the CIA to do that on its own by increasing the pressure on the Agency from various quarters. NSC aide Lawrence Lynn harped on the overall Soviet intelligence estimate, calling it "one of the most badly split estimates in some time; DIA, the Services and State have taken many exceptions to the text in footnotes, and some of the disagreements are fundamental."[41] Kissinger then created a MIRV Working Group to study the issues of Soviet testing and a proposed testing ban. This group of scientists from State, Defense, CIA, the NSC, and Arms Control and Disarmament Agency reviewed many of the reports by other panels and reached roughly the same conclusions. On MIRV capability, they determined that a ban on future testing would not affect the United States as much as the Russians, because the American capability was so much more advanced. The panel's final report on July 23 continued to display the divisions found in the intelligence board's estimate. State, ACDA, CIA, and the Pentagon's Office of Systems Analysis said the Soviets had not tested a MIRV, while the Joint Chiefs of Staff and other Pentagon agencies believed "that the Soviets could deploy a MIRV system without further flight testing." Once again, the Pentagon offices most intimately involved with obtaining and operating an ABM system viewed the data through the most alarmist prism. Nevertheless, the report was published as it was written, and Nixon was again denied a consensus on Soviet MIRVs.[42]

It turned out he did not need it. The Senate voted twice on August 9 on two attempts to kill Safeguard. One was defeated 51–49 and the other 50–50. Although the overall Senate defense-spending bill would not come up for a vote until November, the defeat of the two amendments meant that Safeguard survived to become the bargaining chip Nixon desperately wanted. The following day, Nixon directed Kissinger, Counsel John Ehrlichman, and Chief of Staff Bob Haldeman to "get out the true story" of his victory that should emphasize "that RN made the decision to tackle ABM head on against the advice of most of his major advisers, including particularly the State Department." Nixon wanted his team to hammer home how he pushed hard to "knock down anything in the way of intelligence reports or other things that might be harmful."[43] The push on inconvenient intelligence continued, even after Nixon had secured Safeguard's future. Throughout the summer, Nixon, Kissinger, and Laird kept pushing Helms to give in on the NIE. Helms eventually caved in, telling the US Intelligence Board on September 4 that he would remove the CIA paragraph disputing the lack of proven Soviet MIRV testing.[44] Helms tried to downplay the change by saying he served the president and had to accede to his wishes. If so, Helms could have made that decision months earlier and saved himself the aggravation. In the end, Helms's delay hurt his relationship with Nixon and damaged his reputation with his CIA subordinates. They realized the pressure Nixon had placed on him, but they also saw the risks of independent analysis for a president who did not value it.

By November, Congress had approved the spending for Safeguard, which gave Nixon a significant legislative victory in the Democratic-controlled Congress. Few Americans knew how Nixon demanded intelligence be shaped to conform to his wishes or how Kissinger and Haig would deliver his continued pressure on the intelligence community. Helms, who enjoyed his reputation as a straight shooter, knew the problems for him and the Agency would only get worse. Not long after winning on Safeguard, Kissinger brought in a new member of the NSC—Andrew Marshall, a longtime official at the RAND Corporation—to study the intelligence Kissinger and Nixon received. One item of particular focus was the CIA's analysis on the SS-9 missile, which Kissinger knew was correct. That did not matter. Nixon wanted intelligence that conformed to his desires, and he would use whatever pressure he could to get it.

CHAPTER SEVEN

The Cambodia Sideshow (1970)

THE SECRET B-52 BOMBING OF CAMBODIA THAT STARTED IN MARCH 1969 was aimed at destroying the North Vietnamese and Viet Cong sanctuaries and COSVN, North Vietnam's Central Office for South Vietnam, from which US commanders believed the North directed the war. Early reports, jubilantly reported back to Kissinger at the NSC, were that the bombings had exacted serious damage, which could give the United States more breathing room to negotiate a peace deal and remove troops. Nixon announced his first planned withdrawals shortly after the bombings started as part of Vietnamization, which he hoped would provide cover for the United States to get out of the war while not declaring a unilateral withdrawal and weakening the US negotiating posture. He seemed to forget, however, that he had already signaled through ambassador Dobrynin that his heart was not truly in winning the war but in getting out without creating the impression that the United States was giving up.

By late 1969, it was clear that any damage inflicted on the sanctuaries was temporary. Abrams and the Pentagon wanted more cross-border raids in both Cambodia and Laos. Commanders considered the Dewey Canyon raid in January 1969, which crossed into Laos briefly, a great success. Laos, governed by a shaky coalition of royalists and communists, seemed the most likely site of a major expansion of the fighting. The CIA was already backing a tribal chieftain, General Vang Pao of the Meo tribe, who was fighting the North Vietnamese. By early 1970, the NSC was debating how much more help he would need to keep the fight alive. North Vietnamese supplies and troops continued to pour through Laos and into South Vietnam. Nixon and Kissinger spent hours in the year's first months trying to save Laos without expanding the US commitment there. They were also trying to limit any exposure of the US effort there, which had come under fire by a Senate subcommittee led by Senator Stuart Symington of Missouri. The NSC

met specifically on February 27, 1970, to devise a plan to deal with Symington and his increasing demands about Laos. "Symington knows everything,"
lamented Secretary of State Rogers.[1] Hardly anyone in the White House
paid any attention to Cambodia, even as they knew B-52s were wiping out
huge swaths of the countryside.

Cambodia, however, was crumbling. Not only did the bombings fail to
destroy COSVN, they drove the North Vietnamese and Viet Cong deeper
into Cambodia, which had little to stop them. The effect, one officer told
author William Shawcross, was "the same as taking a beehive the size of
basketball and poking it with a stick. They were mad."[2] Inside Cambodia,
the communists destabilized local towns, which weakened the control of the
national government of Prince Norodom Sihanouk, who had managed to
navigate a tenuous neutrality while war raged to Cambodia's east. The mercurial Sihanouk, in power since 1941, had been an irritant to the United
States for years, and relations between the two countries had gotten worse
after serious fighting started in Vietnam. By January, a desperate Sihanouk
tried to broaden his government by adding two rivals, Prime Minister Lon
Nol, a general, and Deputy Prime Minister Sirik Matak. He also reached out
to the United States, but Rogers and others were leery of doing too much
since Sihanouk had allowed the smuggling of weapons to the communists
hiding in the sanctuaries, which was enabled by Lon Nol, whom the communists had bribed to let the smuggling continue. Kissinger believed a recent
magazine article written by Sihanouk showed a serious change of heart. "It
is an unabashed pitch for aid," Kissinger said, adding that "the mere fact that
Sihanouk had sought a resumption of American aid, and that we had accom-
modated him, would have considerable impact in Southeast Asia."[3] A bigger
challenge, Kissinger noted, was avoiding congressional scrutiny, which they
had evaded so far with the bombing.

At the time, expanding aid and relations with Sihanouk was a moot point.
He had left his country in January for a two-month stint in France. Conditions deteriorated in his absence, and anticommunist riots paralyzed much
of the country. Many suspected his rivals had sparked the riots to undermine
Sihanouk. Yet despite a few CIA reports on the turmoil, no one anticipated
what would come next—a March 18 coup that deposed Sihanouk. The White
House debate quickly turned from Sihanouk to what to do with the new
government. Nixon's initial instinct was to declare neutrality and not overtly
embrace the new government, particularly given the reservations about Lon
Nol's tacit support of the communist arms-smuggling efforts. While the US
military had openly backed Sihanouk's overthrow for years, no one wanted to
take the blame for the coup or appear too eager to exploit it.

Kissinger and Rogers initially believed the United States should keep quiet.[4] At the time, Laos seemed like a greater crisis than Cambodia. Sihanouk's ouster, Kissinger said, "may compensate for Laos." The CIA discounted a communist insurgency in Cambodia, because they already roamed freely throughout the countryside.[5] They did not need to open a second front in a war that was already costing them dearly. Cambodia's coup was a crisis, but Nixon was still more focused on Laos, where he wanted to launch more B-52 strikes. Nixon had competing impulses in Southeast Asia. He wanted to bring more troops home, but conditions on the ground would not let him. He also wanted to simultaneously make a grand military statement while removing the men and equipment that made it possible. Balancing these competing impulses in Cambodia only exacerbated the concern Nixon created among the military leaders responsible for carrying out his orders.

Nixon knew he would be attacked for widening the war if he granted economic and military aid to the new Cambodian government. The B-52 strikes he ordered in 1969 still remained secret. Doing nothing was not an option, either. The continued North Vietnamese use of the sanctuaries hurt the war effort in Vietnam and made it more difficult to withdraw troops. Also, Kissinger wrote Nixon on March 19 that Lon Nol needed to keep his allies happy, so he would most likely do nothing to stop the arms smuggling to the communists in the sanctuaries.

Nixon told Kissinger to tell Helms to have the CIA develop covert actions to prop up Lon Nol but to do it outside official channels.[6] Within a week, Helms gave Kissinger a plan that included covert weapons shipments and the return of US agents to Cambodia.[7] A positive Cambodian response, Helms said, would trigger the sending of financial aid and international support and "develop a clandestine combat control center to coordinate Cambodian military activities with the allied military effort." Nixon agreed, and the CIA quickly expanded its operations inside Cambodia. Soon, the CIA would have one of its biggest intelligence coups, which would have the ironic effect of giving Nixon more ammunition to use to attack the CIA.

Nixon also wanted more military action, which his commanders desired. The B-52 strikes killed enemy troops, damaged their facilities, and destroyed their supplies, which, Kissinger wrote Nixon on March 28, had "a direct bearing on the success of Vietnamization." Laird said even more airstrikes raised possible political risks, Kissinger continued, but that Bunker and Abrams believed the raids have been "one of the most telling operations in the entire war." That was enough for Nixon. "K. Step up menu series immediately (no appeal)," he told Kissinger, and the bombings increased.[8]

The White House's evolving policy toward Cambodia in the three months following the coup epitomized Nixon's emphasis on secrecy and confused lines of communication. The CIA had started covert operations without telling the group meant to oversee them. Nixon talked directly to commanders without informing Laird or Rogers. Haig contacted officials in Saigon, particularly ambassador Bunker, to direct policy while not telling Kissinger. The top military commanders in Washington and Saigon—General Wheeler, Admiral Moorer, and General Abrams—were kept in the dark about many of the developments while they also watched Nixon continue to announce plans to pull more troops from the area. No one other than Nixon had a complete view of developments, and his were often clouded by his evening drinking habits.

Laird met with Nixon and Haig on March 31 to complain that no one had told him of the backchannel messages to Bunker in Saigon.[9] Communications between Phnom Penh and Washington were terrible, Laird said, and the CIA had no station in the Cambodian capital. Nixon told Haig to immediately fix the communications in Phnom Penh, but to say the government needed the improvements to "help US citizens." Nixon also lifted the ban on cross-border raids, telling only Laird, Haig, Abrams, and Admiral John McCain, the commander in chief in the Pacific. Kissinger only found out later. "When the hell did all this happen?" he wrote Nixon.[10]

Haig was particularly active in this period. He shared the military's belief that the troop withdrawals hurt the US war effort. The commanders wanted to delay the withdrawals as they developed their plans for Cambodia. Haig forwarded their thoughts to Nixon on April 3, saying the commanders at the Military Assistance Command Vietnam (MACV) believed that US air support and possibly ground troops were necessary for any operation against the Cambodia sanctuaries.[11] Even Haig saw the MACV plan as an effort to "beat the drum for no US troop withdrawals beyond April 15 levels" and an exaggeration of the threat.[12] Nevertheless, Haig had clearly chosen the side of the commanders in Vietnam and at home against Laird, whom he savaged in notes to Kissinger, particularly in his overview of a Laird April 4 memo in which the Defense Secretary claimed Vietnamization was making progress.[13] Laos and Cambodia lacked leadership or stability, which also offered new possibilities. The United States, Laird continued, should not go into Cambodia, although using South Vietnamese troops would work. Haig attacked Laird, writing Kissinger that Laird had conceded for the "first time that Vietnamization is a farce."[14] Nixon, Haig continued, will "ask what in the hell Laird has been doing all these months" and that "the President will gag upon reading this rambling, purposeless softening effort."

Between April 4 and 22, Lon Nol's government sent increasingly desperate messages to Saigon and Washington asking for money, weapons, or both. Lon Non, Lon Nol's brother, told Michael Rives, the top US diplomat in Phnom Penh, that the Cambodian military needed up to 250,000 arms to survive. Rives considered that figure high but agreed the United States should send some limited aid but no troops.[15] Nixon and Kissinger also wanted to send arms, most likely Soviet-made AK-47 assault rifles through a third country, such as Indonesia. Weapons shipments of another kind, those that passed through the southern port of Sihanoukville to the communist sanctuaries, also drew Nixon's attention. Even as they neared a decision to jump in fully behind Lon Nol, they worried about the support of local chiefs for arms smuggling. Nixon told Kissinger, "I want Helms & State & Defense & your staff to give me some options other than just 'letting the dust settle.'"[16] Kissinger dutifully asked Helms if they could pay off local leaders to prevent the smuggling.[17]

Nixon's plotting reached a zenith on April 13, as he and Kissinger prepared to meet Rogers, Laird, and Wheeler to set the pace of troop withdrawals for the next year. Laird wanted to maintain the planned pace of withdrawals, while the chiefs wanted to backload any withdrawals to the final months of the yearlong period. "You have decided to announce the withdrawal of 150,000 additional US forces over the next year or so," Kissinger told Nixon in his premeeting memo, which also highlighted Nixon's continued deception of his own team.[18] "You have also decided to keep this decision from the members of the Cabinet and the bureaucracy, as well as the troop contributing countries, exclusive of Thieu and Ambassador Bunker." Kissinger continued by highlighting the disagreements between Laird and the commanders. "You should concentrate on the magnitude of the withdrawal increment and its implications in light of what has developed into a substantial disagreement between General Abrams and the Joint Chiefs of Staff on one hand and the Secretary of Defense on the other," Kissinger wrote.[19] Laird favored withdrawing forty thousand troops by August 15, while Wheeler and the chiefs wanted to postpone any withdrawal decision until June 15.

As they developed their plan, Kissinger sent backchannel messages to Bunker and Abrams to determine what they were willing to do.[20] Neither Laird nor Rogers knew of the messages. Abrams and Laird told Kissinger they could live with removing 150,000 troops but wanted to keep "the bulk of these withdrawals to the first half of 1971 and believe Thieu will accept this route," Kissinger wrote.[21] Abrams and the Chiefs did not want to remove any US troops, because they "see the coming months as critical in maintaining Vietnamese confidence." Further withdrawals, they argued, would leave commanders vulnerable to developments in Laos and Cambodia, a feeling Haig and other NSC staff members shared. Haig believed the first three phases of troop withdrawals had cost Abrams's ability to meet any increased North Vietnamese activity, and the South Vietnamese military had not improved under Vietnamization to warrant the removal of US troops. Vietnamization had a better chance of succeeding, Haig said, if most of the US troops remained in place until the end of the fall rainy season. Laird, Kissinger highlighted, wanted to pull out forty thousand troops between April 15 and August 15. That, Kissinger concluded, was what Nixon should do, but he added an extra twist of deception.

"In order to do this, you should suggest at the conclusion of the discussion that you are leaning towards proceeding with the withdrawal of between 35,000 and 40,000 additional US troops between April 15 and August 15," Kissinger wrote.[22] "This decision will likely prove to be a great disappointment to the military and will set the stage for your actual subsequent decision, which will not be made known until just before your announcement." So Nixon and Kissinger were going around Laird, who favored more immediate troop cuts, to Abrams and Bunker in Saigon to signal to them that they favored more backloaded reductions when they actually preferred Laird's suggestion for political reasons. In the end, on April 20, Nixon announced he would try to split the difference by removing 150,000 troops over the course of the year, with the possibility that most would happen at the end of that period. Nixon satisfied no one, and his subterfuge meant no one, neither Laird nor the generals, believed Nixon. They knew they were being deceived. Laird made his recommendations, Kissinger would later write in his memoirs, with the idea that they might stimulate the North Vietnamese to make concessions during the Paris Peace Talks.[23] Laird did not know that Kissinger had already made such an offer in his secret talks with the North Vietnamese and had been rejected.

With the decision made on troop cuts, Nixon turned back to Cambodia. He had made few public statements since the coup. Nixon wanted to help Lon Nol, but did not want to be criticized for widening the war into a neutral country. Abrams and the Chiefs did not believe the South Vietnamese could eliminate the sanctuaries and COSVN on their own, and neither did Helms. Despite Nixon's criticism of the Agency's intelligence from Cambodia, the beleaguered CIA director was his biggest ally in supporting an attack on the sanctuaries. Helms had set up a pipeline to send AK-47s to the Cambodian military while also activating local groups to fight the North Vietnamese, just as the Agency did in Laos.[24] Nixon wanted to avoid using US troops in Cambodia, but each day he learned more about the worsening conditions in

Phnom Penh and heard Lon Nol's increasingly desperate pleadings for help. His views shifted.

They moved because of an unlikely source—Vice President Spiro Agnew, the former Maryland governor whom Nixon ignored unless he wanted Agnew to attack the media for alleged liberal bias and not treating Nixon with enough respect. Nixon did not return the favor. Agnew's counsel was rarely sought, but he was present for an April 22 NSC meeting. Nixon ordered no notes be taken during the meeting, but Kissinger recounted the meeting in his memoirs.[25] Laird and Rogers backed the least aggressive plan, a South Vietnamese offensive into the sanctuary areas for "shallow" operations but with very little, if any, US backing. Kissinger favored using the Vietnamese forces with US tactical and logistical backing, while Abrams, Bunker, and the chiefs wanted an aggressive joint attack with US and Vietnamese ground troops and US air support. Laird and Rogers thought the third option would trigger massive opposition at home but provide little military benefit in either Cambodia or Vietnam.

Nixon made a rare commitment and backed Kissinger's option. Then Agnew, who had remained silent, chimed in. He did not understand "all the pussyfooting about."[26] If the Vietnamese moved into Cambodia, he said, US troops should help them with the full support of the White House. Agnew's sudden volubility surprised Nixon, Kissinger wrote, because the often-ignored vice president had suddenly become the alpha male in the room. Nixon complained to Kissinger later that he thought Agnew had sandbagged him.

Shortly after the meeting, Nixon issued National Security Decision Memorandum 56, which ordered an immediate increase in US military aid to Cambodia, preferably through third countries; a diplomatic surge aimed at attracting more help from other nations, cross-border raids by South Vietnamese forces with US artillery backing, and the movement of ethnic Cambodian forces in South Vietnam back to Phnom Penh.[27]

The trend toward intervention in Cambodia was clear, which triggered a rebellion inside the NSC. Three of Kissinger's best aides—Anthony Lake, Roger Morris, and Winston Lord—wrote a memo warning him about the dangers of invading Cambodia.[28] US intervention had clear limits, they wrote, and using US troops "would probably be militarily ineffective in the long run unless we were willing to become bogged down as a garrison force in another country." The United States needed to determine its true objectives for Cambodia, which, the trio recommended, should "be a return to the status quo ante without Sihanouk." Cambodia, they concluded, was too far gone for a desirable solution. Kissinger knew he had lost their support but hoped Nixon would slow down and enable Kissinger to avoid a breach with his key assistants.

The following day, Kissinger sent Nixon another memo in which he again avoided calling for US troops in Cambodia, but said the fall of the Lon Nol government would endanger both Vietnamization and South Vietnam.[29] Nixon highlighted that section and said Kissinger should remind him to include that in any speech he may have to give. Kissinger also asked Nixon to approve using B-52 strikes and tactical air support for the South Vietnamese troops who would enter Cambodia. Nixon approved, taking another step to a deeper US commitment.

On the morning of April 24, Nixon and Kissinger brought Helms, Moorer, and General Robert Cushman, the deputy CIA director, for another meeting on Cambodia.[30] They specifically excluded Laird and Rogers. Kissinger later said the meeting was only meant to discuss military options and was not a policy debate, but Nixon was just mad at Laird and Rogers for bureaucratic delays over a planned attack in Cambodia's Parrot's Beak region.[31] Helms and Moorer argued for a robust combined US-South Vietnamese operation, while Kissinger remained relatively quiet. Kissinger called Laird after the meeting, and Laird tried some trickery of his own, telling Kissinger that Abrams opposed the larger operation, a claim Kissinger rapidly disproved by calling Moorer.[32] Kissinger then called Wheeler and told him to tell Abrams to start planning for it as if it would happen.

Kissinger also started to reach out to sympathetic members of Congress, starting with Senator John Stennis, the Mississippi Democrat who chaired the Senate Armed Services Committee. He told Stennis the general outlines of the attacks and about the months-long secret bombing campaign. Stennis already knew about the bombing, which was news to Nixon. "The senator knows about Menu?" Nixon asked.[33] Yes, Kissinger, said. Nixon liked Stennis; the wiry Mississippian shared the same belief in a strong military and deference to the White House. Kissinger then put Stennis on the phone, and Nixon laid out his rationale for action: "The first choice is air action including the B-52's which *only* you and [Georgia] Senator [Richard] Russell know about. It's the best-kept secret of the war."[34] Nixon closed by telling Stennis an exaggerated version of reality: "We are not going to fly anybody in to save Phnom Penh—or Cambodia. We are going to do what is necessary to help save our men in South Vietnam. They can't have those sanctuaries there."

That evening, Kissinger called Helms, who said he backed intervention if Nixon was willing to take the political heat it would ignite.[35] Kissinger thanked him and added that if Nixon wanted to go ahead with the larger plan, he needed to tell his cabinet, particularly Laird and Rogers, "even if the decision has already been made and an order is in the desk drawer. You can't ram it down their throats without them having a chance to give their views." Helms agreed, but added that Nixon should not let them think he may change his mind.

On the night of April 25, Kissinger was invited along for what turned into a troubling cruise on the Potomac River on the *Sequoia*, the presidential yacht. Nixon, Attorney General John Mitchell, and Bebe Rebozo, Nixon's longtime friend, turned the trip into a floating bacchanal that ended with another viewing of the movie *Patton*, which Nixon watched as a kind of motivational video.[36]

These conversations built up Nixon to his final decision. He called the NSC into a Sunday afternoon meeting on April 26 in his Executive Office Building hideaway.[37] Helms started off by detailing the conditions in Hanoi and the region. Once again, no official notes exist from the meeting, which Kissinger detailed in his memoirs. Laird and Rogers sat through the meeting, to Kissinger's amazement, without objection, although Kissinger realized that Nixon had spelled out his plans for the invasion. "Nixon tried to avoid confrontation with his Secretaries of State and Defense by pretending that we were merely listening to a briefing," Kissinger wrote. "He would follow with a directive later. To my astonishment, both Rogers and Laird—who after all were familiar with their illusive chief's methods by now—fell in with the charade it was all a planning exercise and did not take a position. They avoided the question of why Nixon would call his advisers together on a Sunday night to hear a contingency briefing." Shortly after the meeting, Nixon and Kissinger retired to the White House family quarters, where Nixon dashed off National Security Decision Memorandum 57, which put the invasion plans on paper. US troops, he wrote, could go thirty kilometers into Cambodia, and any specific operations would have to be approved by him. Nixon had made his call, and the inevitable objections came immediately.

Rogers, Laird, Kissinger, Nixon, and chief of staff Haldeman met the next morning at the White House. Rogers protested that he and Laird had been misled.[38] The Rogers-Kissinger relationship played itself out again. Rogers blamed Kissinger for tricking him and Laird.[39] Rogers said COSVN was not a valid target because it moved constantly and lacked any real infrastructure. Fourteen months of B-52 bombing had not destroyed COSVN, and if it had been destroyed, US troops would not have been needed to invade Cambodia. Rogers also had to testify before Congress the next day and did not want to have to lie if anyone asked him about a planned US invasion. Laird objected to the idea that the Washington Special Actions Group, not the Pentagon, would control the operations.[40] The meeting, which lasted for an hour, ended with Nixon waffling as he often did when confronted by angry subordinates. He said he would think about it and ask Abrams for his opinions again.

Laird went at it again, presenting Nixon with a detailed list of objections. He unsuccessfully tried to sway Mitchell.[41] Laird, Mitchell, Rogers, and Nixon met again on the morning of April 28, and Laird tried again.[42] Nixon was unmoved. It was his call, Nixon said, and Mitchell recorded that Nixon had considered the adverse reaction in Congress and the public from the decision. He also said he dictated a tape that included Laird's and Rogers's objections. Laird's warnings about public reactions were prescient. When Daniel Henkin, the Pentagon spokesman, announced the next day that US planes would provide support for the Vietnamese going into Cambodia, the predictable controversy erupted in Congress about Nixon's illegal expansion of the war effort. That was the easy part.[43]

When Nixon addressed the nation by television the following evening, he lied repeatedly, particularly when he claimed the United States had not violated Cambodia's neutrality. "American policy since then has been to scrupulously respect the neutrality of the Cambodian people," he said, adding that the United States had never attacked the sanctuaries.[44] That ignored the more than 3,500 B-52 sorties over the country since March 1969. The United States would join with the South Vietnamese to go into Cambodia to root out the communist sanctuaries once and for all, Nixon continued, which would enable Vietnamization to continue and thrive. US troops would stay in Cambodia for a maximum of six to eight weeks. "I would rather be a one-term president and do what I believe is right than to be a two-term president at the cost of seeing America become a second-rate power and to see this nation accept the first defeat in its proud 190-year history," Nixon said.

On the ground, the initial results looked positive, as the allied forces kept the initiative and killed hundreds of enemy troops. The North Vietnamese pushed deeper into Cambodia, which exacerbated the chaos. In the United States, the predictions of the NSC's Lake, Morris, and Lord came true. On April 22, they wrote, "US troops in Cambodia would have a strong and damaging political effect in the US which would both hurt the President's Vietnam policies and divide the country further. Fears of widened US involvement in the ground war in Southeast Asia are evident."[45] Protests erupted on college campuses across the country, as students doubted Nixon's claim that the brief incursion would hasten the end of the Vietnam War. On May 4, the protests brought tragedy, as Ohio National Guard troops brought in to control protests at Kent State University shot and killed four students. Nixon's popularity dipped, particularly after he was overheard referring to college protesters as "bums." Protests hit the NSC, too, as Lake, Morris, and

William Watts resigned after the invasion, saying they could not stay in their jobs with a clear conscience.

━━ ❦ ━━

Worst of all, the US invasion did not provide the answers Nixon had hoped. The attacks killed thousands of enemy troops, but COSVN remained unfound and untouched. Nixon was trapped by his rhetoric that the US commitment to Cambodia was limited. He did not want the country or his government to realize just how much would have to be devoted to propping up Lon Nol. In Congress, Senators Frank Church and John Sherman Cooper drafted a proposal that would have ended funding for any US troops in Cambodia or Laos after June 30. Lon Nol's government teetered on the verge of collapse daily. His army lacked the training and weapons to take on the combat-hardened North Vietnamese and Viet Cong troops. By mid-May, just two weeks into the fighting, Nixon had grown desperate. He needed someone in Phnom Penh who could work with the NSC free from the interference of the Defense and State bureaucracies. Haig wrote Kissinger that the United States needed to "have an individual on the ground in Phnom Penh who is fully abreast of the President's thinking and who would hopefully manifest a higher level of diplomatic skill" than the current diplomatic staff.[46] Haig had a candidate in mind—Jonathan Frederic "Fred" Ladd, a recently retired Army Special Forces colonel who had known Haig since 1949. Before retiring, Ladd had created the Khmer Serei, a band of ethnic Khmer living in South Vietnam and fighting with the US forces. After retiring in 1969, Ladd moved to Florida to run a charter fishing boat service, far from Southeast Asia and his old life.[47] His old life never remained that far behind, however, and Haig came calling in May.

Nixon's plan for Ladd was typically deceptive. He wanted Ladd to coordinate the complicated details of helping the Cambodian government and military, but Ladd had to work off the books to enable Nixon to claim the United States was not opening another major front in the Vietnam War. Ladd would report directly to Kissinger and through him to Nixon. That gave Ladd extra clout with Lon Nol, who knew that speaking to Ladd meant speaking directly to the president of the United States. And Nixon wanted to hear from Ladd. On May 25, Kissinger told Nixon they needed Ladd in Phnom Penh as soon as possible.[48] In a May 31 meeting in San Clemente, California, with Laird, Wheeler, Abrams, and Admiral McCain, Nixon said Ladd needed to be in Phnom Penh immediately.[49] "It is essential that the Cambodians know that we are behind them."

Ladd arrived in mid-June and faced immediate demands for information. "Was Colonel Ladd also available to help out yet? Had any reports come in from him?" Nixon asked in a June 15 NSC meeting.[50] When it came to the mysterious Ladd, both State and the military thought he reported to them. Meanwhile, Haig worked the backchannel relationship quickly, particularly in a June 17 message in which he told Ladd that Nixon "wants any and all administrative bottlenecks and red tape cut in order to take those steps now needed to prevent a takeover of Cambodia by Communist forces."[51] The "coming days and weeks," Haig continued, "may be critical and that in large measure the outcome may pivot on psychological issues rather than military power." While the North Vietnamese propaganda suggested they could isolate Phnom Penh militarily, Haig said, "We question whether enemy strength would permit takeover." What did Ladd think?

Ladd's early reports back indicated initial success and that he had managed to skirt much of the bureaucracy and get to Lon Nol quickly. MACV in Saigon, Ladd reported, responded quickly to whatever the Cambodians needed. The South Vietnamese government was also helpful. Lon Nol was encouraged by what the United States was trying to do but also frustrated by the lack of help from other Asian governments. Ladd also agreed with Haig that the North Vietnamese threats to capture Phnom Penh were, at least for the moment, empty propaganda. Ladd knew his shadowy role at the embassy, where he first worked out of an unconverted bathroom, had piqued the curiosity of his colleagues, who wondered "why I was sent here," Ladd wrote Haig in a June 18 backchannel message.[52] Rives at the embassy had been cooperative, but he was overwhelmed. The embassy's military attaches, Ladd wrote, "are not the types to inspire confidence nor are they particularly well organized to tackle the problem at hand. They are now working directly under my control and I am attempting to get them productive." That meant Ladd had crossed over into the Pentagon's realm, which the Chiefs opposed. Nixon cared little about that, if he even realized it. He told Haig shortly after learning of Ladd's report that he wanted more. "Is he on the job and working?" Nixon asked Haig.[53] Yes, Haig responded, adding that Ladd was "going to start screaming for shipments. For stuff they need for psychological reasons." Nixon told Haig "if they need trucks and armored vehicles, get them in there. Just get them in there. There are certainly plenty of them over there. I hope he realizes what we expect of him. Needle the hell out of him. I expect a report every 12 hours."

No one was more vexed by Ladd's curious role than Admiral Moorer, who resented his lack of control in Cambodia and thought that running a major US military aid program through a retired army colonel made little sense. Moorer knew the White House alternated between denying the Chiefs information and using them to go around Laird. During a fall tour to Phnom Penh, Moorer made his move. He took Ladd aside and told him that he had just spoken to Kissinger and that there was a change of plans. "Admiral Moorer got me alone," Ladd told an interviewer in 1982, "and told me that Mr. Kissinger had told him to tell me that damn it I was to stop doing things the way I was to do it and take orders from him and ah . . . So, I told him, I said well, I just received a message from Mr. Kissinger saying just the opposite that ah he was very satisfied and I said I'll be happy to pass on your message to him . . . and try to straighten it out and he said, 'Oh no, well maybe it wasn't Henry. Maybe it was somebody else that said that.' And that was about the last time I ever spoke to Admiral Moorer when I was in Cambodia."[54] That did not mean Moorer had forgotten about Ladd or the other times the White House had deceived him and other commanders. He resolved to find his own sources of information from the NSC. He had one at his fingertips—the Chiefs' liaison office at the NSC, which had already started collecting White House documents and sending them back to Moorer. Soon, the office, which Laird warned Kissinger about in January 1969, started gathering more information to show Moorer what Kissinger and Nixon were hiding from him.

By going into Cambodia, Nixon widened the war in Vietnam while also expanding his fight with his own government. Both the State Department and Pentagon felt slighted by his maneuvering, wounds to their pride that would not heal. Nixon's ongoing war with the CIA found another front, too, and the Cambodia crisis allowed Nixon to turn one of the Agency's biggest successes against it. It involved the communists' use of the Cambodian port of Sihanoukville to smuggle Chinese weapons to the sanctuaries. As with the SS-9 intelligence, the Agency differed with the Defense Intelligence Agency and MACV in Saigon. The CIA analysts believed most of the North Vietnamese supplies moved through Laos. Military intelligence considered Sihanoukville the main conduit for weapons for the sanctuaries.

The debate over Sihanoukville preceded Nixon. Sihanouk denied any weapons went through the port to the Viet Cong. Pentagon and CIA officials knew Sihanouk was lying, but they disagreed over how much. Military analysts pegged the number of weapons moving through the port at the high end, while Agency analysts provided a much lower estimate. The MACV contingent in Saigon believed Agency analysts insisted too much on exact confirmation of weapons shipments. Military intelligence had found too many Chinese weapons in the border areas and in South Vietnam to believe they had come just through Laos. During one of Nixon's first NSC meetings, General Andrew Goodpaster mentioned that any outreach to Sihanouk needed to include "our concern about Sihanoukville and the movement of North Vietnamese arms through that port."[55] A March 22, 1969, intelligence analysis on the war emphasized the continued disagreement between various agencies. "MACV has estimated that some 10,000 tons of arms and ammunition have gone through Sihanoukville to the border between October 1967 and September 1968," the analysis said, adding that CIA and State disagreed.[56] Agency estimates of weapons moving through Sihanoukville were half those claimed by MACV and by Laird. The shipments, and the disagreements about them, continued into the US invasion.

The reopening of the CIA station in Phnom Penh improved intelligence, as operatives no longer had to guess about events outside the capital. One agent developed a relationship with Col. Les Kosem of the Cambodian army, who single-handedly showed the CIA that it had been wrong about Sihanoukville.[57] Kosem provided detailed bills of lading and other shipping records that showed the true scope of the smuggling. Agency officials were proud of their discovery. It reflected, they believed, the best of the CIA's field operatives, and it would help guide future moves in Cambodia. It also meant Helms and his top subordinates would have to admit a major mistake and pay the consequences, which were not long in coming.

To rattle the CIA, Nixon used the President's Foreign Intelligence Advisory Board, an independent group of former government officials and business leaders that helped presidents to ride herd on the intelligence community. In Nixon's case, they existed mainly to tell Nixon what he wanted to hear, and he now wanted to hear the CIA had failed him. Shortly after the CIA admitted its failure with Sihanoukville, a mistake only brought to light through the Agency's own work, he convened the intelligence board on July 18. Haig spelled it out in his notes from the meeting: "Although the military had consistently maintained that Sihanoukville received a very substantial amount of communist material the civilian agencies persisted in discounting its importance until we had begun our sanctuary operations. CIA had described the flow of materials through Sihanoukville as only a trickle while evidence now indicates that about 70% of communist supplies in Cambodia had been brought in through this port." Nixon wondered, Haig wrote, if the CIA could be that wrong about Sihanoukville, what other mistakes had they made?[58] "He emphasized again later in the meeting that the Board should give very close attention to the case of Sihanoukville which represented one of the worst records ever compiled by the intelligence community." George

Carver, one of Helms's longtime deputies, knew what would happen to the Agency next. Helms, he said later, "was vulnerable because in any future major controversy where he really held the line, he would have been vulnerable to: 'Yes, but that's what you said about Sihanoukville.'"[59] That is precisely what happened, as Nixon maintained his pressure on and abuse of the Agency.

CHAPTER EIGHT

Nixon's War with the FBI (1970)

THE EMBERS FROM AMERICA'S BURNING CITIES IN 1968 HAD BARELY COOLED by the time Nixon took office, and nothing about his taking power seemed likely to soothe the nation's urban troubles. College campuses seethed with opposition to the war. Radical groups, such as the Black Panthers and Weather Underground, continued to attack the establishment. Fixing this problem was part of the law-and-order government Nixon promised in his 1968 nomination acceptance speech when he said the United States could not succeed "when the nation with the greatest tradition of the rule of law is plagued by unprecedented lawlessness."[1] Those who voted for Nixon, and even those who supported Hubert Humphrey or George Wallace, wanted protection from growing turmoil. Most Americans thought Nixon, Attorney General John Mitchell, and FBI director J. Edgar Hoover would crack down on criminals, rioters, and student protesters. That expected partnership, however, foundered on Hoover's reluctance to follow Nixon's lead and Nixon's general distrust of Hoover, who he believed would ultimately try to blackmail him.

Hoover told Nixon in early 1969 that Lyndon Johnson had ordered the bugging of Nixon's campaign plane in the final weeks of the 1968 race, because Johnson knew that Nixon was trying to sabotage the Paris Peace Talks. Hoover, as one of his top deputies, Cartha "Deke" DeLoach, said, was exaggerating.[2] The bureau did not bug the plane, although agents did follow Anna Chennault as she relayed messages from the campaign to the South Vietnamese government. Hoover knew Johnson got his information from a combination of National Security Agency telephone intercepts, ground surveillance, and comments from campaign officials, but he added the plane just to stoke Nixon's paranoia. It worked and gave Hoover something with which he could blackmail Nixon if he needed to.

In March 1969, the first of that year's series of student protests and riots broke at San Francisco State College, as students sought an independent black studies department among other demands.[3] In April, students at Ivy League universities Cornell and Harvard rioted.[4] Regardless of their causes, Nixon considered the demonstrations a dangerous sign of social erosion and said "faculties, boards of trustees and school administrators" need "to have the backbone to stand up against this kind of situation."[5] Rioting in black neighborhoods of Chicago on the one-year anniversary of the assassination of Martin Luther King Jr. led Governor Richard Ogilvie to call in seven thousand National Guard troops to patrol the areas and quell the violence.[6] Nixon responded by ordering one of his top aides, White House counsel John Ehrlichman, to determine if the riots and protests had international communist backing.

Ehrlichman, a former Seattle lawyer, had worked as an advance man for Nixon's ill-fated 1962 campaign for governor of California and then signed on again for the 1968 race. Along with H. R. "Bob" Haldeman, the White House chief of staff, Ehrlichman formed the "Berlin Wall" of Teutonic-surnamed aides who controlled much of Nixon's agenda. While Kissinger formed the heart of the secret Nixon national security policy government, Ehrlichman ran a similar shop for domestic policy and Haldeman oversaw the entire operation. Haldeman and Ehrlichman handled the domestic intelligence and political operations for Nixon's White House, and they recruited a small group of aides who focused on riots and protests. Thomas Charles Huston, a young lawyer and former army captain who worked at the Defense Intelligence Agency, joined the White House speechwriting and research staff, reporting to Haldeman. Egil "Bud" Krogh Jr., a former Navy communications officer and Seattle attorney who worked in Ehrlichman's law firm, joined the White House staff to guide security policy. Ehrlichman assigned the investigation of alleged communist support for campus and urban protests to Huston and Krogh, who found few links to any communist country. They, particularly Huston, considered the FBI's intelligence incomplete and wanted better information.

In June, Ehrlichman told Krogh to assign Huston to try again to find foreign assistance for campus protesters.[7] One of Huston's first stops was William Sullivan's office at the FBI on June 19, 1969. Huston told Sullivan about a recent talk with Nixon in which the president said he wanted to know "all information possible relating to foreign influences and the financing of the New Left."[8] Sullivan told Huston he needed to put the request in writing to satisfy Hoover, who required the same process for the wiretaps.[9] Huston wrote the letter and presented it to Hoover the following day, adding that he wanted the FBI to show how it could fix its intelligence reporting. He also asked the same questions of the CIA, NSA, and DIA, and then sent a report to Ehrlichman, who was not satisfied. Ehrlichman, Haldeman, and Krogh kept criticizing the FBI's work and badgered Huston to keep pressuring the bureau.[10] Instead, Huston fell under the sway of Sullivan, who introduced the impressionable aide to the intelligence specialists compiling the reports. The problem was not the reporting, Sullivan told Huston, but the system itself. Nixon needed to get the intelligence agencies to work with each other; if he did that, he would get the intelligence he needed, Sullivan said.[11]

Huston's arrival could not have come at a better time for Sullivan. While Hoover trusted him—he was the only FBI official the director referred to by his first name—the two men disagreed often about Hoover's refusal to work with the CIA and other agencies. Throughout the 1960s, Sullivan argued for more liaisons with the CIA; Hoover wanted less. During the 1965 crisis in the Dominican Republic, Sullivan worked with the CIA's Helms, the Agency's director of operations, without telling Hoover.[12] In October 1968, Sullivan sought Helms's help for a reformed national intelligence system. "There is no need to tell you that we are living in an age of profound and rapid flux," Sullivan wrote Helms in an October 24, 1968, memo.[13] A new administration might give them the chance to make the changes they desired, he continued. Sullivan also chafed at Hoover's decision to stop using a variety of techniques, including illegal break-ins called "black bag jobs." Remove those restrictions, Sullivan told Huston, and overall intelligence will improve. Gradually, Huston became one of Sullivan's chief advocates in the White House. "I do not think there was anyone in the government who I respected more than Mr. Sullivan," Huston would say later.[14]

In October and November 1969, two massive antiwar demonstrations shook the administration. Nixon suspected the hand of North Vietnam was behind the protesters, who he blamed for extending the war. "I think there is a much deeper conspiracy than any of us realize," Nixon told Kissinger in a November 14 telephone call.[15] "I will have to nail these people. I am going to say the protesters will delay the [end of?] war." Mitchell also claimed the protesters were "active militants who want to destroy some of the processes and some of the institutions of our government." Mitchell's intemperate outbursts were hurting the administration's attempts to develop an internal security plan, said Krogh in a January 26, 1970, memo to Haldeman.[16] Huston, Krogh wrote, had developed a new plan that establishes "an apparatus within the White House to monitor and review all intelligence bearing on internal security problems." Huston also wanted greater White House political control over Mitchell, Krogh wrote, because of the attorney general's interference on the antiwar demonstrations and delays in investigating the Black Panthers. Krogh said he and Ehrlichman had cooperated on the protest planning, including recruiting a young Justice Department aide, John Dean, to negotiate with the antiwar protesters the previous fall. The White House, Krogh continued, had to control the details of internal security, but he had doubts about Huston's temperament. He called the young aide "a master at analysis of intelligence, separation of relevant information from hoary scare-projections of the intelligence agencies, and in recommending sound courses of action." But Huston was also uncompromising, acerbic and paranoid about "positions less dogmatic than his own."

Haldeman also wanted Huston to determine the reasons for Johnson's October 1968 decision to stop bombing North Vietnam, which Nixon suspected was done solely to make Hubert Humphrey president. Nixon knew the North Vietnamese had met the conditions Johnson set for the halt, but what he really wanted was evidence of how his campaign colluded with Anna Chennault to sabotage the Paris Peace Talks. Johnson had called Nixon's interference treason, adding that the public exposure of the incident would destroy support for the Vietnam War. Nixon also knew his presidency could be destroyed if the public knew what he had done, so he needed that file. Huston reported to Haldeman on February 25, 1970, that whatever information existed was damaging to the White House. "This paper deals with the Chennault Affair and is highly sensitive," Huston wrote.[17] "As you will note from reading it, the evidence available in the case does not dispel the notion that we were somehow involved in the Chennault Affair and while release of this information would be most embarrassing to President Johnson, it would not be helpful to us either." Huston said he did not send the information to Kissinger at the NSC, because "I think the risks of a leak are too great to send this down to his shop." In a memorandum to Nixon sent the same day, Huston also detailed how Johnson had tracked Chennault and the South Vietnamese and the telephone calls from Spiro Agnew's campaign plane while it was in New Mexico. In the memorandum, which was not released to the public until May 2015, Huston downplayed some of the findings, but added that a November 2, 1968, call between Chennault and the South Vietnamese ambassador "suggested that officials high in the campaign (perhaps the candidate himself or his running mate) were attempting to convince the South Vietnamese to hold out against a bombing halt until after the election," Huston wrote.[18] It is clear from Huston's repeated references to help from the FBI that his mentor Sullivan had fed him information for Nixon, although Huston did not mention Sullivan by name. One thing Huston did not report, however, was that the FBI had bugged Nixon's campaign airplane.

That seemed to satisfy Haldeman and Nixon for the moment, because other crises interfered that would occupy their attention and draw the White House into an attempt to remake the intelligence community.

Nixon's invasion of Cambodia triggered a nationwide wave of student protests that included deadly incidents at Kent State and Jackson State University in Mississippi, which he believed damaged the American bargaining position in the talks with North Vietnam. As in 1969, Nixon told Haldeman to get Huston to get the information he wanted. Huston again went to Sullivan, who now had extra clout to push for a national intelligence service. In March, Hoover killed the formal CIA-FBI liaison over a dispute over a confidential source.[19] His pique reinforced fears of Hoover's instability and provided another argument for greater coordination between agencies. By the time they were done, Huston and Sullivan devised a plan that seriously infringed on the civil liberties of millions of Americans, roiled the leadership of the nation's intelligence agencies, threatened Hoover's control of the FBI, and set off a power struggle for control of the Bureau that contributed to Nixon's eventual downfall. It started with a meeting with Nixon in the Oval Office on June 5, 1970.[20]

That day Nixon summoned Hoover; Helms; Admiral Noel Gayler, the head of NSA; Lt. Gen. Donald Bennett, director of the Defense Intelligence Agency; Ehrlichman, Haldeman, and Huston to ask for a coordinated intelligence plan. They worked off a two-page briefing paper from Huston that Sullivan had actually prepared. No one sitting in Nixon's office other than Huston realized the extent to which Sullivan, who would never actually meet with Nixon, shaped the plan Nixon wanted and that eventually bore Huston's name. Before the meeting, Huston urged Nixon to ask Hoover to put Sullivan in charge of the staff subcommittee that would handle the details. Nixon stuck closely to Huston's script, telling the group he was convinced they were not devoting enough resources to collecting intelligence "on the activities of these revolutionary groups."[21] He asked Hoover and Helms if they had any problems working with each other, and neither said they did. Nixon said he wanted Sullivan to run the subcommittee, and Hoover agreed.

Hoover would now feel the pressure from the White House, and it would be the twenty-nine-year-old Huston who would deliver the punishment, which the seventy-five-year-old Hoover resented intensely. That resentment would escalate on June 8, when Helms, Gayler, and Bennett joined Huston and Sullivan in Hoover's FBI office. The imperious director, never used to having his edicts questioned, started by declaring his alarm at the overall quality of intelligence and said Nixon wanted a historical summary of the political unrest in the United States. He asked Helms and the others if they wanted to say anything. None did except Huston, who accused Hoover of mischaracterizing Nixon's orders. The president did not want just a history but an assessment of security threats and a coherent, coordinated plan to stop them. Huston's remarks gave Gayler, Bennett, and Helms the confidence to challenge Hoover. Nixon wanted more than a history, they said. Hoover blustered and ended the meeting, telling the others to assign their best experts to the project.[22] He then complained to Sullivan about Huston, the "hippie intellectual" from the White House who dared tell him what to do. Hoover did not realize that Sullivan had been guiding Huston all along.

The group met four times over the next two weeks at CIA headquarters in Langley, Virginia, to write a draft that, Huston said, had to create a new format for intelligence gathering. They needed to examine the benefits of keeping or removing restraints in intelligence collection and then let Nixon decide what to do.[23] Huston proposed a permanent interagency committee to coordinate intelligence, which Hoover opposed. By the third meeting, they reached relative unanimity about removing the restraints on intelligence gathering. It looked as if they had finally found a consensus, even with Hoover. That illusion crashed in their fourth meeting on June 23.[24] Hoover wanted to keep many of the restrictions, such as the ban on black bag jobs or illegal mail opening. For years, he said, the FBI had used and condoned such methods, but times had changed and Hoover no longer wanted to have sole responsibility for them. He would only agree to use them if a higher authority, such as the attorney general or the president, ordered him to. At the moment, it was unlikely Attorney General Mitchell would order anything, because Nixon had not told him about the group or its mission. Sullivan tried to persuade Hoover of the difficulty in rewriting the draft after all the other agencies had signed off on it, but his pleas did not work. The draft carried Hoover's objections when the group met for the final time on June 25 in Hoover's office.

Helms, Gayler, and Bennett resisted Hoover's last-minute attempt to kill the plan, but nothing Hoover did surprised them. They had tried to work with him for years. This time Huston's work inside the White House trumped Hoover's opposition, and Hoover signed the June 25 document.[25] Huston talked to Haldeman and called Hoover's objections "generally inconsistent and frivolous" and that Hoover was the sole member of the group opposed to change. At Huston's urging, Haldeman lobbied Nixon, who agreed to sign the plan. On July 14, Haldeman told Huston to tell the others that Nixon had signed it and they should just go ahead as if it was now the new policy.[26] However, Haldeman said, Nixon would not make a formal announcement. Huston and Sullivan wanted to celebrate. For Sullivan, Nixon's signature culminated years of work to build a national intelligence network.

What Nixon signed was, for the time, truly revolutionary. He allowed the FBI to resume surreptitious entries, and "present restrictions should be modified to permit selective use of this technique against other urgent and high priority internal security targets."[27] The CIA could open the mail of people it suspected of espionage, and the NSA could monitor the telephone conversations between people in the United States. FBI agents could infiltrate college campuses and student groups with ever-younger informants, and "CIA coverage of American students (and others) traveling or living abroad should be increased." Intelligence organizations could do more surveillance of "individuals and groups in the United States who pose a major threat to internal security." And all of the groups would work more closely together as part of a "permanent committee consisting of the FBI, CIA, NSA, DIA, and the military counterintelligence agencies." In the eyes of Nixon and the other advocates, they now had a system that allowed them to take the fight to radical groups.

However, they also did not know that each agency was already doing what the new plan gave them the permission to do. They just had never told each other or the president that they were doing it. Since 1956, FBI agents had targeted internal threats, such as foreign spies on US soil, civil rights organizations, black power groups, and students and radicals. Sullivan ran the operation called COINTELPRO, or counterintelligence program, which Hoover knew well.[28] They just never told their colleagues on the panel or the White House. Bureau officials may have debated how well COINTELPRO worked, but it had been a big part of FBI operations for the last fifteen years. Nixon and the others in the group also did not know the CIA routinely opened mail without Court permission or violated its charter by spying on people on US soil. Nor did the president and the others realize that the NSA eavesdropped on domestic communications. Finally, they did not know, but should have suspected, that Hoover was not done trying to stop the plan.

Huston had good reason to suspect Haldeman's statement that Nixon had approved the plan but would not announce it. He realized Nixon would have trouble saying no to Hoover, who was not done trying to stop the plan. He went first to Mitchell, only to learn that Nixon had not told his former law partner about the interagency group's work. Irked at being excluded, Mitchell told Nixon the proposal's risks far outweighed the potential benefits. On July 27, Nixon said he wanted to recall the plan, so he, Mitchell, Haldeman, and Hoover could "reconsider" it, which guaranteed its death, since Hoover and Mitchell were so strongly against it.[29] Nixon told the livid heads of the other agencies what he had done and dispatched Huston to retrieve the documents he had sent by courier to each agency. When Huston collected the documents, he saw that each had been unbound and copied, meaning rogue versions existed that could plague the White House later. Huston also went to Haldeman again to override Hoover. "At one point," Huston wrote Haldeman on August 5, "Hoover has to be told who is President. If he gets his way it is going to look like he is more powerful than the President."[30] Haldeman did nothing. Hoover had won.

Finally, the crestfallen Huston did not know who else had done him in—his mentor and ally, Sullivan. On June 20, Cartha DeLoach, the number-three official in the Bureau behind Hoover and his companion, Clyde Tolson, resigned to take a lucrative security job with PepsiCo in New York.[31] Hoover replaced him with Sullivan, making Sullivan the odds-on favorite to replace Hoover. Sullivan saw little percentage in alienating Hoover with so much at stake. While Huston thought Sullivan was his ally, Sullivan was telling Hoover and DeLoach to oppose "the relaxation of investigative restraints which affect the bureau."[32] Sullivan had been tipping Hoover to the group's work behind Huston's back the entire time. Sullivan, the man who helped build Huston's plan and shepherded the young aide through the wolves of internal administration politics, had been a wolf himself. After Nixon scrapped his creation, a bitter and disillusioned Huston slunk back to his office. He would be out of the White House in less than a year.

~~~

His vision, however, had not died completely. Only the players had changed. Nixon still wanted what he did not know he already mostly had. A new player arrived in late July to become counsel and replace Ehrlichman, who had assumed even greater duties. It was John Dean, the former Justice Department aide who had worked on internal security issues and student protests. Dean also inherited Huston's spot as the White House's internal security and domestic intelligence chief. Haldeman soon asked Dean to "see what I could do to get [Huston's] plan implemented."[33] Dean also had a new ally in Robert Mardian, a Phoenix lawyer and law-and-order Goldwater conservative who was Justice's new head of the Internal Security department. Mardian started pressuring Hoover and the FBI for more information.[34] Mardian also had the backing of Sullivan, who switched back to promoting the plan now that he was Hoover's deputy. Dean, Mardian, and Sullivan created the joint Intelligence Evaluation Committee that would "remove the restraints as necessary to obtain" the intelligence they wanted, Dean told Mitchell in a September 17, 1970, memo.[35] Dean would expand his intelligence gathering as White House counsel, including attempts to collect intelligence on Nixon's political rivals from prostitution rings, because he knew that was the best way to gain the president's favor.

CHAPTER NINE

Chile (1970)

RICHARD NIXON'S PLANS FOR HOW TO RESHAPE THE WORLD AND THE US role in it focused mostly on the war in Vietnam, China, and the Soviet Union, and he viewed most of his policy decisions in the context of those issues. Anything outside that screen rarely attracted his notice unless events demanded it, and so it was with the September 1970 presidential election in Chile, one of the most stable democracies in all of Latin America. Nixon reacted only when he had to, and even then did so so haphazardly that his panicked reactions hurt the administration and hastened the decline of the intelligence community.

Chile stood as a beacon of stability on a continent dominated by class warfare and military dictatorships. A three-thousand-mile-long ribbon of land stretching down the western side of South America, it was blessed with rich copper deposits unearthed by thousands of miners who toiled in harsh conditions and sought help from their powerful labor unions. Its political culture had three almost equally strong factions—organized labor, which allied with the Socialist Party led by Dr. Salvador Allende Gossens, a three-time presidential candidate; a progressive, procapitalist faction embodied by President Eduardo Frei Montalva, and a conservative, pro–big business faction identified by Jorge Alessandri, a former president. Chile was home to numerous American companies, such as Anaconda, Kennecott Copper, and International Telephone and Telegraph (ITT). Allende's popularity with labor and antipathy toward US corporations posed a problem for the Johnson administration in 1964, when Allende waged his third challenge for the office. After his first race in 1952, Allende lost the 1958 election to Alessandri by only thirty thousand votes.[1] In 1964, a massive CIA effort limited the race to just Frei Montalva and Allende, and won Frei Montalva won handily.[2] Term limits prevented Frei Montalva from seeking reelection in 1970, and the conservative-moderate bloc was split between two candidates, Alessandri, who was running as an independent, and Radomiro Tomic, a more liberal Christian Democratic senator. Keeping Allende out of the presidency was a difficult, expensive, and full-time job. CIA analysts had predicted a tough race early in 1969.[3] After all, the US government, either through CIA funds or Agency for International Development grants that were redirected for political purposes spent $3 million to prevent Allende's election in 1964. In 1969, the CIA spent $350,000 at the request of US ambassador Edward Korry to help favored candidates win seats in the March congressional elections in anticipation of a scrambled 1970 presidential campaign in which Congress would have to pick the winner.[4] In an April 15, 1969, meeting to review the successful Agency intervention in Chile's March congressional elections, Agency director Richard Helms said the administration needed to decide what to do for the presidential election, because "CIA has learned through experience that an election operation will not be effective unless an early enough start is made."[5] Helms's warning sparked little interest.

In Santiago, Korry knew Allende remained a threat, as he kept the support of at least one-third of voters in most polls, while neither Alessandri nor Tomic generated any momentum. A former journalist and Kennedy appointee, Korry sent pungent, often digressive, cables to Washington warning of the grave implications of Allende's exploitation of the divided opposition to win the election. Allende would nationalize key industries, ruin the incentives for foreign or domestic investment in Chile, and strip US companies of their expensive assets. The Soviet Union and Cuba would get a foothold where they previously had none. US inaction risked enabling the election of South America's first democratically elected socialist government, Korry warned. White House officials liked Korry, despite the Kennedy pedigree that was usually the kiss of death with Nixon. "He has done an excellent job and is probably the best ambassador we have in Latin America," NSC aide Viron Vaky told Kissinger in July 1969.[6] "It is very much in our foreign policy interest to have Korry remain as Ambassador through the election period and I hope no change will be made."

Even Korry's supporters had grown somewhat immune to his warnings, since he had been making them since arriving in Santiago in 1967. He was the boy who cried *lobo*. Korry always wanted more, either government or corporate money to support some kind of anti-Allende or pro–Frei Montalva campaign, and the Agency usually complied. Still, Allende's support remained solid. For whatever reason, however, the administration did not move against Allende until it was too late. Kissinger later said the polls they received were misleading, while State shied away from direct interference in another country's elections.[7] Nixon declined to overrule State or compel the CIA to do more. Any US intervention would be more difficult and presumably less effective the closer to Election Day. Nixon would learn this lesson too late.

If Nixon was surprised by Allende's strength, it was his fault. He had plenty of warnings, starting with Korry, other diplomats, and the CIA. Korry, in particular, grew more frantic. Finally, on July 24, 1970, Kissinger issued National Security Decision Memorandum 97, in which Nixon "asked for an urgent review of US policy and strategy in the event of an Allende victory in the Chilean Presidential elections."[8] That was barely six weeks before the election, too late for an effective US intelligence intervention. The memorandum sought information on three questions: What would an Allende government do, how big of a threat would an Allende win be to US interests, and what can the US government do "to meet these problems"? But Kissinger asked for answers by August 18, just two weeks before the election. That was far too little time, too late. Once the study was completed, the NSC's Senior Review Group did not consider it until October 19, six weeks after the election. As the CIA would later conclude, "There was no systematic analysis or consideration at the policy-making level on the question of how great a threat an Allende Government would be to US interests."[9]

Three million Chileans voted in the September 4 election, which Allende won by thirty-nine thousand votes. Since no candidate received a majority, the Chilean Congress would decide the winner, and most observers considered it unlikely that it would overturn the popular vote to stop Allende. Nixon snapped awake in a September 15 meeting with Kissinger, Helms, and Mitchell. He spoke for almost twenty minutes and said they needed to keep Allende from taking office. Helms's notes reflected Nixon's intensity:

> *"1 in 10 chance perhaps, but save Chile!*
>
> *worth spending; not concerned risks involved*
>
> *no involvement of embassy*
>
> *$10,000,000 available, more if necessary*
>
> *full-time job—best men we have*
>
> *game plan*
>
> *make the economy scream*
>
> *48 hours for plan of action."[10]*

Kissinger did not believe Nixon actually wanted to spend $10 million but wanted to show everyone he was serious.[11] The following day, the top CIA officials met to determine just how they would carry out Nixon's orders to keep "Allende from coming to power or to unseat him."[12] The White House developed a two-track plan to stop Allende. Track I involved bribing members of Congress to vote for Alessandri, who would then resign, triggering a special election that presumably would be won by Frei Montalva. Track II called for the CIA to start a coup that would then place Frei Montalva back into office. Track I also included bribery and a package of covert operations involving political and economic pressure and propaganda. Korry, the CIA, and State Department would handle this track. Track II was solely a CIA operation.

Track I failed when the Chilean Congress voted 153 to 35 to make Allende president. Track II also fell apart quickly. Agency operatives could not find a willing conspirator or an officer with enough credibility to lead a coup. Their few options were blocked by General Rene Schneider, the military chief of staff, who refused to consider a coup and would not back anyone who did. The CIA's only option was Brigadier General Robert Viaux, the leader of an unsuccessful 1969 barracks uprising against Frei Montalva. Korry considered Viaux an "erratic missile."[13]

Nixon could not stop Allende "unless some tight control and guidance is established," Vaky, the NSC's Chile specialist, wrote Kissinger on September 16.[14] Korry, Vaky continued, was too volatile to control a covert CIA operation. "He is too exposed; it is too dangerous." The White House needed to create a Washington-based task force operating outside the bureaucracy to stop Allende or send a CIA official to run the operation out of the US embassy with Korry's knowledge but not under his direct control.[15]

As Allende's inauguration became imminent, Korry's messages to State grew increasingly dramatic. He was angered by military's reluctance to mount a coup, and he believed they had no sense of the stakes that were involved. "They are a union of toy soldiers who need an order to move and that order can only come from Frei," Korry reported back to Washington.[16]

The ambassador had veered out of control, Vaky told Kissinger, and was "apparently trying to construct something out of whole cloth."[17] Kissinger had to do something, Vaky said. "I believe you have to focus on this. If Korry is not reined in, we are going to be in a mess. . . . I think it now urgent to get somebody down there to assess (a) Korry (and his stability) and (b) the situation."

Kissinger got the message. On September 17, he warned Nixon that the entire effort veered toward total failure.[18] "It is going to be a long shot as it is; if we have to face the additional handicaps of well-meaning but unpro-fessional activism, of lack of coordination and of bureaucratic resistance, we will be dangerously exposed." Kissinger's complaints were rich in irony. He complained about the bureaucracy, but Kissinger and Nixon had exacerbated those problems with their constant end runs around the government. Their delays in following the recommendations of the Agency and the diplomats in Chile made matters worse. The only way they could save the situation, Kiss-inger told Nixon, was to send someone to Santiago to take control. Nixon agreed. That someone was CIA operative David Phillips, who arrived on September 21.[19]

He encountered a confused and direction-less embassy and Agency staff. Phillips's orders were to promote a military coup. "After this we get fuzzy since we have no clear understanding of what we wish Frei to do other than lead a military coup himself, something we can hardly expect of this too-gentle soul," a September 21 telegram from CIA headquarters to Santiago said.[20] Following a coup, Frei Montalva would then seek the resignation of the cabinet, replace them with members of the military, appoint an acting president, leave Chile, and then have a military junta call for new elections. Frei Montalva would then return, run for president, and win the new election with CIA help, just as in 1964. The plan reeked of desperation and a poor understanding of the situation on the ground in Santiago, but the Agency was following Nixon's orders.

Schneider, the Chilean chief of staff, controlled enough troops to stop a coup, so Viaux planned to kidnap Schneider by overwhelming his security detail and flying him to Argentina. The CIA considered that option too risky, dropped Viaux, and recruited another plotter, Brig. Gen. Camilo Valenzu-ela, commander of the Santiago garrison. A Viaux-led coup, Kissinger told Nixon, "looks hopeless. I turned it off. Nothing would be worse than an abor-tive coup."

That left Valenzuela, whose plotters tried and failed twice to kidnap Schneider on October 19 and 20. That seemed the end of any kidnapping or coup attempts, but Viaux ignored the CIA and struck on October 22. At 8:15 that morning, Viaux's team tried to kidnap Schneider, who drew his weapon and was shot and fatally wounded in the chaotic shootout.[21] Instead of kidnapping Schneider, the plotters sparked a full-blown political crisis that ended when Valenzuela locked down Santiago, which guaranteed that Allende would become president.

Allende quickly nationalized foreign-owned industries, and he had the potential to give the Soviet Union and Fidel Castro a foothold in South America. Nixon vowed to crush Allende. Since Nixon would not hold himself accountable, he needed someone to blame, and his eyes turned to Langley, just as he did with the SS-9 estimates and the Cambodia planning.

Once again, Nixon used the President's Foreign Intelligence Advisory Board to pound on Helms. On December 2, Haig sent Kissinger talking points for the following day's board meeting.[22] Haig's memo brutally spelled out the White House plan. "You have expressed the intention of talking to the FIAB about the overall intelligence problem and of refining our current bill of particulars which is proof-positive of the deficiencies with which we are faced." Haig then listed four key areas in which he, Kissinger, and Nixon had taken issue with the Agency—Sihanoukville, the Soviet strategic threat, Middle East ceasefire violations, and Chile. In each, Haig exaggerated the Agency's failures. On Sihanoukville, it was a CIA breakthrough that allowed the military to prove that Chinese supplies were moving through that port to the North Vietnamese. On the Soviet threat, the CIA was right about the Soviet's inability to use MIRVs, while the military and the White House were wrong. On Chile, Haig wrote, "Here again, the intelligence community failed to sharply assess the full implications of the political trends in Chile or, perhaps more seriously, having assessed them with some accuracy, they permitted policy preconceptions to flavor their final assessments and their proposals for remedial action in the covert area." Haig ignored the Agency's record of covert operations against Allende and Helms's April 15, 1969, warning of the need for consistent covert action. It was the White House that delayed action until after the September 4 election. CIA, NSC, and State Department records released in the following forty years all show the White House had plenty of warning about a potential Allende victory and either did little or acted too late.

Nixon did not care about the facts. Just as he had during the SS-9 debate the previous year, he wanted intelligence that allowed him to sell his ideas, not intelligence that had helped to determine them. The PFIAB grilled Helms on December 3 about the alleged intelligence failures.[23] But Helms had information of his own to share with the board. He told them about Nixon's attempts to exclude him from NSC meetings. "He pointed out that at the beginning of this Administration he had been told that he would be excluded from policy making deliberations at the NSC and wondered whether Ambassador [Robert] Murphy," a board member, could explain why. A startled Murphy said he knew nothing about it. Eventually the pressure forced Helms to make changes at Langley.[24] Abbot Smith, the Agency's chief of intelligence estimates, would leave and be replaced by John Huizenga, who "should bring to the national estimates process a new, more imaginative look," Helms told Kissinger on December 7. Smith had led the Agency's work on the SS-9 and MIRV estimate and had angered Kissinger and Nixon. Helms knew Nixon thought the CIA too hidebound to give him what he wanted, and after the beating he took during the Chilean affair and the subsequent PFIAB meeting, Helms knew he needed to throw around the kind of buzzwords aimed to appeal to his mercurial boss. "This is being done to make head-room for the younger generation, to keep the Agency as limber mentally and physically as possible, and to insure the internal shifting, both vertically and laterally, which gives health and resilience to an organization," Helms told Kissinger. "In sum, virtually the entire top level of the CIA will have seen changes within the next year or so."

CHAPTER TEN

Laos and Other Crises (1970–1971)

Along with the crisis in Chile, which ended with a Marxist president, Nixon grappled with two unanticipated flare-ups in different parts of the world. Nixon strove to look tough, but instead he worsened the growing tensions between the White House and the national security bureaucracy. Nixon's drinking fueled much of his belligerent and erratic attitude; his subordinates often reacted by delaying action on his orders in the hope he would either forget them or get distracted by something else.

In the Middle East, terrorists from a radical offshoot of the Palestine Liberation Organization hijacked one Swiss and two American airliners on September 6, 1970, starting a military and diplomatic scramble to keep the passengers in one location. One, Pan Am 93, was flown to Beirut and then Cairo, where the terrorists removed the passengers from the airplane and blew it up. But Swissair 100 and TWA 741 were flown to an airstrip thirty miles from Amman, Jordan. On September 9, they hijacked a British airliner. All of the passengers were held at the airstrip, and the terrorists demanded the releases of all PLO terrorists held in jails in Israel, Great Britain, Germany, and Switzerland. The hijackings precipitated a month of agonizing inside the White House, starting with Nixon's demands to Laird that he "bomb the bastards," which Laird sidestepped by claiming bad weather prevented the scrambling of US jets from the aircraft carrier *Independence* a mere one hundred miles off the coast of Israel.[1] Inside Jordan, the security situation eroded quickly, as Palestinian militants threatened to overwhelm the government of Jordanian King Hussein, the region's most moderate and pro-American leader. By September 15, Hussein had formed a military government and drove the PLO from Jordan. Eventually, the airline passengers were released; the aircraft was destroyed by the terrorists; and the United States managed to stop a Syrian move into Jordan and to keep Israel from intervening on Hussein's behalf. A win for Nixon was damaged by Moorer's discovery that Nixon had excluded him from planning; he only learned that Nixon had planned to aid the Jordanian military after overhearing a telephone call with Laird.[2]

As Jordan erupted, Kissinger told Nixon that US intelligence had spotted what looked like a potential Soviet submarine base being built in Cuba's Cienfuegos Bay. CIA reports in June had detected unusual activity there. By September 18, however, the Soviets had worked on building a possible submarine base there, Kissinger wrote Nixon that day. The Joint Chiefs, Kissinger told Nixon three days later, called it a sign of increased Soviet boldness in the area, although any base in Cienfuegos would add only marginally to Soviet capabilities. Nevertheless, Kissinger called it a significant political challenge that, coupled with the Chilean elections, Latin American leaders would consider a sign of US weakness. Nixon had to force the Soviets to remove the base, just as John Kennedy had done when the Soviets put nuclear missiles in Cuba eight years earlier.

Nixon met with the NSC on September 23 to determine a plan before the Soviet base became public knowledge. Publicly, he said, the United States had to remain calm and avoid a crisis in which both the United States and Soviet Union would take bellicose positions to avoid being seen as weak. Privately, however, he wanted to prepare a series of hard-nosed actions to persuade the Soviets they should roll back their plans. Moorer said the Chiefs had prepared attack plans if Nixon gave the go-ahead; he also told the president the military could either blockade Cuba or mine Cienfuegos Bay, both acts of war.[3] Backed by a rare administration consensus that the base had to go, Kissinger met with Soviet Ambassador Anatoly Dobrynin on September 25 and October 6.[4] Kissinger said a base in Cienfuegos would damage the entire range of US-Soviet relations, particularly the SALT arms control talks. By the October 6 meeting, Kissinger and Dobrynin had "resolved, without a public confrontation, the potentially explosive issue of a Soviet base in Cuba," Kissinger wrote Nixon.[5]

Kissinger, however, had aggravated an existing problem with the Joint Chiefs when he commissioned Rear Admiral Rembrandt Robinson, the Chiefs' liaison with the NSC, to write Nixon's secret memo for the Soviets about Cienfuegos. Robinson, whose job was specifically to tell the Chiefs what Kissinger was doing, showed the memo to Admiral Elmo Zumwalt, Moorer's successor as chief of naval operations, although Kissinger did not want the Chiefs to see it. Zumwalt asked Robinson why he had not shown it to him or Moorer. Robinson said Kissinger "did not want any policy discussion on the matter."[6] The Cienfuegos memo capped off a series of slights that gnawed at Moorer. A year earlier, Kissinger had raised the Chiefs' hopes with the Duck Hook plan to strike North Vietnam, and then Nixon pulled back.

Nixon repeatedly went around either Laird or the Chiefs to talk directly to General Abrams in Saigon or to Ambassador Ellsworth Bunker. Nixon had also established retired Army Special Forces Colonel Fred Ladd in Cambodia to run the US aid effort there, but he kept Ladd out of the chain of command for either the Pentagon or the State Department. Moorer also knew the White House had also bypassed the chiefs on military aid to Jordan, and the constantly shifting troop levels in Vietnam were always a mystery to the commanders in Saigon. Kissinger's hidden SALT negotiations also kept the Chiefs guessing about the future of their nuclear arsenal. Robinson, who was a friend of Haig, had been a reliable conduit of information from the NSC, but recent events convinced Moorer they needed more information, and their efforts got a boost in September 1970 when Robinson got a new assistant at the NSC liaison office, Navy Yeoman Charles Radford.[7]

At twenty-seven, the lanky, slight Radford made for an unlikely spy, but he became one under the tutelage of Robinson and later his successor, Rear Admiral Robert Welander. Robinson told Radford he needed to get the valuable information the White House hid from the Chiefs. Radford told Robinson about anything he saw in the office, and Robinson encouraged the early results by telling Radford to keep the information coming. "The Chiefs' viewpoint was being disregarded," Welander said. "We wondered who the hell is the son of a bitch who is coming up with the information" used to guide Kissinger and Nixon.[8]

~~

Soon, Radford would have much to report, as the situation in Cambodia deteriorated to the point of alarm. By August, communist troops had threatened or overrun sixteen of Cambodia's nineteen provincial capitals and generally had free rein to roam about the nation's highways.[9] Only a major coordinated aid campaign could save Lon Nol's government. By December, it was clear that Cambodia was a disaster. Nixon's handling of the invasion had effectively killed his chances of gaining congressional approval of a major aid effort package. That forced the military, which realized it could not win under Nixon's ground rules, to operate with one hand tied behind its back. From Moorer on down, they resented being forced to cobble together a strategy based on using the unreliable South Vietnamese and Cambodian armed forces. As in March 1969, Nixon's answer was more bombing.

Kissinger told Nixon on December 9 that "in Cambodia the communists have started an attack and have [been] beaten up in Cambodia." The United States needed to strike back or "we will be in a rescue operation." Kissinger said Moorer did not understand Nixon's urgency for results, which was misleading. Moorer just did not agree that territory that had already been bombed repeatedly needed to be bombed again.

Nixon ended the call with another directive to Kissinger to bypass Laird and Moorer: After Kissinger told him Haig was going to Southeast Asia to meet with Abrams and others, Nixon said: "Get a message to Abrams from me on this point. Not from you or Laird or Moorer but from me."[10]

Kissinger then called Moorer, telling him Nixon was "raising Cain with me," and that he had no intention of losing Cambodia.[11] In Kissinger's office, Moorer said Nixon wanted Abrams to "do the impossible." The top commander in Saigon was running the Cambodia operation over the telephone with little support in the country. There were a just a handful of US military advisers in the Phnom Penh embassy, and they were getting reports from the field twenty-four to thirty-six hours late. "There is virtually no way of evaluating the situation in Cambodia or of evaluating Cambodian plans for coping with the situation," Moorer told Kissinger. Meanwhile, 25,000 Cambodian troops around the city of Kampong Cham were being pinned down by about 2,800 Viet Cong and North Vietnamese troops. Nixon feared Congress would kill their bill for extra money to pay for the Cambodia fight if he started a major offensive there, Kissinger said, and asked if they could do it with only Vietnam airlift help and no US troops.

Kissinger sent Nixon a memo in which he said he had told Moorer they had no good intelligence from Cambodia, and that Moorer's response was that bad weather had stymied air operations.[12] "He states that one of the factors which have enabled the enemy to build up in recent weeks is the very poor weather conditions which have limited effective air operations."[13]

That angered Nixon, who called Kissinger later that evening. Nixon, most likely drunk, launched into a long, rambling diatribe. Kissinger could barely say a word as Nixon criticized Moorer's lack of initiative. "I don't think they are trying to do a good enough job in trying to get the intelligence over there," Nixon said.[14]

Nixon also wanted Moorer to bomb everything that moved. "I want a plan where every goddamn thing that can fly goes into Cambodia and hits every target that is open."

They need a World War II–style air force, Nixon said, and more bazookas and anything else that can help take the fight to guerrillas hiding in dense jungles. Find a way to get them to Vietnam, he demanded of Kissinger.

"We have got to do a better job because we are just coming to the crunch," Nixon said. "Right now there is a chance to win this goddamn war and that's probably what we are going to have to do because we are not going to do anything at the conference table. But we aren't going to win it with the people—the kind of assholes who come in here like today saying well now there is a crisis in Cambodia."

Nixon launched into a crescendo of anger and frustration that captured the pressures on him and the office. It reflected a chief executive juggling so many crises, many of his own making, and unraveling under the strain and aided by alcohol. He wanted a new air attack plan, and he approved a ground offensive by the South Vietnamese during the dry season. He wanted to focus on the war and avoid distractions, such as Chile or "a vote on Guinea" that they can let the State Department handle. "I don't want to see any anything about all the other crap. Doesn't make any difference right now. The Pakistan elections; there's not a goddamn thing we can do about any of those things. You understand?"

⤙ ⤚

Kissinger's first move was not to call Moorer, but Haig.

"I just had a call from our friend," Kissinger told Haig.[15] "He wants to do a massive bombing in Cambodia," Kissinger said, adding he was "not eager to do this operation."

Neither, apparently, was Moorer, who met with Haig, Kissinger, Robinson, and Lieutenant General John Vogt of the Joint Staff at the White House the following day, December 10. Moorer told Kissinger the air force was giving the Cambodians all of the air power they asked for. Kissinger replied that Nixon did not care.[16] Kissinger followed up with Moorer the next day, asking him on the phone if the bombing had started. "Now will you bomb around Kampong Cham because the President is driving me out of my mind?" Kissinger pleaded. Moorer said they had tripled the bombing runs in the area, a fact Kissinger reported to Nixon.

This was the environment in which Haig was dispatched to Cambodia and South Vietnam. Moorer had ample reason to wonder what Haig would say while there. The Vietnam War was at a critical point, and Moorer doubted Nixon's commitment to winning as he watched as the president veered from one position to another. They needed more information from the White House than they were getting. At Robinson's recommendation, Haig brought Yeoman Radford on the trip with him. Robinson told Radford to take notes for Haig and to pay attention to everything.[17] The Chiefs had a particular interest in any developments that could lead to an all-volunteer army and any details of upcoming troop withdrawal schedules, information that Nixon routinely kept from them. Radford performed a range of duties, from courier to "baggage boy" to stenographer, and whenever he typed a document for Haig, he made a carbon copy and kept it for himself, stuffing it in a large envelope. At times, he simply kept the carbon paper. If he needed to send a document somewhere, Radford made a Xerox copy first and kept that.

～◦～

On December 15, Haig reported to Kissinger about Abrams and Bunker's plans to cut the North Vietnamese lines of communication and supply to South Vietnam by slicing across southern Laos near the town of Tchepone.[18] The offensive would have the extra benefit of showing how the South Vietnamese army could work without US military help on the ground, which would speed the withdrawal of more US troops.

In another memo to Kissinger, Haig acknowledged that Cambodia was a mess that could only be saved with a massive infusion of US aid.[19] Haig also recommended the Laos offensive. In his memoirs, Haig professed little knowledge of the Tchepone operation, when in fact he was an enthusiastic advocate for it. Of particular interest to the Chiefs, and which Radford most likely forwarded to them, were Thieu's concerns about troop reductions. Haig said Thieu worried about the problems of starting a major offensive while US troops were leaving and asked to slow down the withdrawals. Haig agreed, recommending no more withdrawals until after the operations in Cambodia and Laos.

Upon Haig's return, he met with Kissinger, Moorer, and Robinson on December 22. Moorer outlined the Laos offensive and said Abrams picked the Tchepone area, Moorer said, because "it contains many lucrative targets."[20] Now Kissinger had to tell Laird about the plan, Moorer said. Laird was going to Saigon, where Thieu would obviously ask him about the offensive, which Laird had not been told about.

Kissinger then made the remarkable request that Haig bypass CIA director Richard Helms to tell his deputy, General Robert Cushman, that the Agency not publish any report about the Laos operation until it received White House permission first.[21]

The following morning, Kissinger outlined for Nixon the elaborate charade he created for a meeting Nixon was to have with Laird, Moorer, and Kissinger.[22] That was when, Kissinger wrote, they would tell Laird about the Laos operation for the first time. Kissinger's choreography made it essential, he told Nixon, that Laird not feel as if he had been bypassed and that the Laotian offensive was not already a fait accompli. "Admiral Moorer is aware of the details of this planning which has been proceeding without the full knowledge of Secretary Laird especially with respect to the plan for Southern Laos. Therefore, it is important that at this morning's meeting your decision to proceed with the planning for these operations be conveyed as having resulted from General Haig's trip report to you and not as a result of any prior liaison with the Chairman or the military." In essence, Kissinger said Nixon should tell Laird that Haig has just learned of these ideas during his trip to Southeast Asia and he enlisted Moorer and Laird to help analyze them. "You should then ask me to brief these plans for the group," Kissinger said.

Nixon, Laird, Kissinger, Moorer, and Haig met in the Oval Office at 9:20 a.m.[23] Nixon told Laird and Moorer he wanted to talk to them before they went to Southeast Asia. Haig briefed the others on his findings, and then they reviewed plans for Cambodia and Laos. The Laos operation must succeed, Moorer said, and was worth whatever risks they had to take.

"Let it succeed with a minimum low-key operation so far as US forces are concerned," Nixon said. He then turned to Laird and asked what he thought of the Laotian plan.

"Let's take a crack at it," Laird responded.

Nixon had played Laird masterfully. The Defense Secretary was now on board.

Upon Laird's return, he, Nixon, Kissinger, Helms, Moorer, and Rogers met in the Oval Office on January 18 to complete their planning.[24] The six were convinced the offensive would succeed and help end the war. Nevertheless, Helms said, the South Vietnamese troops would encounter stiff resistance. Moorer agreed but said it would be the enemy's last gasp. Rogers said a South Vietnamese defeat would be costly, to which Nixon replied that it cannot be called a defeat. One way to prevent that was by limiting the goals and keeping the claims modest. Nixon also claimed "that the best way to proceed was to be open on the whole thing," a stunning claim given the duplicity that marked its creation and early planning. Nixon also said the operation "should be conveyed in the context of a raid on an enemy base," according to Haig's notes. "We should avoid all exaggerated claims. Following the operation, we could crow about accomplishments."[25]

Haig would later mischaracterize this meeting in his memoirs and claim that the participants had committed US troops to enter Laos if the South Vietnamese encountered difficulty.[26] Yet his own notes do not reflect that commitment, although they showed that Helms warned the group that "it was probably that the [South Vietnamese] would run into a very tough fight in Laos."

❧

Opposition arose once more officials learned of the Laos plan. State official Alexis Johnson said he had sought a similar operation across southern Laos in 1965, but he recommended six US divisions and not just two South Vietnamese divisions.[27] Even if the attack killed thousands of North Vietnamese troops and destroyed their weapons and ammunition, two South Vietnamese divisions could not finish the job. Johnson criticized the administration for not having a coherent public relations and diplomacy plan that would withstand the anticipated criticism that South Vietnam had violated Laos's neutrality. Laos "was held together by mirrors," Johnson said in a marathon January 21 meeting, and would be destroyed by any kind of invasion.

As the administration deliberated moving into southern Laos, the President's Foreign Intelligence Advisory Board weighed in on January 21 with its report on the CIA failure to gain accurate estimates of Chinese weapons flowing through the Cambodian port of Sihanoukville.[28] Nixon used the mistake to beat up the Agency and the quality of its intelligence. He reinforced his unhappiness by setting loose the advisory board on the Agency. The board's report blamed an overly cautious Agency bureaucracy, the lack of decent collection assets in Cambodia, and Agency analysts unwilling to admit they were wrong. Kissinger told Nixon he was pushing Helms to clean house at the CIA, a move Nixon applauded. "K—give me a report on these changes—I want a real shakeup in CIA, not just symbolism," Nixon wrote in the margins of Kissinger's memo.[29]

The Agency's analysis of the Tchepone operation called it "a difficult target because of high density of enemy security forces and it is probable that enemy caches in the area are widely dispersed." The CIA analysis that Nixon received on January 26 spelled out four major enemy reactions, including anticipation of the allied attack, a desire to "stand and fight" once they realize the scope of the operation, and counterattacks elsewhere in Laos and in South Vietnam.[30] Helms also told Kissinger and others that the North Vietnamese knew about the operation and were prepared for it.[31]

The Tchepone operation, dubbed Lam Son 719, started February 8, 1971, in the middle of the region's dry season. Agency analysts presented policymakers with numerous intelligence reports leading up to the attack, particularly those that noted the North Vietnamese had anticipated the offensive and built up their positions in the area. As predicted, the North Vietnamese let the South Vietnamese move deeper into Laos before reacting. By the end of February, US officials realized the tide had turned. Reports from the field told of panicked ARVN soldiers dropping their weapons and fleeing, including those who grabbed onto helicopter landing supports in order to catch a last-minute ride out of combat.

Nixon and others met February 27, and the president sought answers for the slow progress in Laos. Helms told Nixon that Agency operatives had picked up communications from NVA units that they would "stand and fight," a major change for an enemy that usually relied on its ability to fight and then fade into the jungle. It was also exactly what the Agency had predicted in its report to Nixon. The NVA had decided to finish off the invaders then and there.

Nixon tried to blame the CIA.

"One point, Dick, that concerned me, and I saw on television and so forth, and the news summaries, that our intelligence people are saying that our intelligence is inefficient, inadequate, bad, and that that's the reason that we're, we're running into more resistance than was expected," Nixon said.

Helms would have none of it. "Mr. President, resistance is precisely what we expected. It's—it's been there, we outlined it before the plan ever kicked off."

"They both—they both—they both quote, 'A high official said—,'" Nixon said.

"What if that high official doesn't know?" Helms responded. "When we were in here briefing you long before this operation kicked off, we identified all of those units surrounded on the map, and . . ."[32]

Nixon dropped the point, but he would not forget.

❧

The failure in Laos came as the administration was receiving unwanted scrutiny by the *New York Times* about the State Department's lack of authority in developing foreign policy. That led to a March 2 speech by Senator Stuart Symington in which he accused Kissinger of running a secret government "without any accountability of any kind whatever to the Congress."[33] It was Kissinger, Symington said, who was the real Secretary of State, while Rogers was a mere figurehead and spectator.[34] Nixon defended Rogers in a press conference and accused Symington of taking a cheap shot, while Kissinger told Nixon in a memo that Symington's speech was "a fundamental misunderstanding of how the NSC system actually works. . . . The NSC does not as an entity itself make decisions—only you do." He listed ten more examples of "factual errors and misconceptions" in Symington's speech.[35]

Kissinger and Nixon protested too much, because Symington knew exactly what they had done when they restructured the NSC. He just could do little about it.

By later March, by the time observers on the ground had long deemed Lam Son 719 a failure, the Nixon administration continued to call it a success. Despite the setbacks, a March 30 *New York Times* account said Nixon was "being asked to take comfort from the fact that more time was gained for the defense of South Vietnam and the continuing withdrawal of American forces."[36] Three paragraphs later, reporter Max Frankel raised the same issue Nixon had pressed with Helms in February. "The most conspicuous tactical setbacks are being attributed to intelligence failures," Frankel wrote. "Mr. Nixon is being told that no one expected the North Vietnamese to be able to reinforce their units in Laos as quickly as they did or to supply them with 150 tanks and other heavy equipment in time to stage a massive counterattack," which was blatant White House spin contradicted by the record, which indicates the CIA and its officials had told Nixon the North Vietnamese had the people, arms, and supplies to withstand a South Vietnamese attack. Everyone, including Nixon, knew Lam Son's risks but chose not to listen.

Helms, who had disagreed openly with Nixon's claims of bad intelligence on February 28, quickly refuted the White House leaks in Frankel's story. "As I know you are aware," Helms wrote Kissinger on April 9, "allegations are currently cropping up in the press, and elsewhere, regarding purported 'intelligence failures' in connection with the Lam Son 719 operation."[37] Immediately after reading the March 30 article, Helms said, he asked his staff to assemble a record of the reports they had provided the NSC leading up to Lam Son. Helms took that memo with him to the April 2 meeting of the PFIAB, where he was once again grilled for the Agency's alleged failures. The March 30 memo elaborated in detail the CIA reports leading up to the February 8 attack, particularly a January 21 memorandum that said "Hanoi would be likely to do whatever it could to make the position of the South Vietnamese in Laos untenable and it would be prepared to accept the heavy manpower losses this might entail. . . . For all these reasons Hanoi can be expected to contest the Tchepone raid with whatever resources it can muster." The January 21 memo, Helms told Kissinger, "accurately predicted not only the North Vietnamese response but also the responses of the Lao, Communist Chinese, Soviets and the Thai. In short, there was no 'intelligence failure' so far as this Agency's predictions were concerned. Instead, in this instance we came about as close to calling the shots as one is ever likely to come in the real world."[38]

Nixon kept pushing for changes at the CIA beyond those Helms made at the end of 1970. In March, James Schlesinger, the assistant director of the Office of Management and Budget, presented Kissinger and Nixon a plan he said would improve the quality of intelligence and reduce its costs.[39] His plan would have stripped the heart from much of the CIA. "The role of the DCI should be modified and CIA restructured so that they are separated from direct responsibility for the conduct of intelligence collection and covert action operations," Schlesinger continued. The plan was another shot across the bow for the Agency, and Helms would spend much of 1971 fighting to push it back.

CHAPTER ELEVEN

China (1971)

RENEWING RELATIONS WITH CHINA DOMINATED NIXON'S AGENDA, AND A successful opening there could help end the Vietnam War and give the United States leverage with the Soviet Union. Nixon saw China in sweeping geopolitical terms. By bringing China back into the mainstream of world affairs, Nixon would remove a nation of eight hundred million people from the margins and make it a necessary counterweight to the Soviet Union. Mao Tse-tung, grappling with restive factions in his Communist Party, would be able to neutralize a major international rival and knock his domestic foes off balance. Nixon advertised his interest in China, including it in his pivotal *Foreign Affairs* article in 1967 and during his 1968 convention speech. He issued NSSM 14 in early February, which sought scenarios for improved relations between the two nations. Chinese political rhetoric remained shrill, but as the political upheaval of the Chinese Cultural Revolution faded, the Chinese government signaled through intermediaries that it also welcomed a thaw.

***

A series of border clashes starting in March 1969 between Chinese and Soviet troops spurred Nixon, who considered the fighting a clear sign of the worsening tensions between the communist powers. Others on the NSC staff did, too, but the Joint Chiefs warned that changing the policy made little sense. The Joint Staff was represented by Lieutenant General F. T. Unger, who said on May 15 that he thought any different option would be seen as phony.[1] Unger's objection reflected what would be the Chiefs' longstanding problem with changing China policy. In Vietnam, they fought North Vietnamese soldiers armed with Chinese weapons. Many of them had fought the Chinese in Korea. They also did not want to endanger Taiwan. The CIA, however, reported that the Soviets were extremely worried about China, leading Haig to tell Kissinger that "a concerted effort on our part to at least threaten efforts at rapprochement with the Chicoms would be of the greatest concern to the Soviets."[2] That philosophy had the most momentum inside the NSC, which was reflected in another directive from Nixon on July 3, NSSM 63, which ordered a "study of the policy choices confronting the United States as a result of the intensifying Sino-Soviet rivalry and the current Soviet efforts to isolate Communist China."[3]

~ ~

In late July 1969, Nixon made an around-the-world trip in which he recruited two unlikely helpers for the China opening—Romanian President Nicolae Ceausescu, a megalomaniacal dictator, and the new president of Pakistan, Agha Mohammad Yahya Khan, a former general. Ceausescu wanted to distance his country from the rest of the Soviet bloc. He and Nixon were both smitten with each other. Nixon, who told Ceausescu the United States would not join in a bloc against China, saw Ceausescu as an ally in helping to split the Soviet bloc.[4] In Lahore, the Pakistani leader was even more enthusiastic about any potential China overtures. Yahya, a bushy-browed general who led the Pakistani military in the 1965 war with India, also shared Nixon's desire for stronger ties with China because of their shared antipathy for India. Muslim Pakistan had been split in two by the 1947 partition that divided the British colony of India into two nations, and the Pakistanis felt slighted by their larger, Hindu-majority neighbor. The Pakistanis wanted the mountainous region of Kashmir between the two countries, which Pakistan believed had been granted unfairly to India. China and India's border disagreements had led to a brief war in 1962 that badly scarred the Indian military. Yahya saw China as the stronger ally he needed to ward off India, and he welcomed the chance to help Nixon. Nixon told Yahya he had different ideas about China than most Americans, and that the United States would not join any plans aimed at isolating China. He also asked Yahya to share the details of their discussion with the Chinese but that it was up to him to decide how he wanted to do it. While Nixon wanted to normalize relations with China, he told Yahya, the American people were not ready for it yet. Nevertheless, Nixon promised to help China enter the United Nations from which it had been excluded since 1949 in favor of Taiwan.[5]

Taiwan's government suspected Nixon had told Yahya something, so its envoys immediately sought reassurance about where they stood with the new president. Chow Shu-kai, Taiwan's ambassador to the United States, met with Kissinger on August 6 to investigate reports that Nixon had spoken to Ceausescu and Yahya about opening relations with Beijing.[6] Kissinger lied, telling Chow "there had been no change in the US position regarding Peking and we were not talking with it anywhere."

━ ～ ━

Yahya, however, acted as if Nixon had ordered him to follow through with the Chinese and almost immediately started to contact Beijing. Kissinger sent a message via Haig to NSC aide Harold Saunders directing him to meet with Pakistani ambassador to the United States, Agha Hilaly. Saunders told Hilaly that while Nixon did tell Yahya he wanted to reach out to China, he did not think Yahya had to do anything immediately.[7] Yahya continued to stoke the fire, hoping it would spark into something greater. There was no misunderstanding, Hilaly told Saunders, and "walked to his desk and picked up what looked like 10 legal-sized pages which apparently constituted his record of the debriefing President Yahya had given him on the talk with President Nixon."[8]

━ ～ ━

The deliberations inside the NSC over NSSM 63, the directive to study US policies in the event of greater tensions between the Soviet Union and China, exposed another rift between the Pentagon and the rest of the team. A Defense paper submitted to the NSC said there was "inadequate consideration to two possible outcomes of major Sino-Soviet hostilities, viz the creation of Soviet-sponsored regimes in China and the downfall of the Mao–Lin government."[9] Another concern, General Unger said, was the potential creation of a noncommunist regime in China, which seemed a long shot.[10] Nixon knew early that the military opposed his China plan, so he and Kissinger tried their best to hide it from the Pentagon.

━ ～ ━

On December 23, Hilaly reported back to Kissinger to relay the details of a meeting between Yahya and the Chinese ambassador to Pakistan.[11] Yahya had told the Chinese that the United States would withdraw two naval destroyers from the Taiwan straits as a sign of good faith. In return, the Chinese had released on December 7 two American yachtsmen who had been detained in February after straying into Chinese territorial waters near the Portuguese colony of Macao.[12] Hilaly asked Kissinger if there was anything else he could tell Yahya before Chou visited Pakistan, and Kissinger said the Pakistanis could tell the Chinese that the United States was serious about meeting and wanted to do it outside normal channels.[13]

— ⁓ —

Nixon did not rely solely on Yahya. Major General Vernon Walters, the US military attaché in Paris, was designated as the point man for any backdoor meetings between US and Chinese officials there, including an unsuccessful attempt in 1970 to use a Dutch diplomat as a go-between.[14] Fluent in six languages besides English, Walters had translated for multiple presidents and ran confidential operations around the world; Walters had helped Kissinger open the door to secret peace talks with the North Vietnamese in Paris, and now the administration wanted his help on China. Both were highly irregular missions for an embassy military attaché, but such was Walters's ability and the trust Nixon placed in him.

— ⁓ —

The Pakistan channel flickered back to life in October 1970, starting a nine-month process that would end up with Kissinger making his paradigm-shifting trip to Beijing the following July. During an October 25 visit to Washington, Yahya and Nixon shared their frustrations with India, which Nixon said held an outsized influence over the American people.[15] In turn, Yahya promised to never embarrass the United States. Nixon then cut to the chase.

"I understand you are going to Peking," Nixon said. Yahya said yes.

"It is essential that we open negotiations with China," Nixon told him. "Whatever our relations with the USSR or what announcements are made I want you to know the following: (1) we will make no condominium against China and we want them to know it whatever may be put out; (2) we will be glad to send" a high-level emissary, such as Thomas Dewey, the former governor of New York and two-time Republican nominee for president.

Yahya said he would explain everything to the Chinese.

Two days later, Kissinger met Romania's Ceausescu, who was in Washington to see Nixon.[16] Kissinger said Nixon still wanted to establish relations with China. The Romanian agreed, saying he had been telling the Chinese that in previous conversations and would keep doing so.

— ⁓ —

Yahya went to Beijing in November and shortly afterward told US ambassador to Pakistan Joseph Farland that the Chinese definitely wanted to talk.[17] Yahya told Chou what he and Nixon discussed in October, and Chou said he had raised the issues with Mao and Lin Piao, the Chinese No. 2, and that while both acknowledged significant problems between the two nations, they also believed "a more amiable attitude could develop between the two countries."[18] Two days later, Kissinger sent for Hilaly and told him that Nixon wanted to send a message to Chou through Yahya that the United States was ready to set up a meeting at an early date in a neutral location or in Beijing with a high-level US representative. That could be Dewey or Ambassador David Bruce, the chief US negotiator in Paris. Or it could be him, Kissinger added. Yahya delivered the message to China on January 5, 1971.[19]

Then Nixon did not hear again from Yahya until April, when Chou answered through the Pakistani president, saying the problems between China and the United States can be fixed "only through direct discussions between high-level responsible persons of the two countries." That could either be Kissinger or the Secretary of State or even Nixon himself, if he wanted. The details could be determined by working through Yahya, Chou said.[20] In a second surprise, China invited the US table tennis team, then in Japan for the world championships, to travel to China later in April. It was, the *New York Times* noted, "Peking's first concrete response to a series of American moves aimed at improving relations with China."[21]

Chou's message and the table tennis invitation sent Nixon and Kissinger into overdrive. They needed to pick an envoy and determine where the representatives should meet. Dewey had died in March, which stripped Nixon of one of his top choices. On April 27, Nixon called Kissinger to review developments, a conversation that found both men almost giddy about what they were on the verge of pulling off.[22]

"Mr. President," Kissinger said, "I have not said this before, but I think if we get this thing working, we will end Vietnam this year. The mere fact of these contacts makes that."

Kissinger had difficulty containing himself.

"Once this gets going—everything is beginning to fit together," he said.

"I hope so," Nixon answered.

They discussed media relations and other issues, before Kissinger put the move in context.

"If anyone had predicted that two months ago, we would have thought it was inconceivable," Kissinger said.

"Yeah, yeah," Nixon answered. "After Laos . . ."

"After Cambodia, the same thing," Kissinger said.

"Yeah," Nixon said. "But look at after Laos, the people two to one thought it had failed and yet here comes the Chinese move, the Ping Pong team and something more significant that pales that into nothing. It can have an enormous significance."

Kissinger was the only logical emissary. "I happen to be the only one who knows all the negotiations," he told Nixon and Haldeman the following day.[23]

The White House summoned Ambassador Farland from Pakistan for a secret meeting at the Palm Springs, California, home of Los Angeles developer Theodore Cummings. Kissinger told Farland he had established a secret communications line through the navy.[24] This was the navy's highly classified SR-1 line, which navy lieutenant Bob Woodward, the future *Washington Post* reporter, had monitored when he worked for Moorer at the Pentagon.[25] Kissinger asked Farland to tell Yahya of their plans and they would finalize the rest of the details once they had established the secret communications line.[26] While Kissinger and Nixon thought they had gone to great lengths to conceal the details of their trip, they did not realize their plans had already been penetrated. Taking notes for Kissinger in the meeting with Farland was a young navy officer, David Halperin, who had served under Admiral Elmo Zumwalt, the chief of naval operations, in the Pacific and who had intense personal loyalty to Zumwalt.[27] Halperin regularly informed Zumwalt of Kissinger's activities at the NSC.[28] The secret navy communications line was monitored by the Pentagon's communications office at the Pentagon, which reported to Moorer, who was regularly informed of the traffic on the various channels.

The plan, as finished in June, called for Kissinger to land in Islamabad on July 8 and meet with leaders there. "My official itinerary as sent to posts will show me arriving in Islamabad mid-day July 8 and departing July 10 afternoon," he said in a cable to Farland. "In response to State cable, you should work with Pakistani Government to arrange official schedule in Islamabad during this period. We will adjust schedule while I am traveling."[29] Traveling with him would be NSC aides Harold Saunders, John Holdridge, Winston Lord, Richard Smyser, and David Halperin. The only other person aware of his side trip was Thomas Karamessines, the CIA's deputy director for operations, Kissinger said. Of course, if Karamessines knew, no doubt his boss, Richard Helms, knew as well. Kissinger would then pretend to be sick and go to a remote hill station to rest. Halperin and Farland would go to the hill station, while Kissinger would travel with the other aides to Beijing for meetings from July 9 to 11. Also traveling with him, Kissinger told Farland, would be "Yeoman First Class Charles Radford who will also not be witting."[30] Radford would not travel to Beijing, but that did not mean he did not know what Kissinger was doing. The young yeoman, part of the Joint Chiefs' liaison office at the NSC, was by then liberally sending White House secrets to

Moorer. He would spend the entire Kissinger trip stealing documents from Kissinger's briefcase. Radford's presence on the trip meant the Chiefs had three sources of information on Kissinger's "secret" trip – Radford, Halperin, and the special communications line that went through the Pentagon. Neither Kissinger nor Nixon suspected any of them.

~

All of the secrecy surrounding Kissinger's trip did not stop the Nationalist Chinese government in Taiwan from feeling nervous. Nixon was preparing to minimize dramatically the US commitment to Taiwan. In a June 30 meeting in the Oval Office with Haig and Walter McConaughy, the US ambassador to Taiwan, Nixon continued his deception about his true intentions toward Taiwan.[31] Over the course of seventeen minutes, Nixon told McConaughy that he had no plans to support ousting Taiwan from the United Nations and that Chiang had no greater friend in the United States.

Vietnam, Nixon continued, was where the People's Republic could really help the United States by putting pressure on North Vietnam to end the war. Nixon praised Taiwan's industriousness and added that the economic potential of mainland China was also huge. He also made another gratuitous smear of India. Put eight hundred million Chinese to work, and they would control the world, Nixon said. "The Indians—you could put 200 billion Indians to work, and they wouldn't amount to a goddamn.... You know, they're basically different kinds of people."

Nixon knew he would have to sacrifice Taiwan for the sake of a larger deal with China. On July 1, he told Kissinger and Haig that Kissinger should not "indicate a willingness to abandon much of our support for Taiwan until it was necessary to do so." Nixon spelled out what he wanted from China before he would agree to a presidential summit. The Chinese had to release all US prisoners of war still held in China. They had to accept at least some token shipments of US grain, and they had to make some progress on the Vietnam War. After a summit, he added, the two nations needed to establish a hotline between the two to limit the potential for an accidental nuclear war.

Whatever they agreed on Taiwan, Nixon cautioned, could not look like a sellout of Taiwan. But any US troops on the island, Nixon continued, were only there because of the Vietnam War. Once that was concluded, the troops would leave. In general, Nixon told Kissinger he needed to not make it obvious that the United States was "dumping on our friends" but to be more mysterious about whatever concessions the administration would make on Taiwan.[32]

With these instructions, Kissinger began his trip, stopping first in New Delhi and then to Rawalpindi, Pakistan, where he landed on July 8 and met briefly with Farland and local officials. At 3:30 a.m. on July 9, Kissinger slipped out of his guesthouse and left in a darkened car for Chaklala Airport, where he boarded a Pakistani International Airlines Boeing 707 with a crew of Chinese navigators for the flight to Beijing. He arrived shortly after noon, and his hosts whisked him and his party in dark limousines with curtained windows to the Chinese Government Guest House. Kissinger and his small team of aides encountered Chou En-lai and his group about four hours later. The lean, almost gaunt, and sharp Chou, a savvy survivor of internal Chinese Communist politics, joined them across a green-covered table. Chou opened the talks with a joke: "There is special news—you are lost," he told Kissinger.[33]

Both men grasped the huge stakes of the meeting and the importance of their role in it. Their conversations, spread over twenty hours on three days, showed two masters of geopolitical strategy at work. Chou, always calm and forceful, spoke with a great sense of China's history and its new role in the world. He represented the world's most populous country but one wracked by poverty and internal turmoil about which most outsiders understood little. Kissinger, the son of Jewish refugees fleeing Hitler's Germany, proved every bit Chou's equal. He parried the Chinese prime minister's flights of Maoist rhetoric with a deft hand. Kissinger had prepared for this moment for years, studied Nixon's desires and endured the president's drunken and paranoid nighttime monologues. He knew what Nixon needed and what he had to do. He did not disappoint, at least not Nixon. Others, especially those not represented at the meetings, did not fare so well.

Chiang Kai-shek's Republic of China lost the most, as its officials had sensed before they even knew of Kissinger's secret mission. Chou made it clear, as Nixon and Kissinger expected, that Taiwan was part of China, a point the Chinese considered non-negotiable. "The question of Taiwan becomes one regarding which we cannot but blame your government," Chou said early in the first meeting with Kissinger.[34] "Of course, you are not responsible for this, and you may say that President Nixon wasn't responsible for it either." Chou continued with a detailed history of Taiwan's relationship to China, and then hammered another condition: "The US must withdraw all its armed forces and dismantle all its military installations on Taiwan and in the Taiwan Straits within a limited period. This is the natural logic of the matter."[35]

Kissinger agreed with much of what Chou had to say. "There's no question that if the Korean War hadn't occurred, a war which we did not seek and you did not seek, Taiwan would probably be today a part of the PRC," Kissinger told Chou. "For reasons which are now worthless to recapitulate, a previous administration linked the future of Korea to the future of Taiwan, partly because of US domestic opinion at the time," which, Kissinger declined to add, was stoked by Nixon and his Republican allies. The US military presence in Taiwan, Kissinger said, mattered little. Already, the United States had ended naval patrols in the Taiwan Straits, a move opposed by the Pentagon and Joint Chiefs of Staff, and removed air tankers and military advisers from Taiwan. The Chiefs also opposed withdrawing US troops, arguing that they needed to be there as long as China remained a threat. Two-thirds of the US military presence in Taiwan, Kissinger said, involved matters elsewhere, such as in Vietnam. Once those commitments end, the US troops will leave. That was done on Nixon's orders, he said, not those of Congress or the Pentagon, "so should be treated with great confidence."[36]

At the United Nations, Kissinger assured Chou, Nixon did not want a "two Chinas" solution or "one China, one Taiwan."[37] Any student of history, Kissinger continued, would realize that "the political evolution is likely to be in the direction which Prime Minister Chou En-lai indicated to me." But both nations need to recognize the other's political "necessities." It would be counterproductive, he said, to force the United States into "formal declarations in a brief period of time which by themselves have no practical effect." In other words, do not force the United States to renounce Taiwan openly. Instead, "we will not stand in the way of basic evolution, once you and we have come to a basic understanding." It would not oppose the People's Republic's election to membership in the United Nations, and if mainland China joined the UN, the United States would not oppose the expulsion of Taiwan by a two-thirds vote if the People's Republic could win enough votes at the UN to make that happen. "We would solve the contradiction before our public by withdrawing our opposition to entry of the People's Republic of China," Kissinger said. "But we have not yet announced this because as a sign of our good will, the president wanted me to discuss this matter with you before we adopted a position." The main thing, Kissinger continued, "is that if both countries know where we are going, it will only be a question of time until the end result is acknowledged."[38] Kissinger's words to Chou echoed those he and Nixon told Soviet ambassador Anatoly Dobrynin in February 1969 about Vietnam; once a peace deal was reached between North and South Vietnam and US troops left the area, then it would be up to the people of Vietnam to determine what happened next. Kissinger appeared to make the same pledge to Chou about Taiwan, a commitment that Nixon had assured the Taiwan government he would not make.

But there were limits to what the United States could do now, Kissinger said. "There's no sense deluding ourselves," he said. "There's no possibility in the next one and a half years for us to recognize the PRC as the sole government of China in a formal way."[39] American public opinion would have enough trouble digesting the new reality that "Red China" and the United States had reached some kind of accommodation after twenty-two years of hostility. Veterans of the Korean War and the relatives of those killed fighting the Chinese on the Korean peninsula for almost three years would not be so willing to embrace the Chinese.

Kissinger's presence in Beijing, he told Chou, was only because of Nixon's unique standing in American politics. "The only president who could conceivably do what I am discussing with you is President Nixon," Kissinger said. "Other political leaders might use more honeyed words, but would be destroyed by what is called the China lobby in the US if they ever tried to move even partially in the direction which I have described to you. President Nixon, precisely because his political support comes from the center and right of center, cannot be attacked from that direction, and won't be attacked by the left in a policy of moving toward friendship with the People's Republic of China."[40]

Nixon was prepared to abandon most of his long-held positions on Taiwan for the sake of a world-changing deal with China. The price the Chinese had to pay for such an agreement was not to force Nixon to make any public renunciation of Taiwan but to simply realize that the future would be much to China's advantage.

On Vietnam, Kissinger said the United States would leave but only after a deal that "is consistent with our honor and our self-respect, and if we cannot get this, then the war will continue."[41] China, he told Chou, needs to help make the North Vietnamese understand this. Nixon, Kissinger told him, offered a set date for a complete withdrawal from Vietnam, but there had to be a cease-fire throughout all of Indochina, all prisoners should be released, and the 1954 Geneva agreement that helped partition Vietnam into two countries should be observed. Kissinger said leaving Vietnam without a cease-fire was tantamount to unilateral disarmament. But if the North Vietnamese agreed to the cease-fire, gave back the prisoners, and let US troops leave, then "we will permit the political solution of South Vietnam to evolve and to leave it to the Vietnamese alone." Again, that was another evocation of the "decent interval" doctrine. Kissinger, with Nixon's approval, delivered much of the US position with a wink and a nod. Chou, despite his cool reserve and emphatic bargaining points, seemed to understand.

It was the need to counterbalance India, the world's largest democracy but one slowed by dire poverty and ethnic divisions, which informed much of the meetings. It was Yahya Khan's desire to check India that had driven much of his desire to create the backchannel to China for the United States. As the two men sat in Beijing, Yahya's army was in the middle of a genocidal crackdown that had forced at least five million refugees from East Pakistan into neighboring India. Chou and Kissinger both praised Yahya for his help, and both said they would support Pakistan if India attacked it. Kissinger had warned Indian prime minister Indira Gandhi that the United States would not tolerate an Indian attack against Pakistan. Chou said India's expansionist aims were why China had supplied arms to Pakistan. "We do so because India is committing aggression against Pakistan," Chou said. "They have also committed aggression against us."[42]

The issue of India warped what was Chou's usual clear-eyed view of the world. "Pakistan would never provoke a disturbance against India because in all military fields Pakistan is in a weaker position than India."[43] What neither Chou nor Kissinger seemed to realize at the time was that Pakistan would provoke a regional crisis that year, and it would be Pakistan, not India, that would emerge battered and discredited.

It was also clear by the end of Kissinger's mission that, however grateful the two nations were for Yahya's help, he had outlived his usefulness to Nixon.

"Please tell President Yahya Khan that when necessary we'll still use his channel," Chou said. "We have a saying in China that one shouldn't break the bridge after crossing it."

Kissinger was less enthusiastic.

"We might exchange some communications through him for politeness," he said.

"This is because you have confidence in him," Chou said, "and we also respect him." Maybe so, Kissinger, said, but "there are just some things which we don't have to say through friends, no matter how trustworthy."[44]

The two sides planned for either Kissinger or another US emissary to return to China in the fall and for Nixon to travel there before May 1972 and the commencement of the serious reelection campaign. They would also juggle a future Nixon trip to the Soviet Union to avoid conflicts. General Walters, the US military attaché in Paris, would handle the details. Walters,

Kissinger told Chou, "has direct communications to the White House. He used to be the personal interpreter for the president, and we have used him for contacts with the North Vietnamese. He's completely our man."[45]

—◦—

Even before Kissinger left Beijing he knew he had made history. "Conversations were the most intense, important and far reaching of my White House experience," he told Haig in a July 11 memo that did not mention China or Chou by name. He urged continued secrecy. "Please inform President that I strongly urge no further dissemination even to guest until I return," Kissinger told Haig. "Please keep P.R. types ignorant. A leak or even a hint is almost certain to blow everything."[46] He echoed those comments in a July 14 memorandum to Nixon. The meeting with Chou "resulted in the most searching, sweeping and significant discussions I have ever had in government," Kissinger wrote.[47]

Kissinger rhapsodized about the meetings with Chou, "a moving experience" that "had all the flavor, texture, variety and delicacy of a Chinese banquet." The trip, he continued, made it ready for Nixon and Mao to remake history. Challenges, such as Taiwan, remained and the Chinese "will prove implacable foes if our relations turn sour." The announcement of a new relationship between the United States and China "will send enormous shock waves around the world." The Soviet Union could panic, and Japan could be alienated. "It will cause a violent upheaval in Taiwan. . . . It will increase the already substantial hostility in India." But Kissinger said they knew the benefits of relations with China outweighed the risks. If they could pull it off, he enthused, "we will have made a revolution."[48]

—◦—

Nixon and the Chinese announced on July 15 that Nixon would go to China in the next year, when, Nixon said, he would "seek the normalization of relations between the two countries." The *New York Times* bannered the three-line headline across its entire front page, complete with photos of the three protagonists—Nixon, Kissinger, and Chou.[49] The *Times* story also made prominent mention of Nixon's comment that "our action in seeking a new relationship with the People's Republic of China will not be at the expense of our friends." Taiwan felt differently. Its ambassador to the United States protested immediately, saying the news could "hardly be described as a friendly act."[50] At the Pentagon, the Chiefs also worried about the implications for Taiwan, which they considered a critical part of their Asian defense strategy.

Nixon simultaneously played damage control with Taiwan while also trying to capture public credit for his accomplishment. His message to Taiwan said he deeply regretted not being able to tell Taiwan about the trip in advance. He had to do what he did, Nixon told the Taiwanese, because "it has become imperative in this age to attempt to break down barriers of hostility and suspicion that have grown over the years and could threaten the peace of the world."[51] Asia will benefit from the change, he said, adding that he understood how "disturbing" the news was to the government of Taiwan. That did not mean, however, that the United States would not honor its commitments to Taiwan.

Nixon also wanted the world to know he had made the China breakthrough possible. "One effective line you could use in your talks with the press is how RN is uniquely prepared for this meeting and how ironically in many ways he has similar character characteristics and background to Chou," Nixon wrote Kissinger on July 19.[52] Some of those traits, Nixon wrote, included "strong convictions," rising through adversity, coolness in a crisis, a "tough bold strong leader" who was willing to take chances and a man "who knows Asia and has made a particular point of traveling in Asia and studying Asia." Many of these traits, Nixon said, "are ones you also saw in Chou En-lai."

The president also had to persuade his own staff on July 19. He and Kissinger met in the White House Roosevelt Room to emphasize again the need for absolute secrecy. Without it, Nixon said, "there would have been no invitation or acceptance to visit China."[53]

In the early stages, Nixon continued, "only Henry and I knew. No one else on his staff knew. Later, others on his staff had to know, and the Secretary of State had to know, to be able to brief foreign diplomats. No wife, no other staff member, no other member of the National Security Council knew." Of course, Nixon did not realize that the Joint Chiefs, through Kissinger's aide Halperin, the use of the navy secret communications channel, and the document-stealing Yeoman Radford, knew virtually all of Kissinger's plans and movements, if not the exact words of his meetings with Chou.

The president who had authorized wiretaps on seventeen staff members and journalists, a secret he strove to keep above all others, displayed again his loathing of leaks and obsession with secrecy. His insistence on this day had more meaning, as secrecy had paid off with the coup with China. "I can't emphasize too strongly the passionate obsession people have to talk to the press," Nixon said. Doing so, however, would destroy the China initiative, Nixon warned.

"I have total confidence in all of you—otherwise you wouldn't be here in this room," Nixon said. "But secrecy is essential. Anything in a column, even if not attributed, hurts us. Our Chinese friends read everything of significance coming out of the US No one would want that on his shoulders. The stakes are too high for us to engage in the luxury of seeming to be smart. Thank you."

As Nixon left, Kissinger continued to emphasize secrecy: "There will be no rewards from a trip that aborts." The *New York Times* published a story that identified Kissinger as a possible ambassador to China, which "nearly wrecked it."

Kissinger defended the administration's handling of the Vietnam War. "We needed Cambodia and Laos," he said, ignoring how both he and Nixon had lamented the failures of both operations and tried to blame them on others, particularly the CIA. "The Chinese need a strong American president for the game they are playing. . . . They are playing for very high stakes." Nixon showed the Chinese through the secret meetings that he was the president they needed.

Then, before he took questions from the staff, Kissinger revealed the contempt with which he and Nixon viewed India and how they had skewed their thoughts in favor of Pakistan: "The cloak and dagger exercise in Pakistan arranging the trip was fascinating. Yahya hasn't had such fun since the last Hindu massacre!"

Nixon's opening to China ranks among the top foreign policy achievements of any American president. It ended the relative isolation of what in 2015 was the world's second-largest economy. It brought China onto the world stage and gave Nixon leverage against the Soviet Union and North Vietnam. Nixon fundamentally changed the paradigm of US foreign policy for the last forty years.

He paid costs, however, that were not apparent to him or Kissinger at the time. The secrecy that made the China opening possible also alienated many within his administration, particularly the Pentagon, and his political rivals. The spying by the Joint Chiefs of Staff on the National Security Council heated up, as Yeoman Radford continued to steal more documents for Moorer. The Chiefs knew Nixon had sold out Taiwan, which they considered a necessary bulwark against communism, and feared what he would do to South Vietnam, where US troops were dying each week. Nixon's relationship with Yahya Khan enabled him to use the Pakistani channel to the Chinese, but it also emboldened Yahya to start a genocide in East Pakistan and later start a war with India that would stoke tensions with the Soviet Union. The alienation of India and the US favoritism to Pakistan created opposition inside the Pentagon that eventually turned into leaks in the press that weakened Nixon's hand during the worst of the India-Pakistan crisis and forced him into another coverup that would haunt him for the rest of his presidency. In mid-July 1971, however, as the world watched in wonder at his grand achievement, Nixon did not realize it.

CHAPTER TWELVE

Pentagon Papers and FBI (1971)

THE MORNING AFTER NIXON CELEBRATED THE WEDDING OF HIS DAUGHTER, Tricia, at the White House, the *New York Times* printed on June 13, 1971, an expose of the nation's convoluted Vietnam policy headlined "Vietnam Archive: Pentagon Study Traces 3 Decades of Growing US Involvement." It kicked off a series of stories drawn from a classified Pentagon study of the Vietnam War. "A massive study of how the United States went to war in Indochina, conducted by the Pentagon three years ago, demonstrates that four administrations progressively developed a sense of commitment to a noncommunist Vietnam, a readiness to fight the North to protect the South, and an ultimate frustration with this effort—to a much greater extent than their public statements acknowledged at the time," read the lead of the main story by reporter Neil Sheehan, who had first obtained the documents.

The Vietnam archive, which quickly became known as the "Pentagon Papers," came from a yearlong study commissioned in 1967 by Robert McNamara, the Defense Secretary for Presidents Kennedy and Johnson, who had grown intensely disillusioned by the war he had promoted and perpetuated. A team of between thirty and forty civilian and military experts drew from military documents going back to the 1940s to pull together the history that took up forty book-length volumes and more than seven thousand pages to show how the United States entered the war in Vietnam and why. While it was thorough and often damning in its depiction of the acts of various US officials, the history was not complete. "It displays many inconsistencies and lacks a single all-embracing summary," a June 13 *Times* story said.[1]

What the report did not show, however, was anything about Nixon, because the Pentagon Papers were completed before he became president. "The documents prove once more that truth is the first casualty of war and that war corrupts good men," wrote *Times* columnist James Reston, who was instrumental in getting the papers published. "In fact, the ambiguity of the

Nixon administration's zig-zag withdrawal from Vietnam seems, in the light of these documents, almost innocent compared to the deceptive and stealthy American involvement in the war under Presidents Kennedy and Johnson."[2] If he had bothered to read the story when it first appeared that Sunday morning, Nixon would have realized the papers cast his Democratic predecessors in a far more negative light.

Nixon first tried to reach Kissinger, who was in California. He then spoke to Haig, who complained that the *Times* had exposed "the most highly classified documents of the war."[3] Nixon said he had not read the story, so Haig, who was at the Pentagon when the study was conducted, told him the history was written by the Pentagon's "peaceniks," including Morton Halperin, who advocated for the 1968 bombing halt and who was later wiretapped by the FBI.

Nixon quickly looked for a scapegoat.

"What about Laird, what's he going to do about it?" Nixon said. "I'd, I'd just start right at the top and fire some people. I mean whoever, whatever department it came out of I'd fire the top guy."

Haig said the leak came from the Pentagon and the documents were "stolen at . . . the time of the turnover of the administration." He told Nixon most of the blame for the war would go to Kennedy and Johnson.

Nixon finally caught up with Kissinger shortly after 3 p.m. Kissinger's initial reaction was, at best, tepid and lacked Haig's visceral anger. Nixon had to prod him, and while Kissinger called the leak "unconscionable," he agreed that it damaged Kennedy and Johnson more.

"Haig was very disturbed by that *New York Times* thing," the president said.[4]

Nixon's anger started to simmer, then boil. He wanted Attorney General John Mitchell to start an investigation to find the leaker and then "put to the torch," he said, and he worried about the implications for his files on the secret bombing and invasion of Cambodia and the 1971 Lam Son 719 offensive in Laos that Nixon developed without the knowledge of the Secretaries of Defense and State.

～～

Nixon's concerns were still building. By his first meeting the next morning, he was in full dudgeon.

"I think that story in the *Times* should cause everybody here great concern," Nixon told Haldeman. " . . . bunch of crap. That's the most, that's the most unbelievable thing, well that's, that's treasonable, due to the fact that it's aid to the enemy."[5]

Nixon wanted to stop the *Times* from printing any more stories about the papers, but he also wanted to use the papers to damage his political opponents while also protecting himself from the exposure of his role in sabotaging the Paris Peace Talks. Haldeman had told him that aide Tom Huston believed there was a file kept in a vault at the Brookings Institution, a vaguely liberal think tank, which held the details of Johnson's decision to stop bombing North Vietnam. Also in that file, they believed, was the proof of what Nixon had done to persuade South Vietnam to boycott the peace talks with the help of Anna Chennault. Nixon also believed the FBI had bugged his campaign plane and had information that proved his complicity. Huston had told Nixon and Haldeman in February 1970 that the files contained damaging information about Nixon's campaign involvement in the so-called Chennault Affair.

Nixon's obsession with the bombing halt file started with this meeting with Haldeman on the morning of June 14. He wanted to start a team that would find other information that was damaging to either him or his political opponents. Anything that would hurt him would be covered up, while information that would hurt his opponents would be publicized or used for blackmail. With the bombing halt file, he could blackmail Johnson to keep quiet about the Chennault affair.

"Remember, I talked to you about [the file] a year ago," Haldeman said. "Tom Huston was all alarmed. He was in here, and said they have all this, this file and everything. They've got it over at Brookings. They've moved it out of the Defense Department, copies out of the Defense—the Pentagon—shipped the whole file over there. And he argued—and we had . . . we had some discussions about it. He argued that what we should do is send some people in on a routine—they have a secure safe over there to hold this stuff in. Move some people in on a routine security check, find this stuff and confiscate it and walk out."[6]

"Why didn't we do it, Bob?" Nixon asked.

"I don't know," Haldeman said. "But here, this sure shows it. I'm not sure as a matter of fact that this is precisely the same material. There is other material in there, too."

Haldeman was right. The Pentagon Papers were not at Brookings, but the "other material"—the bombing halt details—might be.

"There's a lot of copies of this one," Haldeman continued, talking about the Pentagon Papers. "There's some other stuff that there are only three copies of, one of which is over at Brookings, according to Huston. Huston is an alarmist, but [foreign policy adviser] Dick Allen was an alarmist when he said he ought to cut out [Missouri Sen. Stuart] Symington's ... and we didn't do that."[7]

Allen, who had left the NSC, had warned the White House about Symington's investigation into the CIA's secret war in Laos and US bombing raids there. Allen had been correct. Symington had bedeviled the White House with his investigations, which then turned into a burning distrust of Nixon, Kissinger, and their secret government at the NSC.

The Pentagon Papers made Nixon think again about the Alger Hiss case, which he did often. The Brookings crowd, just like the Georgetown elitists Nixon despised, "are a bunch of bastards. They'll lie, cheat, anything—and then squeal when somebody else does. See, basically that's what gets back to the whole Hiss syndrome. The intellectual, the intellectuals all defended Hiss because, basically, they have no morals." That crowd, Nixon said, could be defeated, but he needed a staff with some balls to do it, not "these little boys around here" who lacked the kind of experience he earned during the Hiss case.[8]

Nixon wrongly concluded that the leaker of the Pentagon Papers was Leslie Gelb, the former director of policy planning and arms control for the office of International Security Affairs, which helped write the Vietnam archive. He wanted to use the force of the White House to target Gelb, who now worked at Brookings, based on only a hunch and the same anti-Semitism that led him to lash out against *Times* reporter Max Frankel, Halperin, and the other Jews he believed were constantly conspiring against him. Nixon's full-throated expression of paranoia set the tone for the White House's actions throughout the rest of the Pentagon Papers case and beyond. The Nixon who had approved Huston's plan to reshape the nation's intelligence system and condone illegal break-ins, mail openings, and wiretaps wanted to use the same tactics to discredit and defame his imagined enemies.

Nixon wanted Huston's help, but he did not realize that his ardent young aide, embittered by Nixon's refusal to support his plan to reorganize the intelligence system, had resigned from the White House on June 13, the day the *Times* published the first installment of the Pentagon Papers.

By day's end on June 14, Nixon determined that Mitchell would go to court to stop the *Times* from printing more of the papers. Mitchell said he had just talked to Walt Rostow, Johnson's national security adviser, who said Johnson would support whatever they wanted to do.[9] Rostow also had a suspect, but it was not Gelb, but Daniel Ellsberg, a former associate of Kissinger at Harvard and a consultant at the RAND Corporation, a defense-connected think tank.

Ellsberg had worked on the study at the Pentagon and then aided Kissinger on a similar Vietnam study for Nixon in late 1968. Ellsberg, whom Mitchell called a "left winger," had a set of the documents at RAND that Nixon wanted.[10]

❧

That day, after Mitchell asked the *Times* to stop the publication of the papers voluntarily, the Justice Department sued the *Times* to block publication of any more installments of the papers, claiming they would hurt national security. Mitchell said he hoped they had an ace in the hole with US District Judge Murray Gurfein, who was hearing his first case as a federal judge after being sworn in the previous week. Nixon had named Gurfein to the bench on the advice of Mitchell, who thought Gurfein might show his appreciation for the nomination by ruling in the administration's favor.

Gurfein at first seemed to justify Mitchell's confidence by issuing a temporary injunction on June 15 to stop the *Times* from publishing until he made a final ruling. He scheduled a hearing for June 17.

Rostow was correct about Ellsberg, who had gotten a copy of the papers in early 1969 and spent months trying to make them public before giving them in April to *Times* reporter Neil Sheehan. A contingent of *Times* reporters, editors, and lawyers then worked for weeks to prepare the documents for publication. After Gurfein's injunction, Ellsberg then offered the papers to the *Washington Post*, which put more pressure on the White House.

❧

By June 17, the FBI and Justice Department had also identified Ellsberg as the leaker. By then, Kissinger had shed his initial reservations about the danger of the leaks; he embraced the need to stop the paper's publication with gusto and enthusiastically denigrated Ellsberg, his former adviser.

"Curse that son of a bitch," Kissinger said in a meeting in the Oval Office with Nixon, Haldeman, and John Ehrlichman. "I know him well."[11]

Nixon was surprised. "He's nuts," Kissinger continued, calling Ellsberg a genius and his brightest student ever. "He was so nuts that he'd drive around all over Vietnam with a carbine" and shoot at peasants in the fields because he thought anyone who wore black clothing had to be part of the Viet Cong.

"He's a born killer," Ehrlichman said.

Maybe it was because Kissinger feared Nixon had doubts about his loyalty that he made up such lies about Ellsberg shooting Vietnamese civilians. For whatever reason, he eagerly bought into the White House attempt to portray Ellsberg as a drug-addled killer.

Nixon continued to obsess over the mythical bombing halt file at Brookings. No one could find it. He told Haldeman to revive the Huston Plan, which he had killed the previous August, to get the file.

"I mean, I want it implemented on a thievery basis," Nixon said. "Goddamn it, get in and get those files. Blow the safe and get it."[12]

Nixon would never get the file, and there is no evidence that it ever existed, at least not in the form Huston imagined. But if he could not get the file, Nixon would create a team that would help him find other secrets.

As the Nixon administration fought the legal battle to stop the Papers' publication, Nixon wanted to demonize Ellsberg as he did Alger Hiss. This time, however, J. Edgar Hoover did not want to cooperate and put the investigation on a back burner. Hoover's reluctance puzzled Nixon, who had expected Hoover's enthusiastic support.

But the seventy-six-year-old Hoover of July 1971 no longer held the same sway over the Bureau or Congress, where some members had accused him in the last year of spying on them. The media, which once listened to Hoover unquestioningly, had started to scrutinize his record and ethics. A young aide to columnist Jack Anderson even rooted through Hoover's household garbage, which drove Hoover crazy.[13] Anderson also hammered Hoover for hounding Coretta Scott King, the widow of slain civil rights leader Martin Luther King Jr., and hinted that Nixon wanted to fire Hoover.[14] Many of the columns dealt with problems that Sullivan, a legendary leaker to the press, had with Hoover, indicating that Sullivan could have been a source for Anderson, as he was for Rowland Evans and Robert Novak, who cowrote another influential Washington column.

Nixon wanted more than Hoover wanted to give. Hoover grudgingly accepted Nixon's request to tap the telephones of government officials and journalists starting in May 1969, but he fobbed off the responsibility for handling the taps onto Sullivan. Sullivan's relationship with Hoover, once the closest in the bureau, soured in October 1970 when Sullivan told a group of news editors that the Soviet Union's Communist Party did not control the actions of US student and radical groups; Hoover railed that Sullivan had hurt his way of getting Congress to maintain the FBI's funding levels. By the end of 1970, Mitchell had installed Robert Mardian as head of Justice's Internal Security Division. Mardian took over the joint Intelligence Evaluation Committee, a pale version of the Huston Plan, and started working closely with Sullivan. Hoover did not intimidate Mardian, who often badgered Hoover for more information. By February 4, 1971, it was clear to

Nixon, Mitchell, and Haldeman that Hoover had to go; they met for two hours that day to determine how they would fire Hoover and who they would replace him with. Nixon wanted Hoover out by the end of the first term.[15]

The FBI's internal tensions peaked shortly after the White House wanted the FBI to interview Ellsberg's father-in-law, wealthy toy manufacturer Louis Marx, who was also a generous supporter of the FBI and causes favored by Hoover. Charles Brennan, the FBI's intelligence chief and a Sullivan acolyte, thought Marx's connection with Hoover made it necessary to seek Hoover's permission to interview Marx. Hoover denied the request and scribbled "No" on the memo. But Hoover's handwriting was so bad that Brennan thought he had written "OK," and he approved interviewing Marx. An outraged Hoover busted Brennan down in rank and transferred him to the Alexandria, Virginia, field office. Brennan complained to Sullivan, who asked Hoover to change his mind. Hoover refused. Sullivan then went to Mardian, who went in turn to Mitchell, who told Hoover they needed Brennan on the Ellsberg investigation. Hoover agreed, but cut Brennan's rank to inspector, put him on probation, and censured him.

Hoover's behavior reinforced Nixon and Mitchell's feelings about Hoover, but Nixon feared that a fired Hoover would leak Nixon's secrets, such as the FBI wiretaps or Nixon's interference with the Paris talks. Hoover needed to know "that we've got to keep our eye on the main ball," Nixon said. "The main ball is Ellsberg. We've got to get this son of a bitch."[16] Hoover still did not budge, not even after Nixon and Mitchell joined him at an FBI ceremony where Nixon praised Hoover as someone "who stands up when it is tough."[17] But Nixon did not force the issue.

❧

Nixon had worse luck in the courts. The "appreciative" Judge Gurfein ruled against the government and for the *Times*. Testimony behind closed doors from officials with State, Defense, and the Joint Chiefs did not "convince this Court that the publication of these historical documents would seriously breach the national security."[18] The government also lost its fight against the *Post*, which sent the issue to the Supreme Court, which heard arguments in *New York Times v. United States* on June 26.

Nixon had little chance to make it past the Supreme Court, particularly given the previous rulings against the administration. He also faced a Court still heavy with appointees of Democratic presidents, and even Republican appointees, such as Potter Stewart, leaned toward a more open reading of the First Amendment. The details in the Papers were old, and while some documents contained embarrassing details, few contained outright secrets whose exposure would endanger American lives. Solicitor General Erwin Griswold argued the administration's case gamely, saying, "There is no Constitutional rule that there can never be prior restraint on the press or on free speech." The newspapers' lawyers, Alexander Bickel for the *Times* and William Glendon for the *Post*, had an easier time of it, since the majority of the Court had clear records favoring press freedom. The only doubt surrounded the margin of the vote.

That question was answered June 30 when the Court ruled 6–3 for the newspapers. Justices Hugo Black, William O. Douglas, William Brennan, Potter Stewart, Thurgood Marshall, and Byron White backed the press, while Chief Justice Warren Burger and Justices John Marshall Harlan and William Blackmun, all Republican appointees, voted for the government. Nixon, who hoped for a 5–4 ruling in his favor, vowed to Hoover that he would change the Court. White, a friend of John F. Kennedy and former football player, "is of the old Kennedy crowd," Hoover said, while Stewart "is a very wishy-washy individual. He switches from one side to the other."[19] The battle over the Papers was over. Nixon would move to another front.

‑‑‑‑‑

Nixon pivoted back to finding someone to get him the bombing halt documents. Haldeman suggested John Dean, the White House counsel, who ran an investigative team of former New York City police detective John Caulfield, who provided security for the 1968 Nixon campaign, and Tony Ulasewicz, another former New York cop who worked with Caulfield.[20] Dean had already been ordered by Haldeman to gather damaging information on Lawrence O'Brien, the former Kennedy aide who now chaired the Democratic National Committee. Dean was also a main contact for Mardian on the Intelligence Evaluation Committee. Nixon did not sound convinced and wondered if Dean's team knew "how tough it has to be played."

What Nixon really wanted, he told Haldeman on July 1, was the 1948 version of himself. "I've never worked as hard in my life and I'll never work as hard again because I don't have the energy."[21] Part of the job, Nixon said, involved prying loose top secret documents from the CIA so they could leak them "to our friends the stories that they would like to have," such as the Bay of Pigs. That would get "them thinking about the past rather than our present problems."

Later that day, Nixon brought in the one White House aide besides Huston who had the nerve to do many of the things Nixon wanted—Charles Colson, a rough-and-tumble Massachusetts lawyer who handled many of the White House's thorny political issues. While Colson could not tackle Nixon's demand himself, he suggested a recently retired CIA operative, E. Howard Hunt, whom Colson called "hard as nails." Hunt, Colson continued, had written forty books, many of which were pulpy spy novels. Nixon was still not sold, mentioning Huston again and then Vernon Walters, who would soon help set up Nixon's China trip. "He's a spy kind of guy," Haldeman said.[22] Nixon then ruled out Walters, because they needed to run the program out of the White House "without being caught."[23]

After another day of ruminations and monologues about the need for a wily and tough son-of-a-bitch to do the job, Nixon and Haldeman settled on the fifty-year-old Hunt, who had started in the Office of Strategic Services, the wartime forerunner of the CIA, and then joined the Agency for stints in Europe, South America, and Guatemala, where he helped train the rebels who led the CIA-backed coup in 1954. In 1960, he worked with the Cuban exiles preparing for what became the unsuccessful Bay of Pigs invasion of April 1961. By 1969, he was approaching Colson for help getting a job at the White House, although he still worked for the CIA. He officially left the Agency in 1970 but in name only. He joined a Washington lobbying and public relations firm, Robert H. Mullen and Company, which was a CIA front. Helms had endorsed Hunt to Haldeman, calling him "ruthless, quiet and careful, low profile. He gets things done."[24]

That convinced Nixon. Within a few days, Hunt was working for the White House's new Special Investigations Unit, which would soon become known as the Plumbers, after co-leader David Young hung a sign on his office door that said, "D. Young—Plumber," because of the group's mission to stop leaks. Young was a Kissinger protégé and lawyer on the NSC, who wanted to get away from Haig, whom he disliked and distrusted. A patrician New Yorker, Young had come from money and studied at Oxford and Cornell before joining the venerable New York law firm Milbank, Tweed, Hadley and McCloy, which represented the Rockefellers. Young knew many of the NSC secrets the White House wanted to keep. Joining Young was Egil Krogh, who had served in the navy before becoming a lawyer and specializing in antidrug work on Ehrlichman's staff, where he also coordinated much of the White House's domestic security policy. He and Young were natural members of the Plumbers, because they knew the White House but also understood the security secrets the group would have to track and protect. Their fourth member was a volatile, eccentric wild card—former FBI agent G. Gordon Liddy, who was working as a Treasury Department investigator. Short, aggressive, and given to attaching German and/or Nazi terms to many of his activities, Liddy had the ruthlessness Nixon coveted.

The Ellsberg case pushed the steadily building tensions between Hoover and Sullivan at the FBI to the breaking point. After years of carrying out Hoover's toughest assignments, Sullivan rebelled, and Hoover could not tolerate it. On July 1, he announced that he was putting a new person between him and Sullivan on the organizational chart—Mark Felt, head of the Bureau's inspection division and a longtime Hoover loyalist. To the rest of the FBI, the move had a clear meaning: Sullivan's ascent had stopped and Felt's had begun.

At the White House, the problems at the FBI meant the Bureau could not respond to Nixon's demands as fast as he wanted. Sullivan, who had carried out many of the White House's orders, was no longer in a position to even learn, much less act on, them. He had one weapon left to use against Hoover. On July 11, Sullivan told Mardian he had something that Hoover might use to blackmail Nixon into keeping him as FBI director. Mardian knew Hoover knew the secrets of most people in official Washington, but he was stunned when Sullivan told him he had the records of the secret FBI wiretaps of seventeen government officials and journalists conducted between May 1969 and February 1971. Kissinger and Haig had picked the targets, and Hoover had required Mitchell to authorize each tap in writing. Sullivan kept the records for the taps, including the logs for each call, in a safe in his office in the FBI headquarters, but they were not in the official Bureau files, because the taps were conducted "out of channel."[25] The files held tremendous blackmail potential for Hoover. The wiretaps were of questionable legality, and Hoover's requirement that Mitchell approve each tap put the fingerprints of Nixon's closest cabinet official on them.

Mardian realized the damage the wiretaps could cause, so he called Mitchell, who told Mardian to get on the next government mail plane from Washington to meet with Nixon at San Clemente. There, Mardian spent forty-four minutes with Nixon on July 12 and gave him Sullivan's message about the wiretaps.[26] Nixon told Mardian to get the records immediately and give them to Ehrlichman. Then they needed to match Sullivan's files with the summaries kept at the White House by Kissinger and Haig. Mardian gave Nixon's order to Sullivan, who sent Brennan to Mardian's office with the files in a "beat up," olive drab satchel.[27] Mardian then took the satchel to Kissinger and Haig at the White House, where they examined the files and matched them to what they had in their possession. Mardian and Haldeman then checked the list of wiretap records to make sure it conformed to what was already at the White House. It did. Then Mardian took the entire package to the Oval Office. Hoover had lost his blackmail card.

Sullivan, who did not tell Hoover what he had done, still felt besieged by his rivals. On August 12, Sullivan wrote a detailed letter to Mitchell that said his problems with Hoover were crippling the FBI and that Hoover was trying to force him from the Bureau.[28] Sullivan said he was willing to leave the Bureau to save it. If he did leave the FBI, Sullivan continued, he wanted to help Nixon in any way possible, including campaigning for him in 1972. No Democrat, Sullivan said, had the skills to protect the country in the way Nixon had. He had only one reservation, Sullivan wrote Mitchell, echoing the philosophy of his longtime friend Fritz Kraemer: "My only disappointment here is in our military withdrawal from Vietnam. It seems to me we will now ultimately lose all of Asia and will be driven into relative isolation and a weakening of our role as a world leader."[29]

Sullivan's ploy backfired, in part because Mitchell considered Sullivan a sneaky name dropper. Running out of options, Sullivan wrote what became known in the FBI as his "suicide letter," a lengthy memorandum to Hoover criticizing the director's leadership, and copied Mitchell. The letter was for the good of Hoover and the Bureau, Sullivan wrote. "As one official of the FBI has said you claim you do not want 'yes men' but you become furious at any employee who says 'no' to you."[30] The letter precipitated a major argument between the two men in late September before Sullivan left for a brief vacation. He returned to find the locks on his office door had been replaced. Hoover had forced him out.

One piece of business remained unfinished—the status of the wiretap logs. Agents ordered to find them in Sullivan's office encountered an empty safe. Hoover went into a rage and demanded that Felt do something. An internal investigation dated October 20, 1971, spelled out what had happened and the stakes involved. "It goes without saying that knowledge of this coverage represents a potential source of tremendous embarrassment to the Bureau and potential disaster for the Nixon administration," the memo said.[31] "Copies of the material itself could be used for political blackmail and the ruination of Nixon, Mitchell and others of the administration." It was a prescient analysis of the explosive nature of the wiretap logs and a keen prediction of what would come later when Nixon could least afford it.

The Plumbers were busy almost immediately. Not only did they have the Ellsberg case to handle but also Nixon had become apoplectic about a July 23 *New York Times* story that leaked more details about the administration's SALT negotiations with the Soviet Union.[32] The story by William Beecher said the United States was planning to propose a freeze in the construction of land- and submarine-based missiles, an offer that been developed in the previous weeks. The Pentagon, led by Laird, opposed many of the new details,[33] which were elaborated in National Security Decision Memorandum 117 on July 2.[34] It was another indication of how the general themes of White House proposals, if they had not been fully debated, were still leaking out of the White House courtesy of the people trying to stop them.

Since the FBI would not help Nixon demolish Ellsberg as he wanted, the White House turned to the Plumbers. Liddy and Hunt began to build a case against Ellsberg. Hunt suggested to Colson at the White House on July 28 that the unit obtain a psychiatric profile of Ellsberg, just as the Agency used to do for various world leaders.[35] That would give them a better idea of their target and how to build the case against him. Helms got the request, and asked CIA security director Howard Osborn to have the Agency's Office of Medical Services prepare a profile of Ellsberg. The summary, delivered to the investigations unit on August 12, was a single-spaced, one-and-a-half page review of Ellsberg that could have been prepared by anyone reading the press coverage of the Pentagon Papers case.[36] Ellsberg, the Agency psychiatrists determined, had issues with authority figures and may have been going through a midlife crisis. Hunt, Liddy, and Young were not satisfied, but the Agency psychiatrists provided a tip.[37] Ellsberg, they said, had seen a psychiatrist, Dr. Lewis Fielding, in Beverly Hills, California. Perhaps Fielding's files included other secrets Ellsberg had told him. But Fielding would not provide Ellsberg's file voluntarily, so the Plumbers realized they needed to break in and steal it.

Ehrlichman approved the break-in on August 11 by signing a memo prepared by Krogh that authorized a "covert operation" provided that it was "done under [the] assurance that it is not traceable." While Hunt and Liddy had the will for this mission, they lacked the technology. They asked the CIA for more help. Ehrlichman asked Robert Cushman, the Agency's deputy director, to help Hunt. Cushman agreed, but waited two days before he told Helms.[38] The Agency, Ehrlichman said, should realize that Hunt and company had carte blanche to get what they needed. Between August 18 and 27, the Agency outfitted the Plumbers unit with recording equipment and a special Tessina 35 mm camera that was hidden in a tobacco pouch. Liddy, using the name George Leonard, and Hunt, who was called Mr. Warren, then headed for Los Angeles on August 25 to case Fielding's office and prepare for the break-in. They told the cleaning lady in Fielding's office building that they were doctors who needed to leave a message for Fielding. She let them in the office, and they used the Tessina to photograph it and get a better sense of the files they needed to plunder for information on Ellsberg. Hunt and Liddy then took the overnight flight back to Washington, where they gave the film to a CIA official, who had it developed. But the Tessina failed to work properly, making the Plumbers' first critical mission a failure.

CIA officials began to worry that Hunt was putting the Agency in a compromising position. Cushman called Ehrlichman to say that he and Helms thought Hunt wanted too much from the CIA, and then told Ehrlichman on August 27 that the Agency's cooperation was over. "I indicated Hunt was becoming a pain in the neck," Cushman said in an August 31 memo to Helms. "John said he would restrain Hunt." In fact, Ehrlichman said nothing to Hunt, who kept doing what he wanted.[39]

Krogh also worried that Hunt and Liddy's presence in Fielding's office during the first break-in exposed the White House to potential crimes. Krogh wanted someone who did not work at the White House to do the dirty work. So Hunt recruited three of his former Agency colleagues—Cuban exiles Bernard Barker, Eugenio Martinez, and Felipe de Diego.

Over Labor Day weekend, the quintet returned to Los Angeles to break into Fielding's office again. They had enough CIA-supplied cameras to photograph anything they needed, as well as a glass cutter and crowbar in case the more subtle means of entry into the office did not do the job. This time, Hunt and Liddy stayed outside, while the Cubans broke a ground-floor window, pried open the office's front door with a crowbar, smashed windows and doors, and trashed the office. Barker photographed the wreckage, which they had left in an attempt to fool the police into thinking the break-in was the work of addicts looking for drugs. What, if anything, they found inside remains unknown. Barker and Martinez said they never found the Ellsberg file, while de Diego said they had found it and then photographed its contents with the Minox camera. Fielding would also later tell authorities that the Ellsberg file appeared to have been "fingered."[40] Whether the file had been photographed or not made little difference; the film from the Minox never made it to the White House.

The Fielding burglary yielded nothing, but it did open the White House and Nixon to multiple opportunities for exposure. The Plumbers team, however, had made a thorough hash of the job, something that was no secret to the CIA. Helms did not know exactly what the Plumbers were doing, but he knew enough to conclude it could hurt his agency and Nixon. About the Agency, Helms cared a great deal. He had given his life to its mission. About Nixon, who had badgered him for years and made him the scapegoat for many of Nixon's own failures, Helms steadily cared less and less.

Helms's diminished concern for Nixon's wishes came as the president kept pushing the Agency to release information that would damage Nixon's Democratic predecessors and the Agency itself. Of particular interest to Nixon were the alleged "files" that contained the Kennedy administration's handling of the 1963 coup that overthrew South Vietnamese president Ngo Dinh Diem and killed him and his brother, Ngo Dinh Nhu, and the failed 1961 invasion of Cuba by exiles to oust Fidel Castro. Such disclosures, he reasoned, would take the focus from his White House and put it on the excesses and failures of Kennedy and Lyndon Johnson. Nixon told Ehrlichman to get the documents from Helms, who delayed, realizing what Nixon would do with any damaging information he discovered. From the SS-9 missile dispute to Cambodia to Laos, the Agency had been blamed for virtually every White House decision gone wrong, and Nixon had already tried with the Schlesinger plan to gut its budget and strip its power. Helms had already turned over many of his top officials under administration pressure and acquiesced in giving Nixon the intelligence he needed on Soviet missiles. Helms knew the White House had hired Hunt for the Plumbers, because Cushman had told him and Hunt was meeting regularly with his CIA contact officer. Also, Helms told Ehrlichman, the CIA did not have a simple file tucked in a cabinet that provided all of the details of the Bay of Pigs or Diem operations. The documents occupied dozens of cabinets, and they were all highly classified. They detailed Agency sources and methods whose exposure could endanger the lives of US intelligence assets and their foreign collaborators. He would not simply give them to Ehrlichman.

That did not deter Nixon. "We owe Helms nothing. He owes us everything—we kept him on. And we're going to let the CIA take a whipping on this." They needed to show that Kennedy knew about the Diem assassination. Nixon did not care about the security implications of the Diem case. He wanted the files to cause political damage.

Ehrlichman then told Nixon the CIA had files on the Bay of Pigs invasion that they were reluctant to part with. "They will die first before they give us that," he said.

"I want an order to Helms and [deputy CIA director Robert] Cushman that for my purposes, not for public release, I am to have the Bay of Pigs story," Nixon said. "Now that's an order. And I expect it in one week, or I want his resignation on my desk. Put it as coldly as that."[41]

Ehrlichman left Nixon's office with specific instructions, which he had listed in a document for Helms. On the Diem coup, the White House wanted all communications for most of 1963—all situation reports; memoranda from the CIA to the president, Secretaries of State and Defense, and the national security adviser; weekly intelligence bulletins; weekly postmortems; and all relevant national intelligence estimates. Nixon wanted the same information on the Bay of Pigs, as well as the Agency inspector general's report on the operation, and he also sought the same documents for the 1962 Cuban missile crisis, which was universally considered one of Kennedy's finest hours as president. Helms cooperated, but only to a point, giving an envelope to Ehrlichman with some of the documents. Helms would not give up any more documents without talking to Nixon first, a development that created a confrontation with the White House.

October 8, 1971, the day Nixon met with Helms, stands as a critical one in the history of Nixon's secret government, as he grappled with a power struggle at the FBI between Hoover and Sullivan, the keeper of the secret wiretaps, and the potential firing of Helms. Nixon, Ehrlichman, and Mitchell first met for almost forty-five minutes to discuss Supreme Court appointments and the fight between Sullivan and Hoover.[42]

After he realized Sullivan had given the wiretap files to Mardian, Hoover was "tearing the place up over there trying to get at 'em," Mitchell said.

Without the wiretap logs, Ehrlichman added, Hoover lacked blackmail evidence. If Hoover got the wiretap logs back, he said, "he'll beat you over the head with it."

Nixon wanted to fire Hoover, he told Ehrlichman and Mitchell, but did not want to risk the fallout the firing would cause in an election year. Hoover, Nixon said, ought to resign because "he's too old," adding hopefully that he could talk Hoover into resigning.

Meanwhile, Ehrlichman said, they needed to act quickly, "because Sullivan is sitting out there and with a hell of a lot of information," Ehrlichman said.[43]

Ten minutes later, Ehrlichman was back in the Oval Office to tell Nixon that Helms would only release three of the twenty-eight items Nixon wanted. Helms "would not give me any of the Diem stuff until he had an opportunity to talk with you," Ehrlichman said. "He said this is incredibly dirty linen and I just wouldn't feel comfortable about it until talking to the president first."[44]

Nixon did not care. "You can be goddamned sure if a Democrat gets in this chair, they're going to get everything that we've got," he said. Helms's resistance, Nixon continued, made him a liability. "I think maybe the best thing to do would be to just get rid of Helms," he said. "It may come to that pretty soon."

If you do, Ehrlichman answered, "don't replace him from inside."

"I can get [Army Lt. Gen. Vernon] Walters in there," Nixon said.

By invoking Walters's name, Nixon signaled his intention to move some-one he considered a longtime ally into the CIA directorship presumably to do Nixon's bidding. Earlier in the summer, Nixon had contemplated having Walters lead the effort to find damaging information on Ellsberg and to find the Johnson bombing halt memo. Nixon had backed off then, rightly figuring Walters would be too independent. Nixon believed he could trust Walters in situations in which he could not trust Helms.

Nixon's premeeting bravado faded shortly after Helms entered the Oval Office. He seemed almost desperate to seem understanding and sympathetic.

"I am not going to embarrass the CIA," he told Helms, "because I think it's terribly important. Second, I believe in 'dirty tricks.' I think we've got to do it. . . . I haven't told you this, and I want you to talk to Henry about it, but not to state it to anybody else: I want you to strengthen your department in that area where we work on elections, and so forth and so on. I think you've got to do it."[45]

Nixon had turned from threatening to fire Helms less than an hour ear-lier to promising Helms that he wanted to expand the CIA's ability to tamper with foreign elections, such as they had done in Chile in 1964 and failed to do the year before. He could not rely on the State Department for that, Nixon told Helms, because they "don't have their heart in it, but we have got to be in a position where if the Russians or the Chinese are in a particular little country trying to screw it up, we can screw it up, too. Don't you agree?"

"Oh, I agree, I do sir," Helms responded.

Then, in an aside that demonstrated the insincerity of his previous denunciations of the CIA's performance in Chile, Nixon told a surprised Helms that the United States failed to respond to the Agency's warnings there. "Good. I think, and would you not agree, we could have won the Chil-ean [election]?"

"Yes, I think we could, and it was, it was only one," Helms responded.

"Right. Yeah, I know you recommended more money than you got—than we gave them, too? Isn't that right?"

Helms answered reluctantly, saying "Yeah, we just—you know, we . . ."

Nixon ended the awkward encounter not by demanding more informa-tion but by reassuring Helms he would back the CIA. "The point that I want to make is that I want to know we can do things you do. Now, the second point is, I will not embarrass the CIA, because I will defend it."[46]

Helms, who knew how much Nixon distrusted him and his agency, was smart enough not to believe Nixon, and less than a month later he had another reason why. On November 5, Nixon announced he wanted to reorganize the nation's intelligence system.[47] Built in part on James Schlesinger's report from March, the plan called for the director of the Central Intelligence Agency to take a more supervisory role over the entire intelligence community and cede authority to his deputy. A National Security Council Intelligence Committee under Kissinger's direction would be created to review the overall community, which essentially put all of the nation's intelligence agencies under greater White House control.

While some officials considered parts of the plan a necessary improvement, others saw only problems. Laird and the Joint Chiefs rebelled, as did Helms and the CIA. It also stirred up more opposition in Congress, because neither Nixon nor Kissinger told them what they had planned. Those who were already suspicious of the growing secret government inside the NSC, such as Stuart Symington, rebelled. Kissinger had to do damage control, and he did it in his typical combination of half-truths, evasions, and finger pointing at Nixon.

"For somebody I like so much you keep going after me," he told Symington in a November 11 call.[48]

"It's not you; it's the policy," Symington said. "You know that."

"I know," Kissinger said. "You are a good friend and when we are all out of here you will still be. I'm calling about the intelligence reorganization. First, you are absolutely right; I don't know why there was no Congressional consultation before. This wasn't done in my shop. My shop was part of the study . . . but that is no excuse. What I am going to do is to ask George Shultz to come up and see you next week when he gets back in town to explain the Office of Management point of view. Secondly, the purpose of this reorganization wasn't to enhance my office, but to get other members of the committee to state their aims. I can levy requirements now on behalf of the President; I don't need a committee to do that. It, if anything, limits me personally, but the major test of it isn't what it does to me. My role is marginal; it actually tends to enhance the role of Helms."

Symington told Kissinger that it was embarrassing that no one had notified Congress. "So I'm awakened in the morning by an early call from a reporter and I have to say I don't know anything about it," he said. "Then I read the morning paper. I came to the office. I called CIA and asked to speak to Helms. He was out of the country. There was no one there who would talk with me. I got upset about it. I got home and finally there was a call, and there was a member of the CIA staff who was kind enough to deliver the White House press release to me at my house on Saturday afternoon. I said 'what does it mean?' He said, 'we don't know.' Henry, you can't run a railroad like that."

Kissinger scrambled to apologize and assured Symington that Helms would still have authority. "If Helms is only coordinator then it's not doing its job," he said. "I would complain about that. Some people thought of moving Helms out of the CIA; I urged very strongly that he stay."

"He won't be a figurehead," Symington said.

No, Kissinger assured him, Helms would have "more of a voice in military intelligence."[49]

—◦—

While he moved toward success with China, Vietnam, and the Soviet Union throughout the middle of 1971, Nixon's secrecy and hubris during his failed handling of the Pentagon Papers case would cripple him. If he had only tried to block the Papers' publication and then lost in court, he would have avoided many of his subsequent problems. Nixon and his aides knew the Papers contained nothing to embarrass him. The *New York Times*, his nemesis, realized it, too. Nixon's main concern was covering up his sabotage of the 1968 Paris Peace Talks and whether he could get the bombing halt file allegedly hidden inside the Brookings Institution. There was no file, and if there had been, it would have shown that Johnson stopped the bombing in October 1968 because the North Vietnamese met his conditions for one. It was Nixon, which Nixon knew very well, who had broken the law by allowing his campaign to derail the talks.

As for Ellsberg, Nixon cared mostly about making an example of him through a brutal public smear campaign, just as Nixon had waged against Alger Hiss. This time, however, J. Edgar Hoover would not cooperate, and Nixon could not force him. The tensions inside the FBI, which Nixon helped stoke and then backed away from, made that cooperation virtually impossible. So, without Hoover and the FBI, Nixon had created the Plumbers and encouraged their multiple excesses, a lapse in judgment that would provide Nixon nothing but grief.

CHAPTER THIRTEEN

India-Pakistan (1971)

PAKISTANI PRIME MINISTER YAHYA KHAN'S HELP FOR NIXON IN OPENING relations with China had more than just a whiff of enlightened self-interest. Yahya's help gave him rare leverage with Nixon. In turn, Nixon backed Yahya with a fervor that made little sense to anyone outside the few who knew about the Chinese initiative. Yahya was an unlikely benefactor, a soldier with virtually no instinct for democracy. Then, in November 1970, he failed a test for even the most adept politician when a devastating cyclone flooded most of East Pakistan and killed more than 230,000 people there and in India.[1] Yahya had to be bailed out by the United States and its allies, who kept the cyclone's damage from claiming even more lives from disease and starvation. Unfortunately for Yahya, the cyclone happened one month before national elections to pick a new parliament to draft a new constitution for Pakistan, which had been split into two pieces during Great Britain's 1947 partition of India. The Awami League of East Pakistan, which favored the creation of a new nation dominated by the Bengalis of that half of the country, won an overwhelming victory, picking up 160 of the 162 contested seats in the east and a majority of the three hundred seats in the overall assembly.[2] For the first time in Pakistan's history, an Eastern party would control the assembly and the writing of the nation's constitution. The results stunned the Punjabi political class, which had dominated Pakistan from its creation and viewed Bengalis as second-class citizens. "Our country has gone to the dogs, I am telling you," a Punjabi told a *New York Times* reporter days after the election.[3]

The Awami League leader, Sheik Mujibur "Mujib" Rahman had the upper hand. Either he would push for an autonomous East Pakistan—which would be called Bangladesh, or the Nation of Bengal, in Bengali—or he would seek greater control over all of Pakistan. Yahya wanted neither, refusing to convene the assembly that would have made Rahman prime minister, and in March 1971, postponing the opening of the National Assembly that would write the constitution. That threw the country into what Yahya called Pakistan's gravest political crisis, NSC aides Harold Saunders and Samuel Hoskinson told Kissinger in a March 1 memo.[4] Yahya had few decent options and no political power base of his own. While Rahman had swept the east, Yahya's rival, Zulfikar Ali Bhutto and his leftist Pakistan People's Party, dominated the election in the west, which left Yahya with no real political constituency outside the military, wrote Saunders and Hoskinson, who raised the issue of whether the United States should hedge its bets and prepare to recognize the secession of East Pakistan and creation of a new state—Bangladesh.

Nixon could not let that happen, because he still counted on Yahya to deliver on China. Rahman, meanwhile, kept pushing for independence, leading on March 4 to Pakistani military C-130 transport planes filled with troops landing in Dacca to quell the expected uprising.[5] It was apparent to virtually everyone, perhaps even Nixon, that Yahya's efforts would fail and Bangladesh would become independent.

After they failed to reach an agreement on dual governments, Yahya ordered Rahman arrested on March 25. Mujib's supporters feared he would be executed as the Pakistani army began a full-scale crackdown in the east. Kissinger called the army's actions "a reign of terror," even as he told Nixon they needed to avoid doing anything that would "prematurely harm our relationship with West Pakistan."[6] Still, he told Nixon on March 28 that the United States had to do something, because "the full horror of what is going on will come to light sooner or later."[7]

Nixon chose to do nothing.

He considered the US diplomats in the area—consul Archer Blood in Dacca and ambassador to India Kenneth Keating—too soft. "The main thing to do is to keep cool and not do anything," Nixon told Kissinger, who said it would make little difference to the Indians, who "are not noted for their gratitude."[8]

By early April, thirty thousand Pakistani troops were roaming East Pakistan, rounding up intellectuals and opposition leaders and burning Bengali homes and businesses. Blood and other US diplomats in Dacca, who did not know about Yahya's help for Nixon with China, believed their warnings about the growing genocide of ethnic Bengalis at the hands of the Punjabi-dominated military were going unheeded. They sent a scathing memo to State Department headquarters in Washington. "Our government has failed to denounce the suppression of democracy," said the memo, which became known as the Blood telegram. "Our government has failed to denounce atrocities. Our government has failed to take forceful measures to protect its citizens while at the same time bending over backwards to placate the West Pak dominated government and to lessen likely and deservedly negative international public relations impact against them."[9] Blood's telegram, which was signed by twenty other Foreign Service officers in Dacca, called the situation in East Pakistan "genocide," and that the US policy of trying to stay above the fray was only delaying the inevitable—the breakup of Pakistan into two countries, a Punjabi-dominated state in the west and Bengali-controlled Bangladesh in the east.

Blood and his colleagues in Dacca had the agreement of virtually everyone inside the administration working on the crisis. Few believed Yahya's military could gain control over East Pakistan and hold it very long. The Bengalis did not support or trust them, and supply lines from the west to the east were too long and unpredictable. The monsoon season would soon render all of East Pakistan impassable.[10]

Kissinger knew the White House was on the wrong side of events in East Pakistan, writing in his memoirs that "there was some merit to the charge of moral insensitivity" to the crisis there.[11] Kissinger also elaborated that Nixon's main motive was to not do anything that would hurt Yahya or stop the secret channel to China. Nixon was willing to trade the lives of a few thousand Bengalis and Indians for an opening with China that would give the United States a counterweight to the Soviet Union. That feeling gave more clout to the few officials sympathetic to Yahya, such as Joseph Farland, the US ambassador to Pakistan, whose counsel mattered more than Kenneth Keating, the former New York senator and ambassador to New Delhi.

Even Farland had his limits. He knew Yahya had made the disintegration of Pakistan inevitable, as he told State.[12] He urged Washington to do more to stop the crisis.

Farland walked a fine line as he tried to assuage Yahya in Pakistan while telling Washington what was really happening. Outside the NSC, no one knew how much Nixon relied on Yahya and how they needed to prop him up until Kissinger made it to Beijing. But Farland also faced an insurrection among his staff in Dacca, who witnessed firsthand the Pakistani army's genocide in East Pakistan and subsequent refugee crisis. Farland knew the Pakistani government's claims about India and the "success" of their efforts to quell the Bengali rebellion were bogus, while "Bengali grievances" were "now etched in blood."[13]

Nixon's priorities for Pakistan were clear: Take care of Yahya until the secret China visit. Then Nixon had to placate China by backing Yahya, China's ally, over China's longtime rival, India. Meanwhile, hundreds of thousands of innocent people in East Pakistan died.

By mid-April, Yahya's crackdown had stopped the Bengali rebellion long enough for him to brag to Nixon that "the situation in East Pakistan is rapidly returning to normalcy" and that he planned to resume the induction of provincial governments.[14] On April 21, Yahya got what would be his golden ticket for the Nixon White House—a letter sent through him to Nixon from Chinese Prime Minister Chou En-lai giving Yahya the go-ahead to set up the details of a trip to Beijing by a US emissary. That news led to the nighttime call between Nixon and Kissinger on April 27 in which both men gushed about how their plans were finally coming together.

Kissinger, however, realized the fragility of anything that depended on Yahya or Pakistan and essentially begged Nixon in an April 28 memo to take a stand.[15] Kissinger laid out three options for Nixon—unqualified support for West Pakistan; neutrality, which would essentially help the east more; and trying to help Yahya negotiate a settlement with the east and India. Nixon initialed the third option, and then wrote by hand a warning: To all hands, Don't squeeze Yahya at this time. RN." He underlined "don't" three times.[16]

Yahya's value to Nixon rose exponentially after Chou said he was ready for direct talks. The White House summoned Farland to the United States for a special meeting on May 7 with Kissinger in Palm Springs, California. Kissinger then quickly got to business. Since August 1969, Kissinger told Farland, the United States had pursued a backchannel to China. He detailed how the United States removed two destroyers from the Taiwan Straits—which occurred over the Pentagon's objections—to curry favor with the Chinese and how they had responded in kind by releasing two captured boaters.[17] The Chinese had told the Pakistanis the previous week that they wanted to arrange a meeting in Beijing "through the good offices of President Yahya Khan." The Chinese arrangement "could be of great diplomatic significance," Kissinger said, "both with respect to Vietnam and the Soviet Union." Yahya, Kissinger said, "must be kept afloat for six months," and he would ask Robert McNamara, the former Defense Secretary who now led the World Bank, to arrange financing to prop up the Pakistani government.[18]

~~~

Those inside the administration who knew of Yahya's role understood why Nixon went so easy on Pakistan. If Yahya fell, he would take the China initiative with him. Since Nixon had told virtually no one, including the Secretaries of State and Defense, about the Pakistan channel, they thought he had lost his mind and was harming US interests. They also believed that East

Pakistan would become independent, and Yahya's crackdown would only turn the Bengalis toward India. Many, such as Keating in India, saw the United States backing a military dictatorship that was killing its own people with tacit US support. It made little sense, and it hurt the Nixon administration in Congress and in relations with other governments. Keating told Kissinger in a June 4 meeting in Washington that he recognized that Nixon and Yahya had a special relationship, but that he did not understand it.[19] Few people did.

Throughout the late spring and summer of 1971, the situation in East Pakistan continued to deteriorate, as at least five million East Pakistanis fled the country for neighboring India. The refugees and their proliferating health problems taxed an Indian government that could barely support its own people. Nixon made the perfunctory, appropriate comments of concern, but he did little to push Yahya to make real changes. Democrats in Congress, joined by a smaller but growing number of Republicans, expressed horror at the administration's inaction and blocked military aid to Pakistan. Few outside Nixon's inner circle understood his motives. That included Indian prime minister Indira Gandhi and her government. Kissinger's July 7 visit to New Delhi provided little comfort. Only after Kissinger returned from his first China visit did the policy remotely start to make sense. Pakistan, India's great rival, had facilitated the Kissinger trip to China, India's other great rival. Without the help of the United States, the world's dominant superpower, and now hemmed in by China, India looked for help from the next logical source—the Soviet Union—and signed a friendship treaty with the Russians on August 9. The treaty said each nation would protect the sovereignty of the other and would not enter into any military alliance directed at the other.

Nixon, of course, was outraged. "Well, they understand, if they're going to choose to go with the Russians, they're choosing not to go with us," he told Kissinger upon learning of the treaty. "Now, goddamn it, they've got to know this. . . . Goddamn it, who's given them a billion dollars a year?"[20] He and Kissinger still viewed the India-Pakistan issue solely through the prism of China. "At this stage in our stance toward China, a US effort to split off part of Pakistan in the name of self-determination would have implications for Taiwan and Tibet in Peking's eyes," Kissinger wrote Nixon on August 18.[21] Meanwhile, Kissinger continued to tell the Chinese the United States would back Pakistan and China in any conflict. In effect, China's policy had become Nixon's. He believed ties with the People's Republic, regardless of the complaints of the China Lobby, would push the Soviets to reach a better SALT deal and prod North Vietnam to end the Vietnam War.

Nixon's optimism was justified. The Soviets were moving closer on SALT. The North Vietnamese were more forthcoming, too. But the situation in East Pakistan continued to deteriorate, and Yahya launched a series of pre-emptive air strikes on India on December 3 in the hope they would cripple India's ability to fight back. They failed. India quickly gained the advantage over Pakistan, which desperately needed help. Nixon declared the United States neutral but secretly favored a "tilt" toward Pakistan. "I've been catching unshirted hell every half-hour from the President who says we're not tough enough," Kissinger said in a December 3 meeting.[22] "He wants to tilt toward Pakistan, and he believes that every briefing or statement is going the other way."

Nixon tried to evade the embargo of arms shipments to Pakistan by steering aircraft and weapons through Iran and Jordan, and if the word leaked out to the public, "we can have it denied," he told Kissinger on December 4. "Have it done one step away."[23]

Nixon then ordered the movement of a US aircraft carrier group, Task Group 74, into the Bay of Bengal between India and Pakistan. He did it without consulting the navy, alarming Moorer and Admiral Elmo Zumwalt, the chief of naval operations. Zumwalt wanted to make sure the ships had a mission or would not be sent in "harm's way." What followed was a haphazard series of directives that eventually led to the ships moving through the Straits of Malacca into the Indian Ocean "in full view of the world," Zumwalt wrote.[24] The White House said it was to help evacuate US citizens, but Nixon really wanted India to back down. Neither his top military commanders nor the US diplomats in India knew that, however. Instead, they thought Nixon was recklessly inviting a confrontation with the Soviet Union.

━ ⌣ ━

Syndicated columnist Jack Anderson blew the cover off Nixon's alleged neutrality with a December 14 column straight from the White House Situation Room. "A dangerous confrontation is developing between Soviet and American naval forces in the Bay of Bengal," Anderson wrote.[25] "President Nixon has ordered a naval task force into those troubled waters as a restraint upon India," Anderson continued, as he quoted Kissinger and others verbatim as they tried to justify tilting toward Pakistan. The column came directly from meeting records and documents that few people had seen, as if from a mole inside the NSC. Nixon's Olympian levels of paranoia reached new heights.

Anderson's column presented a particular problem for two men—Rear Admiral Robert Welander, the head of the Joint Chiefs liaison office at the NSC, and Yeoman Charles Radford, his assistant. Welander knew the details in Anderson's column could only have come from four specific documents that had all moved through his office—his memo to Haig about contingency forces, notes from the December 3 and 4 WSAG meetings, and the December 10 State Department cables. Welander did not give the documents to Anderson.[26] Welander, just like his predecessor, Rembrandt Robinson, had used Radford to help spy on Kissinger and NSC, because, as the task force incident showed, the Chiefs knew little about Nixon's plans or motives. Welander had prepared the documents to help fill the gaps in what the White House had told Moorer.

Radford also knew Anderson's column posed a problem for him. He had a family connection to Anderson and had served in India, where he had met his wife. That made Radford not only a logical but also perhaps the only suspect, which also threatened to hurt Welander. Radford also knew he did not leak the documents to Anderson and would be happy to tell that to anyone who asked.

Welander first called Haig, his main contact at the NSC, who then called John Ehrlichman, who assigned the leak investigation to David Young, one of the two leaders of the Special Investigations Unit—the Plumbers. Young, a former Kissinger assistant, had suspected the liaison office had leaked to the Pentagon and that Haig, whom he disliked and distrusted, did, too.

At the White House, Young became paired with a Pentagon criminal investigator—Donald Stewart, a middle-aged former FBI agent who looked and acted like a G-man, carrying himself with the black-and-white sense of a man who had spent decades being lied to by criminals and bureaucrats alike. Stewart had also spent three months earlier in 1971 investigating a series of eleven Anderson columns that used classified Pentagon information.[27] Stewart gathered a small team of investigators to work on the latest leak, including Raymond Weir, a National Security Agency polygraph expert. They met with Young and started to interview Radford's navy colleagues and anyone else tied to either Radford, Welander, or the NSC liaison office.

They scheduled a meeting with Radford for December 16, when a second Anderson column revealed how Nixon's tilt toward Pakistan had driven India into the arms of the Soviet Union. Anderson wrote how Kissinger had told reporters that claims of anti-India bias by the United States were "totally inaccurate." Behind the guarded doors of the White House Situation Room, however, Kissinger complained that Nixon told him "every half-hour . . . 'that we are not being tough enough on India.'" Anderson also exposed the White House attempts to circumvent the arms embargo to Pakistan by sending F-104 fighters through Jordan.[28] The two columns did not bode well for Radford, whose interrogators already believed he was guilty.

As they walked into a two-room suite on the second floor of the Pentagon's E-ring, the site of most of the building's high-level offices, Radford surprised the investigators by admitting he had known Anderson for at least a year and that Robinson knew about it. The Radfords and Andersons were Mormons. Radford also said he and his wife had dinner on December 12 with Anderson and his wife at a Chinese restaurant in Washington.[29] Radford said he had become friends with Anderson's parents after he helped them get travel visas three years earlier when he worked at the US embassy in New Delhi. They had corresponded regularly since then. On December 5, Radford told the investigators, Anderson had invited the Radfords to join them a week later for dinner to celebrate his parents' fiftieth wedding anniversary.[30] Radford said he did not tell Anderson about his work other than to mention Welander was his boss and that Anderson appeared to know Welander's name. Radford, investigators noted, "insisted that he only met Jack Anderson on two occasions cited above and at no time did he give Anderson any classified information."[31]

Stewart was irked to learn that Robinson knew about Radford's Anderson connection, which Robinson failed to disclose during their earlier investigation.[32] Stewart's assistant called Robinson to ask about the omission, which Robinson acknowledged. He said he did not know why he did not tell Stewart about it then. Stewart's suspicions, already bubbling, started to reach a boil.[33]

Radford knew he had told the truth, so he readily agreed when Stewart and Young asked him to take a polygraph. He clearly had no idea what would happen next.

Weir, the polygraph examiner, took Radford alone into a separate room. Weir asked nine routine questions, and Radford's answers indicated he was telling the truth, or at least not lying. The lines on the polygraph remained stable when he said he had not given any classified documents to Anderson or had no unauthorized contact with foreign nationals. The machine's needles fluttered when Radford was asked if he had given classified documents to uncleared people. This question rattled Radford.[34] He had no problem answering the questions about Anderson, because he had not given Anderson any classified information. This was different. Radford had been stealing documents from the NSC and Kissinger and Haig's briefcases and rifling through burn bags and sending the documents to the Pentagon. Radford had definitely given classified documents to uncleared persons, and he realized that his interrogators knew it, too.

He paused and then gave his answer: Yes.

Radford declined to give more details, according to the investigators' report, which added that Radford "became emotionally disturbed and it was deemed advisable to continue no further testing on this statement." Radford's questioners asked why, and he said he was worried about "a very sensitive operation which he could not discuss without direct approval of Admiral Welander."[35]

Weir told Stewart and Young of Radford's distress, and Young called Welander, telling him Radford will not say anything more until he talks to Welander. Welander, who believed Radford was about to confess to giving secret documents to Anderson, told his young assistant: "Chuck, all you can do is tell the truth." As Len Colodny and Robert Gettlin wrote in their 1991 account of the affair, *Silent Coup*, it was "one of those small misinterpretations of information on which great events sometimes hinge."[36]

Since Radford had started at the NSC, his superiors had told him not to say anything about his work. Now Welander was telling him to do the opposite. Radford paused, but Stewart pushed him into talking, and once he did, his comments stunned his questioners. Radford admitted where he had stolen documents, and he had typed memos from Robinson and Welander for their superiors—Moorer and Zumwalt. Stewart's blustery, aggressive tone forced Radford to repeatedly collapse in tears. "There was nowhere to draw the line," Radford said later. "I just couldn't say 'I did this' and not talk about that. And I didn't want to quit. I wanted to get it off my chest."[37] He did. The investigators' report noted how Radford had given the stolen documents to Welander, but that neither he nor Robinson had specifically ordered him to do it. Then the stolen documents were given to Moorer, and no one ever reprimanded Radford for what he was doing.

Stewart immediately thought of the bestselling book, *Seven Days in May*, in which rogue military officers tried to oust the president. He was "literally shook" by the "military conspiracy" trying to take down Nixon, Stewart said later.[38] Stewart suspected the military leaders, not the young yeoman who had dissolved into tears in the Pentagon interrogation room. Still, Stewart and Young spent five days building evidence against Radford, who made a compelling suspect for several reasons. He had money problems that forced him to take a second job as a security guard, and his young wife, only twenty-one and under stress at home alone with young children, spent too much money and called Radford at work constantly. Radford knew Anderson, and Anderson's wife had visited their home. He also liked India from his time stationed there, perhaps enough to make Radford want to expose Nixon's tilt toward Pakistan.

Welander also became evasive after Stewart told him about Radford's confession.[39] He declined to discuss anything other than the recent leaks to Anderson, although he did acknowledge receiving the documents Radford stole from the NSC. Welander's reason, the investigators noted, were his "certain confidential relationships with Dr. Kissinger and General Haig."[40] Radford may have given information to Anderson, Stewart concluded, but he did not act alone. Welander also apparently had second thoughts about telling Radford to tell investigators the truth, because on December 17, he told Radford to hire a lawyer.[41]

Stewart and Young realized they had stumbled onto something much bigger than a leak to Jack Anderson. Welander had told them that he was worried about the information to which Radford had access, and that the leaked information to Anderson was just a tiny part of what Radford knew.[42] If Radford wanted, Welander added, he could damage national security by leaking more to Anderson.

Young gave his report on December 21 to Ehrlichman, who quickly realized the military had penetrated Nixon's secret government and then leaked the details to the press. He had to cool his heels until Nixon returned from a trip to the British island of Bermuda in the Atlantic Ocean. When Nixon returned, he went to the Oval Office with Ehrlichman, Haldeman, and Mitchell, who told Nixon the grim dimensions of his problem with the military.[43]

The investigators, Ehrlichman told Nixon, had pinpointed the source of the Anderson leak to "the Joint Chiefs of Staff liaison office of the National Security Council."[44]

"Jesus Christ!" the president said.

It was worse, Ehrlichman continued. Radford was the logical suspect, he said, citing his contacts with Anderson, his time in India, and his strong feelings about the country. He had "motive, opportunity, and access," Ehrlichman said. "The whole thing."

"Does Henry know him?" Nixon asked.

"Everybody knows him," Ehrlichman said.

"He's traveled with Henry," Mitchell joined in.

"He's traveled with Haig," Ehrlichman added.

"Did he go to China?" Nixon asked, worried about whether his main policy achievement had been compromised.

Ehrlichman said no, but that Radford had gone to Vietnam with Haig. "And did all Haig's dealings with . . . So he's been right at the crux of this thing."

Radford, Ehrlichman said, had admitted nothing, but was being cooperative and was "very, very polite." "Right," Nixon said before he asked what seemed to be a standard question whenever he suspected anyone in his administration of being disloyal. "Incidentally, is he Jewish?"

No, Ehrlichman answered, he's a Mormon.

Ehrlichman had more details, which rattled Nixon. He told the president that Radford said Robinson and then Welander had pushed Radford to get information, and he did that and more. Radford and Welander, Ehrlichman said, had directed Radford to get whatever he could, so "he has systematically stolen documents out of Henry's briefcase, Haig's briefcase, people's desks, anyplace and everyplace in the NSC apparatus that he can lay his hands on. And has duplicated them and turned them over to the Joint Chiefs, through his boss. This has been going on now for about thirteen months."

Ehrlichman said he thought the Chiefs had been doing this for a long time, but that when they learned of the Joint Chiefs connection, we "shut the whole thing down."

They did not, however, have Radford wiretapped, Mitchell said, adding that it would be risky to have Radford arrested and charged.

The NSC liaison office, Ehrlichman told Nixon, is the real problem. Robinson told Radford when he first started working at the NSC that he could help provide information about the Pentagon for him and his colleagues. "That office, it seems to me, constitutes a clear and present danger to the, since . . . in the NSC."

The spying went directly to the Joint Chiefs of Staff, Mitchell said, and Nixon said he had to think about prosecuting them. Mitchell agreed but said that invited more problems than it would solve. If they prosecuted, he said, "you would have the Joint Chiefs aligned on that side directly against you." Better "to paper this thing over," Mitchell concluded.

Mitchell said they should close the NSC liaison office and put a security officer at the NSC. Nixon agreed and then asked what they should do about Kissinger.

Someone needs to ride herd on Kissinger, Mitchell said, and they also need to get Welander out of the White House and "transfer him to Kokomo or Indiana, or anywhere we want to have him, along, of course, with this yeoman." Then Mitchell needed to tell Moorer about "this game that's been going on."

Mitchell, had, in essence, proposed covering up the spy ring, just as they had covered up Nixon's tampering with the Paris Peace Talks and the wiretaps on government officials and journalists. Acknowledging the military's spy ring would carry too great a cost, which would enable Radford, Welander, Anderson, or Moorer to evade prosecution. If they prosecuted Anderson, Mitchell said, then Radford could get immunity and "Lord knows where this is going to lead to."

"Yeah," Nixon answered, adding that "it blows the Joint Chiefs right out of the Pentagon, through the roof of the Pentagon, right?"

As he tried to build a relationship with China that would in turn pressure the Soviet Union into an arms control deal and the North Vietnamese to end the war in Vietnam, Nixon could not have the world and Congress know that the military's top officers distrusted him so much that they spied on the White House and stole documents from Kissinger. Such a disclosure would diminish much of Nixon's authority and lead the Chinese and Soviets to not take him as seriously. It could also inspire congressional Democrats to poke around in places Nixon wanted to hide, including his entire secret government inside the National Security Council. Mitchell saw the possibilities inherent in the immunized testimony of just one low-ranking yeoman, and he and the rest of Nixon's inner circle knew they had to let it go.

"I lost more sleep than ... on what to do with this guy," Ehrlichman told Nixon. "And I have finally come to the conclusion that you can't touch him."

Nixon agreed, because the Chiefs "cannot become our enemy. We cannot have it. And also, we can't have this Goddamned security problem!"

So, knowing what he and his administration faced, Nixon decided to paper over the matter: "There is a federal offense of the highest order here," he said. "And you have reported it to the President. The President says you can't discuss it."

~~~

Nixon could not leave the issue alone. He stewed about it overnight and told Ehrlichman the next morning that he wanted to see if Radford and Anderson had a homosexual relationship. Once again, Nixon reached back to the late 1940s and the Hiss case.[45] "Because we got a couple on Hiss and [informant Whittaker] Chambers, you know," Nixon said. "Nobody knows that, but that's the background on how that one began. They were both that way." Anderson could be blackmailing Radford, Nixon added.

Ehrlichman was scheduled to interview Welander that morning. Nixon eagerly wanted to learn what Ehrlichman discovered, particularly if he faced a bigger problem than he realized. Radford, Nixon feared, "is a potential Ellsberg," but one with contemporaneous knowledge of internal White House deliberations. They needed to scare Radford to death, Nixon said, so he did not decide to write a book and expose what he had done. They also needed to keep Kissinger off balance and make him look at his office instead of blaming State for leaks.

Despite his tough talk, Nixon still had difficulty reconciling himself to covering up what he considered the worst security breach of his administration. "What we're doing here is, in effect, excusing a crime," he said.

Ehrlichman and Young had prepared extensively for their meeting with Welander. In a memo, Young recommended that Ehrlichman start with general questions about the leaks and whether Welander believed that Radford had leaked the documents to Anderson. Then, "very obliquely and softly," Young wrote, "we could then bring up the crucial question of what did Welander do with the memoranda he got; i.e. did they eventually find their way to the Chairman of the JCS?" They also needed to learn, Young wrote, if anyone at the Pentagon had received transcriptions of Kissinger's telephone conversations. Also, Young added, "To what extent is General Haig aware of Radford's activities?"[46]

Welander arrived at Ehrlichman's office on the third floor of the West Wing of the White House at 1 p.m. and found Ehrlichman and Young waiting for him. They sat facing a table with a large tape recorder on it. Ehrlichman handed Welander a draft statement that asked Welander to admit obtaining "unauthorized copies of various documents and memoranda" about all manner of secret internal government issues.[47] Welander refused to sign it. Ehrlichman then changed tactics and asked Welander to explain the liaison office and how it worked.[48] Welander said his job was to explain military positions to the White House and act as the "in-house military expert."

Ehrlichman coaxed Welander to tell how Haig informed him about the NSC's activities, including details Nixon wanted to keep secret. Haig could give Ehrlichman a better description of Welander's role, he said. "I had complete copies of memcons from Al's recent trip [to Vietnam]," Welander said. In such a hypersensitive environment, as Nixon worked himself into a state of extreme agitation, such revelations would cast the ambitious Haig in a negative light, but Ehrlichman failed to pick up on the details. Young did not.

Other officers at the Pentagon were envious of Welander's sources and wanted to know what Welander told Moorer. At the White House, he continued, "nine-tenths of the things that I do I give to Al [Haig], and then it's a matter of his judgment whether or not it goes to Henry. . . . We know over the course of time that the things I'm giving them come from the essentially privileged sources. That is, things that have been held very, very closely within the military, private communications to the Chairman. Things of that sort."

Moorer knew Radford was getting information the Chiefs did not receive from other sources, Welander continued, and that much of it came from things Radford picked up on his trips with Haig and Kissinger. Some of that, Welander acknowledged, was information that the White House did not want them to have.

Ehrlichman realized that Radford had successfully penetrated the NSC's cloak of secrecy, particularly with Kissinger's secret trip to China. Welander admitted that he had asked Radford to find information that Welander knew the Chiefs did not have and that Radford had gotten it for him. He also told Ehrlichman and Young that Robinson, his predecessor, had advised him that Haig had set up a system for Radford to travel with him or Kissinger.

Did Haig know what Radford was doing? Young asked.

"You can only ask Al," Welander said. "I've never discussed it with him. Obviously, if to take a man along on a trip like Al makes out in the boon docks, it's a lot easier and Radford does a lot of other chores and everything else which are very helpful on the trip."

Would he have seen memos or any other documents, Ehrlichman asked.

"Well, my conversations with Al," Welander said. "My point is that I've relayed these things often times . . . you know."

For example, Welander said, Haig "has cut me in on what we've been thinking" about contingency plans. He added that Radford did not learn much from the recent trip with Haig that the Chiefs did not already know because "we knew pretty much what the game plan was going to be. Al related to me orally his discussions and some observations that the staff people had made."

Finally, Ehrlichman and Young asked Welander if he thought Radford may have been a homosexual and subject to potential blackmail. "Chuck is not a big manly type or anything else, you know—but 9/10th of the Navy yeomen are that way," he said. After Ehrlichman expressed some surprise, Welander continued. "Who else wants to be a typist? So I would not consider him unusual—he's married—has children." While Radford was not his type of guy, Welander said, he saw no evidence that he may have been a homosexual.

Ehrlichman knew before the Welander interview that Nixon had already ruled they would cover up the spy ring and not prosecute anyone. But Welander's revelations were still explosive for those he implicated, particularly Haig. Nixon had steadily expanded Haig's duties and often relied on him instead of Kissinger, especially when Nixon wanted to keep Kissinger off balance and make him more insecure. The military suspected Kissinger of being behind Nixon's decisions they did not like, but they considered Haig as one of their own and relied on him for information. Young, who had long been suspicious of Haig and his motives, realized what Welander had revealed during the interview, even if his boss, Ehrlichman, did not or discounted Young's interpretations as the result of his animus toward Haig.

Ehrlichman and Young shared their discoveries with Nixon, who was angry that neither Kissinger nor Haig had told him about the security breach from either Kissinger or Haig. "He can't figure out why they didn't do this when they do know at least some of the particulars," Haldeman wrote in his diary of the meeting.[49]

Despite extracting more details from Welander than he imagined, Ehrlichman still needed more information from the Pentagon, but no one there wanted to tell the White House any more than they absolutely had to. That included Laird, who knew how much information Nixon, Kissinger, and Haig hid from him.

Ehrlichman called Laird to ask why they were blocking Young's request to have Radford interrogated again. "This is something in which I have no discretion," Ehrlichman told Laird on the telephone.[50]

Laird said Fred Buzhardt, the Pentagon's general counsel, had concerns about another interrogation and wanted to slow things down. The White House should not have sent one of its investigators to handle what is a Pentagon matter, Laird added, making it clear he had no intention of cooperating. "I'm just the messenger," Ehrlichman pleaded.

Laird would confound Ehrlichman again the next morning, December 23, when Laird refused to cooperate with the investigation into whether Radford and Anderson had a homosexual relationship. Merely asking such a question, Laird said, could blow the lid off their coverup of the spy ring. Plus, he added, this was Nixon's fault, because he had rejected Laird's advice to close the liaison office. It is up to Nixon to fix the problem, Laird continued, "not up to me." The whole issue will embarrass Nixon and the NSC, Laird continued, but that should not "break on the basis of this guy refusing to answer questions on homosexuality."[51]

Ehrlichman let the issue drop and then met with Nixon and Haldeman to determine how to play out the rest of the investigation. They had to close the liaison office and move Welander somewhere, and they needed to ship Radford out of Washington entirely. Mitchell would talk to Moorer and let him know that Nixon knew about the spy operation and did not want it to happen again. They hoped that would make Moorer more compliant, since he would fear the imminent revelation of the spy operation and the threat of either being prosecuted or losing his job. Moorer would be, in Ehrlichman's words, a "pre-shrunk admiral."[52]

Nixon was frustrated, realizing "it will reflect on us because, in the end, we're still going to be accused that we fucked up something." His lament ignored his role in creating the problem through his hiding information from top commanders, such as decisions involving troop levels, arms control, weapons, treaties, and budgets. Instead of analyzing his own behavior, Nixon found a convenient scapegoat—Kissinger. "I'm not sure what to do about the news of this fact that Henry is not in here telling us what the hell he's going to do to find out about that leak!" Nixon told Ehrlichman and Haldeman.[53] Nixon concluded with one more thought about Kissinger, Ehrlichman noted. Don't let Kissinger blame Haig for the problem.

Ehrlichman and Haldeman promptly told Kissinger what had happened. Kissinger did not object and he said he would immediately close the liaison office. He also ordered the seizure of Welander's files, although some remained with Welander, who asked Haig what to do with them. Give them to me, Haig told him, and Welander complied. Whether Haig sanitized the documents is not known.[54]

Haig and Welander spoke that evening, and then an angry, belligerent Haig called Young at home and accused him of denigrating Welander's record. Young concluded that Haig knew nothing about Welander's confession and was lashing out to protect his colleague. Young knew better, because he had listened to Welander describe how Haig had told him about developments inside the NSC and White House. Haig was nervous, Young thought, because Welander had called Haig's loyalty to the White House into question.[55]

At the same time, Kissinger was calling Ehrlichman at home, where he was having a Christmas party. Kissinger wanted to know how strong and hard the evidence was against Welander. Ehrlichman said they had Welander's confession on tape, which he would gladly play for Kissinger the following day.

After Ehrlichman rang off with Kissinger, he received a call from Young, who was rattled by Haig. Ehrlichman told Young he would play the Welander confession for both Haig and Kissinger the next day, but that it would be better if Young stayed away from the meeting. Young agreed, but sent Ehrlichman a memo first thing on the morning of December 24.[56]

"After reflecting on yesterday's events and particularly last night's call to me by Haig, I am all the more convinced that it is now up to only you and Bob to protect Henry; i.e., it is very difficult for him to say no to Haig," Young wrote, adding that he found odd Haig's change of attitude from "enthusiastic retribution against Welander to outrage over the dismissal of Welander."

Young concluded that Haig was nervous about what Robinson and Welander would tell Ehrlichman.[57]

Ehrlichman played Welander's taped confession for Haig and Kissinger at 9 a.m. on December 24. Haig stayed quiet while Kissinger vented and railed at Moorer and Nixon for refusing to do anything about the spying. "They can spy on him and spy on me and betray us and he won't fire them!" Kissinger said. "If he won't fire [Secretary of State William] Rogers—impose some discipline in this administration—there is no reason to believe he'll fire Moorer. I assure you all this tolerance will lead to very serious consequences for this administration!"[58]

At noon, Ehrlichman met with Nixon to tell him that Haig had accused Young of railroading Welander. But Kissinger and Haig were convinced after they heard Welander's confession.[59] Nixon's initial reaction mirrored Young's. "For Christ's sakes! They're just covering up here. That's what Al wanted to do."

Ehrlichman again missed the opening with Haig. "Well, no, I think Al was genuinely concerned. He at least has now sold me that he's loyal. He and Henry both agree in very strong terms that Moorer should go. They're both now satisfied that Moorer is heavily implicated in this. They're doubly concerned because they've been using Moorer's backchannels for all kinds of communications and they're afraid that they've been compromised. Whatever problems that raises I don't know, but the indications are there, but Henry then treated me to a half-an-hour monologue."

While Nixon suspected Haig and Kissinger of covering up, he deflected any attempt to go after Moorer, the architect of the spy operation. "I don't know, it sounds like they're railroading Moorer."

Actually, Ehlichman said, it was Moorer who wanted to railroad Radford.

"Moorer is too good a man," Nixon said. "Moorer stood with us when it was tough, remember?"

Ehrlichman and Nixon betrayed their mutual blind spots. Ehrlichman missed the signs about Haig, which Nixon noticed, while Nixon failed to see what Moorer had done to him and why he had done it. From his first day in office, when he signed NSDM 2 and cut the Pentagon and Laird out of key decisions, the military had doubted Nixon's decisions and motives. Nixon, however, did not realize it.

"You see the problem is that I don't care if Moorer is guilty," Nixon said. "We cannot weaken the only part of the government that for philosophical reasons supports us. We can't do anything with the problem that would just weaken the Joint Chiefs. The military would receive a blow from which it'd never recover. It would never recover if we did do it. We can't do it. The military must survive. We'll see that they, this is not the place to do the disciplining. That's the problem. Now get, take care of the yeoman. We better do something with him, but I don't know what the hell. Have you got any ideas?"

"Yeah, but they're all illegal," Ehrlichman said.

"All of them illegal?" Nixon replied. "Hah, hah. That's good."

"Put [Radford] in a sack and drop him out of an airplane," Ehrlichman said.

"That would do it," Nixon answered. "Yeah."

⁓

Radford would not be dropped out of an airplane, but the White House exiled him to a naval base in Oregon, where the FBI would tap his telephone and monitor his activities. Initially, the navy tried to strip Radford of a security clearance, but he protested, claiming he would be unable to do his job. The navy relented, and Radford went on with his job. The FBI taps, just as those placed between 1969 and 1971, yielded nothing besides a May 1972 telephone call from Radford to Anderson to congratulate him for winning the Pulitzer Prize for his 1971 reporting, including the December columns on the tilt toward Pakistan.

With his office closed, Welander was slated to a sea command to start in mid-January. Until then, he would remain on ice, not part of the fighting navy and not part of the NSC liaison office. The White House considered the issue over.

But the issue was not done. At the Pentagon, Laird had instigated his own investigation led by Buzhardt, who had known Haig since both attended West Point. Buzhardt then joined the air force, where he was a pilot. After law school, Buzhardt joined the staff of the senator from his native South Carolina—archconservative Strom Thurmond, a leader on the Senate Armed Services Committee. That's where Buzhardt met Laird, then a member of Congress, and Mississippian John Stennis, the current Armed Services chairman. As much as anyone else in the Pentagon, Buzhardt knew who kept the secrets and where. After arriving as the Pentagon counsel in August 1970, Buzhardt helped Laird navigate the numerous controversies and crises that befell the military during the Vietnam War, including the fallout from the Pentagon Papers leak. Now he was delving into a case that Nixon believed threatened the core of his government, and that Laird, Haig, and Buzhardt knew could cripple the military if it became public.

Buzhardt ordered another interview of Welander, which would also be conducted by Stewart, who was on vacation in Florida when Buzhardt called him on January 5, 1972, to tell him to return to Washington to interview

Welander on Nixon's orders.[60] That was untrue. Stewart also did not know that Welander had already been interviewed by Ehrlichman and Young. Buzhardt knew, however, as did Laird. Neither told Stewart.

That meant Stewart, when he conducted the second Welander interview on January 7, did not know about Welander's earlier admissions, and he could not pursue those leads. Instead, the second interview seemed geared to blame Radford and only mentioned Haig as a victim of Radford's thievery. "Admiral Welander cited other occasions which he received material from Radford to which he (Admiral Welander) would not normally have access," Buzhardt's report of the interview shows.[61] "He advised that when Radford delivered material from him to General Haig, Radford would ask any of the secretaries in General Haig's office or other offices in the West Wing of the White House whether they had mail which had to be delivered to the EOB. If so, he would volunteer to deliver it." Welander also cast himself as an innocent victim set up by Radford.

Buzhardt's interview of Welander, with Stewart's unwitting assistance, became part of the official record, while Ehrlichman and Young's interview would remain tucked away from the public. With Laird's help, Buzhardt managed to pin most of the spying and leaks on Radford while minimizing the roles of Haig and Moorer. Laird knew what Haig had done, which was "disappointing," he would tell authors Len Colodny and Robert Gettlin. "I didn't think it was fair to the president."[62]

But the Buzhardt investigation, done with Laird's approval, revealed none of that. Perhaps it would have served no purpose, since Nixon had already said he considered the case closed and wanted it to go away. But Nixon continued to obsess about it, including mentioning the case to Haig repeatedly over the next few weeks, making it clear that Nixon felt betrayed by the spying.

Jack Anderson reveled in the problems he caused for Nixon. In early January, he gave the *Post* copies of the documents he had obtained for the India-Pakistan columns. They embarrassed the White House, and Anderson promised more. "My sources—and they are plural—are some of their own boys," Anderson told the *Times*. "And if they want to finger them, they're going to wind up with bubble gum all over their faces. These sources are no Ellsbergs who left the government two years ago."[63] He virtually begged the administration to prosecute him and seemed puzzled when they did little publicly. Anderson did not suspect the real reason, which was that Nixon was covering up the real story.

The initial frenzy about Anderson died down. On January 9, the *Times* printed a short story that was of greater importance than anyone would realize for more than fourteen months. Headlined "White House Took Steps to Stop Leaks Months Before Anderson Disclosure," the article had many of the details of the Plumbers, including how they were led by Krogh and Young. But the impetus for the Plumbers, the *Times* wrote, was not the Ellsberg case but the July 23, 1971, exclusive by William Beecher about the proposed land- and submarine missile moratorium included in the SALT talks.[64]

Krogh and Young never found who leaked to Beecher, and while they tried to pin the Anderson leak on Radford, they never found the real source. Their work would eventually peter out, and two of their team—Hunt and Liddy—would move to Nixon's reelection campaign, a move that in January 1972 seemed innocent but would turn out to be anything but.

CHAPTER FOURTEEN

Triumphs (1972)

FEW PRESIDENTS HAVE HAD SUCH A RUN OF GOOD FORTUNE, MUCH OF IT BY design, as Richard Nixon enjoyed during the first half of 1972. The drama that marked the India-Pakistan war soon faded. The Joint Chiefs spy ring in the NSC that was uncovered in December had been broken, and Admiral Moorer knew his job was on the line. Vietnam was in a lull. The Soviet Union proved more accommodating, no doubt influenced by the fear that the nascent US-Chinese alliance had altered the global balance of power. The events of the previous three years, especially Nixon's secret government, had put all of the pieces in place. Nixon's gamble was paying off.

The first stop was China. Nixon became the first American president on Chinese soil. It almost mattered little what he, Mao Tse-tung, and Chou En-lai planned to discuss. Nixon's presence alone made it momentous. "Over the long term, the intangibles of your China visit will prove more important than the tangible results," Kissinger wrote Nixon just days before the trip.[1] At home, the visit showed how Nixon had evolved from a vocal member of the China Lobby into a statesman. "Despite all the disclaimers about how little can be achieved in a week, President Nixon is flying cloud nine toward the long-forbidden city of Peking, for a round of engagements with Mao Tse-tung and Chou En-lai and other leaders of the long-dreaded and isolated Chinese Communists," Max Frankel wrote in the February 20 *New York Times*.[2]

Nixon's meeting with Mao came on the chairman's timetable. "Nobody ever had a scheduled appointment; one was admitted to a presence, not invited to a government authority," Kissinger wrote later.[3] When Nixon arrived at Mao's residence for his audience on February 21, he was alternately flattering and candid. It would be perhaps his only face-to-face meeting with Mao; Nixon and Kissinger worried repeatedly that Mao might actually die before the summit. "Mao emanated vibrations of strength and power and will," Kissinger wrote.[4] Both men mentioned domestic opposition to their meeting as Mao captured the difference between the two societies. Nixon's opponents remained in Congress, while Mao's "got on an airplane and fled abroad," he said.[5] Nixon also told Mao the United States valued China's friendship and that he would always treat China with respect. Mao accepted Nixon's words but left the complicated work to Chou.

It was in those negotiations that both sides got what Nixon had traveled for. China said it would not do in Vietnam what it had done in 1950, when its intervention in the Korean War turned a US victory into a deadly stalemate. That meant Nixon could step up the fight against the North Vietnamese without Chinese reprisals and give General Abrams more latitude in fighting an anticipated offensive. In return, Kissinger turned over detailed US intelligence on how many troops and weapons the Soviets had massed on the Chinese border. "None of our colleagues here know that we have given you this information and nobody in our government except for the President and these people here know that we have given you this information," Kissinger said.[6] It was a sign of trust aimed at showing the Chinese that the Soviets were a bigger threat than the United States. It worked. It also betrayed the scope of US intelligence, if not the precise methods.

Not all in the US delegation agreed with how far Nixon was willing to go. "They're selling us out to the Communists," Haig complained in Beijing to Dwight Chapin, an assistant to Haldeman.[7] Two decades of intense rivalry, fear, and distrust of the People's Republic could not be washed away by toasts in the Great Hall of the People. The US military that had lost more than thirty thousand men in Korea, many fighting the Chinese, did not shake its history as easily as Nixon. The Chiefs worried whether they could trust the Chinese as Nixon was abandoning the long-held support for Taiwan.

As Nixon prepared to leave, he and Chou reveled in the knowledge they had reshaped the world and history. They also knew they had built another web of secrets. China had a certain image in the communist world it had to maintain, and the United States had one among its allies, Nixon told Chou on February 28. "We will avoid giving any indication that either of us changed our principles. The only indication we will give is that we tried to find here common ground, and as time goes on, we will try to find more common ground. We recognize that between two major countries that have different systems there can never be all common ground. And we will recognize—and this is the last point and perhaps the most important point—the enormous importance of not giving the Soviet Union any grounds to launch attacks of rhetoric against the People's Republic due to the fact that this meeting has occurred."[8]

The Soviet Union knew Nixon's trip reshaped their relationship with the United States. No longer could the Soviets count on US uncertainty about Chinese intentions. On March 1, the day he returned to Washington, Kissinger met secretly with Dobrynin, who unsuccessfully tried to mask his government's concern. Kissinger told Dobrynin that Nixon visited China to normalize relations, but Dobrynin "wondered whether any agreement had been made at the expense of the Soviet Union," Kissinger told Nixon.[9] Dobrynin told Kissinger that he hoped Nixon would respond to the letter the Soviet leadership sent while Nixon was in China in order to put the Soviet Politburo at ease.

While Nixon knew he had gained momentum in arms control and other talks with the Soviets, he still faced a military establishment worried he would give away whatever strategic edge the United States had left over to the Soviets. They had watched him promise them one thing on strategic weapons, such as limits on submarine-based missiles, and then give it away. Nixon also knew he faced another challenge that could derail the Soviet summit he so desperately wanted, and that was in Vietnam, where the North Vietnamese had spent months amassing their forces for an anticipated dry-season offensive. "One massive problem we have is in Vietnam," Kissinger told Nixon on January 20.[10] "We had a message from Abrams today. They are putting in every reserve unit they have. Everything. They're stripping North Vietnam." Nixon and Kissinger knew they had to stop the North Vietnamese just to keep the general stalemate between the North and South and to limit the North's leverage during the peace talks. Doing that, however, would mean the US bombing of North Vietnamese targets, which Nixon had avoided since taking office. Massive bombing raids would stoke domestic opposition to what would be considered the widening of a war most Americans wanted to end while also raising the ire of China and the Soviet Union, the North's patrons.

Abrams wanted permission to strike targets in North Vietnam early in 1972, but the White House held back because Nixon did not want to sidetrack the China summit.[11] Nixon and Kissinger worried the North Vietnamese would attack before or during the China visit and trigger a US response that would overshadow or stop the historic meeting. On February 16, Kissinger reported to Nixon that many of Abrams's air strike requests had been met "with the exception of authority to strike certain areas of North Vietnam freely."[12] Other requests, Kissinger told Nixon, would be considered after March 1, the day after Nixon returned from China. "In addition," Kissinger said, "various plans for other air strikes against North Vietnam have been prepared, but have not yet been authorized. I believe that our preparations are sufficient and that there is no need to grant broader authorities at this time." Nixon agreed, but cautioned that if the North Vietnamese attacked while he was in China, they needed to make sure that Abrams would not criticize them later for delaying air strikes. "The heaviest possible strikes in S.V. Nam, Laos, and Cambodia should be undertaken if an offensive begins and if it will be helpful to blunt it."[13]

The North Vietnamese did not attack until March 30, when two divisions poured across the DMZ into South Vietnam. Their forces quickly overtook key cities and threatened Hue, scene of some of the worst fighting during the Tet Offensive four years earlier. Nixon's first reaction was bombing. "I'm not concerned about the attack," he told Kissinger shortly after learning about the invasion, "but I am concerned about the counterattack. By God, you've got the Air Force there. Now, get them off their ass and get them up there and hit everything that moves."[14]

Military leaders were angry that Nixon had denied their requests for aggressive action for months before the actual attack. "For the past two and one half months, General Abrams and I have consistently requested the authority to conduct those operations deemed necessary to preclude genera-tion of the critical enemy threat which was predicted and has now devel-oped," Admiral John McCain, commander in chief, Pacific, wrote Moorer.[15] "Many of the requests have been denied, or approved with seriously limiting provisions. The effect of the current constraints on the field commander are clearly evidenced by the serious battlefield situation." The delays in approving the strikes came from both the White House and Laird. Kissinger, as he did on February 16, had delayed approving some of what Abrams wanted, while Laird also did not pass along information requests for bombing.[16]

Nixon summoned Moorer to the White House on April 3 to impress upon him the need for bombing strikes, the same raids that Abrams, McCain, and Moorer had sought and which either Nixon or Laird had denied. Moorer could say little as Nixon railed about Abrams, calling him timid and a drunk.

"First, I think there has to be a very clear understanding that—of a mat-ter which I have discussed with the Admiral on occasion before, and that is that I am Commander in Chief, and not Secretary of Defense," Nixon said. "Is that clear? Do you understand that?"[17]

"I do indeed," said Moorer, who knew his job as chairman depended on remaining in Nixon's good graces, particularly after Nixon's discovery of the spy ring.

Nixon said he would not appoint Abrams as army chief of staff "because of his conduct in this business. He's shown no imagination. He's drinking too much. I want you to get an order to him that he's to go on the wagon throughout the balance of this offensive. Is that clear?"

"Yes, sir," Moorer answered.[18]

Nixon had Moorer cowed, although the admiral agreed with Nixon's vision for responding to the attacks. By May, shortly before the Soviet summit, Nixon had decided on a bold package of airstrikes against the North to break the offensive. Called Operation Linebacker, the offensive included B-52 raids over major North Vietnamese cities, while carrier-based aircraft would hammer smaller military targets across the country. The attacks would also feature laser-guided bombs meant to provide closer targeting to avoid hitting civilians and causing unnecessary damage. They would also mine the major port of Haiphong in an attempt to shut down the North's commercial shipping and starve its military of the supplies it needed to maintain the southern offensive longer.

Nixon worried that unprecedented strikes on North Vietnam would derail the Moscow summit set for later in May, but he felt he had to act. "I don't care what the Russian answer is, it is to go," Nixon told Haldeman, Moorer, Kissinger, and John Connally, his former Treasury secretary, on May 4, four days before the the attacks would start. "We've got to get back to the battle."[19] There was heavy fighting around Hue. "I realize that. And then, if the Russians cancel, we'll blockade. We will blockade and continue to bomb. But we are now going to win the war, and that's my position—if it costs the election, I don't give a shit. But we are going to win the war."

Nixon's soliloquy in the Oval Office made for great theater, but Kissinger and Haldeman knew the real story. Nixon had given away his plans for the war in February 1969 when he dispatched Kissinger to tell Dobrynin that the United States was not in the war to win on the ground. Each successive withdrawal of troops from South Vietnam reinforced that philosophy, and the Russians and North Vietnamese knew Nixon's leverage in the war diminished each day. By March 1972 and the start of the Easter Offensive, the United States had fewer than seventy thousand troops on the ground in South Vietnam, hardly enough to push back any North Vietnamese offensive. The United States had to rely on the South Vietnamese military and US air power. The North, while taking considerable losses from US air strikes and whatever resistance ARVN provided, knew it had cut through the South Vietnamese military with little problem. They could withstand whatever air strikes the United States dished out, and when those ended, resume their plan to conquer South Vietnam.

For the Soviets, they had no intention of canceling the Moscow summit. They knew more than anyone of Nixon's real plans for the war. For Leonid Brezhnev and the Soviet Politburo, the Vietnam War represented a problem for the United States and no one else. They could watch events unfold there realizing that they would make the ultimate gains in the arms control talks going on in Helsinki and then finalize them with the summit in Moscow. The nuclear arms race was bankrupting the Soviet Union, not support for North Vietnam, so reaching an arms control deal trumped anything in Southeast Asia. By early 1972, both sides had shaped an arms deal mostly to their liking. The war in Vietnam would not derail it.

While Linebacker provided instant results for the US war effort by knocking out half of the power grid for North Vietnam and relieving allied troops on the ground, it elicited little reaction from Moscow or Beijing. Kissinger would characterize the Russian response as "tepid and mild." His secret talks with Soviet leaders in advance of the summit were predictable, he cabled US ambassador to South Vietnam Ellsworth Bunker. They pushed for their demands as usual, but "without making demands. They did not condition progress in other areas on Vietnam in any way." The summit was on.

— —

US negotiators on the Strategic Arms Limitation Talks (SALT) had worked since late 1969 to reach as sweeping an agreement on nuclear weapons as possible. They faced multiple complications throughout the negotiations, as hawks on both sides worried they would sacrifice more than they gained. The Soviets had spent heavily to reach basic parity with the United States; they resisted anything that would put them in a secondary position again. American hawks, alarmed that the United States had lost its considerable advantage in missiles and warheads during the 1960s, wanted to regain superiority or at least not seem as if the United States was trailing the Soviets. Complicating the US efforts was the Nixon secret government. Lead US arms negotiators Gerard Smith and his team knew Kissinger met often with Dobrynin, although they did not know the scope of the meetings or their contents. They did know, however, that whatever they discussed in Helsinki could be overridden by Kissinger in the White House. Leaks about US negotiating positions in the talks drove Nixon to distraction. He knew his team in Helsinki leaked details they did not like, and Nixon either doubled down on his secrecy or increased his efforts to find the leakers, thereby creating another secret he had to keep.

By the time of the Moscow summit in late May, most of the details had been finalized, but even those remained subject to revision, often without the input of the negotiators, who remained in Helsinki while Nixon, Kissinger, and company were in Moscow. On May 25, Smith complained to Kissinger that "I do not feel sufficiently clued in to Moscow exchanges to give categorical advice" to Kissinger's questions about the evolving deal.[20] Haig advised Kissinger the same day that US negotiators had told Congress about the plans for a limit on submarine-launched nuclear missiles and that any change on the numbers, which were already controversial, "will be more difficult to sell."[21] Haig said Nixon could bring the Joint Chiefs back in line and persuade Congress, even the right-wing Republicans, because "they have nowhere else to go."[22]

Despite the carping from their negotiators, Kissinger and the Soviets led by Dobrynin and Foreign Minister Andrei Gromyko finalized two agreements. One would limit antiballistic missile systems in both countries. Each side would keep a system around their capital cities and another near a complex of nuclear missiles. Nixon had gained the concession he wanted from the beginning. He sought the Safeguard ABM system from Congress because he wanted to trade it away in SALT. He did, although it required him to lie about the threat posed by Soviet SS-9 missiles and their nonexistent ability at the time to put multiple, independently targeted warheads on them. Creating the negotiating position on ABM and the SS-9s ruptured much of the administration's relationship with the CIA, which refused to alter its intelligence to fit Nixon's plan. Now, however, Nixon had gotten what he wanted, and he seemed to care little about the costs.

The second deal focused primarily on the number of submarine-launched missiles each side could have. The United States could keep a maximum of 710 submarine-launched missiles and not more than 44 modern submarines capable of carrying missiles. The Soviets could have no more than 950 submarine-launched missiles and not more than 62 submarines. The numerical imbalance was clear to both sides, and US hawks objected that the deal locked in a permanent disadvantage. Kissinger argued that the considered US technological advantages rendered the numbers meaningless. US missiles had MIRVs, while the Soviets' did not.[23]

Nixon and Brezhnev signed the deals in the Kremlin on May 26, sparking euphoria among the administration, which had now seen two immensely successful summits accomplished in three months. Kissinger puffed up Nixon immediately, telling him on June 2 that "you broke the impasse on SALT."[24]

By early June, it was also clear that successful summits in Beijing and Moscow and the stalling of the North Vietnamese offensive would be followed by another development that was unanticipated at the beginning of the year—the selection by the Democrats of Senator George McGovern of South Dakota as their nominee for president. McGovern, who had received the Distinguished Flying Cross for piloting a B-24 for thirty-five missions over German-occupied Europe in World War II, had become one of the Senate's most committed doves. His campaign had inspired the antiwar youth movement and overwhelmed more traditional Democrats, including the party's 1968 nominee, Hubert Humphrey, who had returned to the Senate from Minnesota. With McGovern, the White House could provide a stark contrast between a president who had successfully negotiated deals with the Chinese and the Soviets and who was well on his way to extricating the United States from Vietnam. They would paint McGovern's domestic policies as overly generous to the poor and lazy, while Nixon represented progress and law and order.

CHAPTER FIFTEEN

Watergate and Early Cover-Up (1972)

Nixon started 1972 immersed in foreign policy but also intensely focused on his reelection campaign. He had trailed potential Democratic candidates in polls throughout much of 1971, and his reelection never seemed assured. He had only won the 1968 election with slightly more than 43 percent of the popular vote, and the right Democratic candidate had the potential to put some of the party's support back in their column in 1972. Nixon left little to chance. Two cabinet officers, Attorney General John Mitchell and Commerce Secretary Maurice Stans, returned to the campaign as its manager and chief fundraiser. The campaign relied on money and political intelligence, which was bolstered by the arrival of Howard Hunt and Gordon Liddy from the White House Plumbers. Campaign leaders had wanted Plumbers co-leader David Young to join them, but Egil Krogh declined, offering Liddy instead.

At the White House, counsel John Dean expanded his mission to include political intelligence. When he took the job in July 1970, Dean inherited Ehrlichman's investigators—former New York City detectives John Caulfield and Tony Ulasewicz, who had been gathering dirt on Nixon's political rivals, particularly Senator Edward Kennedy. Dean knew Nixon's appetite for such information and "encouraged this new specialty, figuring that intelligence would be more valued by the policy-makers than would dry legal advice," he wrote later.[1] In October 1971, Dean sent Caulfield to New York to see if he could tie Democratic politicians to the recently busted Happy Hooker prostitution ring, but Caulfield discovered to Dean's disappointment that the ring had many Republican clients.[2]

In Washington, Dean used another prostitution ring to develop political intelligence. It involved Erika Heidi Rikan, an associate of Washington's top mobster, Joe Nesline, and a very good friend of Dean's girlfriend, Maureen Kane Biner. Also known as Kathie Dieter, Rikan's network of call girls worked from the Columbia Plaza apartments near the Watergate office complex. Rikan's address books, which were found and published in 2013 by author Phil Stanford, listed Dean's private White House telephone number, his unlisted home number, and Maureen's contacts.[3] Maureen lived with Rikan, who also attended the Deans' 1972 wedding. Dean was focused on Rikan's clientele at the Democratic National Committee, which she developed with the help of a shady Washington lawyer, Phillip Bailley. From the fall of 1971 to spring 1972, Bailley lined up Rikan's clients through the DNC.[4] Another Rikan associate was Lou Russell, an alcoholic former FBI agent and former investigator for the House Un-American Activities Committee, who video-taped the johns in their assignations with the prostitutes.[5]

It worked until April 6, when the FBI raided Bailley's apartment and office and seized his notebooks and dozens of incriminating photographs of women. A University of Maryland graduate student Bailley had tried to recruit as a prostitute told two Washington vice cops about his approach, and they told the FBI.[6] Bailley panicked, fled Washington, and tried to hide as much evidence as he could. Meanwhile, the word quickly spread to Dean. Telephone logs from Dean's office, which were obtained as part of a civil lawsuit in the 1990s, show the White House lawyer called Nixon campaign officials whose names were listed in Rikan's address books and who may have had contact with Bailley.[7] They included Stans; Jeb Magruder, Mitchell's deputy; and Fred LaRue, a longtime Mitchell associate and fundraiser. Dean also called Roemer McPhee, a Republican National Committee lawyer and close friend of US District Judge Charles Richey, who would inherit the Bailley case.[8]

Bailley feared the worst and called Rikan. He told her the FBI had his notebooks but not those for the Columbia Plaza operation. Burn those, she said, and meet her the following day at Nathan's, a notorious Washington singles bar.[9]

Bailley arrived at Nathan's and found Rikan already in a booth, wearing a tight blue sweater and fitted black pants. Impatient and angry, she blamed Bailley and his lifestyle fueled by marijuana and promiscuous sex for the mess. Bailley was on his own and had better get a good lawyer, Rikan warned, because she would not be affected by his legal problems. "We can handle all that," she told him. "It's no problem."[10]

Dean needed to know more about what the DNC had in their offices and what, if anything, they knew about the Columbia Plaza ring. He ordered Caulfield to have Ulasewicz case the DNC headquarters to see how easy it would be to break into the offices to tap their telephones. Ulasewicz went to the DNC offices, told a receptionist he was there for a meeting, and sat in the waiting room watching people come and go from offices that were "as open as the sky."[11] Dean then put the DNC atop the list of intelligence targets on April 30. Meanwhile, federal investigators led by Assistant US Attorney John Rudy were interviewing people who were named in Bailley's notebooks, including Lou Russell, who tried to divert Rudy's attention from the Columbia Plaza ring.[12] The Columbia Plaza investigation had the potential to wreck careers and lives.

In May, Dean told Magruder, who worked with Liddy and Hunt, to break into the DNC headquarters to bug two telephones.[13] One belonged to Lawrence O'Brien, the Democratic Party chairman. The other, on a different side of the room, belonged to the secretary of R. Spencer Oliver, the party's liaison with leaders from state parties. Oliver's phone was used to set up dates for party officials with the girls from the Columbia Plaza. The team broke into the DNC on May 28. Their taps, which were monitored from a hotel room in the Howard Johnson hotel across the street, produced nothing from O'Brien. Oliver's phone, however, provided a rich vein of sexual conversations about lining up dates with the Columbia Plaza prostitutes. Those calls, federal prosecutors would later tell a judge handling the case, involved compromising sexual conversations.[14]

Dean's interest in the DNC gained more urgency on June 9, when a grand jury indicted Bailley on twenty-two counts of violating the Mann Act; transporting an underage woman across state lines for immoral purposes; and extortion, pandering, and procuring. The story was on the front page of that afternoon's *Washington Star* with the headline "Capitol Hill Call Girl Ring Uncovered."[15] This was the case Rudy had been investigating since April. After publication of the *Star* story, Dean called Rudy's boss, Earl Silbert.[16] He said he would send a car to bring Rudy and his immediate superior, Don Smith, to the White House with their evidence in the Bailley case.[17]

Dean told Rudy and Smith he wanted to keep the address books over the weekend, but the two prosecutors declined, saying they needed them for the case. So Dean had his secretary copy the address books, and then he circled some names. One listing drew Dean's particular attention, the one belonging to "MB," or Maureen Biner, his girlfriend. Dean also discovered the name of a female White House lawyer who had once dated Bailley. Dean's logs show he called the woman's boss, Darrell Trent at the Office of Emergency Preparedness,[18] and by day's end, Trent had confronted the woman with the evidence and fired her.[19]

Dean was worried about more than Trent's unfortunate employee. His girlfriend's telephone number was in the address book of a man now charged with running a prostitution ring. Dean also knew that Bailley worked with

Rikan, the mobbed-up madam of a Washington call-girl ring.[20] That was the kind of dirt Nixon wanted on his opponents; it would help neither Dean nor the president if that kind of taint extended to the president's lawyer. Again, as he had when Bailley's office and home were raided, Dean called Roemer McPhee, the RNC lawyer and secret contact with Richey.[21]

Shortly after the meeting with Rudy and Smith, Dean told Magruder: The Hunt-Liddy team needed to go into the DNC again. This time, he wanted them to get into the desk of Ida Maxie Wells, Oliver's secretary, who may have had the copies of an address book similar to the one Dean just copied. If so, they needed to take that book and get it out of the hands of the Democrats. Take whatever cameras you need, Magruder told Liddy, but find what O'Brien has "in here," smacking his hand on top of his desk. "The purpose of the second Watergate break-in was to find out what O'Brien had of a derogatory nature about us, not for us to get something on him or the Democrats," Liddy would write later.[22]

Hunt and Liddy gathered their team on the night of June 16. It included Alfred Baldwin, a former FBI agent who had been monitoring the existing taps from the Howard Johnson's across the street. Baldwin would watch the DNC offices and alert the burglars if any problems developed. They were joined by Bernard Barker and Eugenio Martinez, part of the group that broke into Fielding's office; Frank Sturgis, a longtime adventurer and soldier of fortune; and Virgilio Gonzalez, another anti-Castro Cuban. Rounding out the team was the Nixon campaign's security chief—James McCord, a retired CIA agent who was the boss of Lou Russell.[23] Hunt and Liddy would monitor their work from a room at the nearby Watergate Hotel.

The five men finally managed to get into the DNC offices after midnight on June 17. Russell, who was not part of the break-in team, spent much of the night at the Howard Johnson's restaurant or driving around the general area of the Watergate complex.[24] Baldwin, the lookout across the street, was paying intermittent attention and provided little help. Dressed in suits and carrying surveillance equipment, McCord, Barker, Martinez, Sturgis, and Gonzalez got inside the offices and found their way to their target—Wells's desk. Martinez had the key to her desk drawer in his pocket and set up a camera on top of the desk. Suddenly, however, they had unexpected company. Shortly after Baldwin radioed to ask if they had seen "hippie-ish-looking" men with guns, undercover Washington cops rushed into the DNC offices.[25] A building security guard had reported a break-in. As the cops patted down the burglars, Martinez made a quick move, and the cops stopped him before he could put the key in his mouth and swallow it. They took it and added it to their evidence file, proof of Martinez's assignment.

It was shortly after 2 a.m. on June 17. Sleeping at his friend Robert Abplanalp's private island home on Walker's Cay in the Bahamas, Nixon did not know about the arrests or about the planning of the burglary. He could not have realized that the end of his presidency had just begun.[26]

———

Panic set in among the burglary team as the police took the five men into custody. Hunt and Liddy fled the Watergate Hotel and joined Baldwin. Hunt ordered Baldwin to empty the hotel room and take everything to McCord's home in Rockville, Maryland, a Washington suburb, and to tell McCord's wife, who started destroying documents. Baldwin drove through the night to his home in Connecticut. Hunt went home, took a sleeping pill, and went to sleep. Liddy went to the campaign office, where he also shredded documents. He also went to the White House and called Magruder in Los Angeles. The burglars had been arrested at the DNC, Liddy told him, including McCord, whose presence tied the break-in directly to the Nixon campaign.

"You used McCord?" Magruder asked Liddy. "Why, Gordon? Why?"[27]

Magruder's first call was to Dean, who was in Manila, Philippines, for a conference on international narcotics trafficking. Dean said they had to move quickly and persuade Attorney General Richard Kleindienst and get him to spring McCord from jail.[28] Magruder ordered Liddy to find Kleindienst. Liddy grabbed Powell Moore, one of the campaign's press aides, and together they drove to the elite Burning Tree Country Club in suburban Maryland, where Kleindienst was enjoying lunch after a round of golf. The clearly agitated Liddy burst into the club's dining room, surprising Kleindienst, who led Liddy and Moore into a nearby locker room. Liddy spilled out the fantastic story of the arrests and told Kleindienst he had to get McCord out of jail. "Tell them I can't do it—won't do it," Kleindienst said.[29]

Meanwhile, the five defendants were in a Washington courtroom to be charged with burglary. Watching the proceedings was a relatively new *Washington Post* reporter named Bob Woodward, who had been dragged from his home by a call from an editor and was told to cover the hearing. Previously a navy communications officer who worked for the chairman of the Joint Chiefs of Staff, Woodward was covering weekend police news. This day, however, he watched the arraignment and heard McCord list his most recent employer as the CIA. Woodward fed those details to police reporter Alfred Lewis, whose story ran on the front page of the Sunday, June 18, 1972, *Post*.

Dean knew the break-in he authorized would bring unwanted attention from the Democrats and the press. His White House colleagues, who knew nothing about his ties to Rikan or the Columbia Plaza, realized that McCord could become the string that, when tugged, could unravel the administration's entire secret government. McCord would lead to Hunt, the former CIA operative who worked with the White House Plumbers, who would reveal the Plumbers' break-in of the offices of Daniel Ellsberg's psychiatrist. Any further examination of the Plumbers could also uncover their ties to the CIA and their investigation of Admiral Moorer's spy ring at the NSC. Soon, Haldeman, Ehrlichman, and Charles Colson, Hunt's sponsor, were investigating the break-in and Hunt's involvement. Dean, who had by then returned from the Philippines, joined them on June 19. Together they would gin up the administration's cover-up of the Watergate break-in, less to protect the members of the campaign staff who had been involved than to hide Nixon's other activities.

The FBI investigating the break-in was a bureau in transition. After months of resisting the White House's attempts to get him to resign, J. Edgar Hoover died in his sleep on May 2. Nixon named L. Patrick Gray, who had just been nominated as deputy attorney general, to serve as acting director until the November elections. Gray was not embraced by Bureau lifers, many who had waited for years for Hoover to leave and for them to move up.

William Sullivan, forced out by Hoover in October, had moved to his home in rural New Hampshire and plotted to return to the Bureau. Sullivan's main ally was Robert Mardian, the assistant attorney general for internal security to whom Sullivan had given the records of the FBI wiretaps of government officials and journalists. In a series of letters to Mardian, who would shortly move to the Nixon campaign as a political coordinator and counsel, Sullivan offered unsolicited advice for Gray and criticized his own rivals in the FBI. "[Mark] Felt was one of my mistakes," Sullivan told Mardian, claiming that he recommended Hoover bring Felt to Washington from the Kansas City bureau.[30] Gray, Sullivan told Mardian, was walking into "a bucket of worms" that desperately needed reform.[31]

Gray never wanted to be FBI director. He was happy becoming deputy attorney general and working for Nixon, whom he admired since they had first met in the 1940s, when Nixon was a freshman congressman and Gray a young navy officer.[32] Gray left the navy to join Nixon's 1960 presidential campaign, practiced law during the 1960s, and joined the administration in 1969. He wanted to stay at Justice, but his friend Kleindienst said no job in government was more important than FBI director.[33] But Sullivan's warning about the FBI was right about the FBI as a "bucket of worms." So was the

White House. Nixon knew that Gray would follow orders but considered him "too military and straitlaced in his thinking."[34]

Gray would eventually become one of the main casualties of the break-in, and the investigation that quickly uncovered details that worried Dean, Ehrlichman, Haldeman, and eventually Nixon. Gray was in California when he first learned of the break-in. On June 18, he asked Felt if the FBI had jurisdiction in the case. When Felt said he was certain, Gray told him to investigate it "to the hilt with no holds barred."[35]

FBI agents immediately started reviewing documents and interviewing Nixon campaign officials. They unraveled Hunt's involvement early by finding a country club receipt with Hunt's name on it at the Watergate Hotel and his name and White House telephone number in Barker's address book. Dean knew the range of Hunt's pre-Watergate activities, so he rushed to Hunt's office and took the incriminating documents and notebooks from Hunt's safe. When the FBI wanted to interview Colson, Hunt's sponsor, on June 19, Dean delayed them until June 22 and then insisted that he sit in on the interview. Dean knew the FBI's quick work in connecting Hunt and Colson meant they could uncover what Dean had done and the White House's involvement. Meanwhile, the FBI's investigators saw the involvement of Hunt, McCord, and the Cubans and believed the break-in had to be a CIA operation. Gray then called Richard Helms at the CIA to ask if his agency was involved.

No, Helms said, adding that his staff has "been meeting on this every day. My men just can't figure this one out."[36]

Gray then told Dean about the agents' hunch and his conversation with Helms, which gave Dean an idea.

The next morning, June 23, at 8:15, Dean called Haldeman and told him the FBI believed the CIA was behind the break-in, but that Gray could not keep the FBI investigation from spinning out of control.[37] Of course, Gray had no intention of "controlling" the investigation; he had already ordered an all-out investigation. Dean wanted to use the discovery by investigators that Barker had deposited $89,000 in checks from the Mexico City bank account of Manuel Ogarrio, a Mexican national, as evidence the FBI had stumbled onto a CIA operation. After all, Hunt and the five burglars had either worked for the agency, or like Martinez, still did. Dean told Haldeman he had already talked to Mitchell, who said they needed to tell Helms and his new deputy, Vernon Walters, to call Gray and tell him to back off.[38] Mitchell's telephone logs, however, show that he did not talk to Dean on June 22 or on the morning of June 23.[39] Dean came up with the idea on his own to distract the FBI, which was getting too close to learning Dean's connections to the burglary. Haldeman took Dean's word that it was Mitchell's idea and never confirmed it with Mitchell. "Gray doesn't know what to do in controlling the Bureau," Haldeman wrote in his diary for that day.[40]

After talking to Dean, Haldeman spent ninety-five minutes with Nixon in the Oval Office to discuss Dean's recommendation and the lie that it was Mitchell's idea.

The FBI, Haldeman told Nixon, was going "in some directions we don't want to go," and Gray could not control his agents. They have traced money through the Mexican bank, and in Miami an informant told agents that a photographer friend had developed film from Barker that showed documents with DNC letterhead. Haldeman told Nixon about Mitchell's idea, which "John Dean analyzed carefully last night," that the only way to fix the problem was to have Vernon Walters call Pat Gray and tell him to "stay the hell out of this. . . . business here we don't want you to go any further on."[41]

Nixon asked if Gray did not want to cooperate. He did, Haldeman said, even though he had never talked to Gray and was just repeating what Dean had told him. Once Walters called Gray, the FBI chief would have the information he needed to order Mark Felt to tell the rest of the Bureau to fall in line. Felt wants to cooperate, because he's ambitious, and the early indications from the investigation are that it was a CIA operation. That would be enough to shut it down, Haldeman said.

Haldeman explained that investigators had traced the money in the Mexican bank to a Nixon donor named Kenneth Dahlberg from Minnesota. A $25,000 check from Dahlberg had ended up deposited directly in Barker's bank account, where money from some Texas donors had also been deposited. Nixon proposed telling Dahlberg to say the money came from another source.

The only way to do that, Haldeman said, is if they get an order from the White House backed up by Helms and Walters. He and Ehrlichman would call Walters, whom they considered their man, and tell him to call Gray.

"All right, fine," Nixon said. "How do you call him in, I mean you just— well, we protected Helms from one hell of a lot of things." That was, charitably, an exaggeration or an outright delusion. Nixon had pressured Helms repeatedly during the first term, first trying to bar him from NSC meetings and then trying to blame Nixon's failures on bad intelligence from the CIA. Nixon had even contemplated firing Helms the previous October, after Helms denied Ehrlichman's request the previous fall for agency files on Cuba and Vietnam. But Nixon had lost his nerve and ended up reassuring Helms of his commitment to "dirty tricks." Nixon then tried to undercut Helms by installing Walters as his deputy. Nixon had done Helms no favors, but now he expected a huge one in return.

Nixon wanted to stop the FBI, because Hunt was a "scab" with "a hell of a lot of things in it that we just feel that this would be very detrimental to have this thing go any further. This involves these Cubans, Hunt, and a lot of hanky panky that we have nothing to do with ourselves." Then there was Liddy. "Is that the fellow?" Nixon asked. "He must be a little nuts."

"He is," Haldeman said.

"I mean he just isn't well-screwed-on is he?" Nixon continued. "Isn't that the problem?"

There was pressure from the committee, presumably from Mitchell, to get more intelligence, Haldeman said. That led to excesses like the break-in. Nixon said he would not second-guess and expressed relief that Colson, his go-to man for political hardball, was not involved. Haldeman said the FBI interviewed Colson the previous day and concluded from the interview that the burglary was either a White House or a CIA operation.

Nixon told Haldeman to bring in Helms and Walters and "play it tough." They needed to be told that the investigation would "open the whole Bay of Pigs thing" and that the president did not want that uncovered. For the country's sake, Nixon said, they had to tell the FBI "don't go further into this case."

When the tape of this conversation was revealed in August 1974, it would strip Nixon of his remaining political support and force him to resign. At the time of the conversation, however, neither he nor Haldeman knew of the extent of Dean's involvement in planning the break-in or engineering the cover-up. They blamed Liddy for his impulsiveness, which was plausible given Liddy's propensity for bold, often stupid actions, but Liddy had refused to talk to FBI investigators and would do so until after he was released from prison in 1979. That meant the FBI never learned his side of the break-in story, particularly the reasons for which he was sent into the DNC headquarters.

Haldeman and Ehrlichman quickly summoned Helms and Walters to the White House.[42] Nixon wanted Walters there because Nixon mistakenly believed Walters would blindly follow the White House's orders. Helms suspected as much, since Nixon had used his previous deputy, Marine General Robert Cushman, the same way. Haldeman did much of the talking, asking first if the CIA was involved in the burglary. Helms said no. Then Haldeman hit a nerve, asking if the Mexican bank account and the money for the Cubans had anything to do with the Bay of Pigs.[43]

"This has nothing to do with the Bay of Pigs!" Helms all but shouted. Everything involving the Bay of Pigs had been handled years ago, he said.[44] Nevertheless, Haldeman told Walters, not Helms, to visit Gray and tell him to throttle back the Bureau's investigation.

Helms and Walters left the White House confused. The FBI investigation endangered no CIA operations in Mexico. Helms also did not reveal he knew far more about the Plumbers and their work than others believed, including how the White House went behind his back to get the agency to give the Plumbers equipment, disguises, and a psychiatric profile of Daniel Ellsberg. Helms had recommended Hunt to Haldeman the previous year and also knew that Hunt was reporting back to the agency about his work in the White House. Walters was less certain; he had only been on the job for six weeks. Both, however, knew how Nixon operated. Outside the building, Helms instructed Walters to talk to Gray and remind him of the agreement between the agencies that if one learned about another's operations they would inform each other. Helms, however, did not tell Walters that Gray had already called him the day before. Meanwhile, Helms would return to Langley to determine if the agency was doing anything serious in Mexico the FBI investigation would expose. Dean, who had concocted the entire scheme, called Gray and told him that Walters was on his way to his office. When Walters arrived, he told Gray that "if the investigation gets pushed further south of the border, it could trespass into some of our covert projects. Since you've got these five men under arrest, it will be best to taper the matter off here."[45]

Eventually, both agencies would resist the White House pleas. Gray grew increasingly uncomfortable with the interference of Dean and others in the investigation. Helms had endured Nixon's pressures for years and knew Nixon was hiding something. Within days, Helms would tell the White House and FBI the CIA had nothing at risk from a robust investigation. That did not deter Dean or other White House aides. Dean summoned Walters on June 26 and told him that Watergate "was causing a lot of trouble, that it was very embarrassing. The FBI was investigating it. The leads had led to some important people. It might lead to some more important people."[46] Bureau investigators, Dean told Walters, had three main theories—that the break-in had been engineered by the Republicans, the CIA, or an unknown group. The CIA connection was obvious. The burglars and Hunt had either worked for the Agency as agents or contractors. Could the CIA take some of the blame for the break-in? Dean asked. Any doubts Walters had during the June 23 meeting dissipated. He wanted no part of what Dean was proposing, saying CIA interference "would destroy the credibility of the Agency with the Congress, with the Nation." He would resign before doing anything that would implicate the CIA in the break-in.[47]

Back in Langley, Walters told Helms what had happened. Helms asked Walters to write memos for the CIA files detailing the meeting. Dean was also not deterred by Walters's first refusal. He asked Walters to meet him the next day and told him some of the burglars were "wobbling and might talk."[48] That's not our problem, Walters responded. So Dean asked if the CIA could pay the bail and salaries of the burglars. Absolutely not, Walters said, because that would implicate the CIA in something "in which it is not implicated," Walters said.

The CIA had other secrets not shared with Gray. Helms made an odd request of Gray to keep the FBI from interviewing two CIA agents, Karl Wagner and John Caswell, whose names were in Hunt's address book.[49] Wagner was the assistant to Walters and, before that, to Cushman, the deputy CIA directors. Wagner was in a position to know what the Agency had done for Hunt and the Plumbers. Caswell had worked for the Agency in both Vietnam and Europe. Gray agreed and relayed the request to his subordinates.

Dean asked Walters to meet with him again on June 28 and said Walters needed to meet with Gray. Also, Dean asked, did Walters have any suggestions for how to get the Cubans to keep quiet about the break-in? Walters mostly listened and tried to keep the CIA out of it.[50]

By July 5, it was clear the CIA would not participate in any cover-up and that Gray was growing suspicious of the White House attempts to slow the investigation. Dean had already demanded that he sit in on any interviews with White House or campaign officials. Gray wanted the CIA to provide him a document confirming the Agency's reasons for the FBI to not interview Ogarrio or Dahlberg. Without it, the Bureau would go ahead with the interviews. Walters visited Gray on July 6, but he had no letter for Gray. Walters leaned back in a red leather chair in Gray's office and told him he had recently inherited some money. "I don't need to worry about pension, and I'm not going to let these kids kick me around anymore," he said. Something was rotten, they agreed, and someone needed to tell the president.[51]

After Walters left, Gray called a subordinate and told him to authorize the interviews of Dahlberg and Ogarrio. He then contemplated calling Nixon, which he found intimidating. "To me the president of the United States was an awesome figure," Gray wrote later. "I simply didn't have the guts to break protocol, pick up the phone and call him directly."[52]

Instead, Gray called Clark MacGregor, the Nixon campaign manager, through the White House switchboard to reach the president. He and

Walters believed members of the White House were placing inappropriate pressure on the CIA and FBI in ways that would hurt the president. Thirty-eight minutes later, Nixon called Gray, congratulating him and the Bureau for foiling an airplane hijacking in San Francisco the previous day.[53]

"Mr. President, there is something I want to speak to you about," Gray said. "Dick Walters and I feel that people on your staff are trying to mortally wound you by using the CIA and the FBI and by confusing the question of CIA interest in, or not in, people the FBI wishes to interview. I have just talked to Clark MacGregor and asked him to speak to you about this."

Nixon paused. "Pat, you just continue your aggressive and thorough investigation," he said.[54]

Gray and Walters met again on July 12. Walters gave Gray documents the agency had found about its dealings with Howard Hunt. Gray told Walters what Nixon told him the previous week. Walters agreed, saying Nixon needed to be protected from "his self-appointed protectors" who were going to either take down Nixon, Walters, or Gray as they covered their tracks.

"I'll resign before I let that happen to the FBI, Dick," Gray said.[55]

That ended the White House's attempts, which Nixon had endorsed, to use the Agency to block the investigation.

The agitation inside the White House and Nixon campaign about Watergate was exacerbated by the steady parade of negative articles appearing in the press about the break-in, particularly in the *Washington Post*. Woodward, the former navy officer turned cub reporter, had been paired with another young reporter, Carl Bernstein, on the story from the day of the break-in. They combined their ambition to break out of the purgatory of the paper's metro staff with a passion for the story. Their first combined story on June 19 identified McCord as the security coordinator for the campaign committee as well as the Republican National Committee.[56] Many of their best leads came from FBI investigators, who were angry about White House interference, including Dean's insistence, in their work. The agents' leaks were aimed at stopping that interference. Some details came from Mark Felt, while others came from the investigators, including Angelo Lano, a frequent source, and Charles Bates. Felt and his colleagues would gather at the end of each day and decide which reporters would get what.[57] Woodward and Bernstein were on that list, as were Sandy Smith of *Time* magazine, Seymour Hersh of the *New York Times*, and Jack Nelson and Ron Ostrow of the *Los Angeles Times*.

In their 1974 book—*All the President's Men*—Woodward and Bernstein would identify their best confidential source as a man they called Deep Throat. In 2005 and after three decades of denials, Felt claimed through a family lawyer that he was Deep Throat. Woodward acknowledged their relationship that afternoon and then elaborated on it in a quickly published book, *The Secret Man*. But Felt either did not know or could not have known much of the information Woodward and Bernstein claimed Deep Throat provided. For example, Woodward claimed in *The Secret Man* that he met Felt outside the White House basement NSC office of Alexander Haig, where Woodward had been dispatched to deliver a package for his boss, Admiral Moorer. Felt, Woodward speculated, was most likely there to deliver details of the FBI's wiretaps on government officials and journalists.[58] But Felt knew nothing about the wiretaps at the time, because they were a closely held secret handled by Felt's longtime Bureau rival, William Sullivan. In fact, many of the tactics Deep Throat used in the book matched Sullivan's tradecraft, including surreptitious meetings in out-of-the-way restaurants and hotels, such as one columnist Robert Novak described with Sullivan in a hotel bathroom.[59]

In July 1972, Sullivan's exile ended when he became director of the newly created Office of National Narcotics Intelligence. Nixon originally wanted to put the office in the White House as part of the growing network of counternarcotics efforts he had run there, but he moved it to Justice after objections from officials there. Sullivan had to get the job, because Nixon owed him for everything he had done for the White House, Ehrlichman told Walter Minnick, who coordinated much of the White House counternarcotics strategy.[60] The move put Sullivan back in the heart of power with access to his former associates at the White House, starting with Dean, and his remaining acolytes at the FBI who were neither allied with Felt nor Gray.

Before Sullivan moved to Justice, one of his oldest allies proposed a move that could have landed Sullivan in the White House at the NSC. Russell Ash, a former FBI agent and longtime friend of Sullivan's, proposed to Haig that the NSC create a new committee to oversee the FBI's domestic intelligence work.[61] The proposal went nowhere, and Ash eventually left the NSC to work with Sullivan at ONNI, which, author Sanford Ungar wrote, became "a kind of government in exile."[62] Former FBI colleagues would visit Sullivan at ONNI to check in, make sure he knew they still thought about him in case he came back to the FBI, and started to settle scores.

◆━❦━◆

Two parallel cases during the summer of 1972 challenged the White House's ability to control the Watergate investigation. One was the federal case against Phillip Bailley on prostitution charges. The second was the Democratic National Committee's suit against the Nixon campaign for violating its rights with the break-in. As luck would have it for the White House and Dean, both were presided over by newly minted US District Judge Charles Richey, a longtime political associate of Vice President Spiro Agnew. Dean had a direct pipeline to Richey in Roemer McPhee, the RNC lawyer and Richey's old friend.

On June 15, Richey ordered Bailley sent to St. Elizabeth's, Washington's aging mental hospital, pending the availability of a bed. Until then, however, Richey allowed Bailley to continue to practice law, which meant Richey considered Bailley incompetent to represent himself but competent to represent others. Bailley returned to court on August 29, and Richey sent him to St. Elizabeth's starting on September 6, a move that prosecutor John Rudy said was meant "to discredit him."[63] Bailley emerged from the hospital on September 21 and was back in court eight days later, when Richey urged him to plead guilty. Bailley reluctantly agreed and pleaded guilty to one count from the eleven-count indictment, a violation of the Mann Act, transporting someone across state lines for immoral purposes. Richey then ended the case on October 25 by sentencing Bailley to five years in prison and prohibited him from talking to the press, a harsh ruling that far outstripped the punishment meted out to similar defendants.[64] Bailley's plea and sentence got him out of town and unable to tell anyone about his work with Rikan and the Columbia Plaza prostitutes.

Three days after the Watergate break-in, the DNC and party chairman Lawrence O'Brien sued the Nixon campaign for invasion of privacy for its part in the Watergate break-in. The burglars, who worked for the Nixon campaign, had bugged telephones in the Democratic offices without permission. That alone seemed to constitute invasion of privacy. It was also an election-year political case in which any attention paid to its claims could hurt Nixon and boost the Democrats. Unfortunately for the Democrats, Richey had that case, too. Unlike the Bailley case, which remained off the White House's radar for anyone other than Dean, the DNC civil suit had the full attention of the president and his top aides. Dean's job was damage control. He had McPhee's help. Dean's telephone logs show he spoke to McPhee five times in the last two weeks of September, when Richey was to determine Bailley's fate and the DNC case.[65] Dean was also reporting to Nixon and Haldeman that McPhee was talking to Richey constantly and often providing advice.

"Judge Richey is not known to be one of the intellects on the bench," Dean told Nixon and Haldeman in a September 15 meeting in the Oval Office.[66] But Richey was a dependable conduit of information, as he talked to Kleindienst and "his old friend Roemer McPhee to keep Roemer abreast of what his thinking is. He told Roemer he thought that Maury [Stans] ought to file a libel action."[67]

Dean knew a week in advance, courtesy of McPhee, that Richey would sink the Democrats' case. The Democrats, led by attorney Joseph Califano, were confused and outraged by Richey's conduct. "I was convinced that Richey was fixed," Califano wrote. "Someone at the White House or on its behalf was telling Richey what to do."[68] He had effectively shut down the case until after the election, thereby denying the Democrats a chance for any political traction against Nixon. Califano would only later learn that his hunch was right. Richey *had* been in the tank for the Republicans.

Dean also hinted at the real reason for the Watergate break-in, which Haldeman and Nixon still did not realize. Henry Rothblatt, one of the lawyers for the defendants, had raised another issue in the case, Dean said. "This fellow, this fellow Rothblatt . . . he's been getting into the sex life of some of the members of the DNC and . . . ," he said. Rothblatt's justification, Dean said, was "an entrapment theory" and that the Democrats were hiding something, "or they had secret information, affairs to hide . . . It's a way-out theory."[69]

It was no far-out theory. Alfred Baldwin had spent days listening to people use the phone of DNC official Spencer Oliver to line up dates with girls from the Columbia Plaza. That was why Dean and Magruder sent the burglars into the DNC the second time. And it was one of the reasons he worked so hard to get Richey to kill the Democrats' lawsuit.

―◆―

Woodward and Bernstein chipped away at the Watergate story throughout the summer and into September. On September 17 and 18, they published two stories that showed how a small group of Mitchell's aides at the Committee to Re-Elect the President had access to the special fund they used to pay for political intelligence.[70] The articles, guided by FBI sources, kept the pair of reporters and the *Post* in the lead on the Watergate story, but they led a parade with few other followers in the national or Washington media.

By early October, they had two leads for a story that showed the scope of the campaign's dirty tricks operation and which finally put the Watergate story on the national radar. Young staffers traveled from city to city, sending derogatory letters to the editor of local newspapers and planting false stories about Democratic candidates in those papers. Their leader was Donald Segretti, a lawyer who learned dirty tricks while fighting student-body elections at the University of Southern California. Two law enforcement officials told Bernstein they were investigating a letter to the Manchester,

New Hampshire, *Union Leader* that claimed that Democratic frontrunner Edmund Muskie had used a derogatory term, Canuck, to refer to Americans of French-Canadian ancestry. The letter and other issues caused Muskie, who had won the New Hampshire primary, to erupt in an angry postelection news conference that helped sink his candidacy. As Bernstein wrote the final draft of the story, Woodward rushed back to Washington to get his confidential source to confirm his discoveries.[71]

But Deep Throat confirmed neither the tips on Segretti nor the Canuck Letter. Woodward's notes of that October 9 conversation, part of a collection he and Bernstein sold to the University of Texas for $5 million in 2003, show his source would not discuss Segretti and never mentioned the letter.[72] The October 10 story in the *Post* mentions that "law enforcement said that probably the best example of the sabotage was the fabrication—by a White House aide—of a letter to the editor alleging that Sen. Edmund S. Muskie (D-Maine) condoned a racial slur on Americans of French-Canadian descent as 'Canucks.'"[73] In the book, Woodward and Bernstein wrote that two law enforcement sources had given Bernstein shreds of confirmation that the letter was part of their investigation. "Did Segretti have anything to do with the Canuck Letter?" Bernstein asked one investigator. "The official said he couldn't talk about that letter either; it was also part of the investigation."[74] Another investigation told Bernstein that "the Muskie letter is part of it."' Those two tidbits allowed the reporters to mention the letter as the best example of sabotage. As Woodward and Bernstein wrapped the story, *Post* reporter Marilyn Berger told them that White House spokesman Ken Clawson, a former *Post* reporter, had told her that he wrote the letter. The story quoted Berger as the source for Clawson's alleged authorship of the letter and also Clawson's denial.[75] There is no other sourcing in the story for the claim Clawson had written the letter.[76] *All the President's Men*, however, added something not contained in either the notes or the October 10 *Post* story. In the book, after a lengthy discussion, a frustrated Woodward grabbed Deep Throat's arm and asked about the Canuck Letter. "Deep Throat stopped and turned around," the book says. "It was a White House operation—done inside the gates surrounding the White House and the Executive Office Building. Is that enough?"[77]

In the book's dramatic narrative, the comment showed how the Canuck Letter was part of Segretti's White House–sanctioned sabotage campaign. But Woodward's October 9 notes contain no mention of the letter, and the October 10 *Post* article has nothing from the source about the letter.[78] Woodward told author Max Holland in 2011 that he suddenly remembered the quote more than a year later as he was writing *All the President's Men*.[79] That means Woodward rushed back to Washington from New York specifically to talk to his secret source about Segretti and the Canuck Letter, but then forgot to type the critical quote in his contemporaneous notes of the meeting and then failed to tell his reporting partner and his *Post* editors that the source said the letter came from the White House. Instead, the paper relied on two fragmentary confirmations that the letter was part of the FBI investigation and the word of a fellow reporter that Clawson claimed to have written the letter. If Deep Throat was so valuable and had said anything about the letter, it surely would have been included in the story, since the other sourcing was so thin.

As for Segretti, Woodward's source told him twice that he did not know anything about Segretti and could not comment. "Won't talk about Segretti or any others," the notes show. The third page of the notes contains this quote: "I don't know about Segretti. I just don't know. I can't tell you anyway."[80] Nothing in the October 10 *Post* story about Segretti can be traced to Deep Throat. In fact, the only mention of Segretti from a law enforcement source in the story referred to him as "just a small fish in a big pond." Virtually all of the information about Segretti came from one source: Alex Shipley, an assistant attorney general in Tennessee who was quoted as a sole source twenty-one times in the story.[81]

The source also claimed something that eliminated any idea that he worked for the FBI: "Mitchell conducted his invest for 10 days and 'was going crazy—we had guys assigned to him to help.'" As author Ed Gray, Pat Gray's son, has noted in their book, *In Nixon's Web*, the FBI did not have anyone assigned to help Mitchell and company conduct an internal investigation of the Committee to Re-Elect the President. "It was a critical bit of information, but if Woodward wanted to shield his source, he couldn't use it in the book since it identified 'Deep Throat' as being part of a group of insiders 'assigned to help,'" Ed Gray wrote.[82] Woodward's source on October 9 could not have been Felt, because the FBI did not cooperate with the campaign's alleged internal investigation. Dean and the campaign did everything they could to keep the FBI away from them, which was one of the main reasons FBI officials were leaking to the press.

The *Post* was not the only publication covering Watergate, and it was often scooped by one publication to which Felt leaked often—*Time* magazine. Within a week of the *Post* story, *Time* reported that Segretti had been hired by Dwight Chapin, Nixon's appointments secretary and a former fraternity brother. *Time* also reported that Gordon Strachan, the political aide to White

House chief of staff H. R. Haldeman, also had a hand in hiring Segretti, who was paid with $35,000 directed by Herbert Kalmbach, Nixon's lawyer.

Not only was Felt *Time*'s source, but Nixon knew it.

"We know what's left and we know what's leaked and we know who leaked it," Haldeman told Nixon in the Oval Office on October 19.[83]

"Is it somebody in the FBI?" Nixon asked.

Yes, Haldeman said, adding that "the FBI doesn't know who it is. Gray doesn't know who it is . . . And it's very high up."

"Somebody next to Gray?" Nixon asked.

"Mark Felt," Haldeman said.

"Now why the hell would he do that?" Nixon said.

Haldeman said he did not know Felt's motives and that he did not want to endanger their source of the information, who was known only to Mitchell.[84] He knew because *Time*'s outside counsel, former Pentagon official Roswell Gilpatric, told him. Gilpatric also told Mitchell that *Time* had another damaging story about Watergate in the pipeline from the "same source" that tied Magruder and campaign aide Bart Porter to the money that paid for Liddy's activities.

Nixon wanted to retaliate against Felt. He backed off, because he feared Felt would retaliate by spilling more details of the campaign operation to the press. But he urged Haldeman and others to warn Gray about Felt. The White House discovery that Felt was leaking to *Time* closed Felt from any inside information from the White House. Nixon and his top aides considered Felt anathema from October 19, 1972, on, making it very unlikely that anyone at the White House would tell Felt anything he could later tell reporters.

The growing interest in the Watergate story, which surged when Walter Cronkite, the CBS anchorman, devoted thirteen-and-a-half minutes on one broadcast to a detailed explanation of the budding scandal and what it meant, made no difference to Nixon's reelection. On November 7, Nixon beat Democrat George McGovern with almost 61 percent of the popular vote. He carried forty-nine of the fifty states, losing only Massachusetts and the District of Columbia. Nixon capped off a tremendous 1972 with one of the most stunning landslides in American history, and Watergate seemed destined to fade away.

Nixon used his mandate to clean house. He ordered cabinet officials to submit their resignations for a planned reorganization of the entire government. First on his agenda was the CIA, where whatever usefulness Helms had was long gone. On many days, Nixon seemed to think he did not need the Agency at all, as he complained about its elitism and stodgy bureaucracy's lack of creativity. As for Helms's successor, Nixon's focus had shifted. Vernon Walters had fallen out of favor after he refused to block the FBI investigation. Nixon turned to James Schlesinger, the former assistant director at the Office of Management and Budget who was now head of the Atomic Energy Commission. Schlesinger had helped Nixon pressure the CIA with a study to reorganize the intelligence community in 1971, and Nixon knew he would provide even more pressure as director to bring the agency in line.

The end for Helms came two weeks after the election, on November 20. Nixon invited Helms for a meeting at Camp David, which Helms thought would concern the coming year's budget. Nixon started by telling Helms that he had been appointed by Johnson, a Democrat, and that he was looking for new ideas and new blood for the second term. "I had been at the Agency for a long time. It was time to make some personnel changes," Helms would write later.[85] Helms told Nixon he would be sixty in March and at the CIA's retirement age. Nixon, Helms wrote, seemed surprised Helms was that old and that he had been in the intelligence service for thirty years. He then impulsively offered Helms an ambassadorship and mentioned a few countries before they settled on Iran.

On December 21, Nixon made Schlesinger's appointment official. Nixon told Haldeman later that week he had clear goals for his new CIA director. Kissinger and Haig had wasted three years to reform intelligence, Nixon said, so he was delaying the reforms he announced a year earlier. "The Congress is particularly jealous of its authority in the intelligence field," Nixon wrote Haldeman. "If they got the impression that the President has turned all intelligence activities over to Kissinger all hell will break loose."[86] He praised Schlesinger's March 1971 analysis of the intelligence community, with one exception. "On the other hand he does not emphasize as much as I would like the need to improve *quality* as well as reduce *quantity* of top intelligence people in the CIA itself," Nixon told Haldeman. "The CIA, like the State Department, is basically a liberal establishment bureaucracy. I want the personnel there cut in at least half—no, at least by 35 to 40 percent—and I want a definite improvement in so far as attitudes of those in CIA with regard to our foreign policy. There are some very good men there, but the great majority are the old [unclear] Georgetown crowd."[87]

Schlesinger would follow through ruthlessly. The CIA of mid-1973 would look little like the agency that Nixon inherited in January 1969. More than one thousand agents would be terminated, and much of the top leadership would leave. Schlesinger's five months in charge would leave the Agency shaken and vulnerable to future investigations. With his second term secure, Nixon signed off on the evisceration of the intelligence agency that refused to gin up intelligence to suit his needs and the firing of the man who refused to help him cover up the Watergate break-in.

Part II: The Unraveling

CHAPTER SIXTEEN

Early 1973

THE REMAINDER OF NIXON'S FIRST TERM FOCUSED NOT ON WATERGATE, which remained contained, but on Vietnam, where talks with the North Vietnamese had sputtered after Kissinger's announcement in October that peace was at hand. Then the South Vietnamese, who had been excluded from Kissinger's secret talks, balked at the deal. The North Vietnamese used that reluctance to back away, too, leaving Nixon and Kissinger outraged. As he tried to bring South Vietnamese President Nguyen Van Thieu around, Nixon also had to confront the North. Flushed with his reelection success, Nixon had fewer concerns about public opinion on the war. Starting on December 18, he ordered an eleven-day bombing campaign called Linebacker II that mirrored the original series of raids he ordered in May. The raids mostly hit military targets, but they did so with enough ferocity to send the North Vietnamese back to the negotiating table, where they agreed to take the agreement from October. Nixon then had to persuade Thieu. Nixon would not allow Thieu to ruin his deal as he had four years earlier. He dispatched Haig to Saigon, where Haig cajoled Thieu into agreeing with a treaty that Thieu understood was really a choice between future US support and none at all. On January 27, one week into Nixon's second term, all of the parties signed the agreement. All US prisoners of war would return home, while Thieu remained in power in South Vietnam, and North Vietnamese and Viet Cong soldiers kept control of the areas they still held in the south. Kissinger and chief North Vietnamese negotiator Le Duc Tho would eventually win the Nobel Peace Prize for their efforts, but all sides realized it was really the beginning of the "decent interval" between the deal and the fall of South Vietnam.

❧

Despite his successes, Nixon still saw threats all around him, including from within. He resented how Kissinger got the credit for mostly just following

Nixon's orders. Nixon's suspicions that Kissinger boosted his image at Nixon's expense heightened after a December 31 *New York Times* column by James Reston that speculated about a rift between Nixon and Kissinger on the Vietnam negotiations. Nixon, Reston said, would stop the bombing of North Vietnam soon, because Nixon "has made his point to Hanoi, negotiate or suffer, and is ready, as Mr. Kissinger is, to go back to the Paris talks."[1] The president, Reston continued, had also given Thieu a "very hard line" to get him to accept the peace deal. Nixon suspected Kissinger had fed Reston most of the information, and he told Charles Colson to get a record of Kissinger's telephone calls.[2]

Four days later, Colson reported that Kissinger had called columnist Joseph Kraft, whose column was in that day's *Post*. "So you know where that comes from," Nixon said.[3]

On January 10, Nixon returned to the issue again with Haldeman. He wanted a log of Kissinger's calls to track leaks.

"You mean bugged?" Haldeman asked.

"Oh, God, no," Nixon responded, sounding genuinely horrified at the thought. "I don't care what he's saying. I just want to know who he talks to."

Haldeman said he thought they could find a way to get that information, a detail to which Nixon gave one warning:

"Don't do anything that's going to look like we're spying," Nixon said.[4]

— ❧ —

Nixon remade his cabinet for the second term. Elliot Richardson replaced Mel Laird at the Pentagon. James Schlesinger was taking over for Helms at the CIA, but the FBI remained unsettled. Too many of the Bureau's leaders resented acting director L. Patrick Gray for getting the job they wanted. That was especially true for Mark Felt, the top deputy who leaked to undermine Gray. Nixon knew Felt was a leaker, but he was too afraid to fire him. Felt kept leaking into early January, as Nixon still had not signaled who he would pick. In January, Felt told Sandy Smith at *Time* that Gray had started a purge of Hoover allies and, worst of all, was playing politics with the Watergate investigation under White House pressure. "Several agents complained that Gray's spot inspection of the Washington field office in search of the leaks was actually slowing down the Watergate investigation," Smith reported. Gray, the story continued, transferred three FBI officials who pushed the Watergate investigation; one quit instead of moving.[5]

Nixon was livid and so was Gray, who told Felt to investigate the leaks. The result was a memo that Gray suspected was written by a Felt ally, which accused William Sullivan, who was then at the new Office of National

Narcotics Intelligence. The memo also attacked Robert Mardian, the former Justice official who had resurrected Sullivan at ONNI. Nixon's delay in naming a permanent successor to Hoover meant Felt's sniping at Gray and Sullivan would continue. The collateral damage would hit Nixon.[6]

❦

The trial of the five Watergate burglars, plus Howard Hunt and Gordon Liddy, started on January 10. Hunt had threatened the cover-up and the failed break-in as he pressured Colson to pay him, the burglars, and their families if they went to prison. Without the money, the burglars would talk and blow the cover-up. The Cubans knew little about the jobs they were hired to do; they left the details to Hunt, who had also been sharing information with the CIA from the moment he joined the White House in July 1971. Hunt grew more unpredictable after his wife, Dorothy, died on December 8 in the crash of a United Airlines jet near Chicago's Midway Airport. In the wreckage, crash investigators found her purse with $10,000 in cash stuffed inside. Hunt had brazenly showed up the next day in Chicago to try unsuccessfully to claim the money.

Hunt soon realized he had no chance to beat the charges against him. Assistant US Attorney Earl Silbert's case was tightly focused and stuck to the evidence: The burglars had been caught inside the DNC headquarters, and Hunt and Liddy had conspired with them. Hunt pleaded guilty on January 11 to all six counts in the indictment. He did not implicate others and called the break-in something he did "in the best interest of my country."[7] US District Judge John J. Sirica set bail at $100,000. The Cubans followed suit on January 15. They also did not implicate any higher-ups. That frustrated Sirica, who suspected the burglars knew more than they would say and were part of what "looked more and more like a big cover-up."[8] Only Liddy and James McCord remained. Liddy's refusal to talk complicated his case, while McCord claimed that he had only participated because he wanted to protect campaign committee officials from potential harm. The jury believed none of it and took only ninety minutes to convict both men on January 30. Sirica set a sentencing date for March.

Polls showed the public did not take Watergate as seriously as the Washington press corps, despite the increased media attention caused by the trial. Nixon had a 68 percent approval rating in the January Gallup poll.[9] Inside the White House, few felt optimistic. They knew what they were hiding. Sirica's sentencing date meant they had to keep hiding the truth for longer than they believed possible.

On the night of January 30 occurred a random event that would shape the course of the investigation into Nixon's secret government and Watergate, although it was not apparent at the time. Senator John Stennis, the Mississippi Democrat who chaired the Senate Armed Services Committee, was returning to his home in Northwest Washington after dinner with his wife. Three young men appeared in the darkness and confronted the couple. Stennis gave them his watch, wallet, and the change in his pocket before one of them shot Stennis in the left chest and left leg. He collapsed inside his home and was taken to Walter Reed Army Hospital, where he underwent surgery for six-and-a-half hours. His recovery would take months.

Stennis's absence meant that he would be replaced as committee chairman by Senator Stuart Symington, the Missouri Democrat who had been making the White House miserable since the fall of 1969 with his investigation into the secret CIA-led war in Laos and other US commitments abroad. Symington was suspicious of not just the CIA but also Kissinger's continued accumulation of power and the White House's refusal to share what it was doing with Congress. Stennis had already papered over White House problems in Congress, often over Symington's objections. With Stennis in the hospital, Symington would have free rein to run the committee as he saw fit, and he saw no reason to help Nixon.

Preserving the cover-up became more difficult after the Senate voted 77–0 in early February to create a special committee to investigate the Watergate burglary and other 1972 campaign activities. A Senate investigation meant multiple witnesses would testify under oath, increasing the chances that someone would blow Nixon's secrets. Given this atmosphere, it was surprising and reckless that Nixon would pick a permanent director for the FBI and subject him to a potentially dangerous confirmation hearing sure to focus on the Bureau's role in the Watergate investigation.

Since his appointment, Gray had loyally carried out what he thought were Nixon's orders. He had started to clean out some of the dead wood Hoover left behind, and he brought in more female and minority agents. But Gray could not shake the perception, encouraged by Felt, that he was a White House pawn. For example, Gray let Dean sit in on some of the interviews with Nixon campaign officials during the early stages of the Watergate investigation. Dean was the White House lawyer; Gray thought it was not "onerous, just cumbersome" to allow him to represent the officials during questioning.[10] He did not realize Dean was using the information he gathered from those interviews to further the cover-up of the break-in he had ordered. Gray had also acceded to the requests of Richard Helms and Vernon Walters at the CIA to delay interviewing some CIA officials. He did not realize the White House was behind some of the requests. This dedicated, and sometimes naïve, man who could have revived the FBI instead would have to spend years rebuilding his reputation because of his misplaced trust in Nixon. In February 1973, it remained an open question whether Nixon would keep Gray or find another choice to lead the Bureau.

Felt wanted the job but did not know Nixon considered him a traitor. Another aspirant was Sullivan. Sullivan's new job, his oversight of the FBI wiretaps of 1969 to 1971, and his role in the creation of the aborted Huston Plan gave him a unique vantage point; he knew the administration's secrets, its attempts to hide them, and the men trying to unearth them, both in the FBI and the media.

Sullivan was already lobbying potential allies in the administration, including Walters. The two met in early 1973, to which Sullivan followed up with letters on January 23 and February 6 that spelled out their shared vision for a national intelligence system much like that in the aborted Huston Plan. Now, with Hoover dead and Mitchell back practicing law on Wall Street, neither could block Sullivan as they had before. In the January 23 letter, Sullivan told Walters the FBI and CIA should appoint three people to examine the structure of the domestic intelligence community so "the work of one must be directed as to supplement and strengthen the work of the other."[11] He followed up with greater detail on February 6. "As I indicated previously, this country has never actually had a thoroughly professional, high quality, specialized intelligence organization," Sullivan wrote. They had a unique chance to do it with Nixon, because he "recognizes the necessity for valuable intelligence operations, therefore, if we are going to make any real progress here it will have to be done during the next four years while he is at the White House."[12] Sullivan proposed that the government separate intelligence work from criminal matters at the FBI and create a new agency that would cooperate more with the CIA. The beginning of Nixon's second term—with peace on the horizon in Vietnam, arms deals with the Soviets done, and a new relationship with the Chinese—presented a unique chance to do it. "There are storm clouds ahead and I think it would be most unfortunate that when conditions seriously worsen in the future (be it 10 or 20 or 40 years) we had no thoroughly efficient, professional intelligence organization to help our government maintain our historic values and goals," Sullivan continued. "It would seem that in this relative period of quiet, the conditions are as good as they could be to start to build constructively, the kind of intelligence service that this country needs and should have as soon as possible."[13] These were not the words of a man who planned to sit at his newly formed antidrug organization or to drift quietly into retirement. Sullivan was planning his FBI return.

Sullivan had well-placed allies, starting with Alexander Haig, the former NSC deputy who was now the army's vice chief of staff. Haig had long wanted to return to the army, and Nixon granted him his wish in early 1973. Colson suggested Nixon keep Gray for continuity, and for a deputy, Sullivan would be a great candidate. "Al Haig called me yesterday and said Jesus, get Bill Sullivan in there. Al Haig is very high on Sullivan," Colson told Nixon on February 13.[14]

Nixon decided to stick with Gray. He made his official decision after a surreal thirty-minute meeting on February 16 in the Oval Office with Gray and Ehrlichman. Nixon started by asking about Gray's health—he had a serious operation in December—and how he thought he could handle the upcoming wave of Senate hearings on Watergate and the investigation. The meeting then turned into a classic Nixonian rant. He raged about the inability to prove that Johnson had bugged his campaign plane and philosophized about preserving the secrecy that had enabled Nixon's successes. Gray mostly listened, sometimes agreeing to keep the conversation moving and wondering the whole time what had gotten into the president.

Could Gray take the pressure of the confirmation hearings? Nixon wondered.[15] No one could handle it better, Gray said, adding that he thought the FBI had done an excellent job with the Watergate investigation. If Nixon brought in someone new, Gray said, he would be accused of trying to change the subject from Watergate.

Nixon quickly pivoted to his obsession with finding who bugged his campaign plane in 1968. Anyone who knew about the bugging, Nixon demanded, needed to take a lie detector test. But no one had ever bugged Nixon's plane. Hoover had concocted the story because he knew Nixon had derailed a possible breakthrough in the Paris Peace Talks and Hoover wanted to blackmail him with it. It worked; Nixon worried about the bugging constantly. Even Huston's February 25, 1970, memo had no mention of it. The president told Gray that he should bring back Cartha "Deke" DeLoach, the former Hoover deputy who allegedly directed the bugging, for a lie detector, although DeLoach had left the Bureau in 1970. Gray remained noncommittal, but inside "I could not believe what I had just heard," he would write later.

With Gray as director, Nixon wanted to make sure his deputy would also be a loyalist.

"What about this fellow Sullivan, good, bad or indifferent?" Nixon asked. "Would you bring him back?"

"I wouldn't bring him back, at all," Gray said. "I wouldn't touch him at all."

"Why not?" Nixon asked.

"His first words when he came back to Washington, in response to questions from some of the people in the Domestic Intelligence Division as to why he was here, in two words, 'For revenge,'" Gray said. He did not want Sullivan, but he did not tell Nixon he had met with Sullivan twice in the last year, including on July 6 when Nixon called Gray after he had called Clark MacGregor to have Nixon call him.[16] That was when Gray warned him that White House officials were interfering with the Watergate investigation. Gray did not trust Sullivan, which he told Nixon, adding that Sullivan was too nervous and too inarticulate to be in a high position at the FBI. He did not know of Sullivan's contacts with Walters.

Nixon changed the subject to Felt. If Gray kept Felt, Nixon said, he, too, needed to make Felt submit to a polygraph and clear himself. It was another point about trust and loyalty in the one-sided conversation that focused on Nixon's complicated relationships with Hoover and his cabinet. He needed to talk directly with his FBI director, just as he needed the same kind of relationship with the chairman of the Joint Chiefs—Moorer. There had to be total communication with the Bureau, Nixon said, and no leaks. Anyone who leaked should be fired.

"I gotta have a relationship here where you go out and do something and deny on a stack of Bibles," Nixon said. "You gotta get that 'cause I don't have anybody else. I can't hire some asshole from the outside."

The White House announced Gray's appointment the next day.

❦

The first aftershock from Nixon's selection of Gray came a week later when Felt made his most damaging leak to Sandy Smith at *Time*. In Nixon's zeal to find leakers, Smith reported, he had authorized the FBI to listen to the telephone calls of government officials and selected reporters between 1969 and 1971.[17] These were the taps Sullivan coordinated with Kissinger and Haig, and the records Sullivan had taken from the FBI in July 1971 because he thought Hoover would use them to blackmail Nixon. Felt had no operational knowledge of the taps; he had learned of them only in October 1971 after Hoover had fired Sullivan. Only Hoover and Sullivan knew the complete story. Hoover was dead, and Sullivan was not talking. Yet Felt had revealed enough to send the White House into a panic. Attorney General Richard

Kleindienst denied the report. He had never authorized wiretaps, Kleindienst said, and Mitchell told him he had not either.[18] Kleindienst told the truth about his knowledge of wiretaps. They had stopped by the time he became attorney general. Mitchell, however, had lied to Kleindienst. Not only had Mitchell approved the original wiretaps, he had done it in writing.

Inside the White House, Dean tried to find the leaker and reported to Nixon on February 27 and 28. On February 27, Dean said he suspected Felt in part because Felt had tried to pin the leak on Sullivan.[19]

"He said, 'Well, if you talk to Bill Sullivan, he'll tell you all about it,'" Dean told Nixon. "When he did, sort of a general, he painted a general picture about it. Ah, just cool as a cucumber about it."

Despite the accumulation of suspicion about Felt, Nixon determined they could not fire him. He compared Felt to exiled Yeoman Radford, who they sent to a base in Oregon instead of prosecuting him for stealing secret documents.

Not only did Sullivan not leak, Dean said, he was "a wealth-of-knowledge" who can document problems at the FBI. Nixon agreed, saying, "Sullivan knows too much. We owe him something."

Nixon and Dean reiterated their appreciation of Sullivan the next day. Dean said he believed Sullivan's denial about telling *Time* about the wiretaps. "I have watched him for a number of years," Dean said. "I watched him when he was working with Tom Huston on domestic intelligence, and his, in his desire to do the right thing. Uh, I tried to, you know, stay in touch with Bill and to find out what his moods are. Bill was forced on the outside for a long time. He didn't become bitter. He sat back and waited until he could come back in. Uh. He didn't try to force or blackmail his way around, uh, with knowledge he had. So, I, I have no signs of anything but a reliable man who thinks a great deal of this Administration and of, and of you."

Meanwhile, Felt "worries me," Dean said. Even if Gray is confirmed, the problems will only get more complicated, and Felt is not reliable, he said.[20]

Dean continued to rely on Sullivan, who considered Dean another ally to help him to return to the FBI. As Dean told Nixon, he and Sullivan had worked together a handful of times when Sullivan was at the Bureau, and at least once Dean called Sullivan to ask for an FBI background check on a woman Dean was dating. On March 1, Sullivan sent Dean a memo advising the White House to be as open as possible but try to limit the Senate's investigation. Each issue, Sullivan wrote, should "be faced openly, briefly and without equivocation."[21] A lengthy Senate investigation would expose

Sullivan's wiretapping for the White House. He had to discredit the *Time* story, because it implicated him in the unsavory business of spying on the press. He met with Woodward on March 5 at a bar near his longtime home in suburban Prince George's County, Maryland.[22] Inside the bar, which Woodward described as "an old wooden house which had been converted into a saloon for truckers and construction workers," Sullivan pitched Woodward a tale of a "vigilante squad" in the Justice Department run by former Assistant Attorney General Robert Mardian that spied on journalists.[23] Woodward's notes, now archived at the University of Texas in Austin, show that Sullivan told Woodward that "Mardian headed an out-of-channels vigilante squad of wiretappers that did, as *Time* reported, tap phones of reporters, including Hedrick Smith and Neil Sheehan for several weeks after *Times* refused to stop Pentagon Papers publication. authorization by Mitchell and FBI only found out about it indirectly. said this was very closely held knowledge and Gray could deny it under oath because his knowledge was 'out of channels.'"[24] Sullivan, Woodward's notes showed, "said he presumed that Hunt or Liddy, or at least Liddy, worked on the squad. this is part of the reason that Mitchell and Mardian are out. said everything is destroyed about it and only maybe six to eight people have firsthand knowledge of it." Mardian's team, Sullivan continued, eventually became a political operation at Haldeman's request.

In *All the President's Men*, Woodward identified the source of this information as Deep Throat, who Woodward identified in 2005 as Felt. But Felt was not the person who met Woodward at the bar.

Four distinct pieces of evidence point to Sullivan as the source on March 5. Only Sullivan used the term *out of channels* when referring to the FBI wiretaps. Mardian told FBI investigators in May 1973 that Sullivan used that term in reference to the taps, and Mardian repeated that when he testified before the Senate Watergate Committee in July.[25] Sullivan also peddled the false vigilante squad story to others, particularly Senator Lowell Weicker, the Connecticut Republican and member of the Watergate committee. FBI files and Weicker's notes detail Sullivan's allegations about Mardian to Weicker, which were also reported in October 1973 by the *New York Daily News*.[26] "The Sullivan interviews, undertaken over the past several weeks by committee member Sen. Lowell P. Weicker (R-Conn.), reportedly have elicited a number of 'solid leads' from the onetime FBI official," the *Daily News* reported.[27] "Sources said Sullivan had implicated former Assistant Attorney General Robert C. Mardian in the alleged White House dictated spy plot against the Democratic Party." The source's comments on March 5 were completely different from what Felt told Sandy Smith a week earlier. If Felt wanted to damage Gray and Sullivan, he would have repeated the same story to Woodward. The fact the source concocted a false story to divert Woodward's attention from the real FBI wiretaps shows he had something to hide, and Sullivan had more to hide than most. Finally, the bar was close to Sullivan's home in suburban Maryland, while Felt lived in Fairfax, Virginia. The sole beneficiary of Deep Throat's tip to Woodward on March 5 was Sullivan, because it shifted the focus from the wiretaps and him to Mardian, who was under investigation for his connections to Watergate. In that context, the accusation of Mardian made sense. Because Sullivan's tip to Woodward was so misleading, it lingered in the reporter's notes for almost two months, as he and Bernstein struggled unsuccessfully to corroborate it.

Gray was faring poorly during his confirmation hearings before the Senate Judiciary Committee. He had little knowledge of just how much Nixon and company had not told him about Watergate or the cover-up. So Gray honestly answered the committee's questions, which set off meetings inside the White House about how to shut him up and limit the damage. Under questioning from skeptical committee Democrats, the guileless Gray acknowledged that he had allowed Dean to monitor FBI interviews of Nixon campaign aides during the Watergate investigation. Gray told the committee that, despite his initial resistance, he had given Dean some of the FBI's Watergate files. Against the White House's wishes, Gray told the committee he would open the raw FBI files to any member who wanted to come to the FBI to examine them. "We have nothing to hide," Gray said, not realizing just how much Nixon was hiding.

Dean increasingly turned to Sullivan as Gray self-destructed. Sullivan, Dean told Nixon on March 6, had a vast archive of damaging information about previous FBI activities on behalf of Johnson, who had used the Bureau as a private investigative service. Nixon wanted to use that information to discredit Democrats and defend himself. "It doesn't make any difference whether it's hearsay or not," Nixon told Dean. "The game—this game—is not played according to the rules. It's played according to the headlines. . . . Do you understand?"[28]

A week later, Dean and Nixon talked about using a willing Sullivan again. The one risk, Dean said, is what Sullivan would say under oath about the wiretaps or the Huston Plan, which remained a secret. They could limit Sullivan's testimony to national security issues, Nixon said. "And that is totally true."[29]

By March 13, Nixon, Dean, Ehrlichman, and Haldeman all realized the Senate would not confirm Gray, who was pulling them deeper into the growing Watergate quagmire. Gray had exposed Dean's role in the cover-up. Now, the committee wanted Dean to testify, which Nixon fought bitterly. Nixon and Dean spent the next week in the Oval Office trying to repair the cover-up, including the creation of a bogus "Dean report" aimed at absolving the White House of any complicity in the break-in or the cover-up. They discussed on March 13 how Gordon Strachan, one of Haldeman's aides, knew about the Watergate break-in before it happened, which put the White House in the middle of the burglary planning.[30] That revelation shocked Nixon into actively working on the cover-up. Dean expressed confidence their plan would work. "We will win," he told Nixon at the end of a particularly involved meeting on March 16.[31]

Dean presented Nixon with a series of disturbing details that week. On March 17, he told Nixon that "idiots" Hunt and Liddy burglarized the office of Dr. Lewis Fielding, Daniel Ellsberg's psychiatrist, in September 1971. Armed with CIA equipment, they photographed the offices and files and then gave the camera and unexposed film to the CIA, Dean said. The agency still had not determined the meaning of what it had, Dean added, "But it wouldn't take a very sharp investigator very long because you've got pictures in the CIA files that they had to turn over to Justice."[32]

Nixon was shaken. "This is the first I ever heard of this," he said. "Jesus Christ."

Maybe the information would not reach the Senate committee, Nixon speculated, although Dean added that the Justice Department had CIA documents from the Fielding burglary that could end up in the Senate's hands. Dean had already tried to get the CIA to remove the files from the Justice Department, but the agency had refused.

Justice's files, Dean said, included "pictures which the CIA developed and they've got Gordon Liddy standing proud as punch outside this doctor's office with his name on it. And it's this material, it's not going to take very long for an investigator to go back and say, why would this somebody be at the doctor's office, and they'd find out that there was a break-in at the doctor's office, and then you'd find Liddy on the staff, and then you'd start working it back. I don't think they'll ever reach that point," Dean added naively.[33]

~~~

The dam Dean tried to build around the Watergate burglars cracked on March 23. That's when Sirica read in open court a letter McCord had delivered to him on March 20 in which he told the judge there had been political pressure on the burglars to keep quiet, perjury by key witnesses in the trial of the burglars, and knowledge of the cover-up by high-ranking White House officials. "This is it, this is it, this is the break I've been hoping for," Sirica thought to himself when he read the letter in his chambers.[34] He knew the burglars had been paid to keep quiet and that there was more to the break-in.

Gray's situation continued to erode. He had told the Judiciary Committee that Dean had lied to the FBI when agents asked him if Hunt had a White House office. Despite Gray's candor, more committee members said they would not vote to confirm him. Gray acknowledged the inevitable on April 5 and withdrew his name from consideration but would remain as acting director until Nixon named a successor.[35] Sullivan's candidacy, aided by his assistance of Dean and Nixon, had new life. The initial public speculation in the media named Justice Department criminal chief Henry Petersen as a possible replacement, as well as a forty-two-year-old federal judge in California—W. Matthew Byrne.

~~~

Byrne was not immediately available, because he was presiding in Los Angeles over the federal espionage case of Daniel Ellsberg and Anthony Russo for the publication of the Pentagon Papers. Federal prosecutors had stumbled in their efforts to convict the two men. Byrne declared a mistrial in December 1972, ruling that the four months between the seating of a jury and the beginning of the actual trial was too long. The second trial started in January, and the government prosecutors strove to prove that Ellsberg had taken the classified papers and illegally given them to reporters at the *New York Times*. But the defendants' attorneys, who had successfully maneuvered the case into the first mistrial, kept the prosecutors off balance. A series of defense witnesses testified that the disclosure of US programs in the Pentagon Papers did not harm national security.

Gray's withdrawal gave the White House the chance to gain favor with Byrne, whose rulings had already hampered the prosecution, by dangling the FBI job in front of him. Ehrlichman met with Byrne on April 5 in San Clemente, California, site of Nixon's California White House, and again two days later in Santa Monica. Both times Byrne told Ehrlichman he had to see the Ellsberg trial to the end; anything else would be unethical. Byrne said nothing publicly, and neither did the White House. The trial continued, and the government's case continued to unravel.

Back in Washington, Assistant US Attorney and Watergate prosecutor Earl Silbert wrote an astonishing memo on April 16 that told his superiors what Dean had told Nixon a month earlier: Hunt and Liddy had led the burglary into Ellsberg's psychiatrist's office. Nixon and Dean had worried the news would reach the Senate Watergate Committee, and also kill the case against Ellsberg, if the judge or defense learned of it. For whatever reason, they did not learn of it for another eleven days. The White House Plumbers had now officially entered the Ellsberg trial.

—◆—

The White House received two more pieces of bad news on April 27. In Washington, Gray acknowledged that he received papers taken from Hunt's White House office shortly after the Watergate break-in. Instead of turning the papers to his own bureau's investigators, Gray took the papers, which Dean and Ehrlichman said were politically explosive, home and burned them six months later. Before burning the documents, Gray scanned them and determined they were sensitive national security documents from the Kennedy administration. They were actually forgeries Hunt had created to discredit Kennedy in the wake of the Pentagon Papers publication. At the time he was given the documents, Gray had thought little of it. Dean and Ehrlichman said they had nothing to do with Watergate. But in April, a humiliated and embarrassed Gray was shown to have potentially obstructed justice. He had to resign, and his friend Henry Petersen, the head of the Justice Department's criminal division, told him he needed to get a lawyer. "Pat, I'm not kidding," Petersen said. "We're in deep trouble here."[36]

In Los Angeles, Hunt's name appeared in a different context. Byrne announced in court that he had received Silbert's memo detailing the break-in at Fielding's office to steal Ellsberg's files.[37] The revelations Nixon had feared would come in the Senate had now emerged in open court. Ellsberg and Russo exulted, and even though Byrne said the trial would continue, the prosecutors reeled from the damage to their case.

The next day, White House press aide David Gergen, who knew Woodward at Yale, reported to Nixon about conversations he had with Woodward about the leads the reporter was pursuing. "Last night, after receiving an urgent call from reporter Bob Woodward that the *Post* was agonizing over a story would implicate RN in a 'cover-up,' Len Garment and I met with him privately in my office for some 90 minutes," Gergen wrote to press secretary Ronald Ziegler.[38] Woodward was particularly interested in Liddy and Hunt, who had been linked the day before to the Fielding break-in and whom Sullivan had mentioned in his March 5 meeting with Woodward. Under the label "Department of Dirty Tricks," Gergen said, "Interest in this one is accelerating. They have concluded that Hunt and Liddy became 'WH burglers [sic]'; they not only broke into things but also installed a number of wiretaps 'in the guise of national security.' Mardian and Mitchell were both tied into it, according to their sources."[39] In essence, Woodward reported to Gergen the key details of what Sullivan told Woodward on March 5—the bogus story of the Mardian-run vigilante squad that used Liddy and Hunt to tap reporters' telephones. Woodward would talk often with Gergen, tipping him off to the details of his reporting while seeking more information. Finally, Gergen noted, Woodward was acting like more than just a reporter. "It's almost as if he's playing the role of midwife now and wants to help the process," Gergen wrote.[40]

By April 30, the pressures of the Watergate scandal had become too much for Nixon's inner circle. His chief of staff, H. R. Bob Haldeman, and Ehrlichman both resigned. So did Attorney General Richard Kleindienst. Dean, who had begun cooperating with prosecutors because he feared he would become the scapegoat for Watergate, was fired. The core team handling the Watergate cover-up was now gone, and Nixon, who still had no desire to come clean about whatever role he had in Watergate, was alone and exposed.

CHAPTER SEVENTEEN

May 1973

As May 1973 opened, Nixon had lost his most dependable aides—Haldeman and Ehrlichman. Dean's departure also meant Nixon had no staff lawyer who really knew about Watergate and the cover-up. Nixon needed help as each day in May delivered a new disaster to the White House. His problems extended beyond Washington to Los Angeles, where new revelations in the Pentagon Papers case had fused it to Watergate for the first time, which would eventually reveal details at the heart of Nixon's secret government.

◄──✤──►

On May 2, Judge Matthew Byrne had again lost patience with the Justice Department, because it had not answered his questions about the ties between Watergate and Ellsberg.[1] Byrne knew that Hunt and Liddy had burglarized Ellsberg's psychiatrist's office, but he suspected the connections went beyond Ehrlichman. While Nixon had made him a judge, Byrne was no pawn of Nixon's like Charles Richey, who repaid Nixon's appointment by derailing the Democrats' lawsuit against the Nixon campaign for the Watergate break-in. Byrne surprised those in court by saying he had met with Ehrlichman twice in April to discuss the FBI director's job. Both times Byrne said he would not consider the FBI position while the Papers case was pending.

Little in the forty-two-year-old Byrne's background made him a logical candidate to lead the FBI. He had been the US attorney in Los Angeles and in private practice before joining the bench in 1972. Byrne did, however, control the course of the Ellsberg trial and could, as Richey did with the DNC lawsuit, bottle up evidence that would hurt the White House. Byrne's announcement killed that possibility, and the defense team argued that the Ehrlichman overture had damaged Byrne's objectivity.

Frustrated and embarrassed, Byrne told the defense to submit legal precedents that would support either a mistrial or a dismissal. The prosecution was running out of time to save its case.

In Washington, the Plumbers team collapsed. Egil Krogh, who had joined the Transportation Department, took a leave of absence as his role was exposed. David Young resigned from the White House staff. Hunt testified before a grand jury and admitted his role with Liddy in breaking into Fielding's office in pursuit of damaging material on Ellsberg.

~~~

The May 3 *Washington Post* featured a front-page story by Woodward and Bernstein that added a new, but misleading, dimension to the deepening mystery of the Plumbers. "The Nixon administration tapped the telephones of at least two newspaper reporters in 1971 as part of the investigation reportedly ordered by President Nixon into the leaks of the Pentagon Papers to the press, according to two highly placed sources in the executive branch," the story started.[2] It said Hunt and Liddy had been part of a "vigilante squad" of former FBI officials who had tapped reporters to find the Pentagon Papers leaker. Mitchell had approved the team's wiretaps, the story continued, but Mardian ran the operation. Woodward and Bernstein mentioned the February 26 *Time* story by Sandy Smith that first revealed the FBI wiretaps but cited a source saying that "the only wiretapping of reporters and White House aides known to the *Post*'s sources were conducted by the vigilante squads of professional wiretappers and ex-CIA and ex-FBI agents—not by the FBI. 'They were out of FBI channels,' one source stressed."

This story contradicted much of what *Time* reported in February, because Woodward's source—William Sullivan—deliberately misled him to hide his role in the wiretaps. No other source than Sullivan referred to wiretaps as "out of channels," and no other source had the reason to lie about them. Mark Felt had told Smith the truth in February, and it made no sense for him to tell Woodward something completely different a week later. It did for Sullivan, however, because he was working with Dean to cover up the wiretaps. Woodward's notes now at the University of Texas also show his second source, then-Justice official Donald Santarelli, confirmed the wiretaps only obliquely, and Santarelli would later acknowledge that he learned about the taps from Sullivan.[3] The story, as author Max Holland wrote in his 2012 book, *Leak*, was "grossly inaccurate."[4] Mardian never ran a vigilante squad, and Liddy never wiretapped *Times* reporters. There was never a meeting of the campaign committee to discuss bringing over the vigilante team to bug Democratic candidates, as the duo reported, because there was never

a vigilante team to start with. FBI agents, not former Bureau or CIA operatives, conducted the wiretaps between 1969 and 1971. While Woodward and
Bernstein would later insist that Deep Throat only confirmed information
they developed from other sources, the May 3 story was based on an original
tip and quoted Sullivan six times as a sole source.[5]

The story had such an impact because the fascination with the Plumbers
was at its peak. Only Sullivan knew how wrong it was. The story incorrectly
conflated the Plumbers, the 1969 to 1971 FBI wiretaps, the COINTELPRO
program, and Mardian's leadership of the joint Intelligence Evaluation Committee into a stew of alleged illegal activities that smacked of a police state.
Many, starting with Byrne, believed the worst. He asked the FBI's new acting
director, William Ruckelshaus, to see if Ellsberg, Russo, or anyone else connected to the Ellsberg trial were on those taps.[6]

Byrne also demanded Hunt's grand jury testimony from the previous
day, in which Hunt said he and Liddy broke into Fielding's office. "The burden is on the government to prove that neither the Justice Department nor
the White House nor the Watergate conspirators had interfered with the
constitutional rights of Dr. Ellsberg and Mr. Russo" and hurt the case, Byrne
said.[7] Byrne also revealed that unnamed high-ranking administration officials had refused to tell the FBI about the connections between Watergate
and the Pentagon Papers. He gave the defense a letter in which Assistant
US Attorney Earl Silbert refused to say who had told him on April 15 that
Hunt and Liddy had done the Fielding break-in.[8] That source would later be
revealed as John Dean, who had told Nixon of the break-in a month earlier.
"There are holes in the investigation," Byrne told prosecutors in court. "I'm
not going to, day after day, make mention of this to the Government, make
it clear what the burden is on the Government to find out what did occur."[9]

In the White House, Nixon still had no chief of staff or counsel. He
was relying on Leonard Garment, his former New York law partner, to do
some of the counsel's work, but Nixon never completely trusted him. Richard
Kleindienst, the recently resigned attorney general, told Nixon Garment had
done some of the recent legal work, but Nixon said Garment needed to be
kept under control.[10]

Garment entered the Oval Office two hours later. Garment recommended Nixon use executive privilege as a "scalpel, rather than a blunt
instrument," and that while conversations between Nixon and his staff
were privileged, they risked the appearance of trying to cover up embarrassing or criminal activities. Nixon acknowledged the need to prevent the
appearance of a cover-up. He could not believe Hunt and Liddy's careless-
ness. "Crazy Hunt borrowed a camera from the CIA when he was working

there," Nixon said. "He returned it to the CIA. There was a roll of film on it. The roll of film had a picture of these two clowns standing in front of the psychiatrist's office."[11]

Nixon also had to hire a new chief of staff. Haldeman, who still spoke to Nixon every day, had only one suggestion—Haig, who was now a four-star general and vice chief of staff of the army. Chuck Colson also endorsed Haig. Few people knew more administration secrets than Haig. He had coordinated the FBI wiretaps, was Kissinger's White House contact after his secret meetings in China, and he twisted Thieu's arm to get him to agree to the Vietnam peace agreement. Haig knew what he was getting into, including Nixon's fits of drinking and incoherence. Haig knew the military distrusted Nixon and felt he had sold them out in Vietnam and with China. But while Haig knew Nixon's secrets, the president did not know Haig's. Nixon did not know Haig had helped the Pentagon spy on him or that Haig had cooked up a report that whitewashed his connections to the spies. Neither Ehrlichman nor Haldeman knew about that. If he had, Haldeman said later, he would not have recommended Haig.[12] Nixon asked Haig to be his chief of staff after a five-minute meeting before Nixon flew to Florida for a long weekend. Haig would start the next day, when Garment, who was already falling out of favor with Nixon, would also be announced as Dean's replacement.

On May 4, his new acting FBI director William Ruckelshaus was ordering a full investigation into the Bureau's wiretaps. An angry Byrne wanted answers about the alleged vigilante squad, so Ruckelshaus told Mark Felt to find out everything he could, especially who ran them and who had asked for them. Ruckelshaus also noted that Felt's office had provided Sullivan's personnel file, which had confirmed the existence of the taps. Once again, Felt was making sure to pin the blame for the wiretaps on Sullivan, just as he had done with Dean in late February shortly after Felt had told Sandy Smith at *Time* magazine about the taps.

With Gray's withdrawal and resignation, only Sullivan remained of Felt's serious rivals for the director's job. By continuing to tie Sullivan to the controversial wiretaps, which were destroying the Ellsberg prosecution, Felt could undermine Sullivan's chances. He did not realize—and neither did anyone other than Sullivan and Bob Woodward—that the impetus for this final chance to destroy Sullivan had come from Sullivan himself and his bogus claims to Woodward two months earlier.

Nixon remained in Key Biscayne, where his daily logs show he spent most of the day with friends Bebe Rebozo and Robert Abplanalp and had a solitary twelve-minute call with Haig, his new chief of staff.[13] It is also around this time that Haig learned of another of Nixon's deep secrets—the taping system that recorded almost all of his meetings and telephone calls. Alexander Butterfield, the former Haldeman aide who supervised the system's installation in February 1971, was an old friend of Haig. He later said under oath that he told Haig of the system within a few days of Haig taking the job, as did Steve Bull, another aide who knew about the system.[14] Kissinger would also recall that Haig had told him about the tapes in early May. Just when Haig knew about the tapes is critical in understanding his actions as chief of staff, many of which seemed aimed at undermining, not protecting, the man who had just hired him.

At the White House, aide David Gergen was still talking with Woodward. They spoke again on May 5, and, as he did on April 28, Woodward repeated information that Sullivan had provided to him in March. "According to sources they do have—and one in particular, who has a 'cosmic view' and has been their best source throughout—a dirty trick department was set up back in 1969," Gergen wrote Len Garment.[15] "It was run by Mitchell and Mardian and was manned mostly by ex-FBI types, most of whom were very clever." That was essentially a repeat performance of Sullivan's claims of a bogus "vigilante squad" of former FBI agents who spied on journalists. Woodward's source with the "cosmic view" said Mardian/Mitchell tapped the phones of government officials and reporters to track national security leaks, again what Sullivan told Woodward in March. Woodward also told Gergen that his source talked about "infiltration and spying on a number of radical and fringe groups. (Hasn't the government always done that?)"[16] That was again a combination of what Sullivan was telling the committee and a hint at COINTELPRO, which Sullivan helped create and oversee. The source's claims, which would materialize again in a May 17 story, matched closely what Sullivan was telling Senator Lowell Weicker and his staff on the Watergate Committee. Just as in March, the source's claims were riddled with errors. Mardian, for example, could not have run a "dirty tricks" squad with Mitchell in 1969, because Mardian had not yet joined Justice to work for Mitchell.[17]

Gergen would report to Garment again on May 8 and 10 to relay the latest information from Woodward, whom he called "our reporter friend."[18]

The White House's Ellsberg cover-up took another hit on May 7 when Seymour Hersh of the *New York Times* reported that General Robert Cushman, the commandant of the US Marine Corps and the former deputy director of the CIA, had agreed to provide CIA help for the Plumbers in July 1971.[19] FBI agents had questioned Cushman the previous week, which Nixon and his team did not know. The Cushman interview weakened the president's executive privilege claims, since it would be difficult to keep other administration officials from testifying if Cushman had already done so. Cushman showed that not only did Ehrlichman know what the Plumbers planned to do, he had solicited the help of an agency prohibited from working in the United States. Cushman's testimony also implicated the CIA officials in the Plumbers' work and what secrets the White House wanted to keep and the covert operations it was running outside normal government channels.

Hersh's report also showed just how much information Dean had taken with him when he left the White House. Dean, Hersh wrote, had told prosecutors of the Fielding break-in in April when he decided to save himself by going to the prosecutors. That led to Silbert's April 16 memo that finally surfaced eleven days later in the Ellsberg trial.

Both the CIA and a congressional committee used Cushman's revelations to start their own investigations. CIA director James Schlesinger ordered the agency to determine what it did to help Hunt and the Plumbers. Schlesinger also asked Agency employees to come forward if they knew of any activity that may have violated the CIA charter.[20]

◆━━◆

Haig made his first appearance as chief of staff on the morning of May 8. Haig gave Nixon a willing sounding board, and Haig happily told the president exactly what he wanted to hear. Only one person, Dean, was trying to tear down the president, Nixon said, wildly underestimating the number of adversaries he had. Dean posed such a threat, because he was the president's lawyer and knew too much. Dean, Haig said, was "a sniveling coward," to which Nixon responded: "We must destroy him." The situation, Nixon said, was not his fault but was caused by "well-intentioned stupid people."[21]

◆━━◆

In Los Angeles, Byrne received two memoranda from the CIA that confirmed Cushman's ties to the Plumbers, which Byrne promptly gave to the defense. The first memo contained details from two CIA agents about their meetings with Hunt, while the second showed that Cushman's contacts with Hunt started with a July 22, 1971, meeting in which Hunt asked for fake identification papers and disguises. Both documents were also two more pieces of evidence to support the theory that the CIA had organized the Watergate break-in.[22]

That theory was attacked in a memo by burglar James McCord obtained by the *Times* on May 8. McCord said his lawyer, Gerald Alch, had told him his personnel files could be altered to show McCord had been restored to emergency duty by the CIA shortly before the June break-in in order, McCord claimed, to implicate the Agency in the break-in. Schlesinger would be subpoenaed and asked to testify and take responsibility for the agency's role in any trial. McCord said he refused to go along with the plan, which angered Hunt. McCord's memo went beyond the mechanics of the failed burglary. He wrote that Nixon and White House officials wanted to bully the agency and control its intelligence operatives "in order to make them conform to 'White House policy.'" McCord also claimed Nixon fired Helms to install his own man in the agency. Nixon wanted to "lay the foundation for claiming that the Watergate operation had been a CIA operation" and that "Helms had been fired for it."[23]

❦

The FBI investigation into the wiretaps had contacted dozens of current and former Bureau employees. By May 8, it was clear that Sullivan realized that investigators knew his role in the program. Sullivan also knew enough from his friends in the Bureau that both the White House and FBI needed a scapegoat, which Sullivan did not plan to be. He reached out to reporter John Crewdson, who covered the FBI for the *New York Times*. For years, Crewdson did not acknowledge Sullivan's role as a source but told author Max Holland in 2012 that he would still not reveal his source even if he, as Sullivan did, "died in a hunting accident in 1977."[24]

Sullivan told Crewdson that at least three newspaper reporters had been tapped—William Beecher and Hedrick Smith of the *New York Times* and Henry Brandon of the *Sunday Times* of London.[25] Sullivan said Hoover had refused to approve the taps without written authorization, which Mitchell then provided. Much of what Sullivan told Crewdson matched the ongoing FBI probe, but the story allowed him to get ahead of the investigation. Crewdson's story also omitted Sullivan's role coordinating the wiretaps with Haig and Kissinger. Instead, Crewdson wrote that Sullivan had kept the wiretap records at Hoover's request and then, fearing Hoover would try to blackmail Nixon to keep his job, Sullivan had given Mardian the record, which later ended up in a safe in Ehrlichman's office.

Nixon ended May 8 with Haig narrowing his search for a new lawyer to handle the growing Watergate problems. After proposing two Democrats—his former associate at the Pentagon, Joseph Califano, and venerable trial lawyer Edward Bennett Williams, Haig suggested J. Fred Buzhardt, a fellow West Point alumnus who was the counsel to the Defense Department, where he and Haig had helped concoct an "investigation" that whitewashed Haig's role in the Joint Chiefs' spy ring. Buzhardt knew how to put a wall around a growing problem and had enough relationships on Capitol Hill to help Nixon shore up his eroding support there.

In his memoirs, Haig claimed that he "turned, without enthusiasm," to Buzhardt, who had "limited experience and no national reputation as an expert in criminal law."[26] But Haig's taped conversations with Nixon show he enthusiastically recommended Buzhardt, whom Nixon did not know. It took Haig some persuading to get Nixon to come around. By the end of the day, Nixon had agreed, saying that he knew he could count on Buzhardt's loyalty. "I think that's [the] best thing to do, Al."[27]

Buzhardt would take the job while also keeping his post as the Pentagon's counsel. That gave him an immediate conflict of interest, especially since many of the issues plaguing Nixon involved the military.

On May 9, Schlesinger told the Senate Appropriations Committee that Cushman was correct in describing the agency's help for Hunt and Liddy, calling it "an ill-advised act."[28] At the State Department, two officials said they let Hunt copy 240 highly classified documents about Vietnam as he researched Ellsberg. The Pentagon, however, refused to give Hunt access to similar information from its files because his request came from the White House and not the Justice Department.[29]

In the White House, Nixon and Haig continued to prepare for whatever they feared Dean would drop in the Senate or with the prosecutors. Nixon insisted he would not give any ground on executive privilege. Their actions were solely motivated by national security, Nixon said, and releasing too many documents would destroy the government. "I mean Goddamn it, we've got leaks all the time. What the hell do we do?"[30]

One person could help save them, Nixon told Haig—Sullivan. "You get Sullivan in and say, now look here, we're getting it bad down here," Nixon said. "We want to know everything you got on what Johnson and Bobby Kennedy did."[31] Neither realized that Sullivan had already betrayed Nixon by giving Crewdson the details of the FBI wiretaps. Now Nixon, Haig, and soon Buzhardt would be relying on someone who could no longer be trusted.

They would never realize to whom Sullivan was providing information or that Sullivan had betrayed the president.

—◆—

By day's end, Buzhardt joined Haig and Nixon in the Oval Office for their first joint strategy session. Before his arrival, Haig touted his old friend's performance in an earlier meeting that day. Haig also undermined Garment, the nominal White House counsel. Regardless of his flaws, Garment was loyal to Nixon. But Haig had maneuvered Nixon so that he would be relying on a newcomer, Buzhardt, who had greater loyalty to Haig and the military than to the president. "You've got me thinking Buzhardt," Nixon said.[32]

When Buzhardt finally entered the Oval Office, Nixon quickly tried to sway his new attorney by continuing to lie about what he knew about the cover-up and when he knew it. "I just want you to know I didn't know anything about the Goddamn Watergate, as far as the so-called—the whole business of payments and all that crap is concerned," Nixon said. "It was in March when I finally got a whiff of it, on March 21, and started my own investigation. That's it."

Buzhardt responded by demonstrating his own skills at burying controversies. Senator Stennis, he explained, would provide useful cover for Nixon in the Senate, because his colleagues respected him and knew Stennis had helped them entomb bad news. "They call him the conscience of the Senate; others call him the undertaker, depending on which way you look at it," Buzhardt said. "But he has handled almost all of their major problems in the Senate. He's the one voice for their own protection. They've never been in a position to question him when it came to what was the right thing to do for the Senate."[33]

Nixon warmed to the idea. Maybe Stennis could limit what he considered the blood lust of the Senate Democrats. Mitchell was going to be indicted, Nixon said, and his top two aides had been forced to quit. "What the hell more do they want?" he asked. "You know what they want. They want blood."

Nixon ended his day with a final call to Haig. He did not want to give an inch on executive privilege. Buzhardt had also won him over.

"This fellow is our friend, and he's my friend and totally trustworthy," Nixon told Haig. "And if he turns out to be a John Dean, we'll fry your ass, too."[34]

—◆—

In Los Angeles, Byrne released an affidavit from Ruckelshaus that showed the current status of the FBI's investigation into the wiretaps. Ellsberg, Ruckelshaus reported, had been overheard on one wiretap, which was placed on the home telephone of Morton Halperin, the NSC aide who had once been considered Kissinger's main deputy. An FBI employee, Ruckelshaus wrote, recalled that Ellsberg had been overheard on a wiretap on Morton Halperin's home telephone in late 1969 or early 1970. The details were problematic for the White House, because Halperin had left the NSC by September 1969, despite Kissinger's pleading that he stay. Tapping Halperin when he worked at the NSC was legal if Nixon was worried about him leaking information to someone outside the administration. But any tap after September 1969 could have been illegal. Halperin was then a private citizen without access to the White House secrets he once knew about. That made the Halperin wiretap for political, not national security, purposes.

Ruckelshaus's internal investigation reached Sullivan when a written list of twenty-five questions arrived in Sullivan's office at the Office of National Narcotics Intelligence.[35] It focused on who knew and did what as part of the wiretaps. The last question raised the issue that had bedeviled the White House since the *Time* magazine story in late February: "There have been leaks of FBI data concerning this matter to *Time* magazine and possibly other periodicals. Are you aware of the source of any such leaks? If so, provide details."[36]

From the moment the May 11 *New York Times* landed on the doorsteps and desks of administration officials in Washington, Nixon would be besieged on multiple fronts. Sullivan's leak to Crewdson appeared headlined "69 Phone Taps Reported on Newsmen at 3 Papers."[37] Crewdson reported that the FBI wiretaps ordered by Nixon after the *Times* broke the story about the secret bombings in Cambodia in May 1969 involved reporters at the *Times*, *Times* of London, and the *Washington Post*. William Beecher and Hedrick Smith of the *Times* were named as reporters who were tapped, but no one by name at the *Post* was listed. Halperin, who was listed in Ruckelshaus's memo to Byrne, was identified as the one government official under surveillance. Crewdson wrote that the taps seemed to focus on leaks about the conduct of the SALT talks, and Brandon told Crewdson that he had written about SALT in May 1971 and had "a good deal of exclusive information in it and may well have aroused their attention."

Sullivan, Crewdson's main source, appeared in the story as a glorified file clerk who only kept the wiretap records in his office and then gave them to

Mardian to stop Hoover from blackmailing Nixon. One source told Crewdson that Sullivan had given the wiretap records to Mardian in a power play against Hoover, while others said he only gave the details to Mardian upon a legitimate request from the attorney general.[38]

Sullivan's leak threw the White House into disarray. It showed how the White House had improperly targeted journalists who were simply doing their jobs. Nixon, it seemed, knew no limits when it came to trampling on Americans' civil liberties. Sullivan's leak also undermined Felt.

Nixon and Haig continued to believe naively that Sullivan would save them. Haig told Nixon he thought Sullivan would testify that Hoover authorized the wiretaps to stop leaks and that Kissinger received the wiretap memos.[39] Haig knew this was untrue. Hoover only conducted the wiretaps at Nixon's request and only after Mitchell had approved them in writing. Since Hoover was no longer alive to contradict anyone, he became the convenient scapegoat for activity that Kissinger himself had demanded.

Haig pinpointed the White House's real problem with the taps. Nixon could claim they were meant to track national security leaks when they were placed on NSC or Pentagon officials. It was when they veered to other targets, such as White House speechwriter William Safire, that they crossed the line into political spying and illegal activities.

Instead of suspecting Sullivan as the leaker to the *Times*, Nixon focused on Felt. Haig said Elliot Richardson and Sullivan had told him that Felt did it. "Well, [Felt] used to leak to *Time* magazine," Nixon said. "He's a bad guy, you see . . ."

"Very bad," Haig responded. "He's got to go."

"He's got to go," Nixon said. "You still don't have anybody worth a damn at the FBI."

The one person who had been at the FBI who was worth anything was Sullivan, Nixon said. "He knows everything," Haig said. "And he is 100 percent behind you. . . . He's a patriot, that's why." Sullivan was also an old friend of Fritz Kraemer, the hardline Pentagon strategist and mentor to both Kissinger and Haig. "I have great confidence in Sullivan. For years, he's been really the best man in the bureau," Haig said.[40]

While Nixon and Haig discussed his reliability, Sullivan returned his answers to the written FBI questions and denied knowing about any leaks to the press. "However, judging from the nature of this information and the precise details if correct, it would seem that some of it may have come from inside the FBI."[41]

Sullivan played dumb, although he was the leaker for the May 3 *Post* story that spurred the FBI investigation and the May 11 *Times* article that renewed Nixon's suspicion of Felt. He had already succeeded in focusing suspicion on Felt.

❧

Kissinger had kept his distance from Nixon as the president dealt with Watergate. But the merging of the Watergate scandal with the wiretaps drew him into an Oval Office meeting about how to contain the damage Sullivan had created. Kissinger still had many secrets from the first term, such as how he negotiated the Vietnam deal and forced the South Vietnamese to cave in or how he sold out Taiwan in the China talks. Anything that forced these details into the public would devastate future attempts to negotiate with the Chinese or the Soviets. Kissinger, and by extension Nixon, would play with a weaker hand. Kissinger tried to blame the FBI or Justice. Nixon was not buying it. Why did they do the wiretaps? Nixon asked Kissinger.

"To prevent leaks," Kissinger answered.

"Right, and leaks from where?" Nixon asked.

"Well, from here and elsewhere," Kissinger said.

"That's the point," Nixon said, bringing Kissinger around to the work they had done together devising their foreign policy and excluding the rest of the government. The leaks came from the NSC, Nixon said, and they did not have to be defensive about that.

"We didn't have the Congress with us," Nixon said. "We didn't have the press with us. We didn't have the bureaucracy with us. We did it alone, Henry."

Kissinger agreed and blamed Judge Byrne in California for turning public attention on the wiretaps.[42]

❧

No sooner had Kissinger left the Oval Office than Haig walked in bearing a new crisis. The revelations of CIA help for the Plumbers about which Cushman had told the FBI had caused Schlesinger to tell any agency employee to detail if the White House had contacted them about any other similar issues. He heard from Vernon Walters, the CIA's deputy director and longtime keeper of Nixon's secrets, who told him about his contacts with Haldeman, Ehrlichman, and particularly Dean starting on June 23, 1972, about using the CIA to slow down the FBI investigation into the Watergate break-in.

Schlesinger had called Walters back to Washington, and then Walters came to the White House and gave Haig eight memos he had written after he met with Dean, Ehrlichman, and Haldeman in June and July 1972. They were, Haig said, "quite damaging to us." He and Buzhardt read the memos and concluded, "These papers can't go anywhere."

"They deal with Dean's efforts to—to get a CIA cover for the Watergate defendants," Haig said.[43]

Haig continued to tell Nixon what Walters had done the previous June, how he had visited Pat Gray at the FBI to get the Bureau not to investigate the Mexican bank account used by one of the Watergate burglars. The other memcons showed how Dean kept trying to get Walters to use the CIA to pay bail for the burglary defendants or money to provide for their families. Walters turned him down. Instead of dwelling on how Haldeman and Ehrlichman had initially summoned Walters and Helms for a meeting on June 23 to warn them off the Watergate investigation, Haig emphasized the role of Dean, whom Nixon hated.

"These things are very damaging to Dean," Haig said, adding that Walters would help Nixon. "Everything he says is going to help you."

Haig also said Ruckelshaus was almost done with his investigation of the wiretaps. There was more information that pointed to Mark Felt as the leaker.

"Fire his ass," Haig urged.

Ruckelshaus, Haig said, wanted to fire Felt, and Haig said he thought they could do it and destroy Felt's credibility if he tried to hurt Nixon.

Nixon changed the subject back to Walters's memcons and the attempts to get the CIA to tell the FBI to back off. He falsely claimed he knew nothing about the plan, although he had enthusiastically embraced it when Haldeman proposed it to him on June 23. At the time, Nixon thought it was a Mitchell idea, when it had actually come from Dean, who had persuaded Haldeman to recommend it to the president. Although Haig professed to Nixon that he wanted to use executive privilege to keep Walters's memcons secret, he also claimed Walters's testimony would damage Dean and protect the president. Regardless of Dean's motives in contacting Walters, anyone who had seen Walters's memoranda knew the public would conclude instead that the White House, specifically Nixon, had authorized using the CIA to stop the FBI from investigating the Watergate break-in.

In Los Angeles, Byrne dismissed the charges against Ellsberg and Russo entirely and prohibited any further prosecution of them. The government, Byrne said, had "placed the case in such a posture that it precludes the fair, dispassionate resolution of these issues by a jury," and "offended a sense of justice." The defendants and their supporters exulted, and Byrne ducked out the door behind the bench.[44] Byrne was appalled by the Nixon's administration's secrecy and angered by his own missteps, especially his two meetings with Ehrlichman. "We may have been given only a glimpse of what this special unit did," Byrne said about the Plumbers. "The latest series of actions compound a record already pervaded by instances which threatened the defendants' rights to a fair trial."[45]

⌁

The bad news continued. Haig told Nixon that Cushman had presented three different congressional committees a three-page affidavit that repeated much of what Cushman had told the FBI in late April. Cushman testified that he had agreed to Ehrlichman's request for help for Hunt and Liddy and that the Agency provided special cameras, bugging equipment, and disguises. The Agency also provided a psychiatric profile of Ellsberg, which Hunt found wanting enough to warrant breaking into Fielding's office to find incriminating information to use to smear Ellsberg. Cushman added some new details, such as how Helms approved the White House contacts after Cushman said he approved them. The testimony raised new questions about how much Helms knew about the Plumbers.[46]

Cushman's testimony also raised the stakes surrounding Walters and his memcons. If Cushman, his predecessor as deputy CIA director, had been allowed to testify and not claim executive privilege, how could the White House claim privilege to stop Walters? The memcons were very damaging to Haldeman and Ehrlichman, Haig told Nixon, who wondered if they could get Walters to somehow sanitize them. That would not work, Haig said, because everyone knew Walters had a photographic memory. Any truncated memoranda would be immediately suspicious.[47]

Compounding their problems was Symington's leadership of the Senate Armed Services Committee. Unlike Stennis, Buzhardt's favorite "undertaker," Symington had dogged Nixon since his hearings in 1969 about US overseas military commitments and the secret CIA war in Laos. He knew Nixon had tried to put the CIA under Kissinger's control in November 1971 and was not prepared to let anything pass. His leadership of Armed Services during this period put as much pressure on Nixon as virtually anything else that emerged that year from the Senate Watergate Committee.

⌁

Haig continued to give Nixon contradictory advice, saying both that the memcons should not be released while arguing that Walters had to testify because Cushman had. The memcons will look bad, Haig said, because they say that Haldeman told Walters to call off the FBI investigation. But if Walters only delivers direct testimony, he "will build a wall and, to the degree that that kind of innuendo has been stuck from this, then it makes it easier for Bob and John in that context, and hopefully we're going to manage it so that the thing is put in its proper context."[48] Even if Helms is called back from Iran, where he was the US ambassador, he would only present hearsay evidence, Haig argued. Buzhardt will contact Helms, Haig told the president, and he would limit what Helms would say and determine if Helms had any copies of the Walters memcons.

"It will be very embarrassing because it'll indicate that we tried to cover up with the CIA," Nixon said.

He knew that Congress would read Walters's notes as proof of a White House cover-up. He also realized his future depended on the CIA, which he had spent four years abusing. If he wanted to cover up the Watergate break-in, Nixon told Haig, the last person he would have asked was Dick Helms.

"Yeah, you see, my point is, you and I, all of us knew that we thought, we considered Helms to be basically a, well, let's face it, an establishmentarian," Nixon said.[49]

— ❦ —

Haig told Nixon on May 13 that Armed Services already had Cushman's memo, which created a precedent that would likely force the disclosure of Walters's too. Why did Cushman do that? Nixon asked Haig, who said Cushman had been told not to do it again. But it was too late. The committees had reached Cushman before Buzhardt and Haig could plan their strategy, if they even realized the problem of sending Cushman to the Hill with such damaging information. Haig said Buzhardt said Walters would still have to testify, but they could take a broad national security claim to keep the memos private.[50]

— ❦ —

While Nixon worried about Walters, Ruckelshaus received a peculiar telephone call at home. The caller, who said he was John Crewdson of the *New York Times*, expressed concern about what he called a threat to the FBI from leaks. That threat, the caller said, was Mark Felt, who had leaked the information about the wiretaps to him. Ruckelshaus did not think at the time how unlikely it would be for a reporter from any major newspaper, let alone the *Times*, to call a government official and reveal the identity of an unnamed source. He did, however, know of the suspicions that Felt had leaked to not only Crewdson but also to *Time* magazine.[51]

— ❦ —

May 14 brought a convergence of events that made Nixon's demise inevitable. Ruckelshaus released the details of the FBI investigation into the wiretaps, Walters testified before the Armed Services Committee about White House interference in the Watergate investigation, the military spy ring surfaced from an unexpected quarter, and John Dean appeared in US District Judge John Sirica's court and said he had placed several classified documents in a bank safety deposit box, including the controversial Huston Plan for domestic intelligence, which Dean did not name. The accumulated weight of the various revelations, including Nixon's covering of their own tracks, would be too much to overcome.

While many of the details of the wiretaps had already leaked to the press, most of them courtesy of Sullivan, Ruckelshaus still needed to release his investigation's findings. But he had another matter to handle that morning. He summoned Felt to his office and told him about the call he received from the man who identified himself as John Crewdson. Such leaks, Ruckelshaus said, would not be tolerated.

Felt denied leaking.

"You can't deny it," Ruckelshaus said. "I just heard it from the guy you talked to."

Felt said nothing.

"I'm so mad at you, I don't know what to do," Ruckelshaus continued. "I'm going to sleep on it and decide in the morning."

Felt would return to work the following morning, May 15, and submit his resignation. "I would have fired him" if he had not, Ruckelshaus said.[52]

At his briefing, Ruckelshaus read a prepared statement that said FBI officials had conducted forty-two interviews across the country and determined that seventeen wiretaps had been placed between May 1969 and February 1971 on four journalists and thirteen government officials. Mitchell had authorized each tap in writing to Hoover, and Sullivan kept the records in his office on Hoover's orders. Ruckelshaus then told how Sullivan gave the records to Mardian and that when Hoover learned what Sullivan had done he tried to get the records back only to be told they had been destroyed. Ruckelshaus said he then learned from Mardian just days earlier that the records had not been destroyed and were soon located in a safe in Ehrlichman's office.[53]

Ruckelshaus told reporters that Kissinger was responsible for asking for the taps and that he had told Hoover at the time that he was "extremely concerned" about vital national security information leaking from the NSC.[54] That contradicted Kissinger's claims a week earlier that the FBI or CIA had initiated the leak investigations and he had nothing to do with them. He had talked to Hoover about protecting national security information but not about any specific types of investigation. That was a lie, one of many that Kissinger would tell.

More details of the wiretaps were now on the record and public information. Still, much about Kissinger's and Haig's roles in them remained unknown. Neither they nor Nixon seemed inclined to say more about them. For the time being, Nixon believed he could explain away the wiretaps as a necessary evil to protect vital government secrets.

He also wanted to use Sullivan to blunt the claims that the White House had wrongly used the FBI in the wiretaps. Nixon told Ron Ziegler, the embattled press secretary, that he had to get the CIA files on the Diem assassination and the Bay of Pigs to show the excesses of the Kennedy administration. Ehrlichman never got the documents, Nixon said, because Kissinger kept stopping him. But now it was time to get them.[55]

Nixon blamed Kissinger for the wiretaps. He came to Nixon "jumping up and down" about leaks and Nixon agreed to "investigate the sons of bitches." Kissinger then read all of the wiretap reports and "reveled in it, he groveled in it, he wallowed in it. If he quits, starts playing games, we're going to let him have the hook, too. No, no, no, no. . . . Well, I want the story to lead this afternoon that there are hundreds of FBI taps in the Johnson and Kennedy administration that are missing. And that'll force that fucking Ruckelshaus to get in and find them."[56]

With either Haig, Buzhardt, Ziegler, or all of them together, Nixon brought up Sullivan at least five times this day as the man who could give them dirt they sought about the Kennedy and Johnson wiretaps. Haig asked Sullivan to learn more, reporting back to Nixon in the afternoon that Sullivan called the FBI officials around Ruckelshaus "all Hoover men" and that there were files dating back to the 1940s that detailed White House–ordered wiretapping.[57]

<hr />

Walters appeared before Symington's Armed Services Committee, and although the panel knew about the memcons, they were stunned by the details. Walters said on June 23, 1972, he and Helms were summoned to the White House to meet with Ehrlichman and Haldeman, who told them the FBI investigation was threatening to reveal national security secrets. They asked if the agency had any operations in Mexico in danger of being exposed by the FBI probe. Neither man knew of any, Walters testified, but they would check.[58]

Symington saw that Walters had provided another example of the White House's misuse of the CIA. And while they suspected the Agency had overstepped its charter, they knew the ultimate blame went to the White House, whose officials wanted the CIA to lie for them. "I believe that's why Helms was shipped off to Iran," said Sen. William Saxbe, an Ohio Republican and a future attorney general.[59]

Haig soon realized letting Walters testify was worse than he imagined.

"Well, we got a problem with the testimony that Walters gave," Haig told Nixon and Ziegler in the early evening. "He twisted it in a way that was bad for Bob and John."

"Walters deliberately put Haldeman's and Ehrlichman's tit in the wringer on this," said Nixon, who realized what his longtime secret operative, Walters, had done. "That makes me sick."[60]

Nixon engaged in both clear-eyed thinking and incredible denial. "We're just going to take a hell of a battering," he said. "This is difficult shit." But they would bounce back. The only thing to stop that would be if the critics were right. But they are not. "That's the whole point."[61]

But Nixon had tried to use the CIA to stop the FBI. Walters just did not know Nixon had given the order and had tried to pay off the defendants, which Dean was already telling the Senate committee. Even worse for Nixon, he had done those things on tape, which Haig already knew.

⁓

Not only had Symington used his committee to extract Walters's damaging testimony, but he also learned on May 14 about the documents Dean had given to Judge Sirica. That included the Huston Plan, which Sullivan had written the most of and then torpedoed it with Hoover.[62]

The Pentagon learned almost immediately that its work with Huston was now outside the White House, where the illegal activities could become public knowledge. The army's general counsel had obtained a copy of the plan from the Court and then called a meeting for the next day with representatives for the FBI, CIA, National Security Agency, and Defense Intelligence Agency to review their potential exposure.[63] That meant the Defense Department and its chief counsel, Buzhardt, knew what Dean had given Sirica before Nixon did.

⁓

Haig also learned he faced another problem that he and Nixon thought had been dealt with in December 1971—the Joint Chiefs' spy ring at the NSC. Nixon had ordered the scandal buried, Yeoman Charles Radford exiled to Oregon, and Rear Admiral Robert Welander sent to a sea command. Defense Secretary Melvin Laird used the report Buzhardt wrote with Haig's help to bury the issue, and Haig's aid to the spies, at the Pentagon, while the White House report by Plumber David Young was stuck in Ehrlichman's safe. Nixon vented his paranoia about the spying often, including to Haig, but the issue remained dormant.

That was until Donald Stewart, the Pentagon investigator who forced Radford's confession, called the White House. Stewart, unhappy since Buzhardt stopped the investigation, felt stifled at the Pentagon and thought David Young could help. But Young had just resigned, so the call was directed to Richard Tufaro, a young aide to White House counsel Leonard Garment. Tufaro knew nothing about Stewart or the spy ring, so Stewart's call alarmed him, as the voluble Stewart hinted his secret work tracking national security leaks could become public. He also complained about Buzhardt, whom Tufaro already distrusted, and he warned Garment about hiring him to run the Watergate defense because of his ties to the Pentagon. In a memo to Garment sent shortly after the call, Tufaro said, "Stewart clearly is in a position to damage the Administration because of his direct involvement in White House investigations of national security leaks."[64]

Garment told Buzhardt about Stewart's call, and Buzhardt, who was still the Pentagon's general counsel, responded by ordering the seizure of Stewart's files and for him to be reassigned to desk duty. While the cover-up of Watergate crumbled, Buzhardt's cover-up of the spy ring continued.[65]

~~~

A trickle of Walters's testimony had leaked out of the Senate the day before, but Symington left nothing to chance on May 15. Joined by Strom Thurmond, the committee's top Republican, Symington released a statement at a packed news conference that summed up Walters's testimony and implicated the White House in the Watergate cover-up.[66] As Haig had predicted, the testimony damaged Dean. Walters said in June and July, 1972, that Dean tried repeatedly to get the CIA to pay for the bail and salaries of the Watergate burglars and to persuade the FBI to back off the Watergate investigation. Each time, Walters refused and said the White House should fire those responsible for the break-in and cover-up. If Dean or the White House persisted, Walters testified, he threatened to resign.

"It is very clear to me that there was an attempt to unload major responsibility for the Watergate on Director Helms and General Walters, who was at all times operating with the approval of Mr. Helms, who behaved very well with response to this attempt," Symington said.[67]

The White House had no real response. Haig told Nixon after Symington's news conference that Ehrlichman in particular had been especially damaged, and that Ehrlichman believed that Charles Colson had triggered Dean to contact the CIA. "That's just the stupidest Goddamn thing," Nixon said.[68]

Symington was not done. The same day, he met with officials from the FBI, CIA, and NSA and Senator Harry Byrd of Virginia and Armed Services staff members to review the Huston Plan. The FBI wanted Symington's "help in interceding with Senator Ervin's Select Committee to investigate the Watergate matter," according to a May 22 Bureau memo. Symington reviewed the documents and asked for another meeting the following day.[69]

But while Symington had the Huston Plan and other documents that Dean had taken with him from the White House, and Buzhardt knew it, Buzhardt did not tell Nixon.

At the FBI, Felt returned to work the day after his confrontation with Ruckelshaus and submitted his resignation, effective June 12. That meant the end of a thirty-two-year career and stopped at least one of the paths of leaks from the FBI that had bedeviled the White House. In his battle with Sullivan, Sullivan had won.

Haig realized he had another damage-control job when he received a call from Seymour Hersh at the *Times*, who had received more details about the FBI wiretaps that implicated Nixon, Kissinger, and even Haig in picking the targets. Hersh's evidence was solid. At first, Haig tried to bluff Hersh with claims that the wiretaps were necessary for national security. "I have no absolutely no apologies to make," Haig told Hersh. "The wiretaps for the purposes were justified and anyone who claims otherwise is not filled in."[70] The taps were not that important and not worthy of a story, Haig said. Hersh was not swayed. Haig tried again. If the *Times* published Hersh's story, then Kissinger might resign. After all, Kissinger had told a news conference that he had little, if anything, to do with the taps. Hersh's story would expose that lie. When Hersh refused to back down, Haig made his final pitch: "You're Jewish, aren't you, Seymour?" Hersh said he was. "Let me ask you one question, then," Haig said. "Do you honestly believe that Henry Kissinger, a Jewish refugee from Germany who lost thirteen members of his family to the Nazis, could engage in such police-state tactics as wiretapping his own aides? If there's any doubt, you owe it to yourself, your beliefs and your nation to give us one day to prove that your story is wrong." Hersh had no doubt. He had an impeccable source: William Sullivan.[71]

Woodward was also tracking the wiretaps. After the Ruckelshaus announcement, he called an FBI official, who told him that Kissinger had authorized some of the wiretaps. He called a former FBI official, possibly Sullivan, Woodward wrote, who said, "I know Kissinger gave some authorizations."[72] So Woodward then called the White House, and, to his surprise, was connected to Kissinger's office, where the national security adviser answered the phone. Woodward wrote that he told Kissinger he had two sources who said Kissinger had authorized wiretaps. Kissinger lied, saying, "It could be Mr. Haldeman" who signed off on the taps. Did Kissinger authorize any taps? "I don't believe it was true," Kissinger said, another lie. "I frankly don't remember," Kissinger continued.[73] Kissinger mentioned that the names of those who were wiretapped went from Haig to Sullivan, whose name Woodward omitted when he wrote about the call in *All the President's Men*.

Woodward never got a chance to use the interview, because Kissinger complained that he was not speaking on the record, although he never made that clear. He then called Woodward's editor at the *Post*, Ben Bradlee, to complain, and the paper held the story, only to get beat by Hersh.[74]

❧

A tsunami of bad news pounded on the White House on May 16 with the publication in the *Post* and the *Times* of the details of Symington's news conference. "CIA Resisted Lengthy Cover-Up Attempt by White House, Hill Account Reveals," read the *Post* headline, making clear the problem extended to the White House itself, not just John Dean.[75] More importantly, however, Hersh's story on the wiretaps also appeared on the front page. "President Linked to Taps on Aides," the headline said, followed by this lead: "President Nixon personally authorized the wiretapping of more than a dozen of his subordinates on the National Security Council and in the Pentagon beginning in 1969, reliable sources said today (May 15)."[76]

Hersh linked the decision to start the taps to the May 9, 1969, *Times* article by William Beecher about the secret bombing of Cambodia. An unnamed Haig was quoted throughout as defending the wiretaps for national security. Hersh named three Kissinger aides who were tapped—Anthony Lake, who resigned in protest of the Cambodia invasion in 1970; Winston Lord, a China expert who was leaving the White House that week; and Daniel Davidson, the only official who was tapped and then accused of leaking. He quit shortly after the taps were started. Not mentioned in the story was its source—Sullivan. Unlike Crewdson's earlier piece, which described how Sullivan had taken the wiretap records from the White House and given them to Mardian at Justice, Hersh did not name Sullivan at all.[77]

The story detailed much of what the White House had feared. Kissinger's lies about what he knew about the wiretaps were exposed. Kissinger was

Nixon's first visitor that morning in the Oval Office for a conversation that ranged from a pep talk for the worried national security adviser to Kissinger's insistence that Nixon stay in office.

The wiretaps were legal, Nixon said.[78]

Kissinger agreed, saying they had a duty to stop the leaks, which Nixon said could have killed their secret initiatives if allowed to continue. Nixon urged Kissinger not to worry. Nothing found in the taps had ever been disclosed. "I didn't even know what the Christ was in those damn things," he said. Kissinger tried to blame the taps on Hoover.

Regardless of how bad things got, Kissinger reassured Nixon, he could not resign.

"The horror of this thing," Kissinger said, "the disparity between the minor league crap that these guys did and the consequences, the amateur and the stupidity, I mean, nothing they could ever done. That's the worst of it."

Symington met again May 16 with the FBI and Defense officials. Symington brought with him members of his staff and fellow senators Thurmond, Byrd, Henry Jackson of Washington, and Sam Nunn of Georgia. The officials urged the senators to protect the national security aspects of the Huston Plan, but few were persuaded. Jackson, the FBI memo showed, said the White House's claims lacked credibility and that other documents "strongly supported testimony before the committee earlier by former CIA Director Richard Helms, who testified that efforts had been made to involve the CIA in illegal activity." Symington joined in and "denounced what appeared to be efforts by Defense Department to get the committee's support on the one hand and simultaneously hold information bearing on the overall issue of White House efforts to pervert the intelligence community's true mission."[79]

Buzhardt finally told Nixon that the Huston Plan had been revealed that afternoon. It was in the hands of the Senate committee and the prosecutors. He did not tell Nixon that he knew about it earlier and then tried to soft-pedal its implications by saying it had nothing to do with Watergate.

The real problem, Buzhardt said, dealt with the plan's actual suggestions—"a group plan for supplementing domestic intelligence. . . . Some of the language appears quite inflammatory particularly one of Huston's memorandums."[80]

"Everything he wrote was inflammatory," Nixon said.

"So it's very unfortunate," Buzhardt said. "I think it presents a serious problem."

Although Huston had written the memo, it included details from Haldeman that were troubling for the president, Buzhardt continued. Haldeman noted in the memo that Nixon had approved all of the plan's details. That connected Nixon to a series of illegal activities that violated the charters of the nation's intelligence agencies. It showed Nixon approved break-ins that even J. Edgar Hoover had ended and vigorously opposed. Release of the Huston Plan before the Senate would have grave consequences, Buzhardt continued. It could lead the House to consider impeachment proceedings. Buzhardt had one recommendation: The White House needed to get in front of the problem by fighting "this thing head on. Actually, it gives us a better case because the issue can now turn on the threat to national security during this period. The document is a good one. It lays out the threat very well."

Buzhardt did not tell Nixon that Symington, Ervin, Baker, and other senators had seen the plan or about their brutal meeting with the FBI. Instead, Buzhardt pushed hard for what would turn into a May 22 document the White House called the "White Paper" about the president's involvement in the wiretaps, Huston Plan, and Watergate. Buzhardt and Haig would embrace it as the best chance for Nixon to come clean on his role in all of those issues and hopefully put them to rest before the Watergate hearings gained much momentum. Nixon, however, resisted the idea, and he continued to look for justification for his activities.

"I don't ever remember anything about surreptitious entry of selected targets here and there," Nixon said, forgetting that after the Pentagon Papers publication he insisted that Huston be put in charge of a plan to break into the Brookings Institution and steal the imaginary bombing halt file Nixon believed was hidden there. "I mean, that sounds like gobbledygook-gook from bureaucracy or something like that. But I'm sure it was there. You know how this could have happened, though?"[81]

Buzhardt said they needed to prepare for problems with Senator Sam Ervin, the chairman of the Watergate committee, who was "a civil liberties man." Buzhardt would have known, because Ervin had already seen the plan. Nixon said they needed to anticipate what Dean might tell the committee about the plan and how they could explain why they needed to create it. First, Haig warned, they had to make sure the Huston Plan could not be tied to anything related to Watergate, such as the break-in at Ellsberg's psychiatrist's office.[82]

Nixon, Haig, and Buzhardt could see where all of this was headed. Nixon's growing legion of critics, including those on the Senate committee and in the media, would easily conflate the Huston Plan into a White House pickled with paranoia and spying on whatever it considered a security threat, whether they were college students protesting the war, government officials suspected of leaking, a psychiatrist who happened to treat a think tank expert opposed to the war, or Democratic candidates. A president capable of approving an unprecedented abuse of civil rights such as the Huston Plan would be capable of anything, even if he had nothing to do with it, such as authorizing the Watergate break-in. Their one hope was showing that the Huston Plan, even though Nixon had wanted it and approved it, had never actually taken effect. For that reassurance, they reached out again to Sullivan.

"Sullivan thinks he has notes that will give us precise times," Buzhardt said. "But the whole thing was suspended immediately."[83]

That was a thin reed for Nixon to hang on to, Buzhardt determined. Instead, the president needed to take the offensive and spell out everything in detail in the hope of putting the scandal behind him. Such a blanket statement would theoretically absolve the aides who helped promote those activities, such as Haig and Kissinger on the FBI wiretaps, because Nixon would be assuming full responsibility. They, in the words of the Nuremberg defendants, were just following orders.

"We've got a major leak there, we got a threat to the national security," Buzhardt said. "It's either wrap it in there, Mr. President, and hang it on this hat and the whole case than to have to defend it separately. I think we may want to think about whether we just put this one under the umbrella."

The problem, Nixon noted, was that they would have to admit "we approved illegal activities."[84]

❦

That night, in an episode immortalized in the book and movie versions of *All the President's Men*, Woodward met his secret source in an underground parking garage in Arlington, Virginia. Deep Throat was agitated and nervous. He also abandoned his previous practice, as described by Woodward, of only confirming information the reporters had developed elsewhere. Instead, he gave Woodward a thorough dump of original information about White House activities.[85] Woodward listened, quickly wrote down his notes, and then rushed home. He summoned Bernstein to his apartment. Woodward turned up the music to a loud volume and started typing his notes, which were later reprinted in *All the President's Men*. When compared to the White House tapes from May 16, which were not available until 1997, they show the source that evening had to be someone intimately familiar with the fears expressed in the Oval Office that day.[86] That is, if the scene happened at all. The notes show a few kernels of new information. Woodward's source had provided him with old and previously reported information, claims that could not be investigated and tips. As recounted by Woodward and Bernstein in their book and then heightened by screenwriter William Goldman in his script for the movie, the scene makes for great drama. However, little of it is true, and the source could not be the man Woodward now claims it is.

Deep Throat, according to Woodward, said Dean had met with Howard Baker of Tennessee, the Republican leader on the Watergate committee, and that Baker "is in the bag completely" for the White House. Nixon, Deep Throat continued, had threatened Dean with jail if he ever leaked national security details and that John Mitchell had started a series of covert activities at home and abroad. None of the claims was true.[87]

The source was on firmer ground when he claimed that White House investigator John Caulfield had promised Watergate burglar James McCord executive clemency if he kept quiet. McCord would only have to spend eleven months in jail. But that claim had already been reported in the May 13 *Los Angeles Times* and was picked up by the *Post* and other papers. Deep Throat was just rehashing old news.[88]

Deep Throat made another astounding, but outdated, claim. He said CIA officials, starting with Walters and Helms, could testify that Haldeman and Ehrlichman had ordered them to help in the Watergate cover-up. But Walters and Helms had already done that, and the details of Symington's news conference were splashed all over the front of that morning's *Washington Post*. In this case, as with the McCord/Caulfield clemency-for-silence claim, Woodward's magical source might as well have given Woodward the morning newspaper.

Deep Throat also said, the notes showed, that *"The covert activities involve the whole US intelligence community and are incredible. Deep Throat refused to give specifics because it is against the law."*[89] This is a clear reference to the panic that ensued when Buzhardt realized Dean had taken the details of the Huston Plan. Haig and Buzhardt spent much of the afternoon of May 16 in contact with Sullivan and Robert Mardian to learn what had happened with the plan and whether it was ever approved. "Here you've got the CIA, the DIA, the FBI all working together on something," Nixon told Haig and Buzhardt that afternoon. One person they did not contact was Felt.[90]

The source's tips about how the Watergate cover-up was aimed at protecting covert operations and how Nixon was being blackmailed by the burglars were true. The hush money would be one of the main points of Dean's testimony before the Senate committee in June. Also true was Deep Throat's contention that Dean had taken far more documents than anyone had imagined and they were "quite detailed."

Not only did Dean have the Huston Plan, but he had other documents that worried Haig and Buzhardt, who urged Nixon to come clean on all of it. Sullivan knew about their concerns. Felt did not.

Deep Throat concluded his meeting, Woodward and Bernstein wrote, by describing an "unreal" atmosphere at the White House, where Nixon realized he was finished but was also trying to "go on with business." Nixon, the source said, "has had fits of 'dangerous depression.'"

Nixon was definitely unraveling during this time, the White House tapes show. He alternated between telling Haig that he would resign and vowing to fight to the end. Throughout this time, Haig and Buzhardt talked constantly with Sullivan about how to defend Nixon against the onslaught of negative publicity. They did not realize that Sullivan was also leaking to the *New York Times* and most likely to Woodward, too.

According to *All the President's Men*, Woodward and Bernstein rushed with their typed notes to *Post* editor Ben Bradlee's home in Georgetown. They told Bradlee that Deep Throat warned that "everyone's life is in danger" and that the CIA was spying on anyone involved in the Watergate story. They contemplated the seriousness of the story and their next moves until about 4 a.m.

﹏

Woodward and Bernstein gathered at the *Post* a few hours later on the morning of May 17 when Woodward presented Bradlee and other senior editors with copies of the notes he typed the previous evening. Neither *All the President's Men* nor Bradlee's memoirs says if any of the editors commented on the old news Woodward's source was trying to peddle as revelations. Their credibility may have been helped by their story that dominated the front page of the morning's paper that detailed more questionable activities by Nixon's operatives since 1969. "The Watergate bugging and the break-in into the office of Daniel Ellsberg's psychiatrist were part of an elaborate, continuous campaign of illegal and quasilegal undercover operations conducted by the Nixon administration since 1969, according to highly placed sources in the executive branch."[91] Sullivan, who had told Woodward about the bogus "vigilante squad" in March, was clearly a source, and the story doubled down on the false claim of the "use of paid-for-hire 'vigilante squads.'" It also claimed that Mardian had provided information from FBI files to the White House and Nixon campaign operatives during the 1972 campaign. Sullivan was telling Weicker many of these details, too. It was an echo of what Sullivan told Woodward on March 5, and what Woodward told David Gergen two months later. Haig could also have been a source, as he told Nixon on the morning of May 17 that he had received a letter from the doctor of Senator Thomas Eagleton, who was briefly the Democrats' 1972 vice presidential nominee, that his office had been burglarized and Eagleton's records stolen. Eagleton dropped off the ticket after it was revealed he had electric-shock treatments for depression.

"We have some indication the doctor's office was burglarized, Mr. President," Buzhardt said. Haig said they had received a letter from Eagleton's doctor two days earlier with a claim about the burglary. Nixon said he would be shocked if the claim was true, but Buzhardt said the letter was "worrisome."[92]

That meant that Haig, who had known Woodward since the reporter was a young navy officer delivering files to Haig's office at the NSC, had details of the burglary of Eagleton's doctor's office that had just appeared in Woodward's story. It would not be the last time that Haig would guide Woodward's reporting in this period, most of it to Haig's advantage and to Nixon's detriment.

Although Nixon feared that some parts of the *Post* story that morning were true and could sink him, Buzhardt told him that Hunt's recent interviews with the FBI contradicted many of the story's assertions. They also discussed the Senate hearings, which started that morning, and Nixon wanted the White House to have Sullivan and Huston ready in case they needed someone to rebut the claims that were sure to arise in the Senate. He also wanted Sullivan to sign an affidavit to prove the Huston Plan "was turned off."[93]

The hearings provided little drama at first. Woodward, however, set in motion that day what would become the pivotal element of the hearings. He went to the Senate and met with his high school friend Scott Armstrong, whom Woodward had helped get a job on the Watergate Committee staff. Woodward asked Armstrong if the committee had considered interviewing Alexander Butterfield, Nixon's aide who installed the taping system in the White House. They had not, and they did not commit to talking to him. Other than Haig and Buzhardt, who could claim executive privilege and refuse to testify, Butterfield was the best potential witness for the Senate on the taping system, which Haig and Buzhardt already knew about. They knew that revealing the tapes could force Nixon to speak honestly about what he knew about Watergate.

Symington also followed up on May 17 with another round of testimony by Walters and Helms. They repeated what they said earlier about White House attempts to have the CIA block the Watergate investigation. L. Patrick Gray, Walters said, told him that everyone at the White House involved in Watergate should be fired.[94]

It was clear to Buzhardt and Haig that they were in a race with Symington to get out their side of the national security secrets or have the story overwhelm them.

Soon after Donald Stewart contacted the White House seeking help on May 14 for a new job, perhaps even consideration as the new FBI director, Haig and Buzhardt realized they had a problem with the cover-up of the spy ring. Buzhardt had seized Stewart's Pentagon files to keep them from leaking out. But he and Haig knew the former FBI agent was potentially volatile, and while he had kept the secret of the spy ring investigation this long, they could not count on it staying secret.

Rear Admiral Robert Welander, who had returned to Washington from the sea duty to which he was exiled after Nixon learned of the spy ring, received an unexpected telephone call from Woodward, his former subordinate. Could Welander meet him for lunch at the Key Bridge Marriott in Arlington, Virginia? Welander agreed.[95]

Woodward told Welander the details of the spy ring were bubbling up and could become public soon. He asked if Welander could confirm anything, but Welander declined. The revelation of the spy ring, particularly Yeoman Charles Radford's rifling of Kissinger's and Haig's briefcases and the theft of classified documents from the NSC, had scarred his career. He would not tell anything to Woodward, even if he had once been one of his favorite subordinates. Immediately upon returning to the Pentagon after lunch, Welander wrote a memo for Moorer and Admiral Elmo Zumwalt, the chief of naval operations.[96]

Someone had told Woodward enough about the spy ring for him to go directly to one of its key players—Welander—and ask him for more details. That meant Woodward knew enough to report the story and break it. But Woodward sat on the information for almost seven months and only wrote what he knew after others had already reported it in January 1974. This decision had serious ramifications for Nixon, Haig, Buzhardt, and the military. If Woodward had reported that the chairman of the Joint Chiefs of Staff—Moorer—had used a spy operation inside the NSC, it would have exposed the rift between Nixon and the military that distrusted him so much that its top uniformed officer spied on him. By failing to report it, Woodward was protecting two of former superior officers, Moorer and Welander. He was also protecting Haig, one of his best sources. A story that exposed Haig's ties to Welander and his predecessor, Rear Admiral Rembrandt Robinson, could have forced Haig out of the White House.

━◆◆━

At the White House, Nixon, Haig, and Buzhardt were pushing hard to finish their "White Paper" to explain why they started the Plumbers, FBI wiretaps, and the Huston Plan. Haldeman returned to help Nixon and said they needed to acknowledge their fears that the Watergate investigation would uncover the Plumbers. As he crept closer to something like full disclosure, which Nixon could not quite do, he also kept discussing resignation.

"When you come down to it, Bob, I raise this as a devil's advocate," Nixon said. "Don't tell me this unless you believe it, Goddamnit, because I've got to have good advice now. Maybe [I should] resign on the basis you can't do your job because of all this . . . et cetera, et cetera, and you've got to resign in order to clear your name. Shit. I can't do it, Bob."[97]

"My resigning didn't clear my name," Haldeman said. "My resigning proved to everybody in the world except the few people that believe in me that I'm guilty."

They also thought they got a break with Archibald Cox, Attorney General Elliot Richardson's choice as the Watergate special prosecutor. A New England Brahmin, Cox graduated from Harvard Law School and taught on its faculty and had been the US solicitor general for Kennedy and Johnson. He had the same pedigree as Richardson. Haig liked the pick and thought the White House could work with Cox. So did Nixon. "He's not a zealot," Haig said.

━◆◆━

Symington trumped the White House again on May 21 by calling Huston to testify about his proposed domestic security plan. He spent two hours in closed session, and then Symington gave the press a summary of Huston's testimony. The documents the committee reviewed carried Huston's name and appeared to call for "violations of the law in the domestic collection on United States citizens," Symington said. "There didn't seem to be any limitation on the amount of burglary involved."[98]

The senator also released Walters's memcons, which Haig had assured Nixon would never be released.

The steady drumbeat from Symington's committee drove Haig and Buzhardt to turn the White Paper into something they hoped would change the shape of the debate about Watergate. The early days of the Senate Watergate committee hearings provided little that threatened the White House, but Symington was pushing out more damaging information. Nixon also knew that Dean would testify eventually, and even more details they had so zealously tried to conceal would spill out on national television.

Ziegler and Garment released the White Paper in a May 22 news conference, saying it would clear the air of any questions about what Nixon did, when, and why. The FBI wiretaps were done for national security reasons, placed on only seventeen people and obtained vital leads that stopped security threats. They were his responsibility and no one else's, Nixon said. "I authorized this entire program."[99] The Huston Plan was a reaction to the crumbling situation on American college campuses. "Many colleges closed," the paper said. "Gun battles between guerrilla-style groups and police were taking place. Some of the disruptive activities were receiving foreign support." Nixon placed Hoover in the middle of the wiretaps and the Huston Plan. That also extended to the Plumbers, although Nixon did not single out Hoover by name. Nixon said he authorized their creation and "its existence and functions were known only to a very few persons at the White House. These included Messrs. Haldeman, Ehrlichman and Dean." As for Watergate, he knew nothing about the break-in at the DNC, although he worried the investigation into it would reveal secrets he wanted to keep. "I felt it was important to avoid disclosure of the details of the national security matters with which the group was concerned," he wrote. "I knew that once the existence of the group became known, it would lead inexorably to a discussion of these matters, some of which remain, even today, highly sensitive."[100]

Nixon, urged on by Haig and Buzhardt, had essentially admitted to supporting the Watergate cover-up. Instead of clearing the air, the White Paper only inspired suspicion, because it was shot full of lies. The wiretaps involved more people than Nixon, who left the details of the wiretaps to Haig and Kissinger. The Huston Plan may have been stopped, but Nixon always wanted to restore it, including after the Pentagon Papers, when he wanted Huston to lead a break-in of the Brookings Institution. Nixon may not have known about the Plumbers' exact activities, but he helped pick them. Also, many knew about the Plumbers, including Kissinger, and their existence was revealed publicly in a January 9, 1972, report in the *New York Times*. Nixon also knew far more about the plans to pay hush money to the burglars and grant them clemency in exchange for their silence. Dean had laid out the clemency plans, and he and Nixon had worked together to develop more of the cover-up.

The immediate reactions to the White Paper were harsh. The administration's claims of national security rang hollow, particularly just days after the Ellsberg prosecution had failed so spectacularly. "Those denials have to stand the test of time," the *Times* editorialized. "Meanwhile, it is abundantly clear that an inflated and erroneous conception of 'national security' led to criminal behavior which has brought the office of the President into grave disrepute."[101] The *Times* also followed with a detailed story by Hersh about the Huston Plan. "The White House urged the Federal Bureau of Investigation in 1970 to mount a massive counterinsurgency program, involving spying, wiretapping and burglaries, against the Black Panthers, potential Arab saboteurs, antiwar radicals and Soviet espionage agents, well-placed sources said today," the story started.[102] Sullivan seemed to be the obvious source. He had gone from the White House's hoped-for savior to a jilted aspirant for higher office who had nothing to lose. Details of the Huston Plan that could have come only from someone engaged in its creation dotted the story. "One high-level source who worked on the 1970 report said in a telephone interview that 'the facts we had available in this country then showed that we were faced with one of the most serious domestic crises that we've had,'" Hersh reported. Another paragraph cites "a high-level source who was involved in the preparation of the 1970 report," while a third quotes a "former high-ranking FBI official" who criticized Hoover's decision to end black-bag burglaries. "He wiped out the whole domestic security system," Hersh quoted an anonymous source, most likely Sullivan, as saying.

The White Paper and the reaction to it closed out May for Nixon. He had weathered a month the likes of which few presidents had faced, but his presidency was hanging by a thread. Most of the secrets Nixon tried to keep had leaked out, and the main one that remained, the Pentagon spy ring, was on the verge of leaking out. Like Nixon, Haig and Buzhardt wanted to preserve that cover-up but for dramatically different reasons. Nixon wanted to spare himself the embarrassment, while the president's two top aides wanted to hide their culpability. "Crazy Billy" Sullivan, the man who carried out some of Nixon's most secret orders, had conclusively moved from Nixon's team to the opposition. His work had only begun.

CHAPTER EIGHTEEN

The White House Tapes

THE LEAKS ABOUT THE FBI WIRETAPS AND THE HUSTON PLAN, THE FAILURE of the Ellsberg prosecution, and the start of the Senate Watergate hearings pushed Nixon into a defensive crouch. By May, he frequently talked about resigning. His May 22 White Paper, which Haig and Buzhardt urged, had not stopped the daily doses of bad news, and Nixon was in a near panic as he pondered Dean's Senate testimony.

Dean was by then meeting almost daily with the Watergate committee staff to plan testimony that would be devastating. Dean had taken documents such as the Huston Plan with him, and he knew what Nixon knew about the cover-up—when it started and how he discussed raising money to pay off the burglars to keep them quiet. Nixon also realized that the committee and the audience glued to their television sets at home were likely to believe Dean rather than him.

Also meeting with the committee's most aggressive Republican, Lowell Weicker of Connecticut, was Sullivan. Weicker's Senate files show that he became interested in the FBI wiretaps shortly after they were revealed in the *Times*. In a June 4 meeting, Sullivan told Weicker that Mardian routinely used the FBI's intelligence division to monitor antiwar and political groups.[1] Sullivan's tip to Weicker carried an echo of what Sullivan had told Woodward in March about Mardian's mythical "vigilante squad" of former FBI and CIA agents that spied on reporters. Weicker followed up with a letter to acting FBI director William Ruckelshaus for the records of Mardian's requests for FBI data. Sullivan, Weicker wrote, had told him what to look for and where.[2] Ruckelshaus told Weicker the request would be best handled by new Watergate special prosecutor Archibald Cox.[3] Weicker followed with a June 10 news conference in which he said the government was using large parts of the Huston Plan despite Nixon's order to kill it. That was the Intelligence Evaluation Committee that Mardian led with the help of both Dean and Sullivan. Weicker was citing the details Sullivan had provided him just a few days earlier.[4]

Not everyone on Weicker's staff trusted Sullivan as much as their boss did. "Bill Sullivan is a viper," said a memo to Weicker from aide Richard McGowan, a former reporter for the *New York Daily News*. "Outwardly, he is Mr. Peepers—frayed collars, string-attached glasses, unimposing. Underneath, he is tough as nails—a super-sleuth with jugular instincts. Don't get fooled. He's a secret policeman at heart."[5]

McGowan summarized Sullivan's history for Weicker, including his firing by Hoover. McGowan also questioned Sullivan's claims of the "vigilante" squad. "I'm told that it would have been impossible to (1) recruit agents to perform 'wildcat' taps or (2) keep such taps a secret," he wrote.[6]

"I suggest you play cat and mouse with Sully," McGowan continued. "A little flattery and 'emoted' concern over 'just was that the real story' about the radical menace that prompted great Americans like himself and Mardian to do something about the threat. Prime and pump him before he does it to you," McGowan concluded.[7]

Sullivan tried to explain his meeting with Weicker with a letter June 11 to Attorney General Elliot Richardson in which he said Weicker asked to meet and Sullivan merely guided him. Sullivan told Richardson that he had "the highest regard for Mr. Mardian's ability, industry and loyalty to this country" when Weicker asked about Mardian. He added that he referred any questions about Mardian's use of "telephone taps or microphones" to the FBI.[8]

❧

Nixon prepared for Dean by reviewing the tapes of his meetings with his former counsel in February and March. Although they would later claim they still did not know about the taping system, Haig and Buzhardt obviously did. They knew Dean had evidence that would either clear or convict Nixon. They also knew the president had lied to them and was veering into frequent bouts of melancholy and unpredictability. The Dean tapes proved to Nixon and his aides that Dean's upcoming testimony would be devastating, because the two men constantly talked about how to obstruct justice.

The Senate committee delayed Dean's testimony to allow Nixon to host a summit with Soviet leader Leonid Brezhnev. Despite the distraction of Watergate, the summit promised to be successful, a premeeting national intelligence estimate said, because the opening to China had the Soviets worried about "the USSR's isolation in world politics."[9] Between June 19 and 23, the two nations would sign eleven different agreements ranging from agricultural sales to continued nuclear arms limits.[10] The summit's success buoyed Nixon as he braced for the resumption of the hearings.

Dean was the main threat to Nixon's presidency, and the committee's Democrats recognized they needed to enhance their star witness. They turned Dean, once the White House's young, blond playboy, into someone who looked like a junior associate in an accounting firm. Horn-rimmed glasses replaced contact lenses; his hair was noticeably darker and pressed down. Instead of seeing a brash man on the make, the panel and the nation would see a relatively meek young man whose conscience had been shocked by the behavior he witnessed and regretfully enabled.

His testimony had the desired impact. Dean carefully read a detailed statement that laid out his history with the president, starting from his monitoring of student demonstrations at the Justice Department. Dean said he was appearing reluctantly and that "when the facts come out I hope the President is forgiven," Dean said.[11] The senators hung on every word. For Democrats, Dean was the perfect witness. No one knew more about the cover-up and Nixon's role in it. Dean also knew what Mitchell and other campaign leaders had done to create an atmosphere in which the burglars and dirty tricksters had flourished. Republicans, including those in the White House, knew Dean had hurt the president.

But much of it was false. Dean wrongly accused Mitchell and Mardian of devising the plan to have the CIA block the FBI's Watergate investigation. "It was during the meeting in Mitchell's office on June 23 or 24 that Mardian first raised the proposition that the CIA could take care of this entire matter if they wished in that they had funds and covert procedures for distributing funds," Dean said.[12] "I was personally unaware of the workings of the CIA, but Mardian and Mitchell appeared very knowledgeable." It was Dean who developed the idea of having the CIA block the FBI, and he lied to Haldeman on June 23 by claiming it was Mitchell's. Dean had worked with the CIA often as a member of the Intelligence Evaluation Committee. Dean lied when he told the committee that John Caulfield, his staff investigator, had proposed creating a separate firm to handle campaign intelligence.[13] Dean had told Nixon on March 21 that he had asked Caulfield to develop the plan.[14] At virtually every opportunity, Dean minimized his role and amplified the actions of others. For those out to damage Nixon or at least breach the White House's wall of denials, Dean's testimony was too good to check, so they let it go and watched the damage it caused unfold.

Sullivan, however, was not willing to let Dean go unchallenged. He objected to Dean's characterization of the FBI wiretaps as essentially a rogue operation done without Hoover's approval. Sullivan, Dean testified, "explained that after much haggling, that the wiretaps were installed, but as I recall Mr. Sullivan said they did not have the blessing of Director Hoover."[15] Dean's false testimony put Sullivan in a compromising position. Hoover had made sure that each wiretap had Mitchell's written approval, because he did not want anyone to think the FBI was acting alone. Haig had specifically invoked the sanction of a higher authority when he first set up the taps with Sullivan. Sullivan immediately called Weicker to denounce Dean. "First, in regard to Mr. John Dean's statement that I said the wiretaps in question did not have Mr. Hoover's 'blessing,'" Sullivan wrote Weicker. "This is entirely incorrect. I never made this statement and could not have done so because this topic was never discussed in any conversation which I had with Mr. Dean."[16]

⌐∾⌐

There was one way to prove if Dean had told the truth before the Senate committee: the taping system that Nixon had installed in February 1971 in the Oval Office, on his telephone and in his hideaway office in the Old Executive Office Building. Kennedy and Johnson had similar systems, and Nixon planned to use the tapes when he wrote his memoirs after leaving office. Only a handful of people inside the White House knew of the system when it started—Nixon, Butterfield, Haldeman, Haldeman's deputy Larry Higby, and Ron Ziegler. Steve Bull, who replaced Butterfield when he became head of the Federal Aviation Administration, learned when he started his job. Neither Kissinger nor Haig knew of it when they were at the NSC, but Haig was told upon becoming chief of staff. Buzhardt learned of it shortly thereafter.[17] They knew the tapes would prove whether Dean or Nixon was telling the truth. But Nixon had no intention of giving up the tapes. He considered them his private property and covered by executive privilege.

In the first two months in the White House, however, Haig and Buzhardt had demonstrated a poor grasp of how to use executive privilege or lead Nixon's defense. They had let former deputy CIA director Robert Cushman tell Congress about the Agency's help for the Plumbers. Then, having failed to use executive privilege to stop Cushman, they blundered into letting Vernon Walters testify about how the White House tried to use the CIA to block the FBI Watergate investigation. Haig had already tipped off Woodward about investigator Donald Stewart's interest in the Pentagon spy ring. Someone at the White House, presumably Haig, had also insisted that Woodward prod the Senate Watergate committee to interview Alexander Butterfield.

Those details help explain Haig and Buzhardt's behavior in July as Nixon tried to regain his footing after Dean's testimony. So consumed with

Watergate and Dean was Nixon that he could not enjoy the fruits of the successful Soviet summit or shift public opinion. Haig provided the occasional soothing words for Nixon, but he remained more focused on his role in two cover-ups—preserving that of the Pentagon spy ring while helping to unravel the Watergate cover-up and undo the president.

Donald Stewart had not faded away after his May call to the White House that rattled Richard Tufaro. Stewart resurfaced in late June with a letter to William Baroody, a White House aide who shared a mutual friend with Stewart.[18] Stewart told Baroody he was unhappy at the Pentagon, where he believed Buzhardt had sabotaged the spy ring investigation. He was concerned, Stewart continued, that if he was interviewing for another job he might have to describe some of what he did at the Pentagon. While he would never reveal any national security secrets, Stewart did not include the Ellsberg or Jack Anderson cases among them. Those, he said, were influenced by Buzhardt's political concerns, not national security. In the Anderson case, Stewart wrote, "all the culprits are still on board. . . . As you can see, the foregoing is enough to upset an honest investigator and I just want to get the hell out of DoD."

Buzhardt saw the letter and urged Richardson to investigate Stewart for extortion.[19] On June 29, Garment sent a packet to Richardson that included Baroody's notes and Tufaro's memo. The attorney general then gave it to Henry Petersen, the Justice criminal chief, and told him to find a way to charge Stewart. Petersen responded on July 10 to say that Stewart had done nothing wrong and it made no sense to prosecute him. Richardson was not satisfied. The next day, he contacted another deputy, Carl Belcher, to have him review the case.[20]

—◦—

Weicker was frustrated that Cox, the FBI, and Justice Department did not provide the documents related to Sullivan's tips. He, Sullivan, FBI agent James Dunn, and some of Weicker's staff met on July 9, and Sullivan continued to hint at problems with Mardian but did not spell out specifically what they might find. As McGowan warned in his earlier memo to Weicker, Sullivan hinted at more than he could deliver.

"Were there any requests from the White House?" Weicker asked.

"I can't remember specifically, but it's likely," Sullivan said.

Sullivan's caginess was frustrating Weicker, who spelled out clearly what he wanted.

Then Weicker and Sullivan met alone. Weicker asked about the wiretaps, and Sullivan said "there was nothing like this in my 30 years in the FBI.

Letters went to the president and Dr. Kissinger originally and we sent a copy to the attorney general occasionally. In February 1973, John Dean called me over and made it pretty clear he was acting as the president's counsel; he didn't mind pulling rank, and asked about the summaries. I thought the files were at the Justice Department. I didn't know they were over at the White House."[21]

⌐⌐⌐

In early July, it was becoming clear at the White House that the taping system would not be kept secret much longer. Dean had hinted in June that he thought Nixon might have recorded their conversations. Before he met with Senate Watergate staffers on July 5, Haldeman's assistant Larry Higby asked his old boss how to answer any questions about the tapes. Haldeman told him to claim executive privilege. Higby was asked at the meeting if Nixon recorded anything, and he said the president used a dictating machine to record his memories of meetings. When the staffer asked if Nixon recorded anything else, Higby whispered into his lawyer's ear that he would claim executive privilege and not answer. He then massaged his answer to evade the question, and no one followed up.[22]

The next morning, Higby told Haig about his close call. The tapes were going to come out, he said, and Haig responded that he knew about the dictabelt recordings. No, Higby said, all of the tapes were going to be revealed. What should he say if the committee called him back? Haig said he would get back to him, and when he did, Haig told Higby just to tell the truth, not claim executive privilege. Higby was surprised but thought Haig had cleared it with Nixon.[23]

On July 13, a Friday, the committee finally took Woodward's repeated advice to question Alexander Butterfield. As Butterfield met with the three staffers—Armstrong, minority staff member Donald Sanders, and majority staffer Gene Boyce—he realized the conversation was heading into a different area. One handed Butterfield a memo that Fred Thompson, the minority's chief counsel, had written after talking to Buzhardt. The memo included quotes from Nixon during meetings with Dean that appeared verbatim. Buzhardt must have taken the quotes directly from the tapes, Butterfield thought, which only someone familiar with the tapes would have assumed. Sanders reminded Butterfield of Dean's suspicions that he might have been taped and asked if Dean had any reason to think that. Butterfield said no, but the White House did have a taping system that recorded virtually everything said in the Oval Office or on Nixon's telephone. Once prodded, Butterfield continued to unspool the details of the system to the three astonished staffers, who realized almost immediately that they now had a way to determine who was telling the truth—Dean or Nixon. Butterfield then capped off the meeting by saying he had just told them something he had sworn not to tell anyone.[24]

Armstrong and Boyce rushed to tell their boss, majority counsel Sam Dash. They all knew this was the break that would change the committee's investigation and perhaps the presidency. Now they had to get the tapes into the record. Butterfield, however, did not want to testify and was scheduled to fly to Moscow on July 17 to negotiate an aviation treaty. They decided to call Butterfield as a witness on Monday, July 16.[25]

Nixon, who had checked into the Bethesda Naval Hospital the previous night for treatment for viral pneumonia, knew none of this, although he was having regular meetings and telephone calls with staff members between visits with his doctors.[26] Butterfield had not told Haig or Buzhardt of his meeting with the committee staff on July 13. By the next day, Saturday, July 14, Senator Howard Baker, the top Republican on the Watergate committee, knew about the tapes. He and his aides suspected Nixon might be playing some kind of game with the tapes, so they concluded that Butterfield had to testify.[27]

Woodward received a call at home from a staffer with the Butterfield news.[28] Armstrong would later deny he was the source.[29] Woodward then called Bernstein. It was a huge story, but the reporters did nothing. They claimed in *All the President's Men* that they feared a White House hoax, a curious assertion given Woodward's insistence that Armstrong interview Butterfield. They kept the details to themselves until 9:30 that night when they called their editor, Ben Bradlee, at home. The tired Bradlee deemed it only a "B-plus" story and passed.[30]

On the afternoon of Sunday, July 15, Armstrong called Butterfield at home and told him he needed to testify before the committee the next day.[31] Butterfield drove to Baker's home to plead with him to call off the planned testimony. Baker refused. Butterfield then called the White House looking for Garment, who was out of town. Butterfield left him a message. When Garment landed that afternoon at National Airport, he encountered a page that directed him to the White House, where he found Haig, Buzhardt, and Butterfield's frantic message about the testimony scheduled for the next day. Still, no one told Nixon. Haig would later claim that Nixon's hospitalization kept him from telling the president, but White House logs show Haig and Nixon spoke twice on Sunday, and other aides had meetings or telephone calls with the president throughout the day.[32] Nixon himself bragged that he kept a full schedule while hospitalized so as not to appear incapacitated.[33] So Haig had the chance to tell Nixon but did not.

Haig told Nixon about Butterfield's scheduled testimony just hours before Butterfield was set to appear, Nixon wrote in his memoirs.[34] There was nothing they could do about it, Haig said, and Butterfield was most likely going to tell the world about the tapes. Nixon was shocked. He thought the tapes would be covered by executive privilege, which they could have been, if anyone had thought to claim it, as Higby was prepared to do. Haig would claim in his memoirs that he did not tell Nixon anything about the tapes that morning and did not learn about them until after Butterfield had testified.[35]

Butterfield tried to resist testifying, but Senator Ervin warned him that if he did not show up, he would send federal marshals to take him to the hearing room.[36]

By 2 p.m., he sat at the witness table facing Thompson, who asked a series of routine questions. Then he paused and said, "Mr. Butterfield, are you aware of the installation of any listening devices in the Oval Office of the President?"

"I was aware of listening devices," Butterfield replied. "Yes, sir."[37]

Butterfield told about how Nixon recorded himself and that there were also recorders in the Old Executive Building hideaway, at Camp David, and in the Cabinet Room. "There was no doubt in my mind they were installed to record things for posterity, for the Nixon library," Butterfield said. "The President was very conscious of that kind of thing. We had quite an elaborate setup at the White House for the collection and preservation of documents, and of things which transpired in the way of business of state."[38] Virtually everything Nixon or his aides said or put in writing was stored somewhere in the White House.

The committee members and staff grasped the implications of Butterfield's testimony immediately. Dash asked Butterfield the best way to determine who had told the truth. "Well, in the obvious manner, Mr. Dash—to obtain the tape and play it," Butterfield said.[39] That became the mission of the committee. After the hearing, Dash said the committee wanted some of the recordings, particularly those involving Dean, to see who had told the truth. They would tailor the request as narrowly as possible to minimize potential executive privilege issues. Investigators would be "delighted" if the tapes exonerated Nixon, Dash said.[40] The focus turned to a handful of tapes, including the September 15, 1972, meeting between Dean, Nixon, and Haldeman in which Dean gave an update on the cover-up; the February 27, 1973, meeting between Dean and Nixon in which Nixon told Dean to report directly to him about Watergate; the March 13 meeting between Dean and Nixon in which they discussed hush money for the burglars; and the March 21 meeting where Dean told Nixon the blackmail demands were a cancer on the presidency. The committee and special prosecutor Archibald Cox sought those tapes from the White House, and Nixon refused.

Butterfield's admission changed not only the course of the Watergate investigation but effectively ended Nixon's presidency. The tapes contained just what Nixon's enemies believed, what Nixon and his aides knew and what the president's supporters feared—proof that the president of the United States had obstructed justice and then Nixon lied about it. Butterfield could not avoid testifying, and Haig and Buzhardt did nothing to stop him. In fact, they seemed to encourage it, thereby creating a constitutional crisis between the White House, Congress, and Cox that would end with Nixon's resignation thirteen months later. It is difficult to review the record and think that Haig and Buzhardt did not intentionally put Nixon in such a bind. As they did with the appearances before Congress by former deputy CIA directors Cushman and Walters in May, Haig and Buzhardt allowed testimony that devastated Nixon's defense and undermined his presidency. Haig seemed to know it, too. Nixon's "guilt or innocence had ceased to matter," Haig wrote in his memoirs, "because no President could survive the verbatim publication of his most intimate conversations."[41]

Before Butterfield's testimony, the White House was confronted with the official exposure of the secret 1969 to 1970 bombing of Cambodia. Hal M. Knight, a former air force captain who was now a graduate student, had contacted Senator Harold Hughes, an Iowa Democrat on the Armed Services Committee, and told him how pilots falsified their flight plans after bombing targets in neutral Cambodia. Once again, Seymour Hersh had the story on July 15, reporting that the committee had met with Knight behind closed doors and was scheduled to have open hearings led by Symington, who was still the acting chairman in Stennis's absence.[42]

Just as with Watergate and the wiretaps, the initial instinct of those responsible was to lie. "I think it's deplorable," Kissinger said as he disavowed any knowledge of the secret bombing.[43] He not only developed the secret plan but also had told Stennis about the secret bombing three years earlier.

"I want to determine who gave the orders for the bombing and why the public wasn't told about them," Hughes said. Symington agreed and opened a series of hearings that exhumed many of the details of the bombings, particularly how Nixon and Kissinger kept them secret from most of the Pentagon.[44]

As Haig and Buzhardt devastated Nixon's defense, they kept covering up for themselves. With Richardson's help, they continued their attempt to smear Pentagon investigator Donald Stewart by claiming he was trying to extort a job out of the White House. Stewart, who knew nothing of these attempts, continued to agitate for a new job. On July 16, Stewart wrote another angry letter, this time to Pentagon official Martin Hoffman, that condemned the burial of his investigation of the spy ring.[45] Stewart told Hoffman he was looking for a job outside the Pentagon and that he had broken the case of "a rear admiral and a Navy enlisted man engaged in a plot of spying on the President of the US with the purpose of furnishing the results to Adm. Moorer."[46] Despite his findings, Stewart continued, his superiors covered up the case to avoid embarrassing Nixon, the Pentagon, and the military. There was no way this would remain a secret, Stewart said, so James Schlesinger, the new Secretary of Defense, needed to investigate the case further before it exploded around him.

At Justice, Richardson's deputy Carl Belcher continued to investigate whether Stewart could be charged with extortion. Belcher then passed the case to his own deputy, Alfred Hantman, for more probing.[47]

Stewart's emotions boiled over on July 22, when he read a story by Jack Anderson in the Sunday *Parade* magazine newspaper insert. In "My Journal on Watergate," Anderson bragged how the Pentagon and White House Plumbers tried to find his sources and interrogated suspects behind "the forbidding doors of Room 3E993" at the Pentagon. The Plumbers, Anderson wrote, had blamed the wrong person, incorrectly fingering someone on Kissinger's staff. It was the White House, not his sources, that lied about Pakistan, Anderson wrote. "Eventually, an entire section of Kissinger's staff was scattered around the world, and Admiral Robert Welander, who headed it was exiled to the Atlantic fleet."[48]

The mention of the case and Welander's name outraged Stewart, who had believed that Anderson had gotten away with publishing classified information with not even a slap on the wrist. Donald Sanders, one of Senator Baker's aides, also noticed the mention of the Plumbers and the leak investigation. Sanders and Stewart had worked together at the FBI, and Sanders knew about Pentagon's Room 3E993. He called Stewart to set up a meeting.[49] At the White House, Buzhardt was also thinking of the spy ring investigation. Just days before Ehrlichman was scheduled to testify before the Watergate Committee, Buzhardt sent his lawyer, John Wilson, a letter declaring that executive privilege covered anything involving the spy ring. Ehrlichman could not talk about it.[50]

So a week after he and Haig did not use executive privilege to prevent Butterfield from revealing the secret White House taping system, Buzhardt was using it to block testimony about the spy ring, a case in which Nixon was the victim.

Stewart met with Sanders and Howard Liebengood on July 24.[51] He told them the leak investigation went deeper than what Anderson described, and he provided detail about the spy ring. Stewart also recommended they talk to David Young. They prepared a memo for Thompson, who then showed it to a curious Baker, who had long suspected a CIA connection to Watergate. Baker now knew about the military spy ring, a secret almost as closely held as the White House tapes, and he planned to ask Ehrlichman about it when he appeared before the committee.[52]

When Ehrlichman testified, Baker asked about the unnamed national security issues that led to the FBI wiretaps. Ehrlichman said he was prohibited from speaking about the issues because of executive privilege. "I would probably be violating two or three statutes if I disclosed at this point," he said, adding later that "it's one of those collateral matters, senator, that would be interesting and titillating and what not, but it would cause more mischief than the good would be produced from the disclosure." Ehrlichman said he would willingly talk more in executive session, and that "I am under express injunction from Mr. Buzhardt that executive privilege has been invoked as to the other matters."[53]

Stymied, Baker wanted more information. The next day, he and Senator Sam Ervin, the committee chairman, met with Buzhardt and Garment. The senators brought their counsels, Dash and Thompson. The White House lawyers urged the senators not to investigate the matter or talk about it publicly. It would be too explosive, they argued, and they made the dubious claim it was not germane to Watergate. Someone from the Senate mentioned Stewart, whom Buzhardt and Garment smeared by saying he was under investigation for extortion.[54] They neglected to add that Justice had rejected the claims. Ervin, over Baker's opposition, agreed with Buzhardt and Garment that the spy ring was not germane to their investigation and they would not push it.[55]

Baker had one option left. He called Young for a meeting. Young listened to Baker's request but said it was "the one thing that the president told me not to discuss at all, and I won't."[56] Baker would have to ask Nixon himself if he wanted to know more, Young said. With that, the issue died, at least in the Senate.

Shortly afterward, Buzhardt's effort to charge Stewart with extortion also fizzled. Alfred Hantman sent his boss, Carl Belcher, a memo on August 2 that said Stewart's June letter to Baroody was something anyone looking for a job would do. "It certainly strains credulity to believe that if a former

FBI agent, such as Stewart, intended to 'commit or attempt an act of extortion' he would" do it in writing, Hantman wrote. Richardson tried to keep the matter alive, but another aide also told him there was no case. Richardson finally took no for an answer.[57]

◆━◆

Secretary of State William Rogers had long been unhappy about how Nixon and Kissinger treated him. By July, rumors started that Rogers would resign. In what turned out to be his final news conference, Rogers criticized the abuses uncovered by the Watergate investigation, particularly citing the "extralegal" actions used by the White House to investigate Daniel Ellsberg and others.[58] In essence, Rogers criticized the very tools used to support the secret government that too often excluded him. Rogers resigned on August 22. Nixon made the obligatory compliments about Rogers's service and then named his nemesis, Kissinger, to replace him.

As national security adviser, Kissinger was protected by executive privilege. He never had to testify before Congress, one reason why Nixon funneled much of his national security decisions through the NSC. Nominating Kissinger as Secretary of State removed that protection; Kissinger's actions as national security adviser were fair game for the Senate Foreign Relations Committee. Unlike Pat Gray, who was brutalized by his Judiciary Committee hearings, Kissinger faced a more supportive committee. He had often met informally with William Fulbright, an Arkansas Democrat and the panel's chairman, and many of the committee members backed his nomination. But Kissinger lacked practice in coping with probing senators or the spotlight of a packed hearing room. He had much to explain, starting with the administration's policies, including the secret bombing of Cambodia, and moving to his role in initiating the wiretaps by the FBI of seventeen government officials and reporters. Nixon had taken responsibility for the taps in his May 22 White Paper, but few took that statement seriously. Questions remained, and now Kissinger would be forced to answer them.

Fulbright complicated the hearings by seeking the Justice Department's report on the wiretaps, which had been compiled after the FBI finished its investigation in May. Richardson delayed releasing it, because he thought it would invade the privacy of those who were improperly tapped.[59] Under oath, Kissinger lied when Fulbright asked about the extent of his involvement in the wiretaps. Kissinger claimed he had little to do with them.[60] It was Kissinger who talked to FBI director J. Edgar Hoover four times on May 9, 1969, after the *New York Times* story about the Cambodia bombings. It was Kissinger who told Hoover he wanted to find the leaker and "destroy" him.

It was Kissinger who picked the names of the people to be tapped and gave them to Haig to deliver to Sullivan. Under oath in front of the Senate, his chances to be Secretary of State threatened by a curious committee, Kissinger covered up his part in Nixon's secret government. He succeeded with help from Richardson, who provided the Justice report that portrayed Kissinger as a minor participant in the wiretaps.

The full Senate voted 78–7 to confirm Kissinger on September 22. The wiretap incident, however, left a mark. Among those who voted no were Senators Weicker and Gaylord Nelson, a Wisconsin Democrat, who said their votes were influenced by the wiretaps. Another, Senator James Abourezk, a South Dakota Democrat, said, "We know enough about Dr. Kissinger to know that he is capable of deceiving the Congress and the public."[61]

Weicker remained fixated on the wiretaps and Kissinger's role in them. Mardian testified in late July before the Senate Watergate Committee, and Weicker said he wanted Sullivan to testify before the committee. But Ervin questioned the wiretaps' relevance to the committee's investigation, because they did not involve the 1972 campaign. Weicker, determined to have Sullivan testify, brought him back for another interview on October 7 with him and five staff members. By this time, Sullivan was openly resistant to testifying, and he started the interview by "stating that he had no knowledge relating to the responsibilities of this committee."[62] Since he first met with Woodward on March 5 and in subsequent meetings with Weicker and his staff, Sullivan had talked about White House and Justice-related spying on Democrats and Democratic candidates. Now he had a convenient case of amnesia as he faced being called as a witness. Sullivan lied again when he told the group that he did not know the Plumbers had existed until "it was made public" and that he had only met Gordon Liddy "five or six years ago" and did not know him or the other defendants.[63] That claim was contradicted by a memo Liddy wrote August 2, 1971, after meeting with Sullivan to discuss help investigating Daniel Ellsberg. "I explained the functions of Messrs. Krogh and Young, and myself in responding to" the leaks.[64]

Sullivan lied about his relationship with Haig, which had existed for years. Kissinger, he told Weicker, was the only person he knew at the White House, where Haig was now the chief of staff. Sullivan spent the rest of the meeting backpedaling on what he knew and when and presenting a false picture of his work with Hoover and the FBI. "Sullivan made it clear that he does not think that the investigation of the wiretaps is within the scope of this committee," the notes said. "Sullivan said he has been harassed all summer by leaks in the newspapers."[65] He also changed his motive for telling Mardian about the wiretap logs. Instead of being worried that Hoover would use them as blackmail against Nixon to keep his job as FBI director, Sullivan told Weicker that he "knew that the people on whom the taps were placed were innocent and did not want these names to become public." In a further bit of revisionism from Sullivan, he told Weicker that he told Hoover in 1964 that Lyndon Johnson was relying too much on wiretaps and that it "could damage Hoover. Robert Novak called Sullivan at the time to verify information that Novak already had, but Sullivan did not give Novak a column."[66]

Despite Sullivan's evasions, Weicker still wanted to call him as a witness and wrote Ervin on October 11 to ask him to put Sullivan on the witness list to detail "FBI activities . . . undertaken to affect the climate of the 1972 presidential campaign."[67] Meanwhile, someone involved with Weicker's investigation, most likely staffer and former New York *Daily News* reporter Richard McGowan, leaked the details of the probe to *Daily News* writer Frank Van Riper, who had been one of the most aggressive reporters covering the Watergate hearings. On October 13, Van Riper reported that "William C. Sullivan, an assistant FBI Director until his ouster by the late J. Edgar Hoover in 1971, has been secretly interviewed by the Senate Watergate Committee in connection with an alleged FBI spy operation."[68] Sullivan, Van Riper continued, had been cooperating with Weicker "reluctantly" but had been "hinting strongly" that the committee should get the files from Mardian's division of the Justice Department.

The *Daily News* story exposed the machinations of Sullivan, the man McGowan described as a "viper," and caused Sullivan to erupt in anger. He wrote the *Daily News* a letter on October 16 demanding a retraction of the story he called "a malicious falsehood it its entirety. I have not had any such interviews and do not intend to do so with Senator Weicker at any time in the future."[69] He admitted to talking with Weicker twice earlier in the year but not since then, an obvious lie given his October 7 meeting with Weicker and top committee aides. Sullivan followed up the same day with a letter to Weicker, saying he had been the victim of partisan sniping during much of the year, and "I do not intend to take any more of it."[70]

On October 19, Ervin told Weicker he would not allow Sullivan to testify, because he had nothing relevant to say about 1972 campaign activities.[71]

Butterfield's revelation about the White House tapes led Cox and the committee to subpoena them. Nixon was determined not to give them up. He particularly resisted Cox, whom he now viewed as an enemy backed by a legal team of Ivy League liberals out to get him. Eventually the legal battle focused on nine tapes, most of them conversations between Dean and Nixon. US District Judge John J. Sirica had ordered the White House to give up the tapes, and the White House had appealed. The appeals court ruled 5–2 against Nixon on October 12, but still Nixon resisted. Cox pressed on, putting his nominal boss, Richardson, in a difficult position. Nixon wanted to fire Cox; Richardson resisted and threatened to resign.

Then Buzhardt devised a possible solution. Instead of giving the tapes directly to Cox, the White House would first give them to friendly Senator John Stennis, who would then listen to the tapes and then provide written summaries for Judge Sirica. Such a gambit made sense only to Nixon and his loyalists. At seventy-two, Stennis was healthy, but he was hard of hearing and had been shot in a mugging attempt in January. He had only returned to work in September. But Buzhardt knew Stennis well and that the senator, whom he called the Senate's "undertaker," could help bury some of their problems.

Cox was initially unwilling to accept the offer. Richardson also had problems but wavered between resigning and staying on to see if he could persuade Cox, his former professor at Harvard Law School, to remain. The two entered into negotiations with Buzhardt and Haig over what Cox was willing to accept to get the tapes. Nixon wanted to fire Cox and be done with it, but Richardson wanted to keep him in fear of the fallout from such a high-profile dismissal.

Complicating matters was the start of another war in the Middle East. Egyptian and Syrian forces had attacked Israel on October 6, the high holy day of Yom Kippur, and swept into territories Israel had occupied after their war in 1967. Israel appeared in jeopardy. The United States responded by sending weapons and supplies to Israel, which triggered an embargo on oil sales to the United States. The Soviet Union moved to back its Arab clients, Egypt and Syria, and tensions escalated enough to spark world fears of a superpower confrontation. Nixon was drinking heavily enough that he barely functioned. On October 11, Kissinger did not bother waking him to accept a call from British prime minister Edward Heath because Nixon was too drunk. "Can we tell him no?" Kissinger asked his deputy, Brent Scowcroft. "When I talked to the president he was loaded."[72] On their own, Haig and Kissinger raised the nation's nuclear-alert level to DEFCON 3, which only increased fears the crisis would spread beyond the Middle East. Israel eventually gained the advantage and recaptured its territory, and its forces crossed the Suez Canal and threatened Cairo. The crisis preoccupied Nixon as he fought the legal challenge over the tapes and again showed how it was Haig, not Nixon, who made most of the decisions, often to Nixon's detriment.

That was never truer than in the fight with Cox over the tapes. Haig told Nixon he had reached a deal with Cox in which the prosecutor would accept Stennis's review of the nine tapes, and Cox and Richardson would not resign. Then Haig changed the deal without telling Nixon.[73] Cox could only have the tapes if he agreed to never ask for more than the nine at issue. Haig led Nixon to believe Cox and Richardson would take this deal, too, although Richardson had already told Haig such a proposal was unacceptable. Haig pushed that deal anyway, and Cox and Richardson refused to take it. On Saturday, October 20, Nixon ordered Richardson to fire Cox, and Richardson refused. He went to the White House to see Nixon and resign in protest. Nixon begged him to stay, citing the Middle East crisis as the need for stability. Richardson declined and thanked Nixon for having the faith in him to name him to three cabinet posts. Firing Cox fell to Richardson's deputy, William Ruckelshaus, who refused and quit. Next in line was Solicitor General Robert Bork, who was now the acting attorney general. He agreed to fire Cox, because he knew that Nixon would burn through Justice's hierarchy until he found someone willing to dump the special prosecutor.

Dubbed the Saturday Night Massacre, the firing of Cox and the resignations of Richardson and Ruckelshaus wiped out any goodwill Nixon had with Congress. The House immediately began impeachment proceedings. Representative B. F. Sisk, a Democrat from California, said Nixon's "actions raise real questions to me of whether or not he's thinking straight."[74] Nixon now had to find a new special prosecutor and attorney general. His ability to influence either would be minimal, since the price of getting anyone to take the jobs would be more independence than their predecessors had enjoyed. Once again, Nixon was the victim of his continued flawed judgment and his reliance on Haig and Buzhardt. They had maneuvered him into the crisis with Cox, and Haig had misled Nixon into believing Richardson would not quit. That error precipitated the chain reaction of resignations that pushed Congress to the next level of confrontation—impeachment—that had been last tried more than one hundred years earlier.

Haig concluded that Nixon had lost confidence in him after the tapes debacle. "Although he said nothing about this, I was quite sure that he felt that he had been let down not only by Richardson but by me and everyone else who had urged him to accept the Stennis compromise rather than trusting and acting on his own instincts," Haig wrote later.[75]

Nixon then reversed field and said he would turn over the tapes. He was acting erratically, and Buzhardt concluded Nixon had to resign. He flew to Key

Biscayne on November 3 to make the case, but Haig, who later claimed he had no idea what Buzhardt planned, refused to let him see the president.[76] At the White House, Nixon's secretary, Rose Mary Woods, was preparing transcripts of the White House tapes to give Sirica. By late October, she had already acknowledged to Nixon that she had accidentally erased about five minutes of one tape. She and other White House officials were due in Sirica's court on November 8 as part of the legal proceedings surrounding the attempts to obtain the tapes. That morning Woodward and Bernstein had another scoop. The tapes were of questionable quality, the duo reported, but more ominously, one of their sources told them the tapes contained gaps "of a suspicious nature" and that "conversation on some of the tapes appears to have been erased or obliterated by the injection—inadvertent or otherwise—of background noise."[77]

The November 8 story raised the question of whether Nixon or someone else in the White House was intentionally destroying incriminating evidence. It tipped off the public to a potential crime—the intentional destruction of evidence in a law enforcement investigation. The tape was one of those subpoenaed by Congress and the special prosecutor. Also, someone inside the White House was spilling Nixon's secrets about the "suspicious nature" of the gaps.

"Portions of the seven White House tapes that President Nixon has agreed to turn over to the US District Court here are 'inaudible' and thus will probably fail to definitively answer questions about Mr. Nixon's role in the Watergate affair, according to White House sources," Woodward and Bernstein wrote.[78] They cited White House sources questioned over the last three days, a sign that interviews started on November 5, just after Buzhardt's failed attempt to get Nixon to resign. Between the lead and the sixth paragraph, only White House sources are cited in the story. The sixth paragraph quoted one of the five White House officials saying the gaps were suspicious. The other four, the story said, did not confirm that the gaps were suspicious or intentional.

The story alerted Sirica to problems with the tapes, and Woods, when asked about them in court, said some parts were inaudible. "The quality is very bad on some, depending on the room," Woods said in court.[79] Woods's testimony coupled with the *Post* story increased the belief by congressional investigators and prosecutors that Nixon was hiding something on the tapes. Those suspicions became even greater on November 21, when Buzhardt told Sirica that he had detected an eighteen-and-a-half-minute gap on one of the tapes.[80] Sirica then demanded the White House turn over the tapes to prevent any further damage, intentional or otherwise, to what had become evidence in a growing case against Nixon.

Woodward and Bernstein went even further in *All the President's Men*, which was released the following spring. The tip, they wrote, came from a newly revived Deep Throat, who had not spoken to Woodward since May.[81]

"In the first week of November, Woodward moved the flower pot and traveled to the underground garage." There he met Deep Throat, whose "message was short and simple: one or more of the tapes contained deliberate erasures."[82]

The book said Bernstein immediately contacted four White House aides; none would confirm the tip that the tapes contained suspicious gaps, but they printed the claim anyway. Between the November publication of the story and the spring release of the book, however, the pair had also erased their source's White House connection. Instead, the shadowy figure of Deep Throat, whose job in government was never really defined, was described in the book as providing the initial tip about the erased tapes.[83]

Woodward and Bernstein had altered the true identity of a source, a White House official, to fit their fictional composite Deep Throat character. They also violated two of their often-flexible rules of reporting. In the November 8 story, Deep Throat was an original source, not a confirming one, for the tip about the intentional erasure. He gave the tip to Woodward and then Bernstein sought confirmation, which he could not find, from the only people who would know about the problems with the tapes—the White House staff. That was why Woodward and Bernstein relied on an anonymous, uncorroborated source to claim that someone had committed an illegal act, in this case the destruction of evidence. The reporters also changed the account of the tape gap between the November 8 story and the book; again, the book features a more definitive claim.

Overriding everything, however, is the original sourcing in the story from five White House sources. There is no mention anywhere in the November 8 story that someone outside the White House provided any information about the tapes. Sourcing throughout the *Post*'s Watergate-related stories, even if they relied on anonymity, was consistent, according to an analysis of other stories that involved the Deep Throat composite. The paper would not reveal a source's name or specific job but it never said a source worked in one part of the government when he or she worked somewhere else. A White House official would never be described as someone working at the Justice Department, for example. A September 17, 1972, story for which Deep Throat was a source included an explanatory paragraph spelling out the overall sourcing: "The *Post*'s information about the funds and their relationship to the Watergate case was obtained from a variety of sources, including investigators, other federal sources and officials and employees of the Committee for the Re-election of the President."[84] A September 18, 1972, follow-up about the campaign attributed the information from "sources close to the investigation," which was accurate.[85] The May 3, 1973, story derived from a March 5 interview with William Sullivan of the FBI, and a Justice Department official cited "two highly placed sources in the executive branch."[86] Woodward and Bernstein claimed in their book that information came from Deep Throat. Finally, the November 8 article cited five White House sources and no one else.

That sourcing ruled out Felt, who not only had never worked at the White House but also was not working at all at the time.

Woodward's attempts to explain how Felt could have known about the tape gap make little sense. In *The Secret Man*, Woodward attributed Felt's knowledge to the mysteries of the FBI: "With Felt out of the FBI, I figured he would not be up-to-date," Woodward wrote in 2005. "But in the first week in November 1973 I contacted him in order to set up a meeting in the underground garage. It was brief. He had retired from the Bureau, but he was in touch with many friends there. That's the way the place worked."[87]

In other words, a gossipy FBI official told Felt, a former colleague. However, no evidence exists to show that any of the five people who knew about the gap—Haig, Buzhardt, Woods, Steve Bull, and Haig assistant John Bennett—ever told the FBI about it. The tape had been subpoenaed as evidence. Erasing it would have been tantamount to admitting to a crime. FBI documents do not show that anyone from the White House informed the Bureau about the tape gaps before Woods acknowledged the problem in court. If no one told the Bureau, no one at the Bureau could have told Felt. If someone at the Bureau believed evidence was being destroyed, they would have gone to Sirica, not Felt or Woodward.

Believing Woodward's claim also means accepting that the sixty-year-old Felt would have spent every day for five months driving from his home in northern Virginia to look for a flower pot on Woodward's balcony on the off chance the young reporter wanted a meeting. Since Woodward's notes show he had called Felt at home in July for an on-the-record telephone interview, why would he need the flower pot?[88] Felt had no direct knowledge of the tape, because no one who did know told him.

Woodward and Bernstein already told their *Post* readers that the tip came from the White House. Of the five people there who knew about the tape, the most likely source was the person who erased the tape. Bull, Woods, and Bennett did not talk to Woodward, but Buzhardt and Haig did. Woodward and Haig knew each other from when Woodward would deliver packages and briefings to Haig at the NSC offices in the White House basement.

Buzhardt would become one of Woodward's best sources for *The Final Days*, Woodward and Bernstein's 1976 book about Nixon. Among those who knew about the gap, Haig or Buzhardt seem the most likely source.

Nixon's fortunes faded with virtually every day as Haig and Buzhardt, either intentionally or through incompetence, made a series of missteps that weakened Nixon. Those who helped enable Nixon's gamble were now helping to unravel it.

CHAPTER NINETEEN

Spy Ring Cover-Up (1973–1974)

JOHN EHRLICHMAN'S SENATE TESTIMONY, PARTICULARLY HOW HE AVOIDED talking about national security issues, piqued the curiosity of Jim Squires of the *Chicago Tribune* and Dan Thomasson of Scripps Howard newspapers.[1] They wondered what Ehrlichman had been forbidden to mention, and although they worked for different news organizations, their editors allowed them to collaborate to dig out what Ehrlichman was hiding.

It was slow going. Few people knew about the spy ring, and those who did were not talking. Yeoman Charles Radford and Rear Admiral Robert Welander had been exiled to remote assignments. Admiral Thomas Moorer had been cowed into silence and would not have been given a second term as chairman of the Joint Chiefs if he did not cooperate. Donald Stewart had kept his silence other than talking to Senators Baker and Ervin. Still, the chance of detection remained. Then, seemingly out of the blue, Woodward and Bernstein published a story that came dangerously close to breaking the spy ring open. Published on page A27 of the October 10 *Post* and headlined "Military Aide Phone Was Tapped," the story focused on how the FBI put a wiretap on the telephone of a low-level military aide—an unnamed Radford—ten months after Nixon had said all wiretaps had stopped.[2] It did not mention the spy ring, about which Woodward had known about since May. The story merely emphasized how Nixon had been misleading when he said the wiretaps had stopped in February 1971. The story also mentioned that the wiretaps were tied to Jack Anderson's India-Pakistan columns from December 1971.

The point of the October 10 story is mysterious. As Len Colodny and Robert Gettlin wrote in *Silent Coup*, the story seemed aimed at smoking out Squires and Thomasson.[3] The wiretap story got lost in that day's *Post* because of the crisis surrounding Vice President Agnew, who would resign later that day after pleading no contest to federal charges of tax evasion. Agnew, a former governor of Maryland, had been under federal investigation for months, but the first public word that Agnew was a target surfaced in August. As long as Agnew remained vice president, few believed Nixon would resign and make Agnew president. Now, Agnew's resignation had removed that obstacle, and Nixon's nominee for vice president, House Minority Leader Gerald Ford of Michigan, was deemed far more acceptable and someone Americans could see as a potential president.

Haig faced another problem on October 31, when Egil Krogh, the codirector of the Plumbers, filed a motion in the perjury case against him to use the fruits of the Plumbers' work to defend himself.[4] He wanted tapes of conversations between Nixon, Ehrlichman, and David Young from December 1971 through February 1972 related to the Plumbers' work on the India-Pakistan leaks and the instructions calling for secrecy. If he had lied, Krogh claimed, it was only because Nixon told him to. Haig and Buzhardt had already seen how these details about the Plumbers had destroyed the Pentagon Papers case. Krogh's case portended something even worse, because the release of the documents he sought would eventually implicate Haig in the spy ring and Buzhardt in its cover-up.

Haig was also in the final phases of hiring a replacement for Archibald Cox, and he had settled on Leon Jaworski, the veteran Texas trial lawyer, longtime adviser to Lyndon Johnson, former head of the American Bar Association, and a named partner of a powerhouse Houston law firm. Cox's fate made Jaworski reluctant to consider the job, but Haig appealed to his patriotism and promised independence. Haig also told Nixon that Jaworski understood the difference between legitimate Watergate-related issues and national security matters better left alone. Jaworski accepted the offer on November 1.

Haig and Buzhardt called Jaworski for a meeting on November 13. They discussed the scope of Krogh's motion, which meant "trouble," Jaworski's notes show, and then an explanation of the spy ring.[5] Haig and Buzhardt told Jaworski that a young yeoman had taken the records from the NSC and given them to the chairman of the Joint Chiefs of Staff. A complete report of the incident existed, but they referred only to the sanitized report that Buzhardt gave to Mel Laird. Haig knew Young had done a more complete report, because he and Kissinger had listened to Ehrlichman's interview of Welander. That meant Haig knew how much Welander had told Ehrlichman about how Haig shared information with the chiefs. That interview was now buried in the White House files. By giving Jaworski the sanitized report, Haig and Buzhardt were withholding evidence the prosecutor could have used to decide potential cases.[6]

Their concerns about Krogh would come to nothing. US District Judge Gerhard Gesell rejected Krogh's motion, and Krogh eventually pleaded guilty to the lesser charge of conspiracy to violate Daniel Ellsberg's civil rights and received a six-month prison sentence. The perjury charge was dropped.

By December, Squires and Thomasson had gotten close to discovering the mysterious issues Ehrlichman could not mention. They knew someone had prepared a report about a security breach at the White House involving the military. In late December, Buzhardt called them to a White House meeting, where they managed to bluff Buzhardt into believing they knew more than they actually did. They finished reporting in early January and only needed a White House comment before publishing. Aldo Beckman, the *Tribune*'s White House correspondent, asked Haig in California about the report, and the surprised chief of staff muttered that he was afraid the story would get out. Then Haig returned and told Beckman: "There's not a word of truth to it."[7]

Meanwhile, Woodward seemed to be at least two steps ahead of Squires and Thomasson. On January 7, he called Radford and told him the story was going to get out. Stunned, Radford felt "sick to my stomach" the affair would become public but did not comment.[8] Woodward then called Donald Stewart to ask what he knew about the tap on Radford's phone. Stewart told Woodward to call the Pentagon press office, but the questions kept coming. Stewart started taking notes of his own. Woodward's questions showed he knew that documents about the India-Pakistan war had been leaked and that someone was passing classified information from the NSC to the chairman of the Joint Chiefs. Stewart did not realize that Woodward had once worked for both Moorer and Welander. He also did not know Woodward had known about the spy ring since at least May. Woodward then called Welander. Once again, Woodward told Welander the story was going to come out and asked what Welander could tell him. Welander just denied he had done anything wrong.[9]

Again, however, Woodward sat on the story, just as he had the previous May.

Both Squires's and Thomasson's stories appeared on January 11. "A still-secret White House investigation in 1971 disclosed that top-ranking military officials engaged in a spying and eavesdropping campaign against Henry Kissinger, *The Tribune* learned today," read the lead of Squires's story.[10] They included Haig's denial and then a reversal of the denial by Buzhardt. They also included Moorer's denial that he was involved in spying. While neither reporter knew the names of Welander or Radford, they had overcome the White House stonewalling to reveal the spy ring that Nixon had tried so hard to conceal.

Woodward and Bernstein finally had a story the next day,[11] January 12, as did Hersh in the *New York Times*.[12] Hersh's account was more accurate, while the *Post*'s story seemed as if it was dictated directly from sources at the White House and Pentagon.

Hersh led with the Young report and how the White House Plumbers had uncovered a military spy ring "attempting to relay highly classified information on the China talks and other matters" to Pentagon officials. Hersh noted that some of the officers involved were assigned to the NSC and that Young's investigation was triggered by the December 1971 leaks to Jack Anderson. The story named Welander, but not Radford. One reason for the spying, Hersh wrote, was how the White House denied the Pentagon information it needed. It included the White House's attempt to blame Radford alone for the leaks and Anderson's statement that Welander was the wrong person to blame for the leaks. Hersh also noted how the *Chicago Tribune* and Scripps Howard had broken the story the day earlier. Finally, it ended with the concerns by Stewart, who was not named, that the spy ring could have been part of a potential military plot to seize control of the government.[13]

The *Post* report, on the other hand, gave the impression that the *Post* had broken the story on its own. They mentioned neither the Squires nor Thomasson stories published a day earlier. Despite Woodward's head start—it noted that Welander and Radford had been interviewed up to two weeks earlier—it was less complete than the first two articles or Hersh's.[14] It named Radford as "the central figure in the matter." Woodward, who had worked at the NSC, had to have known better than to believe that an enlisted man could steal documents for the chairman of the Joint Chiefs of Staff on his own and against the chairman's wishes. In 1989, Woodward claimed in an interview that his story was "an example of the newspaper's and my independence. He was a former skipper and somebody I knew, but names were being taken and we went ahead and did it."[15] But Woodward and Bernstein were not the first to name Welander. Hersh did, too, and Jack Anderson named Welander in his July 1973 *Parade* magazine article that mentioned the leak investigation. Hersh also quoted Anderson, saying Welander was the wrong man and "gave me nothing."[16] Woodward and Bernstein mentioned only Buzhardt's sanitized report for Laird, not Young's more detailed report to Nixon.[17] Buzhardt, they wrote, "never established that Welander or Radford did anything wrong." Nixon never knew about Buzhardt's report, which was done after Nixon ordered the cover-up of the spy ring. He had seen Young's report and then ordered Welander and Radford transferred and the issue buried. Woodward also did not disclose that he had worked for both

Welander and Moorer. There is no indication that he ever told his colleagues or superiors of his connection to either officer.

Everyone involved in the spy ring case had something to hide. Nixon did not want the world to know the military was spying on him, and Haig wanted to hide that he had helped the spies. Buzhardt had covered up for Haig. Moorer did not want to advertise that he was so out of the loop that he had to rely on a young enlisted man, Radford, who was often looting Haig's and Kissinger's briefcases for secrets. Only Donald Stewart, who had been yanked from the Pentagon investigation he had started, had reason to talk, and the White House had plans for him.

Haig and Buzhardt's campaign to discredit Stewart started with Hersh's story on January 13.[18] White House officials, he reported, had told members of the Senate Watergate Committee that an unnamed government official—Stewart—had threatened to blackmail the White House into giving him a job or he would expose the spying. Haig and Buzhardt knew that by September the Justice had declined to prosecute Stewart for extortion, but they wanted to smear Stewart by labeling him a blackmailing, disgruntled office seeker. Hersh would call this story his greatest regret about his spy ring coverage.

The *Post* followed with two stories, including a Woodward and Bernstein piece that concluded that Nixon had made "unwarranted use" of the national security claim for eighteen months in order to cover up the Plumbers.[19] The spy ring was the final national security item to be revealed, which one source called just another part of the continued Watergate cover-up.[20] Sources claimed Nixon cited national security in reference to the Plumbers and Ellsberg, when he was really just hiding that the Plumbers had burglarized Ellsberg's psychiatrist's office.[21]

In January 1974, after eighteen months of White House lies about Watergate, the national security claims seemed like just another part of the cover-up. In December 1971, however, Nixon had legitimate national security fears arising from the spy ring. He was then negotiating the China summit, the heart of his foreign policy gamble. Anything that jeopardized that summit, including Anderson's columns, had national security implications. Nixon could say none of that publicly, and prosecuting anyone involved in the spy ring would have weakened Nixon's hand against the Soviet Union and China, who would have seen a weak US president unable to exert his will with his own military.

Everyone involved in the case spent the next weeks scrambling for cover. The White House tried to pin everything on Radford, claiming he had acted alone. Moorer denied he received anything improper, and told NBC's *Today* show on January 18 that Nixon still had confidence in him.[22] That was only because Nixon had, in Ehrlichman's words, turned Moorer into a "preshrunk admiral" by holding his involvement in the spy ring over him. Moorer's claims about Radford made no sense. He knew the yeoman was stealing classified documents for him, but Moorer never told him to stop, because he was getting information from Radford that the White House had denied him.

Although Kissinger was the spy ring's victim, he, too, had much to hide. He had denied for months that he knew anything about the Plumbers, even though Young, one of his closest aides, directed them. Those denials started to crumble on January 22, when Kissinger had to acknowledge he had listened to Young and Ehrlichman's interview with Welander.[23] That admission contradicted Kissinger's claim to the Senate Foreign Relations Committee that he knew nothing about Young's work.[24] Kissinger not only knew about Young's investigation of Welander, but he was outraged that Nixon decided not to prosecute Moorer or Welander, claiming the administration would regret it later.

The administration-wide lack of curiosity extended to the Pentagon, where Defense Secretary James Schlesinger said that while there were "clearly improprieties" with the stolen documents, he doubted there was a spy ring.[25] He also made the stunning claim that Buzhardt had denied the Pentagon access to Young and Ehrlichman's interview of Welander by saying it could be used as evidence in any impending trial of members of the Plumbers. That made little sense. Buzhardt and Haig had already tried to limit the use of the spy ring in any of the Plumbers trials. Krogh had already pleaded guilty in his perjury case after he had originally sought the spy ring documents for his defense. Young had been granted immunity in May, so he did not need them. Since the spy ring had been revealed, there was no longer a national security excuse for hiding it. The only reason to keep the first Welander interview from anyone, including the Defense Secretary Welander worked for, was to protect Haig and Buzhardt.

The next break for the White House came with the decision on January 31 by the friendly John Stennis, who was back in charge of the Senate Armed Services Committee, to investigate the spy ring. The Senate's "undertaker" was a friend of Buzhardt, but an even greater friend of the military, which Stennis believed could not endure a lengthy investigation. Stennis had no plans for one.

Stennis's initial instinct was to call only a few witnesses in a closed, one-day hearing, but liberal members of the committee, led by Democrat Harold Hughes of Iowa, demanded full committee hearings.[26] They could tell by the White House and Pentagon's nonsensical claims about the spy ring that the case was bigger than they let on. Hughes wanted to see Young's report on the spy ring, which unnamed White House officials—read Haig and Buzhardt—were now calling overblown. Meanwhile, Hersh kept uncovering new and embarrassing details, including a February 3 piece that showed how the spying had started in 1970, shortly after Radford joined the NSC liaison office with Robinson as his commander.[27]

The hearings started February 6 with Moorer, who testified that he wanted to court martial Radford and was overruled, but he did not know who made that decision.[28] That was another lie, because Moorer knew any trial of Radford would expose how the yeoman was stealing secrets for him. Moorer had to admit that he received more than just "two batches" of information from Radford, as he originally claimed, and that the pipeline of stolen documents had flowed freely for months.[29]

Kissinger's testimony continued the perjury. He said that while some White House documents were not meant to be shared with other officials, it was absurd to insist he had hidden anything from the Joint Chiefs. "I was never conscious of any disagreement between myself and Admiral Moorer," Kissinger said.[30] But Kissinger did admit how angry he was to learn just how much Radford had taken when he listened to Ehrlichman and Young's interview with Welander. That was enough for Stennis, who said he saw nothing wrong in what Kissinger and Moorer had said in closed testimony, and he announced he would only call three more witnesses—Welander, Buzhardt, and Radford, who was being flown to Washington from Oregon.

Hersh tracked down Radford as he was changing planes in Denver, and Radford told him a much different story than what Kissinger and Moorer had told the committee. He took "hundreds" of documents to Moorer's office, Radford said, adding that "I had everyone's confidence."[31] Moorer knew exactly what he was getting and where it came from, Radford told Hersh. "Admiral Moorer was pleased with the information. I always got feedback." Radford was far more credible than Moorer, the *Times* wrote in a February 11 editorial. "Enlisted men do not take it upon themselves to embark on unauthorized missions against the White House. Nor are they likely to drop in on admirals with the secret booty."[32] Radford repeated what he told Hersh when he met later in February with the full committee. Not only did Moorer know he was stealing documents, Radford said, so did Moorer's staff, who urged him to keep it up.[33]

The committee could have cleared up many of the unanswered questions by calling Stewart as a witness, but he never testified, perhaps because Haig and Buzhardt had tarnished his reputation. The Justice Department had already rejected the claim that Stewart had tried to extort a job out of the

White House. On February 7, Donald Sanders, the Senate aide and Stewart's former FBI colleague, had contacted him again to ask if he would talk to Sanders's boss, Baker, a request that Stewart detailed the next day in a memo to his boss, Martin Hoffman.[34] Shortly thereafter, Stewart received another call from Woodward, who again had information that Stewart knew was still secret. He asked Stewart if he knew that Radford and Anderson had dinner together two nights before Anderson's first column about India and Pakistan. Two hours later, Woodward called Stewart again, this time to ask him if Buzhardt told the committee what he knew, would it "contradict Adm. Moorer and bring about Moorer's court-martial." Stewart said he did not know and ended the call.[35] Woodward wrote nothing about the Stewart interview or anything more about the spy ring case.

Buzhardt was the committee's final witness on March 7, and he continued the White House cover-up by giving the panel the sanitized report he delivered to Laird on January 10, 1972, not Young's more complete investigation. He claimed the two interviews of Welander were virtually identical and that he did not give Schlesinger the first interview when he had asked for it because he no longer worked for Schlesinger.[36] Buzhardt had quit as the Pentagon's general counsel on January 4, ending the seven months in which he served as both the Pentagon's lawyer and Nixon's Watergate attorney. Buzhardt also made the astounding claim, which contradicted months of White House arguments, that the spy ring case had no real national security implications. Instead, the reports contained private conversations that should not be revealed. Some senators wanted to compare the Buzhardt and Young reports, but Buzhardt continued to stall, and Stennis let him. Eventually only Hughes and Stennis remained in the hearing room, and Stennis persuaded his colleague to back off, or they might never get to see the Young report. Buzhardt's cover-up was complete.

The military spy ring case had much in common with Watergate. The actual "crime," except for the leak of classified documents to Anderson, was minor. The documents that were stolen from the NSC were those that Moorer had the clearance to see. Kissinger and Nixon just did not want him to see them or know what they were hiding from him. The leak to Anderson was the security breach that Nixon and Kissinger wanted to stop, which was why they had the Plumbers track it down. The cover-up was the real problem. Haig knew he had violated Nixon's cardinal rule of secrecy, and Haig could not afford to have Nixon learn the truth.

Kissinger and Moorer also had secrets to keep. As Secretary of State, Kissinger now thoroughly dominated American foreign policy and operated almost free of Nixon's control. He could not afford anything that tarnished his reputation or weakened his authority, so he lied under oath to maintain the fiction that he and Moorer worked in perfect synchronization. Moorer's tortured explanations were his attempt to hide what he and his Pentagon knew from the first day of the Nixon administration—the White House had forced them to fight a war in Vietnam with one hand behind their back because the president had no commitment to winning. Nixon only wanted the war as a bargaining chip in his grand plan to resume relations with China and to broker an arms deal with the Soviet Union. Moorer could not acknowledge that. He lied, because he had bigger secrets to keep and more important institutions to protect than the Nixon presidency, which, as was apparent to everyone aside from the president himself, was doomed.

CHAPTER TWENTY

Impeachment (1974)

DESPITE THE WIDESPREAD BELIEF THAT EVERYONE WHO TESTIFIED EXCEPT Yeoman Radford was hiding something, Stennis's Armed Services Committee wrapped up its hearings and buried the results. Nixon paid little attention. By the spring of 1974, he was increasingly a bystander in his own administration and spent more time at Camp David, Key Biscayne, or San Clemente than at the White House. When he was in Washington, Nixon still managed to talk a good game, telling a news conference on February 25 that he did not expect to be impeached. The accumulating evidence, particularly the tapes that had emerged, suggested otherwise.

On March 1, the Watergate grand jury indicted seven former White House or campaign committee aides on twenty-four counts of conspiracy, lying, and obstructing justice. Haldeman, Ehrlichman, Mitchell, Colson, Mardian, Gordon Strachan, and Kenneth Parkinson had been the heart and soul of the Nixon campaign and White House. The indictments could have been worse if the grand jury had heard the June 23, 1972, tape in which Nixon and Haldeman conspired to have the CIA block the FBI's Watergate investigation. The grand jury also voted unanimously to name Nixon as an unindicted coconspirator, which would not be revealed until June. That meant Nixon's conversations with the accused could be used as evidence in the upcoming trials. Special Prosecutor Leon Jaworski's appetite for more tapes would only increase, as he sought more evidence for convictions and to bring more indictments.

The tapes determined Nixon's future. He fought attempts to provide more than those he had already given up in October 1973 after the Saturday Night Massacre, when Richardson and Ruckelshaus resigned rather than fire Archibald Cox. Jaworski knew that Nixon fired Cox because he wanted more tapes, but that did not stop him. Nixon fought back, since he knew what the tapes would reveal. The House Judiciary Committee joined the fight by asking for forty-two more tapes for its impeachment investigation. The White House refused. The committee then voted 33–3 to subpoena the tapes, an overwhelmingly bipartisan result that showed how much Nixon's Republican support had cracked. They gave Nixon until April 25 to produce the tapes. Never before had a House committee hit a US president with a subpoena, which the committee followed by asking for another 142 tapes. James St. Clair, Nixon's Watergate lawyer, asked for and received an extension, which gave Nixon until April 28 to turn them over.

Nixon spent the weekend of April 27 and 28 at Camp David pondering his options. He knew that simply complying with the subpoena would have had devastating repercussions. Nixon had to seize the initiative, which he did on April 29 in the Oval Office with binders filled with more than 1,300 pages of typed transcripts of the tapes the committee wanted that sat on the desk beside him. "In giving you these, blemishes and all, I am placing my trust in the basic fairness of the American people," he said.

Nixon's ploy had an immediate, but momentary, effect. Republicans who hoped to stave off impeachment grasped at the transcripts as a possible rope to lift them from danger. Their constituents, however, were not satisfied. Republican Robert McClory of Illinois was willing to take the transcripts, but his constituents deluged his office with telegrams, letters, and calls demanding he hold firm for the tapes and "nothing but the tapes," as one constituent wrote.[1]

Nixon also underestimated the reaction to the embarrassing details throughout the transcripts. Many Americans had never seen a president curse as routinely as Nixon. Despite the editing—the transcripts added the phrase *expletive deleted* to the American lexicon—readers saw how Nixon discussed paying the burglars to keep quiet and how to hide White House involvement in Watergate. The details, said Senator Hugh Scott, a Nixon loyalist, were "deplorable, disgusting, shabby, immoral."[2] They also did not satisfy the committee, which rejected the transcripts on May 1 as a substitute for the tapes and demanded again that Nixon produce them. Instead of putting Watergate in the rearview mirror, Nixon was back where he started, hounded by the committee and Jaworski and now further damaged by his own backfired gambit.

The tapes case went back to Judge Sirica, who had spent almost two years on Watergate. He had never wavered from his suspicion of Nixon and the White House. The former lawyer for the Republican political machine turned judge had become one of Nixon's worst nightmares. "I figured the president was doomed," Sirica wrote about this period.[3] The White House had little confidence Sirica would rule in its favor.

It was with that in mind that Haig and Jaworski met in the White House Map Room on the afternoon of May 5. Jaworski told Haig the grand jury had voted to name Nixon an unindicted coconspirator, which Jaworski said he would keep secret if Haig met his price. He wanted eighteen of the forty-two subpoenaed tapes, including that from June 23, 1972, and he would stop the court fight if he got them. If Nixon refused, Jaworski would reveal the grand jury vote. While St. Clair opposed the deal, Haig was intrigued. He went to Camp David to tell Nixon.

Nixon started to review the tapes again. By May 6, he had reached the June 23 conversation in which he approved using the CIA to block the FBI's Watergate investigation. At Camp David, Nixon listened to his own words and realized the tape proved what he had denied since June 17, 1972: He had obstructed justice and embraced the Watergate cover-up. He would spend the last three months of his presidency trying to keep the American people from seeing the evidence.

As expected, Sirica ruled on May 20 that Nixon had to give up the tapes. St. Clair said they would go to the appeals court in Washington, but Jaworski decided to go straight to the US Supreme Court, and on May 31, the Court agreed to hear the case.

While Nixon's survival depended on not giving up the tapes and other documents, his tactics were crippling the defenses of some of his most loyal aides. John Ehrlichman, who was indicted for perjury for lying in the case of the break-in of Dr. Lewis Fielding's office, wanted to use the tape of his interview with Welander about the spy ring. It would show, Ehrlichman and his lawyers believed, that Ehrlichman was working on secret national security issues and lied to keep them secret on Nixon's orders. Ehrlichman had few alternatives. He had lied about the Fielding break-in, because Nixon had declared the Plumbers' work a national security secret. In the Fielding/Ellsberg case, those claims were mostly bogus; by the time of the Labor Day 1971 break-in, Ellsberg posed no national security threat. Haig and Buzhardt were determined to stop Ehrlichman's defense. Unlike their earlier failures to use executive privilege to stop former CIA officials Cushman and Walters from testifying, Haig and Buzhardt claimed executive privilege to block Ehrlichman, who then tried to use that claim as a reason to dismiss the case against him. Ehrlichman also went to the White House to hear the tape, and as he sat outside Buzhardt's office, Ehrlichman could hear Buzhardt listening to the tape. "I could hear it through the door because it was turned up loud," Ehrlichman said.[4] Ehrlichman never got the tape; a federal judge rejected his claim, and he had to plead guilty.

Starting in April, the publishing and political worlds anticipated the publication of *All the President's Men*, Woodward and Bernstein's book about Watergate. The breathless tale of political intrigue told how the two reporters went from sitting on the back benches of the *Post*'s metro staff to covering the nation's hottest story through luck, curiosity, and hard work. Woodward had been a *Post* reporter for less than a year when he was first assigned to cover the arraignment of the Watergate burglars, while Bernstein had spent six years honing a reputation as the staff screw-up. But he was a tenacious reporter and a clean, fast writer. The book showed how they got the Watergate story and also introduced to the public Woodward's shadowy super source—Deep Throat, who was named after the popular 1972 X-rated movie, because he spoke only on "deep background" and would only meet with Woodward in an underground parking garage late at night.

Deep Throat, they wrote, had extensive government connections and would only confirm information they had developed elsewhere. He "could be contacted only on very important occasions. Woodward had promised he would never identify him or his position to anyone. Further, he had agreed never to quote the man, even as an anonymous source. Their discussions would be only to confirm information that had been obtained elsewhere and to add some perspective."[5]

The public was all too willing to believe that Nixon was capable of what Deep Throat claimed, but even so, questions about Deep Throat arose immediately.

"The climate of fear is best illustrated in episodes involving Woodward's meetings with a confidential source—Deep Throat," wrote historian Doris Kearns Goodwin in her *New York Times* review of the book.[6] "(Anonymous even now—one man or possibly several—Deep Throat had access to information from the White House, the Justice Department, the FBI and the CRP.)" Richard Whalen, a former Nixon adviser, wrote in his complimentary review in the *Post*'s Book World that Deep Throat seemed like more than one person.[7] "If I did not have such respect for the integrity of Woodward and Bernstein, I would be tempted to suspect that Deep Throat is a composite character made up of several sources—he is too knowing about too many very closely held subjects in widely separated political quarters to ring quite true," Whalen wrote.

The book's release at the height of impeachment proceedings also influenced those trying to determine Nixon's guilt or innocence. Most landed on the side of guilt, such as Representative M. Caldwell Butler, a Virginia

Republican on the House Judiciary Committee. His wife read passages to him each night before he voted to impeach.[8] As a history, *All the President's Men* is a flawed work with questionable sourcing. As a drama, it captured the Washington zeitgeist of the spring of 1974 and nudged Nixon closer to the exit.

～～

The Judiciary Committee's closed-door hearings had started in early May, and the leaks quickly spilled forth. Committee chairman Peter Rodino and his staff had access to documents obtained from the Watergate grand jury, and investigators had collected files from the FBI and other agencies. While many of those leaks, coupled with the transcripts Nixon released, dealt with Watergate, others pointed at Kissinger or Haig. The new Secretary of State thought he had finished off the speculation about his role in authorizing the FBI wiretaps when the Senate confirmed him the previous September. While Nixon was increasingly unpopular, the public considered Kissinger the architect of Nixon's popular policies and no one wanted to see him go. Still, Kissinger's explanation of the wiretaps did not make sense. He could never adequately explain what he had done to pick the targets or why. Even the FBI could not provide the definitive story.

On June 6, the *Post* chipped away at Kissinger's wiretaps claims with a story that quoted Nixon from February 28, 1973, in which he told John Dean that Kissinger "asked that it (the wiretaps) be done. And I assumed that it was."[9] That fragment was enough to raise new questions about Kissinger's credibility. It also set up a confrontation in a news conference later that afternoon in which an unsuspecting Kissinger ran into a disbelieving gaggle of reporters. One reporter asked Kissinger if he had hired a lawyer to prepare him for a potential perjury indictment tied to his previous Senate testimony.[10] Kissinger had lied to the Senate, and now those lies had resurfaced, leaving Kissinger desperate to save himself.

The wiretaps became the heart of what became impeachment Article II, and Jaworski was investigating possible criminal charges. That made anyone connected to the program vulnerable, whether they pushed for their creation, as Kissinger did, or relayed messages and helped picked targets, as did Haig. As Kissinger floundered in his attempts to explain himself, Sullivan made another well-timed leak. He told Hersh of the *New York Times* that Kissinger was behind the orders to stop the wiretaps in February 1971 and used Haig as his messenger. Hersh's article, published June 9, quoted sources involved with the program, who said Haig relayed Kissinger's orders to the FBI.[11] The latest revelations contradicted Kissinger's testimony at his confirmation hearings. Kissinger, Hersh reported, was in charge of the wiretaps. "The official also said it was General Haig who relayed most, if not all, of the White House requests for wiretaps," Hersh wrote. "General Haig made clear that the requests originated with Mr. Kissinger, the official added." Hersh also reported that the message to Sullivan was the leaks had to be stopped in order to preserve Kissinger's foreign policy.[12] Everything about Hersh's story implicated Kissinger and not Haig, who bore much of the responsibility for the wiretaps. As Nixon's presidency collapsed and others were faced with the possibility of going down with him, Sullivan, perhaps with Haig's blessing, was pointing the finger for the taps at Kissinger and away from Haig and himself.

Sullivan was talking to both Hersh and Woodward at the time. Woodward's notes show he talked to Sullivan in early June. The notes indicate the interview could have taken place on June 6, but the numeral six is crossed out.[13] That was three days before Hersh's story. Woodward had also interviewed Sullivan in March 1974, shortly after the *Times* published another story about the wiretaps.[14]

～～

Nixon hoped his foreign policy expertise would save him, so on June 10 he started a Middle Eastern trip that included Austria, four Arab nations, and Israel. Even on the road, Kissinger could not escape the wiretaps, as members of the Judiciary Committee said on June 11 they had received FBI reports that showed Kissinger initiated some of the wiretaps. Previously Kissinger had testified that the genesis of the wiretaps was a May 9, 1969, meeting at the White House.[15] There was no May 9 meeting, because Nixon and his staff were in Key Biscayne. The inconsistencies surrounding Kissinger's role continued to accumulate, and the pressure was getting to him. It boiled over on the afternoon of June 11.

Kissinger told reporters in Salzburg, Austria, that he had "said everything I need to say about" the wiretaps. He told the Foreign Relations Committee everything he knew and would answer questions from any other committee or "investigating agency."[16] But, Kissinger warned, if the attacks on him did not stop, he would resign as Secretary of State.

It was a bold move, particularly because Kissinger *had* committed perjury before a Senate committee. In Washington, members of Congress considered Kissinger the puppeteer who pulled Nixon's strings to create détente with the Soviet Union and the opening to China. They did not realize that Kissinger had carried out Nixon's plans, and Kissinger was in no hurry to tell them otherwise. Most of official Washington realized Nixon would not last for very long, so Kissinger's departure was considered a disaster by those who supported the current US foreign policy.

By June 12, almost fifty members of the Senate had signed a letter backing Kissinger almost without reservation.[17] Republicans, led by Vice President Ford, accused the Democratic leadership of the House and the Judiciary Committee of leaking information to push impeachment. Ford said it would be a catastrophe for Kissinger to resign. State Department officials thought Kissinger was bluffing and was hypersensitive and that his ego would not let him quit.[18] They also probably realized that few in Congress had the stomach for forcing Kissinger out of office.

Kissinger received his first major break on June 13, when Jaworski said he had not seen anything to indicate that Kissinger had any criminal liability with the wiretaps.[19] His major focus, Jaworski said, was on those who had used wiretap information for purposes not related to national security, such as the development of political intelligence to guide legislative or campaign strategy.

With the wiretaps back in focus, FBI investigators turned again to Sullivan, who tried to deflect attention from himself to Kissinger. Although the FBI agents interviewing him had the memos he had written to Hoover in May 1969, Sullivan's memory grew faulty.[20] He claimed that a heart attack he suffered in April made it impossible for him to testify in person, although Sullivan had no problem detailing to Hersh and Woodward in early June more of the details of the wiretaps. Sullivan followed a well-worn pattern, telling journalists anonymously a more damaging and sometimes more honest version of what happened and then backpedaling when forced to talk on the record. That allowed Sullivan to manipulate events while evading official responsibility.

The jubilant greetings for Nixon on the Middle East trip, where giant crowds packed city streets in Alexandria and Cairo, boosted his spirits and gave him the false sense of hope that he could stay in office. In his diaries, Nixon told himself that Watergate had been put in its proper perspective and that his policies made for a strong America and would affect "the well-being of people everywhere."[21]

Kissinger was more skeptical. Reporters in each city they visited asked him how Watergate had affected US foreign policy, if other governments still took Nixon seriously, and if he had the staying power to remain as president. Each day demonstrated that the answer was no, and Kissinger realized Nixon had turned into a liability. China was starting to wonder if its confidence in Nixon was misplaced. The Soviet Union's leaders did not understand how Nixon's seemingly minor domestic problems threatened the progress the two nations had made on arms talks and a general reduction in Cold War tensions. In Moscow, Leonid Brezhnev and the rest of his leadership were cordial to Nixon; they appreciated how he slowed the arms race and improved relations between the two nations. But they could reach no concrete agreements, as they had in 1972 and 1973. Perhaps that was inevitable, because the progress in the first two summits outpaced anything else that had happened since 1945. It also showed the limits of Nixon's ability to negotiate and the questions the Soviets had about the United States' continuing commitments to arms talks and reductions in a post-Nixon world.

They had reasons to wonder. Even before the trip, Nixon was feeling more internal dissent than normal. A June 20 cabinet meeting showed how the Pentagon and Joint Chiefs pushed back at Nixon's desire for more arms reductions. Defense Secretary Schlesinger showed Nixon a proposal for SALT the military wanted Nixon to present to the Soviets in Moscow. Nixon knew the Russians would never accept the changes Schlesinger and Moorer wanted in the ABM agreement that had taken years to devise.[22] Nixon held them off in the meeting, but it was obvious the Pentagon felt emboldened to push a harder line with a weakened president. Unlike 1972, when Nixon went to Moscow with a position of strength backed by years of secret negotiations, Nixon could no longer hide his dealings with anyone. His internal critics on the Right knew they could stop Nixon from making a deal they thought would weaken the United States militarily.

Nixon returned to the United States on July 3, a day after the House Judiciary Committee started its open hearings on impeachment, and went to San Clemente, not Washington. The atmosphere in the capital during the hot summer was not conducive to Nixon or his future. His longtime aides were either on trial, imprisoned, or appearing before the committee. Nothing in the Judiciary Committee hearings led anyone to believe the outcome would favor Nixon. The president had hoped he could avoid impeachment if three of the panel's southern Democrats bucked their party and voted against the articles, thereby killing them in committee, if all of the Republicans voted no. On July 23, he learned that would not happen, and that Democratic Alabama governor George Wallace would also not support him. Nixon knew then he had little chance to survive, and he told Haig, "Well, Al, there goes the presidency."[23] He got another blow the next day, when the Supreme Court ruled 8–0 that Nixon had to turn over to Sirica the sixty-four tapes sought by the prosecutors. That included the June 23 tape, which implicated Nixon in the Watergate cover-up.

The committee voted 27–11 on July 27 for Article I of impeachment, which was for obstruction of justice. That covered the June 23 tape and the myriad other activities that John Dean and others had testified about. More critical for Haig and Buzhardt was Article II for abuse of power, which included the FBI wiretaps, Plumbers, and other national security–related issues. Nixon obstructed justice to protect these activities, not whatever his errant campaign staff had done. Article II passed 28–10 on July 29, a margin that made Nixon's impeachment by the full House inevitable and then a trial in the Senate, where his support dwindled each day.

Haig had matters of his own to worry about as well as Nixon's. He appeared July 30 before the Senate Foreign Relations Committee as it reviewed Kissinger's involvement in the wiretaps and whether he had lied to Congress. Most committee members wanted to clear Kissinger, particularly if Nixon had to resign or was impeached. Haig also needed to clear himself. He had helped Kissinger pick the wiretap targets, and he had met often with Sullivan at the FBI. With Buzhardt beside him, Haig testified for more than three hours in closed session, and he again tried to dump the entire matter in Kissinger's lap.[24] Haig said if Kissinger had the name of someone he wanted to tap, Haig would deliver it to Sullivan. So much did the committee want to believe Kissinger that even a skeptic such as Stuart Symington of Missouri bought it. Kissinger and Haig, Symington said, were cleared because "any taps were not originated by them but at a higher authority."[25] It was all Nixon's fault, and he would be gone soon. On August 6, the committee voted unanimously to clear Kissinger, because "there are no contradictions between what Dr. Kissinger told the committee last year and the totality of the new information available." "He is needed," said Senator Hubert Humphrey of Minnesota. "His role is good. He's a tremendous national asset."[26]

By July 31, everyone involved in Nixon's defense had listened to the June 23 tape except Haig, who made the hard-to-believe claim that he had not heard it. That tape held the key to the president's survival, and not listening to it was a kind of malpractice. Plus, Haig had acted for months as if Nixon was guilty. On that day, he went to see Kissinger and told his former boss about the tape, and Kissinger told Haig he had concluded long ago that Nixon had to quit.[27] Later that afternoon, Haig called Robert Hartmann, his counterpart in Vice President Ford's office. Haig wanted to visit Ford the next morning, and Hartmann said he would arrange it. Hartmann told Ford that Haig would be there. They decided that Hartmann should be there as a witness.[28]

On August 1, Nixon told Haig he knew he had to resign.[29] He asked Haig to contact Ford, not knowing that Haig had already set up the meeting with Hartmann. Shortly after talking to Nixon, Haig arrived at Ford's office, where he was unhappy to see Hartmann. Haig told Ford he had not seen the evidence himself, but he gathered that the June 23 tape was the smoking gun everyone feared. That was not, however, what Haig had told Nixon, who wrote that Haig had told him the day before that he, too, had read the transcript and concluded Nixon was finished.

After the morning meeting with Ford, Haig called the vice president back in the afternoon to set up a meeting with just Ford alone. He arrived at 3:30 and quickly got to business with Ford by laying out Nixon's shrinking number of options.[30] Nixon could either hope to survive impeachment, quit, or pardon himself and the other Watergate defendants. Nixon had also told Haig to tell Ford he was planning to resign. Haig then added another option: Ford could pardon Nixon if Nixon agreed to quit. Ford would write later that Haig said those were not the options that he had developed and that he was not recommending one option over another. Haig then told Ford that they needed to keep in close contact as events unfolded quickly. Ford repeated this story under oath when he testified before the House Judiciary Committee in October 1974,[31] while seven years later, under oath during his confirmation hearings to be Secretary of State, Haig denied that he ever talked to Ford about a resignation-pardon deal.

Haig had hidden his second meeting with Ford. When he slipped into Ford's office, he told the receptionist not to mark down his name but that of Rogers Morton, a former House member and now the Interior Secretary. Haig seemed surprised when he emerged from the second meeting and saw one of Ford's aides standing there. Hartmann knew why Haig wanted to keep the meeting secret: He had pitched to Ford the idea of pardoning Nixon. "So that's the pitch Haig wouldn't make with me present!" Hartmann wrote in his memoirs.[32]

That night, Ford's wife, Betty, told him he should not make any recommendations about Nixon, and Ford agreed. He called Haig, with three witnesses in his office, and said he would not recommend to Nixon what he should do. Haig agreed, but he had already planted the idea with Ford.[33]

Nixon's family wanted him to fight, and he decided to make another attempt to see if he could ride out the impeachment in the House. Over the weekend of August 3 and 4, he decided to release a transcript of the June 23 tape to the public on Monday, August 5. Inside the White House, the pressure for him to quit continued to build. When St. Clair heard that Nixon had listened to the June 23 tape in May and did not tell him, St. Clair threatened to quit if Nixon failed to resign.

Haig still had to work to do. He called Jaworski on the morning of August 5 before Nixon released the transcript of the "smoking gun" tape.[34] He told Jaworski he did not know what the tape said and that Nixon had political, not national security, reasons to use the CIA to stop the FBI investigation into the Watergate break-in. Jaworski wrote in his memoirs that Haig went on in detail about his ignorance of Nixon's activities the morning of June 23, 1972. "I'm particularly anxious that you believe me, Leon," Haig told him. "I didn't know what was in those conversations." Jaworski told Haig he believed him.[35]

Nixon then released the tape with a statement that acknowledged it would most likely damage his case, but that he put it out in the interest of full disclosure. The full record, he said, would show that he should not be impeached. The public disagreed. Instantly, members of Congress who were on the fence about Nixon's future jumped off and into the impeachment or resignation column. He spent August 6 and 7 meeting with congressional Republicans, including some of his staunchest defenders, such as Barry Goldwater of Arizona. Hugh Scott of Pennsylvania, the Republican leader in the Senate, told Nixon he might have fifteen votes in his favor in the Senate if an impeachment trial got that far. "I don't have many alternatives [other than resignation], do I," Nixon told them.[36]

As Nixon told his family his decision, Haig called Jaworski. If he resigned, Nixon would not face trial in the Senate, where the details of the spy ring and wiretaps, two issues of great concern to Haig, could be aired in devastating detail. But the special prosecutor's office was still in action, and Jaworski and his staff were pushing forward with Nixon as their main target. A Nixon trial could expose Haig.

Jaworski's staff suspected Haig's motives when he met with Jaworski on the morning of August 8. Three of them urged Jaworski before the meeting not to make any deal with Haig. A driver picked up Jaworski at his hotel and took him to Haig's home in northwest Washington. At the same time, Nixon was at the White House telling his family that he would resign that night in a nationally televised speech. Haig, who was Nixon's closest aide for the last eighteen months, was not there. He was cutting a deal with Jaworski.[37]

Nixon was taking his tapes and personal papers with him when he resigned, Haig told Jaworski. The special prosecutor's office could have access to them if they wanted them, he continued. Jaworski said he did not object but only added that he and his staff needed to be able to see the documents. They ended the meeting with a strong and heartfelt handshake, and Jaworski headed to his office, where he was immediately confronted by his top lawyers, who feared he had made some kind of deal with Haig. Jaworski said he had not, and his office released a statement that said so.

Not even Jaworski's closest associates at the special prosecutor's office believed the release. James Doyle, Jaworski's spokesman, wrote in his memoirs that they found it impossible to believe that Haig would spend two hours with Jaworski on the day that Nixon decided to quit and not come away with some kind of deal.[38] Haig could have called Jaworski and given him advance notice of the resignation over the telephone.

Nixon was not sure what Haig had done, either. When his chief of staff returned to the White House on August 8, he told the president that he did not think Nixon had to worry about Jaworski and criminal charges. Nixon "had little reason to feel assured," he wrote, because of the prosecutor's aggressive attitude leading up to the resignation, which he would announce that night.[39]

Ford's staff soon learned that Nixon's remaining team was packing up boxes of documents to ship to California and was burning others. They knew they had to act quickly or else they could find a White House stripped of the important documents needed to keep the presidency moving. Hartmann called Benton Becker, a lawyer who had worked in the Robert Kennedy Justice Department before representing Ford during his confirmation hearings to be vice president. Becker realized there was little they could do until Nixon actually left office and Ford became president. Meanwhile, the packing continued, the final stages of a Haig-engineered White House cover-up.

Nixon went on camera at 9 p.m. the night of August 8 to give his final national address as president. Nixon said he wanted to continue to fight, because he was not a quitter. But the events of the recent days, especially after the release of the June 23 tape, made it obvious "that I no longer have a strong enough political base in the Congress" to keep fighting. So, it was Congress's fault, not his own, that he had to quit. "I regret deeply any injuries that may have been done," Nixon continued. "If some of my judgments were wrong—and some were wrong—they were made in what I believed at the time to be in the best interest of the nation."

He truly believed that, because Nixon *had* accomplished virtually everything he set out to do as president. His secret government, signed into action on his first day in office, created the framework for the China opening, reduced tensions with the Soviet Union, a groundbreaking nuclear weapons agreement, and eventually an end to the war in Vietnam with South Vietnam still standing, however shakily. Considering the dire condition in which Lyndon Johnson had left office, such accomplishments should have put Nixon in the pantheon of the nation's greatest presidents. But the secrecy that had enabled Kissinger to open a backchannel to the Soviet Union through Anatoly Dobrynin or for Nixon to use Pakistan's Yahya Khan to broker the opening to China had created great fissures inside the government. From the CIA to the Pentagon to the State Department, officials who had once had great influence and access to power soon learned they had little. They soon learned the White House routinely cut them out of critical information and decisions or simply lied to them. The military realized he was bleeding the nation out of Vietnam and setting up South Vietnam, for which they had given the lives of fifty-eight thousand US troops, for failure. They often reacted in the few ways they had, by either telling a sympathetic reporter what they knew and feared or by dragging their feet to slow Nixon's agenda. Those reactions created Nixon's counterreactions, as he approved spying on his own officials and the press. He authorized special teams to investigate and harass his opponents. He relied on men with questionable motives to do his dirty work, and when they were threatened with the exposure of what they had done, often without Nixon's knowledge, they rushed to save themselves, often at Nixon's expense. That chain reaction that started on January 20, 1969, had led Nixon to where he sat the night of August 8, sweat glistening on his brow under his TV makeup, giving up the office he strove so long to achieve.

~~~

The following morning, Nixon gathered his staff in the East Room of the White House for his final farewell. His face wet with tears, his family quietly weeping behind him, Nixon summoned the human emotion he used when he was at his most desperate. "Always remember, others may hate you, but those who hate you don't win unless you hate them—and then you destroy yourself," he said, dispensing wisdom he too often failed to heed himself. His lust to destroy his enemies, starting with Alger Hiss and continuing to Daniel Ellsberg or Ted Kennedy, led Nixon to spy on his own staff, mislead his own government, and lie to the American people. Those traits, which fueled Nixon's drive to succeed, eventually destroyed him.

He and his family walked to the South Lawn of the White House to his awaiting marine helicopter. After they boarded the helicopter, Nixon stood in the doorway, turned, and delivered his iconic pose—his arms outstretched and his fingers forming a V for victory—before he stepped into the helicopter and flew to Andrews Air Force Base and then home to San Clemente for the start of his exile from office.

Ford stepped into the White House shortly afterward and was given the oath of office by Chief Justice Warren Burger. He asked the nation to "help bind up the internal wounds of Watergate. Our Constitution works. Our great Republic is a government of laws and not of men. Here the people rule."

As Ford said those words, Haig was still trying to hustle Nixon's documents and tapes out of the White House and get Nixon a presidential pardon. Doing both moves would protect Haig as much as Nixon, who was already gone. Haig had a career and his freedom to protect.

Becker knew there were tons of papers on the fourth and fifth floors of the Executive Office Building next to the White House. He saw dozens of bags packed with documents in burn bags outside the White House burn room in the basement. Another aide told him the chemical shredding machine was cranking at five times capacity. The day after Nixon left, Becker looked outside the White House and saw crews loading three air force trucks with file cabinets and other Nixon materials. He rushed outside to tell the air force colonel in charge of the operation to stop, but the colonel told Becker he answered only to Haig. Together they went to Haig's office where Becker told Haig it had to stop. Haig professed ignorance and acquiesced. The papers stayed at the White House.[40]

On August 14, Ford's spokesman, Jerry terHorst, said Nixon's lawyers and the special prosecutors had agreed that Nixon would get his tapes and papers. terHorst backed off the next day after a huge uproar, and Buzhardt, who had remained White House counsel, quit as a result. Haig had laid the groundwork for this move on August 8, which the public did not then realize, and Haig continued to agitate to have the documents sent to Nixon. Becker was just as determined not to let that happen.

Less than a month later, Ford had concluded that he had to explore pardoning Nixon, the idea that Haig had first raised on August 1. He dispatched Becker to San Clemente to negotiate with the fallen president and the few remaining aides, including Ron Ziegler, who had accompanied him to California. Their main sticking point was the custody of the tapes and papers. Nixon wanted them; Ford did not want them to leave Washington. Eventually a federal court would make the issue moot by declaring that everything would be placed under the control of the National Archives.[41]

By agreeing to the pardon, which came before any formal charges had been brought against him, Nixon acknowledged his guilt. Ford announced the pardon almost immediately after Nixon agreed. On Sunday, September 8, he told the nation that he spared Nixon to spare the nation of years of turmoil from any kind of trial. "I feel that Richard Nixon and his loved ones have suffered enough," Ford said, "and will continue to suffer no matter what I do."[42] While Ford believed he had made the correct decision, it had real costs. He threw away much of the good will he had accumulated during his first month in office. Many voters smelled a deal in which Nixon quit to allow Ford to succeed him and then let him off. Ford denied it, and it was true he never made an explicit deal. It was, however, an outcome Haig coveted. He had coaxed Nixon out of office, which avoided an impeachment vote and Senate trial that could have uncovered everything Haig tried to hide, and then engineered a pardon that spared Nixon, and ultimately Haig, from having those same issues emerge during a criminal trial. Alexander M. Haig, one of the enablers of Nixon's secret government, would leave Washington with his own secrets intact.

Epilogue: Ramifications

NIXON DECAMPED TO HIS EXILE IN SAN CLEMENTE, WHERE HE STEEPED IN the disapproval of the citizens who less than two years earlier reelected him with more than 60 percent of the vote. He remained controversial even out of the public eye. Ford's approval rating in the Gallup poll had dropped from 70 percent to 48 percent after the pardon, which would be one of the reasons he would lose his bid for a full term to Democrat Jimmy Carter in 1976. Ford and Kissinger would try to keep Nixon's foreign policy intact, but the pressure from the Right that started to build throughout Nixon's presidency became too much to overcome. Ford became bogged down in fights over the direction of the second round of SALT, which failed to come off before he left office.

Ford spent much of his tenure coping with the residue left by his predecessor. A special Senate committee chaired by Frank Church, a liberal Democrat from Idaho who harbored presidential ambitions, began hearings in 1975 into the multiple abuses of civil liberties by the CIA, FBI, National Security Agency, and Nixon White House. Coupled with the fallout from the firing of more than a thousand CIA agents Nixon ordered in early 1973, the investigations by Church and a House committee led by Otis Pike, a New York Democrat, forced multiple reforms on the intelligence community. Committee investigators discovered multiple CIA-led assassination plots and agency tests of LSD on unsuspecting subjects, including one who jumped from a window to his death. The committee also exhumed abuses from the Nixon White House, including more details on the FBI wiretaps between 1969 and 1971 and the aborted Huston Plan. The committee also exposed William Sullivan's harassment of Martin Luther King Jr., and COINTELPRO, the counterintelligence program that Sullivan helped start and then led through the 1960s. For his part, Sullivan told the panel he had few regrets. The FBI considered itself at war. By 1978, Congress had taken many of the committee's recommendations and passed a landmark regulation of wiretaps and intelligence collection. The Foreign Intelligence Surveillance Act required the FBI to get a court order for each telephone wiretap its agents wanted to install and created a special FISA court to hear the requests. Nixon had so tainted the image of the nation's intelligence community that intelligence veterans, who disliked the idea of having anyone ride herd over their work, had little chance to stop it.

◆~~◆

Woodward and Bernstein followed their success with *All the President's Men* with an even more gossipy and attention-getting book in 1976—*The Final Days*, which examined Nixon's fall as president. It was the full flowering of the anonymous, background sourcing they used to great effect in their *Post* reporting and in their previous book. The two authors claimed to have interviewed almost four hundred people on background for a book that ultimately leaned on two key sources—Fred Buzhardt, Nixon's White House lawyer for his last fifteen months in office, and Haig, who denied talking to them but who was nevertheless an obvious source.[1] The Haig links are clear, including passages that describe his emotions and the overall sense that Haig was the man who saved the Republic while gently coaxing Nixon out of office. Woodward confirmed Buzhardt as a source in 1984, six years after Buzhardt had died of a heart attack. The book was dominated by Woodward, who enlisted the help of Scott Armstrong, his old high school friend and former member of the Senate Watergate committee staff.

◆~~◆

Richard Helms became collateral damage in the aftermath of Nixon's abuses of the intelligence system. While Nixon received a pardon for everything he had done, Helms found himself accused of lying to Congress during his February 1973 Senate confirmation hearings to be ambassador to Iran. When asked about his agency's involvement in the 1970 election in Chile, Helms was evasive. A subsequent internal CIA review concluded Helms had lied. The matter went to the Justice Department in 1974, which spent three years investigating it, moving from the Ford to the Carter administrations. Helms learned shortly before he left Iran that a grand jury would indict him for perjury. Months of negotiations throughout 1977 concluded with an October 31 court date in which Helms pleaded no contest to a misdemeanor.[2] He was fined $2,000 and sentenced to two years in prison, suspended. He left the courthouse for a reception at the Kenwood Country Club in Bethesda, Maryland, where four hundred CIA alumni passed around two wastebaskets and collected enough cash to pay his fine.[3] It was an agonizing end to a career in which Helms oversaw agency abuses but also many successes. His refusal to manufacture intelligence to suit the desires of Richard Nixon, who always resented Helms and the CIA culture, led to many of his problems. Nixon had broken much of the CIA and tried to break Helms.

—◆—

On November 9, 1977, William Sullivan walked through the woods about one mile from his home in Sugar Hill, New Hampshire, hard by the Connecticut River that separated the state from Vermont. Just after dawn, a shot rang out, hitting Sullivan in the back just below his neck and killing him almost instantly.[4] A hunter, twenty-one-year-old Robert Daniels Jr., the son of a New Hampshire state policeman, had mistaken Sullivan for a white-tailed deer. Daniels would plead guilty to a misdemeanor, pay a $500 fine, and lose his hunting license for ten years. Sullivan's life in the shadows was over. It was ending anyway, as he was scheduled to testify before the House committee investigating the assassinations of John F. Kennedy and Martin Luther King Jr. He had been named as a defendant in multiple civil suits arising from the FBI wiretaps and was an upcoming witness in the case being brought by the Watergate special prosecutor against L. Patrick Gray, Mark Felt, and Edward Miller for their alleged bugging and break-in work at the FBI. Gray would eventually be dropped from the case, while Felt and Miller would be convicted and then pardoned. During his career in Washington, Sullivan had once told columnist Robert Novak that he believed he would die under strange circumstances, and if anyone claimed it was an accident, not to believe it. But Sullivan's family said they believed it had been an accident, as so did the police. There were no further investigations once Daniels pleaded guilty.

"It seems to me that our Lord thought Bill had suffered enough from government harassment and civil lawsuits so called him home. Now he is at peace," wrote his widow to FBI director Clarence Kelley.[5]

—◆—

After leaving the White House, Haig was named the supreme US commander of NATO, based in Brussels. It was the highest post he could achieve without undergoing a Senate confirmation hearing, which Ford and Schlesinger believed would be disastrous for Haig and the young Ford administration. He served there until 1979, when he left the army for a think tank and eventually the presidency of United Technologies, a major defense contractor. After Republican Ronald Reagan won the 1980 presidential election, Haig was mentioned as a potential cabinet official in the new administration, although he had virtually no connection with Reagan. Nevertheless, Reagan nominated Haig to be Secretary of State. As he did after Nixon's resignation, Haig still had the problem of his record in the Nixon administration. This time, senators wanted to hear the White House tapes on which Haig was recorded providing advice to Nixon on foreign policy and other matters. Most of those tapes were still in limbo at the National Archives. Haig did not want to cooperate. He then received help from someone most Americans would consider an unlikely benefactor—Woodward. In an op-ed column in the *Post*, Woodward wrote that the Senate should forget about the tapes, because whatever Haig told Nixon, it was only to placate the president.[6] It was a modified version of the Nuremberg defense. Instead of following orders, Haig would have only been telling Nixon what he wanted to hear. Woodward, whose reporting had been helped by the White House tapes, was now telling Americans that those tapes should be off limits when considering the nomination of his longtime source, Haig, as Secretary of State.

The tapes were never released, and Haig was confirmed. Haig knew from experience how the White House staff could marginalize the Secretary of State. He wrote and presented Reagan with a plan that would make Haig the "vicar for the community" of foreign policy decision makers. Reagan did not sign it, and the White House staff banned Haig from ever being alone with Reagan. It was one of the first signs that Haig would never fit in with the Reagan crowd. The most glaring came on March 30, shortly after Reagan had been shot following an appearance at the Washington Hilton. A rushed Haig appeared in the White House briefing room and made what struck everyone there and watching on television as a blatant power grab. "Constitutionally, gentlemen, you have the President, the Vice President, and the Secretary of State in that order, and should the President decide he wants to transfer the helm to the Vice President, he will do so," Haig said. "He has not done that. As of now, I am in control here, in the White House, pending return of the Vice President and in close touch with him. If something came up, I would check with him, of course."[7] The Speaker of the House was third in line of succession, not the Secretary of State, and Haig's statement stuck with him for the rest of his life. It never set well with the rest of the Reagan administration, and after one clash too many he offered his resignation to Reagan on June 25, 1982. The president accepted on July 5 and replaced Haig with George Shultz, the former Labor and Treasury Secretary for Nixon.

～～

The administrations that followed Nixon's tried with varying degrees of success to devise a National Security Council structure that worked. None would ever repeat the system in which Kissinger, acting out Nixon's wishes, was the focal point for all national security policy. Carter's national security adviser,

Zbigniew Brzezinski, seemed a Democratic version of Kissinger: A Polish refugee from communism, former Harvard professor, and anticommunist hardliner, Brzezinski had Carter's ear on many issues and often clashed with his counterpart at State, Cyrus Vance. Reagan cycled through six national security advisers during his eight years as president, and their failure to watch over their shop allowed a marine colonel, Oliver North, to run a secret policy aiding the Nicaraguan Contra rebels and handling a complicated arms-for-hostages deal with the Iranian government that had only recently held US diplomats hostage for 444 days. Reagan's runaway NSC mired him in the worst controversy of his administration—the Iran Contra scandal that led to extensive hearings throughout the summer of 1987. The administrations of George H. W. Bush, Bill Clinton, and George W. Bush all had strong national security advisers working in concert with influential cabinet members. None outshone the cabinet as Kissinger had. All, however, had the ear of the president and spent more time in the Oval Office than anyone else.

In June 2005, one of the biggest mysteries of the Nixon era seemed to end. For the thirty years following the publication of *All the President's Men*, journalists, former officials, and even college journalism classes had examined the book's text with Talmudic intensity to identify Deep Throat. They had various explanations. Authors Jim Hougan, Len Colodny, and Robert Gettlin concluded that Deep Throat was most likely a composite character made up of contributions from different officials, including Haig, John Dean, and Mark Felt of the FBI. In early June 2005, Felt's family made its move with an article in the magazine *Vanity Fair* claiming that Felt was Deep Throat.[8] Felt, then 91 and suffering from dementia, could not speak for himself, but the article by John O'Connor, an attorney for the family, detailed how Felt had met with Woodward a few years earlier and described the close relationship between the retired FBI official and the reporter. After a few hours, Woodward acknowledged it was true, and the *Post* published a lengthy article by Woodward the following day that told of how Woodward met Felt and how they worked together.[9] The following month, Woodward published a thin volume, *The Secret Man*, which expanded on the *Post* article.

Woodward said he met Felt outside Haig's office in the White House basement in late 1969 and early 1970. He took great pains to say that he was not there to meet Haig, whom he did not meet until 1973, regardless of what anyone else said. "I've tried to establish the date of this first encounter but I can't be sure," Woodward wrote. "It is possible that Felt was there to see someone about" the FBI wiretaps on seventeen government officials and reporters.

"Perhaps Felt was just bringing one of those Top Secret letters which had to have been handled very carefully, and were probably delivered by courier. Felt later denied that he knew of the Kissinger wiretaps at this time."[10]

Felt, however, did not know about the wiretaps until October 1971 after Hoover had fired Sullivan. FBI records and multiple investigations have detailed Sullivan's role and how Felt had contemporaneous knowledge of only one similar wiretap, the one placed on Yeoman Charles Radford in January 1972 after the discovery of the military spy ring in the NSC. Beyond that, Woodward interviewed Sullivan about the wiretaps on several occasions, including in March and June 1974, when the wiretaps had surfaced again in the House Judiciary Committee's impeachment investigation.[11] Felt's denials about knowing about the wiretaps at the time were true. The person responsible for them was Sullivan, Felt's bitter rival and the man who would engineer Felt's forced retirement from the FBI. Sullivan had carried the letters to the White House, and he told Woodward so in March 1974, according to Woodward's own notes.

⌐∼⌐

Richard Nixon, the president whose secrets William Sullivan helped keep and then exposed, spent the last twenty years of his life trying to resurrect his reputation. He published multiple books about the world leaders he had met and worked with, foreign policy challenges, and life in the political arena. Eventually, he moved from San Clemente to the East Coast, settling in an estate in Saddle River, New Jersey, closer to New York and the epicenter of finance and politics. Nixon started to venture into the public, including a surprise stop at a New Jersey fast food restaurant that startled the patrons. Gradually, he became known more as an elder statesman. Presidents, including Bill Clinton, sought his counsel.

Finally, on Friday, April 22, 1994, it was over. Nixon had suffered a massive stroke at home on Monday, April 18, and was taken to New York Hospital-Cornell Medical Center in Manhattan. There he remained until he fell into a deep coma on Thursday and then died Friday night at 9:08. His two daughters, Julie and Tricia, were at his bedside.

Official Washington quickly lauded Nixon as a statesman who had changed the world, which he had. "He understood the threat of Communism, but he also had the wisdom to know when it was time to reach out to the Soviet Union and to China," Clinton said.[12] They had to acknowledge why he left office and the disgrace involved, but the initial reaction was that a lion had passed. Clinton and the living former presidents—Gerald Ford, Jimmy Carter, George Bush, and Ronald Reagan—all paid homage at the funeral in Yorba Linda, California, which was now part of the suburban expanse east of Los Angeles and no longer the citrus grove land of Nixon's youth. The ceremony was dignified. Clinton spoke, as did California governor Pete Wilson, a Republican who broke into politics as a Nixon advance man. So did Kissinger. "So let us now say goodbye to our gallant friend," he said. "He stood on pinnacles that dissolved into precipice. He achieved greatly, and he suffered deeply. But he never gave up. In his solitude, he envisaged a new international order that would reduce lingering enmities, strengthen historic friendships and give new hope to mankind—a vision where dreams and possibilities conjoined."[13] It was the sendoff Nixon desired, and many of his failings seemed forgotten.

But not for long. Shortly afterward, the diaries kept by Bob Haldeman while Nixon's chief of staff were published. While they showed Nixon as an innovative policy mind quick to take a risk, they also showed the bitter, vindictive, and paranoid man who kept a chip on his shoulder each day he entered the Oval Office. The philosophical eulogies over, those who were paying attention remembered again why Nixon had accumulated so many enemies in his almost thirty years in public office and why so many were driven to push him from office and into exile.

Nixon died with his legacy unsettled, where it still remains. Too many details remain to be sorted, too many opinions need to be reexamined. Watergate and what John Mitchell, his law partner and attorney general, dubbed the "White House horrors," meant that fixing Nixon's place in history would always be difficult.

As president, Nixon reversed two decades of his own philosophy to reach out to China and bring the world's most populous nation into the world community. To do that, he needed to balance the political demands to get US troops out of Vietnam while maintaining enough of a war effort there to provide a bargaining chip to use with the Chinese and the Soviet Union. Both of those nations wanted the United States out of Vietnam. If Nixon had simply removed US troops from South Vietnam, he would have lost the leverage he needed for his other goals. So he bled the United States out of Vietnam; more than twenty-one thousand Americans paid for his policy agenda with their lives, as did millions of Bengalis in Bangladesh and Pakistan. Nixon did not want to risk anything that would upset China, the longtime rival of India, as India and Pakistan fought a bloody war that sent more than ten million people fleeing into India and killed hundreds of thousands more.

To make it happen, Nixon had to create a government devoted to secrecy. He kept his own cabinet in the dark, while he and Henry Kissinger handled foreign policy out of the White House and National Security Council. This stoked envy, resentment, and curiosity, as those shut of out of the decision making strove to learn what they could and then leaked what they did not like to the press. In turn, Nixon and Kissinger doubled down on the secrecy and spied on the suspected leakers. Cover-up begat cover-up; Nixon had too much to hide and too many lies to remember, even as he rushed toward a revolutionary arms deal with the Soviet Union, the opening to China, and the end of the Vietnam War. Few presidents had accomplished so much. Few had accumulated so many enemies. Nixon's gamble was that he tried to do it all in secret before the weight of the secrets crushed him. That he succeeded at the first part is to his everlasting credit. That he failed to avoid the inevitable collapse is to his everlasting shame.

The results of his policies are there for all to see. China is now the world's second-largest economy and the United States' largest creditor. The arms race between the United States and the Soviet Union slowed, which helped speed up the ultimate collapse of the Soviet Union. Vietnam is now a US ally and rival of China. These all could have happened without Nixon, but hardly as rapidly as he accomplished them.

Few politicians would openly say they wanted to emulate Nixon's style, but the American national security state owes much to his presidency. The Huston Plan and its seemingly revolutionary goal to forge a unified national intelligence network was the forerunner of the Patriot Act passed after the September 11 attacks. Intelligence agencies that rarely coordinated with each other before now share information in intelligence fusion centers around the country. The National Security Agency, which monitored the communications of Americans at home during Nixon's time, now collects the metadata of telephone calls made by people inside and outside of the country. White House control over national security policy, usually guided by the NSC, has grown stronger than ever. Few cabinet secretaries enjoy the kind of autonomy of John Foster Dulles under Eisenhower or James Baker under George H. W. Bush. Nixon created that structure with NSDM 2, and much of it remains to this day. Only the names have been changed.

Nixon's gamble was that he would achieve his goals before the consequences of his policy changes got the better of him. He did it, but just barely. He also helped kill faith and trust in the US government. The United States is still living with the results.

Acknowledgments

This book would not exist if not for Len Colodny. His exhaustive research for *Silent Coup* provided the foundation for many historians, including me, and is an invaluable resource. He inspired me with his friendship, steadfast spirit, and energy. It's only fitting that his work for *Silent Coup* and *The Forty Years War* is now collected at Texas A&M University, where they will be available to future scholars. Len's wife, Sandy, and his children, Sherry and John, have also been rocks throughout this entire project, and my thanks go out to them.

Ed Gray, author and son of former acting FBI director L. Patrick Gray, provided years of research and encouragement. He was the first to mine the Woodward and Bernstein papers at the University of Texas and expose the numerous inconsistencies between their notes and books. His insights led me to dig further into the life and work of William C. Sullivan, which yielded many of the new details here. He helped make this book what it is today.

Authors, officials, scholars, and advisers essential to the existence of *Nixon's Gamble* include Robert Gettlin, who put his heart and soul into *Silent Coup*; Luke Nichter of Texas A&M University, who will become one of history's greatest Nixon scholars; Max Holland; Evan Thomas; James Rosen; Brian Robertson; Martin Lobel; and Fred Graboske.

The resources at the University of Texas, the Harold Weisberg Collection at Hood College in Frederick, Maryland, the Lowell Weicker papers at the University of Virginia, the Richard Nixon and Lyndon Johnson presidential libraries, the Defense Department, FBI, CIA, and the State Department Office of the Historian were incredible aids. Their collections provided much of the documentation upon which this book stands.

Friends and colleagues provided incredible support and encouragement. Much of the inspiration came from more than thirty years of conversations with Lee Landenberger, whose fascination with the events of the Nixon era kept me going. Michael Fechter helped expose the flaws in earlier collections of White House tapes and provided critical help with all stages of the manuscript. Gene Brissie at Lyons Press helped shape the book where it needed the most help, and James Jayo helped make it possible by accepting the proposal. Warren and Sandy Johnston have been incredible friends for more than 25 years and insightful critics. Mike Casey, Peter Kelley, and Griff Thomas were great sounding boards at the Present Moment Retreat in Troncones, Mexico. Peter Viles, John Jeter, Allan Katz, Peter Eisler, Fredreka Schouten, Tom Vanden Brook, Chrissy Terrell, David Jackson, Gregory Korte, Jim Michaels, Lee Horwich, Susan Page, Paul Singer, Linda Kauss, Julie Mason, and Cooper Allen provided personal and professional assists along the way. Special thanks to Kelly Kennedy for support and encouragement that extended to introducing me to my agent, the incredible Scott Miller of Trident Media, and to *USA TODAY* Editor David Callaway for helping with op-eds and overall support.

Any project of this magnitude depends on the help and patience of family. Throughout the researching, thinking, and writing of this project, Margaret Talev has been an incredible sounding board, critic, and cheerleader. I would not have made it without her. My daughters Maggie and Abbey have put up with my time hidden in the office and the various distractions. My parents, Bob and Marge Locker, who voted for Richard Nixon for president three times, provided tremendous support and encouragement. They are everything anyone would want in parents. Finally, to the rest of my extended family, Lauren, David, Marina, Julia, and Henry Piper; Lydia, Steve, Ian, and Paul Josowitz; and Debbie and Richard Etchison, thanks for the kind thoughts and help.

Notes

PROLOGUE

1   "That is what . . . :" Nixon's grand jury testimony, June 25, 1975.
2   Nixon's instinct for the jugular. Kissinger, Henry A. *White House Years*. Boston: Little, Brown, 1979, p. 163.

PART I, CHAPTER 1

1   "Hard but happy," Nixon. *RN: The Memoirs of Richard Nixon*. New York: Grosset & Dunlap, 1978, p. 4.
2   "My father," Nixon, *RN*, p. 6.
3   "Lacking in aggressiveness," Roger Morris. *Richard Milhous Nixon: The Rise of an American Politician*. New York: Henry Holt, 1990, p. 184.
4   "I had to win," Morris, *Richard Milhous Nixon*, p. 341.
5   "The most influential Communist," Cronin, John. *The Problem of American Communism in 1945: Facts and Recommendations*, 1945.
6   "I don't think there is any doubt," Morris, *Richard Milhous Nixon*, p. 412.
7   Roosevelt Hotel and Dulles. Morris, *Richard Milhous Nixon*, p. 415.
8   El Capitan Theater. Morris, *Richard Milhous Nixon*, p. 825.
9   Checkers Speech. Morris, *Richard Milhous Nixon*, pp. 827–33.
10   "You're my boy!" Nixon, *RN*, p. 106.
11   1967 *Foreign Affairs* article. *Foreign Relations of the United States, 1969–1976, Volume I, Foundations of Foreign Policy*, Document 3.
12   Ibid.
13   "Nixon on communism," *New York Times*, August 10, 1968.
14   "Pledges End of War, Toughness on Crime." *New York Times*, August 9, 1968.
15   "Nixon Would Bar Forced Coalition in South Vietnam," R. W. Apple Jr., *New York Times*, October 28, 1968.
16   Oct. 7, 1968, Johnson/Nixon conversation. *Foreign Relations of the United States, 1964–1968, Volume VII, Vietnam, September 1968–January 1969*, Document 54.
17   "Johnson Calls Nixon 'Unfair' in Implying Cynical Peace Move." Neil Sheehan, *New York Times*, October 28, 1968.
18   Ibid.
19   October 30, 1968, Johnson/Russell conversation, LBJ Library.
20   November 2, 1968, Johnson/Dirksen conversation, LBJ Library.
21   November 3, 1968, Johnson/Nixon conversation, LBJ Library.
22   Johnson calmed down. Nixon, *RN*, p. 329.

23   November 4, 1968, telegram from Rostow to Johnson, *Foreign Relations of the United States, 1964–1968, Volume VII, Vietnam, September 1968–January 1969*, Document 194.
24   May 29, 1991, Nixon memorandum to Aitken, Nixon Library.
25   November 9, 1968, Johnson/Rusk conversation, LBJ Library.

PART I, CHAPTER 2

1   Rays out of his eyes; Haldeman, H. R. *The Haldeman Diaries: Inside the Nixon White House.* New York: G. P. Putnam's Sons, 1994, p. 18.
2   "From Partisan to President of All," *New York Times*, January 21, 1969.
3   Richard Nixon's first inaugural speech text.
4   "Nixon Rules Out Agency Control by Staff Aides," Robert B. Semple Jr., *New York Times*, November 14, 1968.
5   "Kissinger Named a Key Nixon Aide in Defense Policy," R. W. Apple Jr., *New York Times*, December 3, 1968.
6   Colodny, Len, and Tom Shachtman. *The Forty Years War: The Rise and Fall of the Neocons, from Nixon to Obama.* New York: HarperCollins, 2009, p. 16.
7   "The Iron Mentor of the Pentagon," Nick Thimmesch, *Washington Post*, March 2, 1975.
8   Richard Allen oral history, May 28, 2002, Miller Center of Public Affairs.
9   Morris, Roger. *Uncertain Greatness: Henry Kissinger & American Foreign Policy.* New York: Harper & Row, 1977, p. 46.
10   January 9, 1969, Laird to Kissinger memorandum, *Foreign Relations of the United States, 1969–1976, Volume II, Organization and Management of Foreign Policy*, Document 6.
11   Rough roads, Johnson, U. Alexis, with J. O. McAllister. *The Right Hand of Power.* Englewood Cliffs, NJ, Prentice-Hall, 1984, p. 514.
12   Richardson memo, *Foreign Relations of the United States, 1969–1976, Volume II, Organization and Management of Foreign Policy*, Document 4.
13   Van Atta, Dale. *With Honor: Melvin Laird in War, Peace, and Politics.* Madison: University of Wisconsin Press, 2008, p. 157.

PART I, CHAPTER 3

1   January 21, 1969, NSC meeting minutes, *Foreign Relations of the United States, 1969–1976, Volume II, Organization and Management of Foreign Policy*, Document 15.
2   Ibid.
3   Ibid.
4   January 22, 1969, Laird to Kissinger memorandum, *Foreign Relations of the United States, 1969–1976, Volume II, Organization and Management of Foreign Policy*, Document 16.
5   Nixon, *RN*, p. 390.
6   February 1, 1969, Haldeman to Rogers memorandum, *Foreign Relations of the United States, 1969–1976, Volume II, Organization and Management of Foreign Policy*, Document 20.
7   Joseph Califano interview with author.
8   February 7, 1969, Haig to Kissinger memorandum, *Foreign Relations of the United States, 1969–1976, Volume II, Organization and Management of Foreign Policy*, Document 22.
9   Ibid.
10   1967 *Foreign Affairs* article, *Foreign Relations of the United States, 1969–1976, Volume I, Foundations of Foreign Policy*, Document 3.
11   Ibid.
12   Ibid.
13   Ibid.
14   February 4, 1969, Nixon to Rogers letter, *Foreign Relations of the United States, 1969–1976, Volume XII, Soviet Union, January 1969–October 1970*, Document 10.

15   National Security Decision Memorandum 9, *Foreign Relations of the United States, 1969–1976, Volume XII, Soviet Union, January 1969–October 1970*, Document 4.

16   February 13, 1969, Rogers and Dobrynin meeting, *Foreign Relations of the United States, 1969–1976, Volume XII, Soviet Union, January 1969–October 1970*, Document 12.

17   February 15, 1969, Kissinger to Nixon memorandum, *Foreign Relations of the United States, 1969–1976, Volume XII, Soviet Union, January 1969–October 1970*, Document 13.

18   Ibid.

19   February 18, 1969, Toon memorandum to Kissinger, *Foreign Relations of the United States, 1969–1976, Volume XII, Soviet Union, January 1969–October 1970*, Document 16.

20   Every confidence, Dobrynin, Anatoly. *In Confidence.* New York: Times Books, 1995, p. 199.

21   Tough confrontation, Kissinger, *White House Years*, p. 143.

22   Unprecedented, Dobrynin, *In Confidence*, p. 200.

23   Dobrynin memorandum of conversation with Kissinger, February 21, 1969.

24   Ibid.

25   Gradual evolution, Dobrynin, *In Confidence*, p. 200.

26   Dewey Canyon, Colodny and Shachtman, *The Forty Years War*, p. 34.

27   Pentagon lunch, Colodny and Shachtman, *The Forty Years War*, p. 34.

28   Actual or feigned, Colodny and Shachtman, *The Forty Years War*, p. 35.

29   April 22, 1969, Kissinger memorandum to Nixon, *Foreign Relations of the United States, 1969–1976, Volume VI, Vietnam, January 1969–July 1970*, Document 62.

30   March 2, 1969, Haig to Kissinger memorandum, *Foreign Relations of the United States, 1969–1976, Volume XXXIV, National Security Policy, 1969–1972.*

31   February 19, 1969, Kissinger to Nixon memorandum, *Foreign Relations of the United States, 1969–1976, Volume VI, Vietnam, January 1969–July 1970*, Document 22.

32   Ibid.

33   Ibid.

34   Ibid.

35   Ibid.

36   Ibid.

37   February 25, 1969, Laird memorandum to Nixon, *Foreign Relations of the United States, 1969–1976, Volume VI, Vietnam, January 1969–July 1970*, Document 25.

38   Shawcross, William. *Sideshow: Kissinger, Nixon and the Destruction of Cambodia.* New York: Simon and Schuster, 1979, p. 32.

39   Bombing order, Haldeman, *The Haldeman Diaries*, p. 38.

40   March 16, 1969, Kissinger memorandum to Nixon, *Foreign Relations of the United States, 1969–1976, Volume VI, Vietnam, January 1969–July 1970*, Document 40.

41   Cambodia strikes, Kissinger, *White House Years*, p. 246.

42   Halperin told to keep quiet, Hersh, Seymour. *The Price of Power: Kissinger in the Nixon White House.* New York: Summit, 1983, p. 63.

43   High state of alarm, *Foreign Relations of the United States, 1969–1976, Volume VI, Vietnam, January 1969–July 1970*, Document 41.

44   March 16, 1969, Kissinger memorandum to Nixon, *Foreign Relations of the United States, 1969–1976, Volume VI, Vietnam, January 1969–July 1970*, Document 40.

45   December 24, 1968, Sneider memorandum to Bundy, *Foreign Relations of the United States, 1964–1968, Volume XXIX, Part 2, Japan*, Document 138.

46   March 29, 1969, Wheeler memorandum to Laird.

47   April 2, 1969, Haig memorandum to Kissinger.

48   "US Perplexed by Okinawa Issue," Hedrick Smith, *New York Times*, March 30, 1969.

49   "US Scout Plane with 31 is Lost, Reported Downed by 2 North Korean MiGs," William Beecher, *New York Times*, April 16, 1969.

50   Park assassination attempt, Cheevers, Jack. *Act of War: Lyndon Johnson, North Korea, and the Capture of the Spy Ship* Pueblo. New York: NAL Caliber, 2013, pp. 55–58.

51   Nixon Daily Diary, April 15, 1969.
52   Ibid.
53   April 15, 1969, Joint Chiefs of Staff memorandum, *Foreign Relations of the United States, 1969–1976, Volume XIX, Korea, 1969–1972*, Document 7.
54   Ibid.
55   April 15, 1969, Kissinger to Nixon telephone conversation, *Foreign Relations of the United States, 1969–1976, Volume XIX, Korea, 1969–1972*, Document 8.
56   Ibid.
57   Ibid.
58   Ibid.
59   April 15, 1969, Kissinger to Nixon telephone conversation, *Foreign Relations of the United States, 1969–1976, Volume XIX, Korea, 1969–1972*, Document 9.
60   April 16, 1969, Helms intelligence briefing, *Foreign Relations of the United States, 1969–1976, Volume XIX, Korea, 1969–1972*, Document 10.
61   April 16, 1969, Haig to Kissinger memorandum, *Foreign Relations of the United States, 1969–1976, Volume XIX, Korea, 1969–1972*, Document 11.
62   April 17, 1969, CIA intelligence memorandum, *Foreign Relations of the United States, 1969–1976, Volume XIX, Korea, 1969–1972*, Document 14.
63   April 17, 1969, Nixon to Kissinger telephone conversation, *Foreign Relations of the United States, 1969–1976, Volume XIX, Korea, 1969–1972*, Document 15.
64   April 18, 1969, Sneider memorandum to Kissinger, *Foreign Relations of the United States, 1969–1976, Volume XIX, Korea, 1969–1972*, Document 16.
65   April 18, 1969, Laird memorandum to Nixon, *Foreign Relations of the United States, 1969–1976, Volume XIX, Korea, 1969–1972*, Document 17.
66   Kraemer's reaction, Colodny and Shachtman, *The Forty Years War*, p. 45.
67   Nixon drunk, Hersh, *The Price of Power*, p. 108.
68   Number of directives, Nixon Library.
69   Ibid.
70   "Ky Said to Discuss US Troop Withdrawal Plans," Hedrick Smith, *New York Times*, April 4, 1969.
71   "Nixon Has Begun Program to End War in Vietnam," Max Frankel, *New York Times*, April 6, 1969.
72   National Security Decision Memorandum 8, Nixon Library.
73   Ibid.
74   "A Series of Limited Pacts on Missiles Now US Aim," Peter Grose, *New York Times*, April 22, 1969.
75   "Posting of US Intelligence Ship Off Korea Believed Under Study," William Beecher, *New York Times*, April 24, 1969.
76   "US to Sell Jordan a 2d Jet Squadron," Hedrick Smith, *New York Times*, April 25, 1969.
77   April 25, 1969, Nixon schedule, Nixon Daily Diary.

PART I, CHAPTER 4

1   "Raids in Cambodia by US Unprotested," William Beecher, *New York Times*, May 9, 1969.
2   Outrageous, Isaacson, Walter. *Kissinger: A Biography*. New York: Simon & Schuster, 1992, p. 212.
3   "Administration Gets Study of Global Nuclear Strategy," William Beecher, *New York Times*, May 1, 1969.
4   "Aides Say Nixon Weighed Swift Korea Reprisal," William Beecher, *New York Times*, May 6, 1969.
5   Laird call, Van Atta, *With Honor*, p. 181.
6   May 9, 1969, Hoover memo to Clyde Tolson, Cartha DeLoach, Sullivan and Bishop, FBI files.

7   May 13, 1969, Hoover letter to Kissinger about press office, *Foreign Relations of the United States, 1969–1976, Volume II, Organization and Management of Foreign Policy*, Document 41.

8   *Final Report of the Select Committee to Study Governmental Operations with Respect to Intelligence Activities, US Senate, Book III, Supplementary Detailed Staff Reports on Intelligence Activities and the Rights of Americans*, 1976 (Church Committee), p. 324.

9   Ibid.

10   Hoover and wiretaps, Nixon, *RN*, p. 387.

11   Haig, *Inner Circles*, p. 212.

12   Church Committee, Book III, p. 324.

13   April 25, 1969, Nixon Daily Diary.

14   April 25, 1969, Hoover calendar, FBI files.

15   April 25, 1969, Haldeman, *The Haldeman Diaries*, p. 53.

16   Hersh, Seymour, "Kissinger and Nixon in the White House," *The Atlantic*, May 1982.

17   May 11, 1969, Sullivan to DeLoach memorandum, FBI files.

18   Sullivan and Haig, Haig, *Inner Circles*, p. 215.

19   Ibid.

20   May 7, 1963, Sullivan to Belmont memorandum about Kraemer, FBI files.

21   Sullivan description, Haig, *Inner Circles*, p. 215.

22   Wiretap targets, FBI investigation, May 1973, FBI files.

23   Davidson Paris, Hersh, *The Price of Power*, p. 18.

24   Sonnenfeldt and Kraemer, Colodny and Shachtman, *The Forty Years War*, p. 22.

25   Morris interview with Colodny, Colodny Collection.

26   Hoover memorandum on Pursley, May 1969.

27   Laird NSA intercepts, Van Atta, *With Honor*, p. 224.

28   Pursley and Haig, Hersh, *The Price of Power*, p. 90.

29   Church Committee, Book III, p. 326.

30   July 19, 1966, Sullivan to DeLoach memorandum on black bag jobs, FBI files.

31   Sneider and Moose, Hersh, *The Price of Power*, p. 91.

32   March 6, 1969, Sneider memorandum to Kissinger, *Foreign Relations of the United States, 1969–1976, Volume VI, Vietnam, January 1969–July 1970*, Document 30.

33   April 10, 1969, Sneider memorandum to Kissinger, *Foreign Relations of the United States, 1969–1976, Volume VI, Vietnam, January 1969–July 1970*, Document 63.

34   Moose, Hersh, *The Price of Power*, p. 34.

35   Sensitive material, May 28, 1969, Sullivan memorandum to DeLoach, *Foreign Relations of the United States, 1969–1976, Volume II, Organization and Management of Foreign Policy*, Document 47.

36   Davidson, Haig, *Inner Circles*, p. 219.

37   Sullivan urging end to taps, Sullivan, William C., with Bill Brown. *The Bureau: My Thirty Years in Hoover's FBI*. New York: W. W. Norton & Co., 1979, pp. 221–22.

38   Kissinger call to Halperin, Hersh, *The Price of Power*, p. 95.

39   Kissinger bragging about firing Halperin, February 18, 1971, Nixon conversation with Kissinger, Brinkley, Douglas, and Luke A. Nichter. *The Nixon Tapes*. New York: Houghton Mifflin Harcourt, 2014, p. 13.

40   October 20, 1971, Miller memorandum to Mark Felt, FBI files.

41   Church Committee, Book III, pp. 349–51.

42   Haig and Sullivan, Sullivan, *The Bureau*, p. 219.

43   Cartha DeLoach oral history, 2005.

44   April 25, 1969, Kissinger memorandum to Nixon.

45   Sullivan FBI personnel file.

46   Ibid.

47   Weinstein, Allen. *Perjury: The Hiss-Chambers Case*. New York: Random House, 1978, p. 347.

48   Ibid.

49   *Final Report of the Select Committee to Study Governmental Operations with Respect to Intelligence Activities, US Senate, Book II, Intelligence Activities and the Rights of Americans,* 1976 (Church Committee), p. 65.

50   *Final Report of the Select Committee to Study Governmental Operations with Respect to Intelligence Activities, US Senate, Book I, Foreign and Military Intelligence,* 1976 (Church Committee), p. 112.

51   Church Committee, Book II, p. 61.

52   Sullivan on USIB, June 30, 1961, Hoover letter to Allen Dulles about USIB.

53   Sullivan and Helms, Riebling, Mark. *Wedge: The Secret War Between the FBI and CIA.* New York: Knopf, 1996, p. 275.

54   Dominican Republic, Sullivan, *The Bureau,* p. 71.

55   Sullivan's friends, Ibid., p. 170.

56   May 7, 1963, Sullivan to Belmont memorandum about Kraemer, FBI files.

57   Sullivan and young reporters, Novak, Robert. *The Prince of Darkness: 50 Years Reporting in Washington.* New York: Crown, 2007, p. 208.

58   Church Committee, Book III, COINTELPRO, p. 79.

59   Ibid., p. 160.

60   Church Committee, Book II, p. 231.

61   Church Committee, Book III, p. 360.

62   Ibid., p. 8.

63   Ibid., p. 9.

64   DeLoach oral history.

65   Hoover and OSS, Riebling, *Wedge,* p. 33.

66   Sullivan and Angleton, Riebling, *Wedge,* p. 276.

67   October 24, 1968, Sullivan letter to Helms, *Foreign Relations of the United States, 1964–1968, Volume XXXIII, Organization and Management of Foreign Policy, United Nations,* Document 287.

PART I, CHAPTER 5

1   Walters told Kraemer, Colodny and Shachtman, *The Forty Years War,* p. 35.

2   NSA communications, Van Atta, *With Honor,* p. 224.

3   Laird told Nixon, Van Atta, *With Honor,* p. 224.

4   Ibid.

5   "US Said to Plan an Okinawa Deal Barring A-Bombs," Hedrick Smith, *New York Times,* June 3, 1969; "Nixon-Thieu Talk May Bring Accord on US Troop Cuts," Hedrick Smith, *New York Times,* June 4, 1969.

6   March 13, 1969, Laird memorandum to Nixon, *Foreign Relations of the United States, 1969–1976, Volume VI, Vietnam, January 1969–July 1970,* Document 38.

7   Ibid.

8   Xuan Thuy, April 24, 1969, Kissinger note to Nixon, *Foreign Relations of the United States, 1969–1976, Volume VI, Vietnam, January 1969–July 1970,* Document 68.

9   Ibid.

10   "Nixon Asks Troop Pullout in a Year and Would Join Vietnam Political Talks," Robert B. Semple Jr., *New York Times,* May 15, 1969.

11   May 15 NSC meeting, *Foreign Relations of the United States, 1969–1976, Volume VI, Vietnam, January 1969–July 1970,* Document 68.

12   Ibid.

13   September 12 NSC meeting minutes, *Foreign Relations of the United States, 1969–1976, Volume VI, Vietnam, January 1969–July 1970,* Document 120.

14   Ibid.

15   Ibid.

16   Ibid.

17   Ibid.

18   Ibid.
19   October 2, 1969, Duck Hook documents.
20   CNO office on Duck Hook, Hersh, *The Price of Power*, p. 120.
21   Robinson to Moorer, Colodny and Robert Gettlin, *Silent Coup: The Removal of a President*. New York: St. Martin's, 1991, p. 4.
22   September 29, 1969, Lake and Morris memorandum to Robinson.
23   October 2, 1969, Duck Hook documents.
24   Ibid.
25   Ibid.
26   Ibid.
27   Laird and Rogers threatened to quit, Colodny and Shachtman, *The Forty Years War*, p. 64.
28   Duck Hook, H. R. Haldeman, *The Haldeman Diaries*, p. 95.
29   Kraemer memo, *Foreign Relations of the United States, 1969–1976, Volume VII, Soviet Union, January 1969–October 1970*, Document 148.
30   Ibid.
31   Ibid.
32   Nuclear alert, Colodny and Shachtman, *The Forty Years War*, p. 64.
33   Ibid.
34   Ibid.
35   Ibid.
36   Richard Allen oral history, 2002.
37   Ibid.
38   Ibid.
39   Nixon drinking, Hersh, *The Price of Power*, p. 109.
40   John Ehrlichman interview with Colodny, Colodny collection.
41   Morris and Nixon's drinking, Hersh, *The Price of Power*, p. 108.
42   Woodward, Colodny and Gettlin, *Silent Coup*, p. 75.
43   Meeting Felt, Bob Woodward, *The Secret Man: The Story of Watergate's Deep Throat*. New York: Simon & Schuster, 2005, p. 17.
44   Briefing Haig, Colodny and Gettlin, *Silent Coup*, p. 70.

PART I, CHAPTER 6

1   National Security Study Memorandum 3.
2   Stop Where We Are, Hersh, *The Price of Power*, p. 545.
3   June 23, 1969, US Intelligence Board, Soviet Strategic Attack Forces estimate.
4   February 12, 1969, National Security Council meeting minutes, *Foreign Relations of the United States, 1969–1976, Volume XXXIV, National Security Policy, 1969–1972*, Document 5.
5   February 14, 1969, National Security Council meeting minutes, *Foreign Relations of the United States, 1969–1976, Volume XXXIV, National Security Policy, 1969–1972*, Document 7.
6   Ibid.
7   Ibid.
8   Ibid.
9   Ibid.
10   "Laird Sees 'Rapid' Soviet Missile Gains," John W. Finney, *New York Times*, February 21, 1969.
11   February 19, 1969, *National Security Council meeting minutes, Foreign Relations of the United States, 1969–1976, Volume XXXIV, National Security Policy, 1969–1972*, Document 8.
12   Ibid.
13   Ibid.
14   "Laird Sees 'Rapid' Soviet Missile Gains."
15   February 26, 1969, Wheeler memorandum to Laird, *Foreign Relations of the United States, 1969–1976, Volume XXXIV, National Security Policy, 1969–1972*, Document 11.

16   March 5, 1969, Kissinger memorandum to Nixon, *Foreign Relations of the United States, 1969–1976, Volume XXXIV, National Security Policy, 1969–1972*, Document 15.

17   March 5, 1969, National Security Council meeting minutes, *Foreign Relations of the United States, 1969–1976, Volume XXXIV, National Security Policy, 1969–1972*, Document 16.

18   Ibid.

19   March 6, 1969, Richardson and Smith memorandum to Rogers, *Foreign Relations of the United States, 1969–1976, Volume XXXIV, National Security Policy, 1969–1972*, Document 19.

20   March 9, 1969, Smith and Johnson memorandum to Rogers, *Foreign Relations of the United States, 1969–1976, Volume XXXIV, National Security Policy, 1969–1972*, Document 20.

21   March 10, 1969, Harlow memorandum to Nixon, *Foreign Relations of the United States, 1969–1976, Volume XXXIV, National Security Policy, 1969–*1972, Document 21.

22   March 11, 1969, Haldeman note to file about DuBridge meeting, *Foreign Relations of the United States, 1969–1976, Volume XXXIV, National Security Policy, 1969–1972*, Document 22.

23   March 13, 1969, Nixon memorandum to Klein, *Foreign Relations of the United States, 1969–1976, Volume XXXIV, National Security Policy, 1969–1972*, Document 25.

24   March 14, 1969, Buchanan memorandum to Nixon, *Foreign Relations of the United States, 1969–1976, Volume XXXIV, National Security Policy, 1969–1972*, Document 24.

25   "Reorientation of Sentinel Envisioned by Nixon as Guarding US from All Directions," William Beecher, *New York Times*, March 15, 1969.

26   ABM as bargaining chip, Nixon, *RN*, p. 416.

27   "SS-9 Helps Administration Score Points in Missile Debate," John W. Finney, *New York Times*, March 24, 1969.

28   "Study Backs Foes of Missile Shield," John W. Finney, *New York Times*, April 9, 1969.

29   April 14, 1969, Nixon memorandum to aides, *Foreign Relations of the United States, 1969–1976, Volume XXXIV, National Security Policy, 1969–1972*, Document 25.

30   May 26, 1969, Helms memorandum to Nixon, *Foreign Relations of the United States, 1969–1976, Volume XXXIV, National Security Policy, 1969–1972*, Document 30.

31   May 28, 1969, Packard memorandum to Kissinger, *Foreign Relations of the United States, 1969–1976, Volume XXXIV, National Security Policy, 1969–1972*, Document 31.

32   Ibid.

33   May 29, 1969, review group meeting minutes, *Foreign Relations of the United States, 1969–1976, Volume XXXIV, National Security Policy, 1969–1972*, Document 32.

34   "Administration Critics Say 'Intelligence Gap' Clouds ABM Issue," John W. Finney, *New York Times*, June 1, 1969.

35   June 2, 1969, Nixon note to Kissinger, *Foreign Relations of the United States, 1969–1976, Volume XXXIV, National Security Policy, 1969–1972*, Document 33.

36   Ibid.

37   June 5, 1969, Kissinger memorandum to Nixon, *Foreign Relations of the United States, 1969–1976, Volume XXXIV, National Security Policy, 1969–1972*, Document 33.

38   June 12, 1969, Nixon call to Kissinger, *Foreign Relations of the United States, 1969–1976, Volume XXXIV, National Security Policy, 1969–1972*, Document 33.

39   Ibid.

40   Hathaway Robert M., and Russell Jack Smith, *Richard Helms as Director of Central Intelligence*, Washington: Center for the Study of Intelligence, 1993, p. 39.

41   June 30, 1969, Lynn memorandum to Kissinger, *Foreign Relations of the United States, 1969–1976, Volume XXXIV, National Security Policy, 1969–1972*, Document 40.

42   July 23, MIRV Working Group recommendations, *Foreign Relations of the United States, 1969–1976, Volume XXXIV, National Security Policy, 1969–1972*, Document 43.

43   August 10, 1969, Nixon memorandum, *Foreign Relations of the United States, 1969–1976, Volume XXXIV, National Security Policy, 1969–1972*, p.88.

44   Changing NIE, Helms, Richard, and William Hood, *A Look Over My Shoulder*. New York: Random House, 2003, p. 387.

PART I, CHAPTER 7

1   February 27, 1970, National Security Council meeting minutes, *Foreign Relations of the United States, 1969–1976, Volume VI, Vietnam, January 1969–July 1970*, Document 194.

2   Beehive, William Shawcross, *Sideshow*, p. 25.

3   Pitch for aid, February 12, 1970, Kissinger memorandum to Nixon, *Foreign Relations of the United States, 1969–1976, Volume VI, Vietnam, January 1969–July 1970*, Document 179.

4   March 18, 1970, Kissinger call to Rogers, *Foreign Relations of the United States, 1969–1976, Volume VI, Vietnam, January 1969–July 1970*, Document 205.

5   March 19, 1970, National Security Council meeting minutes, *Foreign Relations of the United States, 1969–1976, Volume VI, Vietnam, January 1969–July 1970*, Document 205.

6   March 19, 1970, Kissinger memorandum to Nixon, *Foreign Relations of the United States, 1969–1976, Volume VI, Vietnam, January 1969–July 1970*, Document 205.

7   March 23, 1970, Helms memorandum to Kissinger, *Foreign Relations of the United States, 1969–1970, Volume VI, Vietnam, January 1969–July 1970*, Document 208.

8   March 27, 1970, Kissinger memorandum to Nixon, *Foreign Relations of the United States, 1969–1976, Volume VI, Vietnam, January 1969–July 1970*, Document 215.

9   April 1, 1970, Haig memorandum to Kissinger, *Foreign Relations of the United States, 1969–1976, Volume VI, Vietnam, January 1969–July 1970*, Document 217.

10   Ibid.

11   April 3, 1970, Haig memorandum to Kissinger, *Foreign Relations of the United States, 1969–1976, Volume VI, Vietnam, January 1969–July 1970*, Document 219.

12   Ibid.

13   April 4, 1970, Laird memorandum to Nixon, *Foreign Relations of the United States, 1969–1970, Volume VI, Vietnam, January 1969–July 1970*, Document 221.

14   Ibid.

15   April 10, 1970, memorandum for the record, *Foreign Relations of the United States, 1969–1970, Volume VI, Vietnam, January 1969–July 1970*, Document 225.

16   April 19, 1970, Kissinger memorandum to Nixon, *Foreign Relations of the United States, 1969–1976, Volume VI, January 1969–July 1970*, Document 226.

17   Ibid.

18   April 13, 1970, Kissinger memorandum to Nixon, *Foreign Relations of the United States, 1969–1976, Volume VI, Vietnam, January 1969–July 1970*, Document 228.

19   Ibid.

20   Ibid.

21   Ibid.

22   Ibid.

23   Laird recommendation, Kissinger, *White House Years*, p. 478.

24   April 15, 1970, Helms memorandum to Kissinger, *Foreign Relations of the United States, 1969–1976, Volume VI, Vietnam, January 1969–July 1970*, Document 232.

25   Agnew's recommendations, Kissinger, *White House Years*, pp. 491–92.

26   Ibid.

27   National Security Decision Memorandum 56, April 22, 1970, *Foreign Relations of the United States, 1969–1976, Volume VI, Vietnam, January 1969–July 1970*, Document 249.

28   April 22, 1970, Morris, Lake, and Lord memorandum to Kissinger, *Foreign Relations of the United States, 1969–1976, Volume VI, Vietnam, January 1969–July 1970*, Document 250.

29   April 23, 1970, Kissinger memorandum to Nixon, *Foreign Relations of the United States, 1969–1970, Volume VI, Vietnam, January 1969–July 1970*, Document 253.

30   Nixon Daily Diary, April 24, 1970.

31   Editorial note, *Foreign Relations of the United States, 1969–1976, Volume VI, Vietnam, January 1969–July 1970*, Document 254.

32   Laird's claims about Moorer, Kissinger, *White House Years*, pp. 495–96.

33   April 24, 1970, telephone call minutes between Kissinger, Nixon and Sen. John Stennis, *Foreign Relations of the United States, 1969–1976, Volume VI, Vietnam, January 1969–July 1970,* Document 256.

34   Ibid.

35   April 24, 1970, telephone call between Kissinger and Helms, *Foreign Relations of the United States, 1969–1976, Volume VI, Vietnam, January 1969–July 1970,* Document 254.

36   Sequoia cruise, Kissinger, *White House Years,* p. 498.

37   April 26, 1970, NSC meeting, Kissinger, *White House Years,* p. 499.

38   April 27, 1970, meeting with Rogers, Laird, Kissinger, Nixon, and Haldeman notes, *Foreign Relations of the United States, 1969–1976, Volume VI, Vietnam, January 1969–July 1970,* Document 261.

39   April 27, 1970, meeting notes, H. R. Haldeman, *The Haldeman Diaries: Inside the Nixon White House,* p. 155.

40   April 27, 1970, meeting, Haldeman, *The Haldeman Diaries; Foreign Relations of the United States, 1969–1976, Volume VI, Vietnam, January 1969–July 1970,* Document 261.

41   April 27, 1970, Laird memorandum to Nixon, *Foreign Relations of the United States, 1969–1976, Volume VI, Vietnam, January 1969–July 1970,* Document 263.

42   April 28, 1970, Mitchell memorandum on meeting between Nixon, Laird, Rogers, and Mitchell, *Foreign Relations of the United States, 1969–1976, Volume VI, Vietnam, January 1969–July 1970,* Document 267.

43   "Rising Peril Seen," William Beecher, *New York Times,* April 30, 1970.

44   "Nixon Sends Combat Forces to Cambodia to Drive Communists from Staging Zone," Robert Semple Jr., *New York Times,* May 1, 1970.

45   April 22, 1970, Morris, Lake, and Lord memorandum to Kissinger, *Foreign Relations of the United States, 1969–1976, Volume VI, Vietnam, January 1969–July 1970,* Document 250.

46   Undated Haig memorandum to Kissinger, *Foreign Relations of the United States, 1969–1970, Volume VI, Vietnam, January 1969–July 1970,* Document 294.

47   Fred Ladd, Shawcross, *Sideshow,* p. 168.

48   May 25, 1970, Kissinger memorandum to Nixon, *Foreign Relations of the United States, 1969–1970, Volume VI, Vietnam, January 1969–July 1970,* Document 306.

49   May 31, 1970, minutes of meeting with Nixon and others in San Clemente, *Foreign Relations of the United States, 1969–1976, Volume VI, Vietnam, January 1969–July 1970,* Document 313.

50   June 15, 1970, Washington Special Action Group meeting minutes, *Foreign Relations of the United States, 1969–1976, Volume VI, Vietnam, January 1969–July 1970,* Document 326.

51   June 17, 1970, Haig backchannel message to Ladd, *Foreign Relations of the United States, 1969–1976, Volume VI, Vietnam, January 1969–July 1970,* Document 328.

52   June 18, 1970, Ladd backchannel message to Haig, *Foreign Relations of the United States, 1969–1976, Volume VI, Vietnam, January 1969–July 1970,* Document 328.

53   June 18, 1970, Haig meeting with Nixon, *Foreign Relations of the United States, 1969–1976, Volume VI, Vietnam, January 1969–July 1970,* Document 328.

54   Fred Ladd interview, January 25, 1982, WGBH interview.

55   January 25, 1969, National Security Council meeting minutes, *Foreign Relations of the United States, 1969–1976, Volume VI, Vietnam, January 1969–July 1970,* Document 10.

56   March 22, 1969, summary of interagency responses to NSSM 1, *Foreign Relations of the United States, 1969–1976, Volume VI, Vietnam, January 1969–July 1970,* Document 44.

57   Ahern, Thomas L. Jr., *Good Questions, Wrong Answers: CIA's Estimates of Arms Traffic Through Sihanoukville, Cambodia, During the Vietnam War,* Center for the Study of Intelligence, 2004, p. xi.

58   July 18, 1970, President's Foreign Intelligence Advisory Board meeting minutes.

59   Hathaway and Smith, *Richard Helms as Director of Central Intelligence,* p. 36.

PART I, CHAPTER 8

1   "Pledges End of War, Toughness on Crime," *New York Times,* August 9, 1968.
2   Cartha "Deke" DeLoach oral history, January 11, 1992, LBJ Library.
3   "Widening Rebellion," Fred M. Hechinger, *New York Times,* March 14, 1969.
4   "400 Police Quell Harvard Uprising," Robert Rheingold, *New York Times,* April 11, 1969.
5   "Nixon Diverts 200-Million to Fix Up Riot-Torn Areas," John Herbers, *New York Times,* April 9, 1969.
6   "Troops Patrol in Chicago As Slum Violence Erupts," Donald Janson, *New York Times,* April 4, 1969.
7   Church Committee, Book III, p. 928.
8   Ibid., p. 929.
9   Ibid., p. 929.
10   Ibid., p. 929.
11   Ibid., p. 930.
12   Riebling, *Wedge,* p. 228.
13   October 24, 1968, Sullivan letter to Helms, *Foreign Relations of the United States, 1964–1968, Volume XXXIII, Organization and Management of Foreign Policy; United Nations,* Document 281.
14   Church Committee, Book III, p. 930.
15   November 14, 1969, telephone call between Nixon and Kissinger, *Foreign Relations of the United States, 1969–1976, Volume VI, Vietnam, January 1969–July 1970,* Document 149.
16   January 26, 1970, Krogh memorandum to Haldeman on internal security.
17   February 25, 1970, Huston memorandum to Haldeman on bombing halt.
18   February 25, 1970, Huston memorandum to Nixon on bombing halt and Chennault affair.
19   Church Committee, Book III, p. 924.
20   Ibid., p. 925.
21   Ibid., p. 937.
22   Ibid., p. 938.
23   Ibid., p. 939.
24   Ibid., p. 942.
25   Ibid., p. 945.
26   Ibid., p. 955.
27   Ibid., p. 948.
28   Ibid., p. 985.
29   Ibid., p. 960.
30   Ibid., p. 966.
31   Ibid., p. 966.
32   Ibid., p. 974.
33   Ibid., p. 977.
34   Ibid., p. 975.
35   Ibid., p. 974.

PART I, CHAPTER 9

1   Allende in 1958, Hersh, *Price of Power,* p. 259.
2   CIA aid to Frei Montalva in 1964, Hersh, *Price of Power,* p. 260.
3   April 15, 1969, minutes of 303 Committee meeting on Latin American covert operations.
4   March 14, 1969, minutes of 303 Committee meeting, *Foreign Relations of the United States, 1969–1976, Volume XXI, Chile, 1969–1973,* Document 3.
5   April 15, 1969, minutes of 303 Committee meeting.
6   July 10, 1969, Vaky memorandum to Kissinger, *Foreign Relations of the United States, 1969–1976, Volume XXI, Chile, 1969–1973,* Document 16.
7   Chile polls, Kissinger, *White House Years,* p. 667.

8 National Security Decision Memorandum 97, July 24, 1970.

9 March 4, 1971, CIA analysis of US policy on Chilean elections.

10 September 15, 1970, meeting details, *Foreign Relations of the United States, 1969–1976, Volume XXI, Chile, 1969 -1973*, Document 93.

11 $10 million, Kissinger, *White House Years*, p. 674.

12 September 16, 1970, Broe memorandum for the record, *Foreign Relations of the United States, 1969–1976, Volume XXI, Chile, 1969–1973*, Document 94.

13 September 1, 1970, Korry backchannel message to State, *Foreign Relations of the United States, 1969–1976, Volume XXI, Chile, 1969–1973*, Document 59.

14 September 16, 1970, Vaky memorandum to Kissinger, *Foreign Relations of the United States, 1969–1976, Volume XXI, Chile, 1969–1973*, Document 95.

15 Ibid.

16 September 16, 1970, Korry backchannel to Alexis Johnson, *Foreign Relations of the United States, 1969–1976, Volume XXI, Chile, 1969–1973*, Document 96.

17 September 16, 1970, Vaky memorandum to Kissinger, *Foreign Relations of the United States, 1969–1976, Volume XXI, Chile, 1969–1973*, Document 98.

18 September 17, 1970, Kissinger memorandum to Nixon, *Foreign Relations of the United States, 1969–1976, Volume XXI, Chile, 1969–1973*, Document 100.

19 September 16, 1970, Broe memorandum for the record, *Foreign Relations of the United States, 1969–1976, Volume XXI, Chile, 1969–1973*, Document 94.

20 September 21, 1970, CIA telegram to Santiago station, *Foreign Relations of the United States, 1969–1976, Volume XXI, Chile, 1969–1973*, Document 107.

21 Schneider killing, Church Committee interim report, 1975; October 22, 1970, Embassy report to State Department, *Foreign Relations of the United States, 1969–1976, Volume XXI, Chile, 1969–1973*, Document 161.

22 December 2, 1970, Haig memorandum to Kissinger for President's Foreign Intelligence Advisory Board meeting.

23 December 4, 1970, PFIAB meeting, *Foreign Relations of the United States, 1969–1976, Volume II, Organization and Management of US Foreign Policy, 1969–1972*, Document 219.

24 December 7, 1970, Helms memorandum to Kissinger, *Foreign Relations of the United States, 1969–1976, Volume II, Organization and Management of US Foreign Policy, 1969–1972*, Document 220.

PART I, CHAPTER 10

1 "Bomb the bastards," Van Atta, *With Honor*, p. 272.

2 Moorer kept in the dark, Colodny and Shachtman, *The Forty Years War*, p. 87.

3 September 22, 1970, Kissinger to Nixon memorandum, *Foreign Relations of the United States, 1969–1976, Volume XII, Soviet Union, January 1969–October 1970*, Document 212.

4 September 25, 1970, Kissinger and Dobrynin meeting memorandum of conversation, *Foreign Relations of the United States, 1969–1976, Volume XII, Soviet Union, January 1969–October 1970*, Document 215.

5 October 6, 1970, Kissinger and Dobrynin meeting memorandum of conversation, *Foreign Relations of the United States, 1969–1976, Volume XII, Soviet Union, January 1969–October 1970*, Document 224.

6 October 10, 1970, Kissinger memorandum to Nixon, *Foreign Relations of the United States, 1969–1976, Volume E-10, Documents on American Republics, 1969–1972*, Document 230.

7 Radford joins NSC, Colodny and Gettlin, *Silent Coup*, p. 4.

8 Welander on spying, Colodny and Gettlin, *Silent Coup*, pp. 25–26.

9 August 6, 1970, Special National Intelligence Estimate, The Outlook for Cambodia, *Foreign Relations of the United States, 1969–1976, Volume VII, Vietnam, July 1970–January 1972*, Document 9.

10 December 9, 1970, transcript of telephone call between Nixon and Kissinger, *Foreign Relations of the United States, 1969–1976, Volume VII, Vietnam, July 1970–January 1972,* Document 83.

11 Ibid.

12 December 9, 1970, Moorer diary entry, *Foreign Relations of the United States, 1969–1976, Volume VII, Vietnam, July 1970–January 1972,* Document 84.

13 December 9, 1970, Kissinger memorandum to Nixon, *Foreign Relations of the United States, 1969–1976, Volume VII, Vietnam, July 1970–January 1972,* Document 85.

14 December 9, 1970, transcript of telephone call between Nixon and Kissinger.

15 December 9, 1970, transcript of telephone call between Kissinger and Haig.

16 December 10, 1970, Moorer diary entry, *Foreign Relations of the United States, 1969–1976, Volume VII, Vietnam, July 1970–January 1972,* Document 86.

17 Radford's trip with Haig, Colodny and Gettlin, *Silent Coup,* pp. 24–25.

18 December 15, 1970, Haig message to Kissinger, *Foreign Relations of the United States, 1969–1976, Volume VII, Vietnam, July 1970–January 1972,* Document 89.

19 Unified but weak, Undated Haig memorandum to Kissinger, *Foreign Relations of the United States, 1969–1976, Volume VII, Vietnam, July 1970–January 1972,* Document 92.

20 December 22, 1970, Memorandum of conversation, Kissinger, Moorer and Robinson, *Foreign Relations of the United States, 1969–1976, Volume VII, Vietnam, July 1970–January 1972,* Document 93.

21 Ibid.

22 December 23, 1970, Kissinger memorandum to Nixon, *Foreign Relations of the United States, 1969–1976, Volume VII, Vietnam, July 1970–January 1972,* Document 95.

23 December 23, 1970, Memorandum for the record of meeting with Nixon, Laird, Moorer, Kissinger, and Haig, *Foreign Relations of the United States, 1969–1976, Volume VII, Vietnam, July 1970–January 1972,* Document 96.

24 January 18, 1971, Memorandum for the record of meeting with Nixon, Laird, Kissinger, Helms, Moorer, and Rogers, *Foreign Relations of the United States, 1969–1976, Volume VII, Vietnam, July 1970–January 1972,* Document 104.

25 Ibid.

26 US troops, Haig, *Inner Circles,* p. 273.

27 January 19, 1971, Memorandum for the record from WSAG meeting, *Foreign Relations of the United States, 1969–1976, Volume VII, Vietnam, July 1970–January 1972,* Document 105.

28 January 21, 1971, Kissinger memorandum to Nixon about PFIAB report on Sihanoukville, *Foreign Relations of the United States, Volume II, Organization and Management of US Foreign Policy, 1969–1972,* Document 224.

29 Ibid.

30 January 26, 1971, Kissinger memorandum to Nixon on CIA report on Laos, *Foreign Relations of the United States, 1969–1976, Volume VII, Vietnam, July 1970–January 1972,* Document 111.

31 January 28, 1971, WSAG meeting minutes, *Foreign Relations of the United States, 1969–1976, Volume VII, Vietnam, July 1970–January 1972,* Document 113.

32 February 27, 1971, Minutes from meeting with Nixon, Kissinger, Laird, Rogers, Moorer, and Helms, *Foreign Relations of the United States, 1969–1976, Volume VII, Vietnam, July 1970–January 1972,* Document 140.

33 "Nixon Accuses Symington of 'Cheap Shot' at Rogers," John W. Finney, *New York Times,* March 5, 1971.

34 Ibid.

35 Undated Kissinger memorandum to Nixon, *Foreign Relations of the United States, Volume II, Organization and Management of US Foreign Policy, 1969–1972,* Document 133.

36 "Nixon's Aides Insist Drive in Laos Was Worth Price," Max Frankel, *New York Times,* March 30, 1971.

37 April 9, 1971, Helms memorandum to Kissinger about Laos.

38 March 30, 1971, CIA memorandum for the director about Lam Son intelligence.

39   Undated Schlesinger intelligence reorganization plan, *Foreign Relations of the United States, Volume II, Organization and Management of US Foreign Policy, 1969–1972*, Document 229.

PART I, CHAPTER 11

1   May 15, 1969, Senior Review Group meeting minutes, *Foreign Relations of the United States, 1969–1976, Volume XVII, China, 1969–1972*, Document 13.

2   June 24, 1969, Haig memorandum to Kissinger, *Foreign Relations of the United States, 1969–1976, Volume XVII, China, 1969–1972*, Document 15.

3   National Security Study Memorandum 63, July 3, 1969.

4   August 2, 1969, memorandum of conversation between Nixon and Ceaucescu, *Foreign Relations of the United States, 1969–1976, Volume XVII, China, 1969–1972*, Document 20.

5   September 2, 1969, Harold Saunders report to Kissinger, *Foreign Relations of the United States, 1969–1976, Volume XVII, China, 1969–1972*, Document 20.

6   August 6, 1969, memorandum of conversation between Kissinger and Taiwan ambassador, *Foreign Relations of the United States, 1969–1976, Volume XVII, China, 1969–1972*, Document 21.

7   August 21, 1969, Grant and Saunders memorandum to Kissinger, *Foreign Relations of the United States, 1969–1976, Volume XVII, China, 1969–1972*, Document 26.

8   August 28, 1969, memorandum of conversation between Saunders and Hilaly, *Foreign Relations of the United States, 1969–1976, Volume XVII, China, 1969–1972*, Document 28.

9   September 25, 1969, Defense paper on NSSM 63, *Foreign Relations of the United States, 1969–1976, Volume XVII, China, 1969–1972*, Document 36.

10   September 25, 1969, minutes of Special Review Group meeting, *Foreign Relations of the United States, 1969–1976, Volume XVII, China, 1969–1972*, Document 36.

11   December 23, 1969, Kissinger memorandum to Nixon, *Foreign Relations of the United States, 1969–1976, Volume XVII, China, 1969–1972*, Document 54.

12   Ibid.

13   Ibid.

14   February 5, 1970, Kissinger memorandum to Nixon, *Foreign Relations of the United States, 1969–1976, Volume XVII, China, 1969–1972*, Document 66.

15   October 25, 1970, memorandum of conversation between Nixon and Yahya, *Foreign Relations of the United States, 1969–1976, Volume E-7, Documents on South Asia, 1969–1972*, Document 90.

16   October 27, 1970, memorandum of conversation between Kissinger and Ceausescu, *Foreign Relations of the United States, 1969–1976, Volume XVII, China, 1969–1972*, Document 94.

17   December 14, 1970, telegram from Farland to State, *Foreign Relations of the United States, 1969–1976, Volume XVII, China, 1969–1972*, Document 98.

18   Ibid.

19   December 16, 1970, record of discussion between Kissinger and Hilaly, *Foreign Relations of the United States, 1969–1976, Volume XVII, China, 1969–1972*, Document 100.

20   April 21, 1971, Chou message to Nixon, *Foreign Relations of the United States, 1969–1976, Volume XVII, China, 1969–1972*, Document 118.

21   "15 Invited by Peking," Takashi Oka, *New York Times*, April 8, 1971.

22   April 27, 1971, transcript of telephone call between Nixon and Kissinger, *Foreign Relations of the United States, 1969–1976, Volume XVII, China, 1969–1972*, Document 120.

23   April 28, 1971, transcript of meeting between Nixon, Kissinger and Haldeman, Brinkley and Nichter, *The Nixon Tapes*, pp. 113–14.

24   May 7, 1971, memorandum of conversation between Kissinger and Farland, *Foreign Relations of the United States, 1969–1976, Volume E-13, Documents on China, 1969–1972*, Document 6.

25   SR-1 line, Colodny and Gettlin, *Silent Coup*, p. 70.

26   May 7, 1971, memorandum of conversation between Kissinger and Farland, *Foreign Relations of the United States, 1969–1976, Volume E-13, Documents on China, 1969–1972*, Document 6.

27   Ibid.

28   Berman, Larry. *Zumwalt: The Life and Times of Admiral Elmo Russell "Bud" Zumwalt, Jr.* New York: HarperCollins, 2012, p. 319.

29   June 22, 1971, draft telegram from Kissinger to Farland, *Foreign Relations of the United States, 1969–1976, Volume XVII, China, 1969–1972,* Document 135.

30   Ibid.

31   June 30, 1971, conversation between Nixon and McConaughy, *Foreign Relations of the United States, 1969–1976, Volume XVII, China, 1969–1972,* Document 136.

32   July 1, 1971, memorandum for the file on meeting between Nixon, Kissinger and Haig, *Foreign Relations of the United States, 1969–1976, Volume XVII, China, 1969–1972,* Document 137.

33   July 9, 1971, memorandum of conversation of meeting between Chou En-lai and Kissinger, *Foreign Relations of the United States, 1969–1976, Volume XVII, China, 1969–1972,* Document 139.

34   Ibid.

35   Ibid.

36   Ibid.

37   Ibid.

38   Ibid.

39   Ibid.

40   Ibid.

41   Ibid.

42   Ibid.

43   Ibid.

44   July 10, 1971, memorandum of conversation of meeting between Chou En-lai and Kissinger, *Foreign Relations of the United States, 1969–1976, Volume XVII, China, 1969–1972,* Document 140.

45   July 11, 1971, memorandum of conversation of meeting between Chou En-lai and Kissinger, *Foreign Relations of the United States, 1969–1976, Volume XVII, China, 1969–1972,* Document 143.

46   July 11, 1971, Kissinger memorandum to Haig.

47   July 14, 1971, Kissinger memorandum to Nixon, *Foreign Relations of the United States, 1969–1976, Volume XVII, China, 1969–1972,* Document 144.

48   Ibid.

49   "Nixon Will Visit China Before Next May to Seek a 'Normalization of Relations'; Kissinger Met Chou in Peking Last Week," John Herbers, *New York Times,* July 16, 1971.

50   July 16, 1971, State telegram to embassy in Taipei, *Foreign Relations of the United States, 1969–1976, Volume XVII, China, 1969–1972,* Document 145.

51   July 17, 1971, State telegram to embassy in Taipei, *Foreign Relations of the United States, 1969–1976, Volume XVII, China, 1969–1972,* Document 146.

52   July 19, 1971, Nixon memorandum to Kissinger, *Foreign Relations of the United States, 1969–1976, Volume XVII, China, 1969–1972,* Document 147.

53   July 19, 1971, minutes of White House staff meeting.

PART I, CHAPTER 12

1   "Vast Review of War Took a Year," Hedrick Smith, *New York Times,* June 13, 1971.

2   "The McNamara Papers," James Reston, *New York Times,* June 13, 1971.

3   June 13, 1971, Nixon and Haig conversation, Brinkley and Nichter, *The Nixon Tapes,* pp. 170–71.

4   June 13, 1971, Nixon and Kissinger conversation, White House tape 005-059.

5   June 14, 1971, Nixon and Haldeman conversation, White House tape 519-001.

6   Ibid.

7   Ibid.

8   Ibid.
9   June 14, 1971, Nixon and Mitchell conversation, White House tape 005-070.
10   June 15, 1971, Nixon and Mitchell conversation, White House tape 005-086.
11   June 17, 1971, Nixon, Ehrlichman, Kissinger, and Haldeman conversation, White House tape 525-001.
12   Ibid.
13   "Hoover's Trash Shows He's Human," Jack Anderson, *Washington Post*, March 27, 1971.
14   "Nixon Would Like to Replace Hoover," Jack Anderson, *Washington Post*, April 22, 1971.
15   February 4, 1971, Nixon Daily Diary; Hoover's future, Haldeman, *The Haldeman Diaries*, p. 243.
16   June 29, 1971, Nixon and Mitchell conversation, White House tape 006-021.
17   "Nixon Sees End of Permissiveness Era," Robert M. Smith, *New York Times*, July 1, 1971.
18   "What Judge Gurfein Rules," *New York Times*, June 20, 1971.
19   July 1, 1971, Nixon and Hoover conversation, White House tape 006-084.
20   June 30, 1971, Nixon and Haldeman conversation, White House tape 006-062.
21   July 1, 1971, Nixon and Haldeman conversation, White House tape 534-2.
22   July 1, 1971, Nixon, Colson, and Haldeman conversation, White House tape 534-5.
23   Ibid.
24   July 2, 1971, Nixon, Ehrlichman, and Haldeman conversation, White House tape 260-21.
25   May 11, 1973, Jacobson memorandum to Walters about Mardian interview, FBI files.
26   July 12, 1971, Nixon Daily Diary.
27   May 11, 1973, Jacobson memorandum to Walters about Mardian interview, FBI files.
28   August 12, 1971, Sullivan letter to Mitchell, Mardian files.
29   Ibid.
30   August 28, 1971, Sullivan letter to Hoover, Mardian files.
31   October 20, 1971, Edward Miller memorandum to Alex Rosen about FBI wiretaps, FBI files.
32   "US Urges Soviet to Join in a Missiles Moratorium," William Beecher, *New York Times*, July 23, 1971.
33   July 12, 1971, Laird memorandum to Kissinger, *Foreign Relations of the United States, 1969–1976, Volume XXXII, SALT I, 1969–1972*, Document 174.
34   July 2, 1971, National Security Decision Memorandum 117.
35   July 28, 1971, Hunt memorandum to Colson on Ellsberg.
36   September 25, 1973, Hunt testimony before Senate Watergate Committee.
37   August 11, 1971, Krogh and Young memorandum to Ehrlichman.
38   "CIA Link to Hunt Confirmed by US," Martin Arnold, *New York Times*, May 9, 1973.
39   August 31, 1971, Cushman note to Helms about Hunt.
40   June 5, 1973, Lewis Fielding grand jury testimony, *People v. Ehrlichman*.
41   July 1, 1971, Nixon and Mitchell, White House tape. "Word for Word/Presidential Tapes; Nixon Wanted to Show Up J.F.K. and Wouldn't Let It Go," Tim Weiner, *New York Times*, February 28, 1999.
42   October 8, 1971, Nixon, Ehrlichman, and Mitchell conversation, White House tape 587-3.
43   Ibid.
44   October 8, 1971, Nixon and Ehrlichman conversation, White House tape 587-7.
45   October 8, 1971, Nixon and Helms conversation, White House tape 587-7.
46   Ibid.
47   "Nixon Reorganizes Intelligence Work," UPI, *New York Times*, November 6, 1971.
48   November 5, 1971, Kissinger and Symington conversation, *Foreign Relations of the United States, 1969–1976, Volume II, Organization and Management of US Foreign Policy, 1969–1972*, Document 244.
49   Ibid.

PART I, CHAPTER 13

1   "Thousands of Pakistanis Are Killed by Tidal Wave," *New York Times*, November 15, 1970; Bass, Gary J. *The Blood Telegram: Nixon, Kissinger, and a Forgotten Genocide*. New York: Knopf, 2013, p. 22.
2   "Bengali and Leftist Parties Lead in Pakistani Election," Ralph Blumenthal, *New York Times*, December 9, 1970.
3   "Vote in Pakistan Jolts Punjabis," Ralph Blumenthal, *New York Times*, December 12, 1970.
4   March 1, 1971, Saunders and Hoskinson memorandum to Kissinger, *Foreign Relations of the United States, 1969–1976, Volume XI, South Asia Crisis, 1971*, Document 2.
5   March 4, 1971, Saunders and Hoskinson memorandum to Kissinger, *Foreign Relations of the United States, 1969–1976, Volume XI, South Asia Crisis, 1971*, Document 5.
6   March 26, 1971, Kissinger memorandum to Nixon, *Foreign Relations of the United States, 1969–1976, Volume XI, South Asia Crisis, 1971*, Document 10.
7   March 28, 1971, Hoskinson memorandum to Kissinger, *Foreign Relations of the United States, 1969–1976, Volume XI, South Asia Crisis, 1971*, Document 13.
8   March 30, 1971, Nixon and Kissinger telephone conversation, *Foreign Relations of the United States, 1969–1976, Volume XI, South Asia Crisis, 1971*, Document 15.
9   April 6, 1971, Blood telegram to State Department, *Foreign Relations of the United States, 1969–1976, Volume XI, South Asia Crisis, 1971*, Document 19.
10   April 9, 1971, Senior Review Group meeting minutes, *Foreign Relations of the United States, 1969–1976, Volume XI, South Asia Crisis, 1971*, Document 23.
11   Moral insensitivity, Kissinger, *White House Years*, p. 854.
12   April 6, 1971, Farland telegram to State Department, *Foreign Relations of the United States, 1969–1976, Volume XI, South Asia Crisis, 1971*, Document 21.
13   April 8, 1971, Farland telegram to State Department, *Foreign Relations of the United States, 1969–1976, Volume XI, South Asia Crisis, 1971*, Document 22.
14   April 17, 1971, Yahya letter to Nixon, *Foreign Relations of the United States, 1969–1976, Volume XI, South Asia Crisis, 1971*, Document 29.
15   April 28, 1971, Kissinger memorandum to Nixon, *Foreign Relations of the United States, 1969–1976, Volume XI, South Asia Crisis, 1971*, Document 36.
16   Ibid.
17   May 7, 1971, Kissinger conversation with Farland, *Foreign Relations of the United States, 1969–1976, Volume XI, South Asia Crisis, 1971*, Document 42.
18   Ibid.
19   June 3, 1971, Kissinger, Keating, and Saunders meeting minutes, *Foreign Relations of the United States, 1969–1976, Volume XI, South Asia Crisis, 1971*, Document 64.
20   August 9, 1971, Nixon, Kissinger, and Haldeman conversation, Brinkley and Nichter, *The Nixon Tapes*, p. 208.
21   August 18, 1971, Kissinger memorandum to Nixon, *Foreign Relations of the United States, 1969–1976, Volume XI, South Asia Crisis, 1971*, Document 127.
22   December 3, 1971, Washington Special Actions Group meeting minutes, *Foreign Relations of the United States, 1969–1976, Volume XI, South Asia Crisis, 1971*, Document 218.
23   December 4, 1971, Nixon and Kissinger conversation, *Foreign Relations of the United States, 1969–1976, Volume XI, South Asia Crisis, 1971*, Document 222.
24   Zumwalt, *On Watch*, p. 367.
25   "US, Soviet Vessels in Bay of Bengal," Jack Anderson, *Washington Post*, December 14, 1971.
26   Secret documents and Anderson, Colodny and Gettlin, *Silent Coup*, p. 14.
27   Stewart's earlier investigation, Colodny and Gettlin, *Silent Coup*, p. 17.
28   "US Moves Give Soviets Hold on India," Jack Anderson, *Washington Post*, December 16, 1971.
29   "Unauthorized Disclosure of Classified Defense Information Appearing in the Jack Anderson Columns in *The Washington Post* dated December 14 and December 16, 1971," Young report.
30   Ibid.

31   Ibid.
32   Stewart irked at Robinson, Colodny and Gettlin, *Silent Coup*, p. 20.
33   Ibid.
34   Radford rattled, Colodny and Gettlin, *Silent Coup*, p. 22.
35   Radford and sensitive operation, Young report.
36   Misinterpretation, Colodny and Gettlin, *Silent Coup*, p. 22.
37   Get off my chest, Colodny and Gettlin, *Silent Coup*, p. 23.
38   Stewart and conspiracy, Colodny and Gettlin, *Silent Coup*, p. 23.
39   Welander evasive, Young report.
40   Welander's relationships with Haig and Kissinger, Young report.
41   Radford and a lawyer, Young report.
42   Radford's access, Young report.
43   December 21, 1971, Nixon Daily Diary.
44   December 21, 1971, Nixon, Mitchell, Haldeman, and Ehrlichman conversation, Brinkley and Nichter, *The Nixon Tapes*, pp. 327–31,
45   December 22, 1971, Nixon, Mitchell, and Ehrlichman conversation, Brinkley and Nichter, *The Nixon Tapes*, pp. 331–35.
46   December 22, 1971, Young memorandum to Ehrlichman.
47   December 22, 1971, Ehrlichman draft statement for Welander.
48   December 22, 1971, Welander interview with Ehrlichman and Young.
49   December 22, 1971, Haldeman diary entry, Haldeman, *The Haldeman Diaries*, p. 386.
50   December 22, 1971, Laird and Ehrlichman telephone conversation.
51   December 23, 1971, Laird and Ehrlichman telephone conversation.
52   Preshrunk admiral, Colodny and Gettlin, *Silent Coup*, p. 51.
53   December 23, 1971, Nixon, Mitchell, and Ehrlichman conversation, *The Nixon Tapes*, pp. 335–38.
54   Haig and Welander's documents, Colodny and Gettlin, *Silent Coup*, p. 57.
55   Haig and Young, Colodny and Gettlin, *Silent Coup*, p. 58.
56   December 24, 1971, Young memorandum to Ehrlichman.
57   Ibid.
58   Kissinger's anger, Colodny and Gettlin, *Silent Coup*, p. 60.
59   December 24, 1971, Nixon, Ehrlichman, and Mitchell conversation, Brinkley and Nichter, *The Nixon Tapes*, pp. 338–41.
60   Buzhardt calls Stewart, Colodny and Gettlin, *Silent Coup*, p. 62.
61   Buzhardt report, Colodny and Gettlin, *Silent Coup*, p. 64.
62   Laird on Haig, Colodny and Gettlin, *Silent Coup*, p. 64.
63   "Anderson Ready for Battle with Government but Appears Unlikely to Get One," Jack Rosenthal, *New York Times*, January 6, 1972.
64   "White House Took Steps to Stop Leaks Before Anderson Disclosures," Robert M. Smith, *New York Times*, January 9, 1972.

PART I, CHAPTER 14

1   February 19, 1972, Kissinger memorandum to Nixon, *Foreign Relations of the United States, 1969–1976, Volume XVII, China, 1969–1972*, Document 193.
2   "Historic Visit by an Unlikely Guest," Max Frankel, *New York Times*, February 20, 1972.
3   Mao's schedule, Kissinger, *White House Years*, p. 1057.
4   Ibid., p. 1059.
5   February 21, 1972, Nixon, Mao Tse-tung, Chou En-lai, Kissinger memorandum of conversation, *Foreign Relations of the United States, 1969–1976, Volume XVII, China, 1969–1972*, Document 194.

6   February 23, 1972, Kissinger and Yeh Chien-ying memorandum of conversation, *Foreign Relations of the United States, 1969–1976, Volume E-13, Documents on China, 1969–1972,* Document 92.

7   They're selling us out, Colodny and Shachtman, *The Forty Years War,* p. 134.

8   February 28, 1972, Nixon, Kissinger, and Chou En-lai memorandum of conversation, *Foreign Relations of the United States, 1969–1976, Volume XVII, China, 1969–1972,* Document 204.

9   March 1, 1972, Kissinger and Dobrynin memorandum of conversation, *Foreign Relations of the United States, 1969–1976, Volume XIV, Soviet Union, October 1971–May 1972,* Document 54.

10   January 20, 1972, Nixon and Kissinger conversation, *White House Tape,* 652-17.

11   Ibid.

12   February 16, 1972, Kissinger memorandum to Nixon, *Foreign Relations of the United States, 1969–1972, Volume VIII, Vietnam, January 1972–October 1972,* Document 28.

13   Ibid.

14   March 30, 1972, Nixon conversation with Kissinger, *White House Tape,* 697-2.

15   April 1, 1972, McCain message to Moorer, *Foreign Relations of the United States, 1969–1972, Volume VIII, Vietnam, January 1972–October 1972,* Document 49.

16   April 2, 1972, Kissinger conversation with Moorer, *Foreign Relations of the United States, 1969–1972, Volume VIII, Vietnam, January 1972–October 1972,* Document 49.

17   April 3, 1972, Nixon, Kissinger and Moorer conversation, *White House Tape,* 700-5.

18   Ibid.

19   May 4, 1972, Nixon, Connally, Moorer, and Kissinger conversation, Brinkley and Nichter, *The Nixon Tapes,* p. 537.

20   May 25, 1972, Smith backchannel message to Haig, *Foreign Relations of the United States, 1969–1972, Volume XXXII, SALT I, 1969–1972,* Document 309.

21   May 25, 1972, Haig backchannel message to Kissinger, *Foreign Relations of the United States, 1969–1972, Volume XXXII, SALT I, 1969–1972,* Document 310.

22   Ibid.

23   May 27, 1972, Kissinger backchannel message to Haig, *Foreign Relations of the United States, 1969–1972, Volume XXXII, SALT I, 1969–1972,* Document 320.

24   June 3, 1972, Nixon, Kissinger, and Haldeman conversation, Brinkley and Nichter, *The Nixon Tapes,* p. 581.

Part I, Chapter 15

1   Dean, John W. *Blind Ambition: The White House Years.* New York: Simon & Schuster, 1976, p. 40.

2   Liddy, G. Gordon. *Will: The Autobiography of G. Gordon Liddy.* New York: St. Martin's, 1980, p. 181.

3   Stanford, Phil. *White House Call Girl: The Real Watergate Story.* Port Townsend, WA: Feral House, 2013, p. 61.

4   Hougan, Jim. *Secret Agenda: Watergate, Deep Throat and the CIA.* New York: Random House, 1984, p. 114.

5   Lou Russell, Hougan, *Secret Agenda,* p. 117.

6   Raid on Bailley, Colodny and Gettlin, *Silent Coup,* p. 132.

7   Stans, Stanford, *White House Call Girl,* p. 94.

8   April 6, 1972, Dean White House telephone logs.

9   Burn notes, Stanford, *White House Call Girl,* p. 109.

10   Ibid.

11   Open as the sky, Stanford, *White House Call Girl,* p. 98.

12   Russell's interference, Hougan, *Secret Agenda,* p. 118.

13   Dean and first break-in, Colodny and Gettlin, *Silent Coup,* p. 134.

14   January 2, 1973, transcript from *US v. Liddy* on content of Watergate phone intercepts.

15   "Capitol Hill Call Girl Ring Uncovered," *Washington Star,* June 9, 1972.

16 June 9, 1972, Dean White House telephone logs.
17 Dean sent car for Rudy, Colodny and Gettlin, *Silent Coup*, p. 145.
18 June 9, 1972, Dean White House telephone logs.
19 Woman fired, Colodny and Gettlin, *Silent Coup*, p. 146.
20 February 4, 1965, FBI interview with Erika "Heidi" Rikan, FBI files.
21 June 9, 1972, Dean White House telephone logs.
22 Magruder slapped desk, Liddy, *Will*, p. 237.
23 McCord and Russell, Hougan, *Secret Agenda*, p. 185.
24 Ibid.
25 Hippies, Hougan, *Secret Agenda*, p. 202.
26 June 17, 1972, Nixon Daily Diary.
27 Why McCord, Liddy, *Will*, p. 250.
28 Magruder calls Dean, Colodny and Gettlin, *Silent Coup*, p. 169.
29 Kleindienst's refusal, Liddy, *Will*, p. 253.
30 Undated Sullivan letter to Mardian, Mardian files.
31 June 8, 1972, Sullivan letter to Mardian, Mardian files.
32 Gray meets Nixon, Gray, L. Patrick, III, and Ed Gray. *In Nixon's Web: A Year in the Crosshairs of Watergate*. New York: Henry Holt, 2008, p. xx.
33 No job is more important, Gray and Gray, *In Nixon's Web*, p. 22.
34 June 23, 1975, Nixon grand jury testimony, *United States v. John Doe*, p. 295.
35 Investigate it to the hilt, Gray and Gray, *In Nixon's Web*, p. 60.
36 No CIA involvement, Gray and Gray, *In Nixon's Web*, p. 65.
37 Dean called Haldeman, Haldeman interview with Colodny.
38 June 23, 1972, Nixon and Haldeman conversation, White House Tape 741-2.
39 Mitchell phone logs, Colodny and Shachtman, *The Forty Years War*, p. 142.
40 June 23, 1972, Haldeman entry, *The Haldeman Diaries*, p. 474.
41 June 23, 1972, Nixon and Haldeman conversation, White House Tape 741-2.
42 Walters and Helms summoned, August 3, 1973, Walters testimony, Senate Select Committee on Presidential Campaign Activities.
43 Bay of Pigs, August 2, 1973, Helms testimony, Senate Select Committee on Presidential Campaign Activities.
44 Ibid.
45 Taper off, Gray and Gray, *In Nixon's Web*, p. 72.
46 Important people, August 3, 1973, Walters testimony, Senate Select Committee on Presidential Campaign Activities.
47 Ibid.
48 Wobbling, June 28, 1972, Walters memorandum for the record.
49 Wagner and Caswell, Gray and Gray, *In Nixon's Web*, p. 78.
50 CIA help, June 28, 1972, Walters memorandum for the record.
51 Tell the president, Gray and Gray, *In Nixon's Web*, p. 89.
52 Call directly, Gray and Gray, *In Nixon's* Web, p. 89.
53 Hijacking, Gray and Gray, *In Nixon's Web*, p. 90.
54 Thorough investigation, Gray and Gray, *In Nixon's Web*, p. 90.
55 I'll resign, Gray and Gray, *In Nixon's Web*, p. 91.
56 "GOP Security Aide Among Five Arrested in Bugging Affair," Bob Woodward and Carl Bernstein, *Washington Post*, June 19, 1972.
57 FBI sources, Weiner, Tim. *Enemies: A History of the FBI*. New York: Random House, 2012, p. 315.
58 Felt and wiretaps, Woodward, Bob. *The Secret Man: The Story of Watergate's Deep Throat*. New York: Simon & Schuster, 2005, p. 22.
59 Sullivan and Novak meeting, Novak, *The Prince of Darkness*, p. 208.
60 Ehrlichman and Sullivan, Walter Minnick interview with author, August 5, 2014.

61   May 12, 1972, Latimer memorandum to Haig.
62   Sullivan and ONNI, Ungar, Sanford. *FBI: An Uncensored Look Behind the Walls*. Boston: Little, Brown, 1976, p. 312.
63   Bailley and St. Elizabeth's, Colodny and Gettlin, *Silent Coup*, p. 153.
64   Bailley's sentence, Colodny and Gettlin, *Silent Coup*, p. 231.
65   September 1972, Dean White House telephone logs.
66   September 15, 1972, Nixon, Dean, and Haldeman conversation, White House Tape 779-2.
67   Ibid.
68   Richey, Califano, Joseph A., Jr. *Inside: A Public and Private Life*. New York: PublicAffairs, 2004, p. 274.
69   Rothblatt, September 15, 1972, Nixon, Dean, and Haldeman conversation, White House Tape 779-2.
70   "Spy Funds Linked to GOP Aides," Carl Bernstein and Bob Woodward, *Washington Post*, September 17, 1972; "Secret Fund Tied to Intelligence Use," Carl Bernstein and Bob Woodward, *Washington Post*, September 18, 1972.
71   Canuck Letter, Woodward, Bob, and Bernstein, Carl. *All the President's Men*, New York: Simon & Schuster, 1974, p. 130.
72   October 9, 1972, Woodward notes with "X," University of Texas.
73   "FBI Finds Nixon Aides Sabotaged Democrats," Carl Bernstein and Bob Woodward, *Washington Post*, October 1, 1972.
74   Segretti and Canuck letter, Woodward and Bernstein, *All the President's Men*, p. 127.
75   Ibid.
76   "FBI Finds Nixon Aides Sabotaged Democrats," Bernstein and Woodward.
77   White House and Canuck Letter, Woodward and Bernstein, *All the President's Men*, p. 134.
78   October 9, 1972, Woodward notes with "X," University of Texas.
79   October 12, 2011, Woodward interview with Max Holland.
80   October 9, 1972, Woodward notes with "X," University of Texas.
81   Shipley quotes, "FBI Finds Nixon Aides Sabotaged Democrats," Carl Bernstein and Bob Woodward, *Washington Post*, October 1, 1972.
82   Guys assigned to help, Gray and Gray, *In Nixon's Web*, p. 293.
83   October 19, 1972, Nixon and Haldeman conversation, White House Tape 370-9.
84   Ibid.
85   Helms fired, Helms and Hood, *A Look Over My Shoulder*, p. 411.
86   December 27, 1972, Nixon memorandum to Haldeman, *Foreign Relations of the United States, 1969–1972, Volume II, Organization and Management of US Foreign Policy, 1969–1972*, Document 290.
87   Ibid.

Part II, Chapter 16

1   "Nixon and Kissinger," James Reston, *New York Times*, December 31, 1972.
2   January 1, 1973, Nixon and Colson conversation, White House Tape 829-12.
3   January 5, 1973, Nixon and Colson conversation, White House Tape 160-2.
4   January 10, 1973, Nixon and Haldeman conversation, Kutler, Stanley. *Abuse of Power*, New York: Free Press, 1997, p. 202.
5   FBI leaks and stories, Gray and Gray, *In Nixon's Web*, p. 141.
6   Leaks memo, Gray and Gray, *In Nixon's Web*, p. 147.
7   "Hunt Admits All 6 Charges as Judge Bars Partial Plea," Walter Rugaber, *New York Times*, January 12, 1973.
8   Big cover-up, Sirica, John J. *To Set the Record Straight: The Break-in, the Tapes, the Conspirators, the Pardon*. New York: W. W. Norton & Co., 1979, p. 74.
9   Nixon January 1973 approval, Gallup.

10   Dean's interference, Gray and Gray, *In Nixon's Web*, p. 64.
11   January 23, 1973, Sullivan letter to Walters, CIA files.
12   February 6, 1973, Sullivan letter to Walters, CIA files.
13   Ibid.
14   February 13, 1973, Nixon and Colson conversation, White House Tape 854-17.
15   February 16, 1973, Nixon, Gray, and Ehrlichman conversation, White House Tape 858-3.
16   Sullivan, Gray and Gray, *In Nixon's Web*, p. 164.
17   FBI wiretaps, *Time*, February 26, 1973.
18   "Wiretap Report by *Time* Rejected," *New York Times*, February 27, 1973.
19   February 27, 1973, Nixon and Dean conversation, White House Tape 864-4.
20   Ibid.
21   March 1, 1973, Sullivan memorandum to Dean.
22   Sullivan's home, Sullivan FBI personnel file.
23   March 5, 1973, meeting, Woodward, *The Secret Man*, p. 12.
24   March 5, 1973, Woodward interview with "X," University of Texas.
25   "Out of channels," May 9, 1973, FBI interview with Mardian, FBI files.
26   June 4, 1973, Weicker letter to William Ruckelshaus, Weicker files.
27   "FBI and Political Spying," Frank Van Riper, *New York Daily News*, October 14, 1973.
28   March 6, 1973, Nixon and Dean conversation, White House Tape 869-13.
29   Ibid.
30   March 13, 1973, Nixon, Dean, and Haldeman conversation, White House Tape 878-14.
31   March 16, 1973, Nixon and Dean conversation, White House Tape 037-134.
32   March 17, 1973, Nixon, Haldeman, and Dean conversation, White House Tape 882-12.
33   Ibid.
34   McCord letter, Sirica, *To Set the Record Straight*, p. 96.
35   "Nixon Withdraws Gray Nomination as FBI Director," John M. Crewdson, *New York Times*, April 6, 1973.
36   Deep trouble, Gray and Gray, *In Nixon's Web*, p. 7.
37   "Trial Will Go On," Martin Arnold, *New York Times*, April 28, 1973.
38   April 28, 1973, Gergen memorandum to Nixon.
39   Ibid.
40   Ibid.

Part II, Chapter 17

1   "Ellsberg Judge Confirms 2 Talks with Ehrlichman," Martin Arnold, *New York Times*, May 3, 1973.
2   "Wiretaps Put on Phone of 2 Reporters," Bob Woodward and Carl Bernstein, *Washington Post*, May 3, 1973.
3   March 24, 1973, Woodward interview with Santarelli, University of Texas.
4   Riddled with errors, Holland, Max. *Leak: Why Mark Felt Became Deep Throat*. Lawrence, KS: University of Kansas Press, 2012, p. 143.
5   "Wiretaps Put on Phone of 2 Reporters," Woodward and Bernstein.
6   May 4, 1973, Ruckelshaus memorandum to Felt, FBI files.
7   "Ellsberg Judge Orders Hunt Data," Martin Arnold, *New York Times*, May 4, 1973.
8   Ibid.
9   Ibid.
10   May 3, 1973, Nixon and Kleindienst conversation, Kutler, *Abuse of Power*, p. 396.
11   May 3, 1973, Nixon and Garment conversation, Kutler, *Abuse of Power*, p. 403.
12   Haig recommendation, July 25, 1986, Colodny interview with Haldeman, Colodny Collection.
13   May 5, 1973, Nixon Daily Diary.
14   Haig and taping system, Colodny and Gettlin, *Silent Coup*, p. 326.

15   May 5, 1973, Gergen memorandum to Garment.
16   Ibid.
17   May 8 and 10, 1973, Gergen memoranda to Garment.
18   Ibid.
19   "Cushman Named," Seymour M. Hersh, *New York Times*, May 7, 1973.
20   May 9, 1973, Schlesinger memorandum to CIA employees.
21   May 8, 1973, Nixon and Haig conversation, Kutler, *Abuse of Power*, p. 407.
22   "CIA Link to Hunt Confirmed by US," Martin Arnold, *New York Times*, May 9, 1973.
23   "M'Cord Charges Plot Against CIA," Seymour M. Hersh, *New York Times*, May 9, 1973.
24   Hunting accident, Holland, *Leak*, p. 8.
25   "'69 Phone Taps Reported on Newsmen at 3 Papers," John M. Crewdson, *New York Times*, May 11, 1973.
26   Buzhardt, Haig, *Inner Circles*, p. 340.
27   May 8, 1973, Nixon and Haig conversation, Kutler, *Abuse of Power*, pp. 418–19.
28   "CIA Head Admits 'Ill-Advised' Act," Marjorie Hunter, *New York Times*, May 10, 1973.
29   Ibid.
30   May 9, 1973, Nixon and Haig conversation, Kutler, *Abuse of Power*, p. 423.
31   Ibid.
32   May 9, 1973, Nixon and Haig conversation, Kutler, *Abuse of Power*, p. 431.
33   May 9, 1973, Nixon, Haig, and Buzhardt conversation, Kutler, *Abuse of Power*, p. 437.
34   May 9, 1973, Nixon and Haig conversation, Kutler, *Abuse of Power*, p. 440.
35   May 10, 1973, Ruckelshaus list of written questions to Sullivan, FBI files.
36   "Data Introduced in the Ellsberg Trial," *New York Times*, May 11, 1973.
37   "'69 Phone Taps Reported on Newsmen at 3 Papers," Crewdson.
38   Ibid.
39   May 11, 1973, Nixon and Haig conversation, Kutler, *Abuse of Power*, p. 456.
40   Ibid.
41   May 11, 1973, Sullivan-written answers to questions, FBI files.
42   May 11, 1973, Nixon and Kissinger conversation, Kutler, *Abuse of Power*, p. 460.
43   May 11, 1973, Nixon and Haig conversation, Kutler, *Abuse of Power*, p. 461.
44   "New Trial Barred," Martin Arnold, *New York Times*, May 12, 1973.
45   Ibid.
46   "Cushman Says Helms Assented to CIA Aid to Hunt for Break-in on Coast," Marjorie Hunter, *New York Times*, May 12, 1973.
47   May 12, 1973, Nixon and Haig conversation, White House Tape 165-19.
48   Ibid.
49   May 13, 1973, Nixon and Haig conversation, Kutler, *Abuse of Power*, p. 487.
50   Ibid.
51   Crewdson call to Ruckelshaus, Holland, *Leak*, p. 6.
52   July 27, 2005, Ruckelshaus interview with Ed Gray.
53   "Statement by Acting FBI Director About Wiretap Documents," *New York Times*, May 15, 1973.
54   "Week-Long Hunt," John M. Crewdson, *New York Times*, May 15, 1973.
55   May 14, 1973, Nixon and Ziegler conversation, White House Tape 436-5.
56   Ibid.
57   Ibid.
58   "Bid to CIA Cited," Marjorie Hunter, *New York Times*, May 15, 1973.
59   Ibid.
60   May 14, 1973, Nixon and Haig conversation, Kutler, *Abuse of Power*, p. 495.
61   Ibid.
62   May 22, 1973, T.J. Smith to Edward Miller memorandum.
63   Ibid.

64   Tufaro memorandum, Colodny and Gettlin, *Silent Coup*, p. 306.
65   Buzhardt reaction, Colodny and Gettlin, *Silent Coup*, p. 306.
66   "CIA Resisted Lengthy Cover-Up Effort by White House, Hill Account Reveals," Laurence Stern, *Washington Post*, May 16, 1973.
67   Ibid.
68   May 15, 1973, Nixon and Haig conversation, White House Tape 46-57.
69   May 22, 1973, Smith to Miller memorandum.
70   Haig on wiretaps, Hersh, *The Price of Power*, p. 89.
71   Sullivan on wiretaps, Hersh, *The Price of Power*, p. 90.
72   FBI wiretaps, Woodward and Bernstein, *All the President's Men*, p. 314.
73   "I frankly don't remember," Woodward and Bernstein, *All the President's Men*, p. 314.
74   May 15, 1973, Woodward interview with Kissinger; *All the President's Men*, p. 315.
75   "CIA Resisted Lengthy Cover-Up Effort by White House, Hill Account Reveals," Laurence Stern, *Washington Post*, May 16, 1973.
76   "President Linked to Taps on Aides," Seymour M. Hersh, *New York Times*, May 16, 1973.
77   Ibid.
78   May 16, 1973, Nixon and Kissinger conversation, Kutler, *Abuse of Power*, p. 503.
79   May 22, 1973, Smith to Miller memorandum, FBI files.
80   May 16, 1973, Nixon, Buzhardt, and Haig conversation, Kutler, *Abuse of Power*, p. 507.
81   Ibid.
82   Ibid.
83   Ibid.
84   Ibid.
85   Deep Throat meeting, Woodward and Bernstein, *All the President's Men*, pp. 317.
86   May 16, 1973, White House Tapes; Kutler, *Abuse of Power*, pp. 502–17.
87   Baker, Woodward and Bernstein, *All the President's Men*, p. 318.
88   "New Watergate Figure Leaves," *San Francisco Chronicle*, May 14, 1973.
89   Covert activities, Woodward and Bernstein, *All the President's Men*, p. 318.
90   May 16, 1973, Nixon, Buzhardt, and Haig conversation, Kutler, *Abuse of Power*, p. 514.
91   "Vast GOP Undercover Operation Originated in 1969," Carl Bernstein and Bob Woodward, *Washington Post*, May 17, 1973.
92   May 17, 1973, Nixon, Buzhardt, and Haig conversation, Kutler, *Abuse of Power*, p. 521.
93   Ibid.
94   "Symington Doubts That Nixon Didn't Know of CIA Role," William Claiborne, *Washington Post*, May 18, 1973.
95   Welander and Woodward, Colodny and Gettlin, *Silent Coup*, p. 306; May 29, 1987, Colodny interview with Welander.
96   Welander memorandum, Colodny and Gettlin, *Silent Coup*, p. 307.
97   May 18, 1973, Nixon and Haldeman conversation, Kutler, *Abuse of Power*, p. 532.
98   "Nixon Aide Proposed Espionage, Burglaries," William Claiborne, *Washington Post*, May 22, 1973.
99   "Text of a Statement by the President on Allegations Surrounding Watergate Inquiry," *New York Times*, May 23, 1973.
100   Ibid.
101   "More of the Truth . . . ," *New York Times*, May 24, 1973.
102   "A Broad Program," Seymour M. Hersh, *New York Times*, May 24, 1973.

Part II, Chapter 18

1   June 4, 1973, Weicker letter to Ruckelshaus, Weicker papers.
2   Ibid.
3   June 5, 1973, Ruckelshaus letter to Weicker, Weicker papers.

4 "Weicker Charges FBI Used a Part of 1970 Spy Plan," *New York Times*, June 11, 1973.
5 Undated McGowan staff memorandum to Weicker, Weicker papers.
6 Ibid.
7 Ibid.
8 June 11, 1973, Sullivan letter to Richardson, FBI files.
9 The Soviet Approach to Summit II, National Intelligence Estimate 11-9-73, June 1, 1973.
10 July 23, 1973, Department of State *Bulletin*, pp. 161–62.
11 June 25, 1973, Dean testimony.
12 Ibid.
13 Ibid.
14 March 21, 1973, Nixon, Haldeman, and Dean conversation, White House Tape 886-8.
15 June 29, 1973, Sullivan letter to Weicker, Weicker papers.
16 Ibid.
17 Haig and taping system, Colodny and Gettlin, *Silent Coup*, p. 326.
18 Stewart letter, Colodny and Gettlin, *Silent Coup*, p. 307.
19 Buzhardt and extortion, Colodny and Gettlin, *Silent Coup*, p. 308.
20 Belcher, Colodny, and Gettlin, *Silent Coup*, p. 309.
21 July 9, 1973, Sullivan interview with Weicker and staff, Weicker papers.
22 Higby and tapes, Colodny and Gettlin, *Silent Coup*, p. 321.
23 Ibid.
24 Butterfield meeting, Colodny and Gettlin, *Silent Coup*, p. 328.
25 Ibid.
26 July 12–16, 1973, Nixon Daily Diary.
27 Baker and staff, Colodny and Gettlin, *Silent Coup*, p. 329.
28 Woodward called, Woodward and Bernstein, *All the President's Men*, p. 330.
29 Armstrong denies he called, Colodny and Gettlin, *Silent Coup*, p. 332.
30 Bradlee passed, Woodward and Bernstein, *All the President's Men*, p. 332.
31 Butterfield called, Colodny and Gettlin, *Silent Coup*, p. 333.
32 July 15, 1973, Nixon Daily Diary.
33 Nixon's schedule, Nixon, *RN*, p. 899.
34 Butterfield's testimony, Nixon, *RN*, p. 900.
35 Butterfield, Haig, *Inner Circles*, p. 373.
36 Ervin's threat, Lukas, J. Anthony. *Nightmare: The Underside of the Nixon Years*. New York: Viking, 1976, p. 410.
37 July 16, 1973, Butterfield testimony, Senate Select Committee on Presidential Campaign Activities.
38 Ibid.
39 Ibid.
40 "Surprise Witness," James M. Naughton, *New York Times*, July 17, 1973.
41 Nixon's innocence, Haig, *Inner Circles*, p. 374.
42 "Cambodian Raids Reported Hidden Before '70 Foray," Seymour M. Hersh, *New York Times*, July 15, 1973.
43 "Kissinger Denies White House Role in False Raids Data," Seymour M. Hersh, *New York Times*, July 20, 1973.
44 "Inquiry Pressed in Secret Raids," Seymour M. Hersh, *New York Times*, July 16, 1973.
45 Stewart letter, Colodny and Gettlin, *Silent Coup*, p. 307.
46 Ibid.
47 Ibid.
48 "My Journal on Watergate," Jack Anderson, *Parade*, July 22, 1973.
49 Sanders call, Colodny and Gettlin, *Silent Coup*, p. 312.
50 Buzhardt letter, Colodny and Gettlin, *Silent Coup*, p. 313.
51 Stewart meeting, Colodny and Gettlin, *Silent Coup*, p. 313.

52   Baker's mood, Colodny and Gettlin, *Silent Coup*, p. 314.
53   July 26, 1973, Ehrlichman testimony, Senate Select Committee on Presidential Campaign Activities.
54   Baker and Ervin meeting with Buzhardt, Colodny and Gettlin, *Silent Coup*, p. 314.
55   Ibid.
56   Young and Baker, Colodny and Gettlin, *Silent Coup*, p. 315.
57   No charges for Stewart, Colodny and Gettlin, *Silent Coup*, p. 310.
58   "Rogers Quits, Kissinger Named," Bernard Gwertzman, *New York Times*, Aug. 23, 1973.
59   "Kissinger's Role in Wiretaps Snags Senate Approval," Bernard Gwertzman, *New York Times*, September 8, 1973.
60   "Excerpts from Kissinger's Testimony to Senators," *New York Times*, September 8, 1973.
61   "Senate Confirms Kissinger, 78 to 7," Bernard Gwertzman, *New York Times*, September 22, 1973.
62   October 7, 1973, Sullivan interview with Weicker and staff, Weicker papers.
63   Ibid.
64   Ibid.
65   Ibid.
66   Ibid.
67   October 11, 1973, Weicker letter to Ervin, Weicker papers.
68   "FBI and Political Spying," Frank Van Riper, *New York Daily News*, October 14, 1973.
69   October 16, 1973, Sullivan letter to the editor of the *New York Daily News*, Weicker papers.
70   October 16, 1973, Sullivan letter to Weicker, Weicker papers.
71   October 19, 1973, Ervin letter to Weicker, Weicker papers.
72   October 11, 1973, Scowcroft conversation with Kissinger.
73   Haig and tapes deal, Colodny and Gettlin, *Silent Coup*, p. 350.
74   "Outcry in House," Richard L. Madden, *New York Times*, October 21, 1973.
75   Lost confidence, Haig, *Inner Circles*, p. 407.
76   Buzhardt mission, Haig, *Inner Circles*, p. 427.
77   "Tapes Have Puzzling 'Gap'; Parts Inaudible," Carl Bernstein and Bob Woodward, *Washington Post*, November 8, 1973.
78   Ibid.
79   "Miss Woods Says Tapes Contain Inaudible Parts," Warren Weaver Jr., *New York Times*, November 9, 1973.
80   "Tapes Have Puzzling 'Gap'; Parts Inaudible," Bernstein and Woodward.
81   "Another Section of Tapes Is Blank, a Nixon Aide Says," David E. Rosenbaum, *New York Times*, November 22, 1973.
82   Deep Throat on tapes, Woodward and Bernstein, *All the President's Men*, p. 333.
83   Ibid.
84   "Spy Funds Linked to GOP Aides," Carl Bernstein and Bob Woodward, *Washington Post*, September 17, 1972.
85   "Secret Fund Tied to Intelligence Use," Carl Bernstein and Bob Woodward, *Washington Post*, September 18, 1972.
86   "Wiretaps Put on Phones of 2 Reporters," Bob Woodward and Carl Bernstein, *Washington Post*, May 3, 1973.
87   Felt and tapes, Woodward, *The Secret Man*, p. 103.
88   July 1973, Woodward interview with Felt, University of Texas.

PART II, CHAPTER 19

1   Squires and Thomasson, Colodny and Gettlin, *Silent Coup*, p. 376.
2   "Military Aide Phone Was Tapped," Bob Woodward and Carl Bernstein, *Washington Post*, October 10, 1973.

3   Smoke out, Colodny and Gettlin, *Silent Coup*, p. 376.
4   Krogh case, Colodny and Gettlin, *Silent Coup*, p. 374.
5   November 13, 1973, Jaworski notes of meeting with Haig and Buzhardt.
6   Sanitized report, Colodny and Gettlin, *Silent Coup*, p. 375.
7   Haig answer, Colodny and Gettlin, *Silent Coup*, p. 379.
8   Ibid.
9   Ibid.
10   "Probers Charge Pentagon Spied on Kissinger in 1971," Jim Squires, *Chicago Tribune*, January 11, 1974.
11   "Pentagon Got Secret Data of Kissinger's," Bob Woodward and Carl Bernstein, *Washington Post*, January 12, 1974.
12   "A Military 'Ring' Linked to Spying on White House," Seymour M. Hersh, *New York Times*, January 12, 1974.
13   Ibid.
14   "Pentagon Got Secret Data of Kissinger's," Woodward and Bernstein.
15   March 5, 1989, Woodward interview with Colodny and Gettlin, Colodny Collection.
16   "A Military 'Ring' Linked to Spying on White House, Hersh,.
17   "Pentagon Got Secret Data of Kissinger's," Woodward and Bernstein.
18   "Blackmail Laid to Official in Pentagon 'Spy' Inquiry," Seymour M. Hersh, *New York Times*, January 13, 1974.
19   "The Plumbers," Bob Woodward and Carl Bernstein, *Washington Post*, January 13, 1974.
20   Ibid.
21   Ibid.
22   "Moorer Concedes He Received 'File' of Secret Security Papers," Seymour M. Hersh, *New York Times*, January 19, 1974.
23   "Kissinger Says He Heard Tapes of 'Plumbers' Inquiry," Seymour M. Hersh, *New York Times*, January 23, 1974.
24   Ibid.
25   "Plumbers Ousted Him, Krogh Says," Seymour M. Hersh, *New York Times*, January 25, 1974.
26   "Senator Breaks with Stennis on Closed Kissinger Session," Seymour M. Hersh, *New York Times*, February 4, 1974.
27   "Spy in the White House Said to Have Begun in '70," Seymour M. Hersh, *New York Times*, February 3, 1974.
28   "Kissinger Scores Military Spying," Seymour M. Hersh, *New York Times*, February 7, 1974.
29   Ibid.
30   Ibid.
31   "Radford Contends Moorer Knew About His Snooping," Seymour M. Hersh, *New York Times*, February 11, 1974.
32   "Yeoman and Admiral," *New York Times*, February 11, 1974.
33   Radford testimony, Colodny and Gettlin, *Silent Coup*, p. 396.
34   Sanders and Stewart, Colodny and Gettlin, *Silent Coup*, p. 394.
35   Ibid.
36   March 7, 1974, Buzhardt testimony, Senate Armed Services Committee.

PART II, CHAPTER 20

1   "Nixon Will Give Edited Tape Transcripts on Watergate to House and Senate and the Public; Notes Ambiguities, Insists He Is Innocent," John Herbers, *New York Times*, April 30, 1974.
2   "Senator Brands Conduct as 'Immoral'; GOP Leader in House Is Also Critical," Christopher Lydon, *New York Times*, May 8, 1974.
3   Doomed, Sirica, *To Set the Record Straight*, p. 223.
4   Welander tape, Colodny and Gettlin, *Silent Coup*, p. 409.

5   Deep Throat rules, Woodward and Bernstein, *All the President's Men*, pp. 71–72.
6   "A Whodunit without an Ending," Doris Kearns, *New York Times*, June 9, 1974.
7   "Putting It All Together," Richard J. Whalen, *Washington Post*, June 2, 1974.
8   "Three Republicans for Impeachment," *People*, August 12, 1974.
9   "Nixon Attributed Taps to Kissinger," Laurence Stern, *Washington Post*, June 6, 1974.
10   "Kissinger Threat Culminates Long Dispute," Bernard Gwertzman, *New York Times*, June 12, 1974.
11   "Kissinger Linked to Order to FBI Ending Wiretaps," Seymour M. Hersh, *New York Times*, June 9, 1974.
12   Ibid.
13   June 1974, Sullivan interview with Woodward, University of Texas.
14   March 1974, Sullivan interview with Woodward, University of Texas.
15   "FBI Tied Tap Requests to Kissinger or Gen. Haig," John M. Crewdson, *New York Times*, June 12, 1974.
16   "Kissinger Threat Culminates Long Dispute," Bernard Gwertzman, *New York Times*, June 12, 1974.
17   "Capital Rallying Round Kissinger; Vindication Asked," Bernard Gwertzman, *New York Times*, June 13, 1974.
18   Ibid.
19   "Wiretap Inquiry Is Said Not to Aim at Kissinger Role," John M. Crewdson, *New York Times*, June 14, 1974.
20   April 29, 1974, T.J. Feeney to Mr. Walsh letter about Sullivan's heart attack, FBI files.
21   Middle East trip, Nixon, *RN*, p. 1018.
22   June 20, 1974, minutes of National Security Council meeting, *Foreign Relations of the United States, 1969–1976, Volume XXXIII, SALT II, 1972–1980*, Document 68.
23   Walter Flowers, Haig, *Inner Circles*, p. 471.
24   "Haig Testimony: He Acted for Kissinger on Wiretaps," John M. Crewdson, *New York Times*, September 29, 1974.
25   "Kissinger Backed on Wiretap Issue," *New York Times*, July 31, 1974.
26   "Fulbright Panel Clears Kissinger on Wiretap Role," Bernard Gwertzman, *New York Times*, August 7, 1974.
27   Haig and Kissinger, Lukas, *Nightmare*, p. 597.
28   "The Pardon," Seymour M. Hersh, *The Atlantic*, August 1983.
29   Ibid.
30   Ibid.
31   Ibid.
32   Ibid.
33   Ibid.
34   Haig call to Jaworski, Colodny and Gettlin, *Silent Coup*, p. 421.
35   Ibid.
36   No alternatives, Colodny and Gettlin, *Silent Coup*, p. 422.
37   Haig and Jaworski, Hersh, "The Pardon."
38   Doyle's suspicion, Colodny and Gettlin, *Silent Coup*, p. 424.
39   Jaworski, Nixon, *RN*, p. 1080.
40   Documents and Becker, Hersh, "The Pardon."
41   Archives, Hersh, "The Pardon."
42   "No Conditions Set," John Herbers, *New York Times*, September 9, 1974.

Epilogue: Ramifications

1   "Nixon's Private Tapes: A Key to His Character," Bob Woodward, *Washington Post*, August 5, 1984.

2   "Helms Accord: Balancing Secret and Justice," Nicholas Horrock, *New York Times*, November 1, 1977.

3   Fine paid, Powers, Thomas. *The Man Who Kept the Secrets: Richard Helms and the CIA*. New York: Knopf, 1979, p. 305.

4   "William C. Sullivan, Once High FBI Aide, Killed by Hunter," J. Y. Smith, *Washington Post*, November 10, 1977.

5   December 16, 1977, Mrs. Sullivan letter to Kelley, FBI files.

6   "Don't Subpoena the Tapes," Bob Woodward, *Washington Post*, January 15, 1981.

7   "Reagan Wounded in Chest by Gunman; Outlook 'Good' After 2-Hour Surgery; Aide and 2 Guards Shot; Suspect Held," Howell Raines, *New York Times*, March 31, 1981.

8   "'I'm the Guy They Called Deep Throat,'" John D. O'Connor, *Vanity Fair*, July 2005.

9   "How Mark Felt Became 'Deep Throat,'" Bob Woodward, *Washington Post*, June 20, 2005.

10   FBI wiretaps, Woodward, *The Secret Man*, p. 24.

11   Sullivan interviews with Woodward, University of Texas.

12   "The 37th President; President Clinton; 'He Had an Incredibly Sharp and Vigorous and Rigorous Mind,'" *New York Times*, April 28, 1994.

13   Kissinger eulogy for Nixon, April 27, 1994.

Bibliography

Books

Ahern, Thomas L. Jr. *Good Questions, Wrong Answers: CIA's Estimates of Arms Traffic Through Sihanoukville, Cambodia, During the Vietnam War*. Washington: Center for the Study of Intelligence, 2004.

———. *The Way We Do Things: Black Entry Operations into North Vietnam, 1961–1964*. Washington: Center for the Study of Intelligence, 2005.

———. *Undercover Armies: CIA and Surrogate Warfare in Laos*. Washington: Center for the Study of Intelligence, 2006.

Ahlberg, Kristin L., and Alexander Wieland, eds. *Foreign Relations of the United States, 1969–1976, Volume XXXVIII, Part 1, Foundations of Foreign Policy, 1973–1976*. Washington: US Government Printing Office, 2011.

Baker, Russ. *Family of Secrets: The Bush Dynasty, the Powerful Forces that Put It in The White House, and What Their Influence Means for America*. New York: Bloomsbury, 2009.

Bass, Gary J. *The Blood Telegram: Nixon, Kissinger, and a Forgotten Genocide*. New York: Knopf, 2013.

Bennett, M. Todd, ed. *Foreign Relations of the United States, 1969–1976, Volume XXXIV, National Security Policy, 1969–1972*. Washington: US Government Printing Office, 2011.

———, ed. *Foreign Relations of the United States, 1969–1976, Volume XXXV, National Security Policy, 1973–1976*. Washington: US Government Printing Office, 2014.

Berman, Larry. *No Peace, No Honor: Nixon, Kissinger, and Betrayal in Vietnam*. New York: Free Press, 2001.

———. *Zumwalt: The Life and Times of Admiral Elmo Russell "Bud" Zumwalt, Jr.* New York: HarperCollins, 2012.

Bird, Kai. *The Chairman: John J. McCloy; The Making of the American Establishment*. New York: Simon & Schuster, 1992.

———. *The Color of Truth: McGeorge Bundy and William Bundy: Brothers in Arms*. New York: Simon & Schuster, 1998.

Bradlee, Ben. *A Good Life: Newspapering and Other Adventures*. New York: Simon & Schuster, 1995.

Branch, Taylor. *Parting the Waters: America in the King Years 1954–63*. New York: Simon & Schuster, 1988.

———. *Pillar of Fire: America in the King Years, 1963–65*. New York: Simon & Schuster, 1998.

———. *At Canaan's Edge: America in the King Years, 1965–68*. New York: Simon & Schuster, 2006.

———. With Eugene M. Propper. *Labyrinth*. New York: Viking, 1982.

Brinkley, Douglas, and Luke A. Nichter. *The Nixon Tapes*. New York: Houghton Mifflin Harcourt, 2014.

Bundy, William. *A Tangled Web: The Making of Foreign Policy in the Nixon Presidency*. New York: Hill & Wang, 1998.

Califano, Joseph A., Jr. *Inside: A Public and Private Life*. New York: PublicAffairs, 2004.

Carland, John M., ed. *Foreign Relations of the United States, 1969–1976, Volume VIII, Vietnam, January–October 1972*. Washington: US Government Printing Office, 2010.

———. *Foreign Relations of the United States, 1969–1976, Volume IX, Vietnam, October 1972–January 1973*. Washington: US Government Printing Office, 2010.

Cheevers, Jack. *Act of War: Lyndon Johnson, North Korea, and the Capture of the Spy Ship* Pueblo. New York: NAL Caliber, 2013.

Clifford, Clark, with Richard Holbrooke. *Counsel to the President: A Memoir*. New York: Random House, 1991.

Coleman, Bradley Lynn, ed. *Foreign Relations of the United States, 1969–1976, Volume X, Vietnam, January 1973–July 1975*. Washington: US Government Printing Office, 2010.

Colodny, Len, and Robert Gettlin. *Silent Coup: The Removal of a President*. New York: St. Martin's, 1991.

———. And Tom Shachtman. *The Forty Years War: The Rise and Fall of the Neocons, from Nixon to Obama*. New York: HarperCollins, 2009.

Corn, David. *Blond Ghost: Ted Shackley and the CIA's Crusades*. New York: Simon & Schuster, 1994.

Crouse, Timothy. *The Boys on the Bus: Riding with the Campaign Press Corps*. New York: Random House, 1973.

Crowley, Monica. *Nixon Off the Record: His Candid Commentary on People and Politics*. New York: Random House, 1996.

———. *Nixon in Winter*. New York: Random House, 1998.

Cullen, Leslie Julian. *Brown Water Admiral: Elmo R. Zumwalt Jr. and United States Naval Forces Vietnam, 1968–1970*. Lubbock, TX: Texas Tech University, 1998.

Dallek, Robert. *Nixon and Kissinger: Partners in Power*. New York: HarperCollins, 2007.

Dean, John W. *Blind Ambition: The White House Years*. New York: Simon & Schuster, 1976.

Dobrynin, Anatoly. *In Confidence*. New York: Times Books, 1995.

Drea, Edward J. *McNamara, Clifford, and the Burdens of Vietnam, 1965–1969*. Washington: Office of the Secretary of Defense, 2011.

Ellsberg, Daniel. *Secrets: A Memoir of Vietnam and the Pentagon Papers*. New York: Viking, 2002.

Emery, Fred. *Watergate: The Corruption of American Politics and the Fall of Richard Nixon*. New York: Simon & Schuster, 1994.

Feldstein, Mark. *Poisoning The Press: Richard Nixon, Jack Anderson, and the Rise of Washington's Scandal Culture*. New York: Farrar, Straus and Giroux, 2010.

Felt, Mark. *The FBI Pyramid: From the Inside*. New York: G. P. Putnam & Sons, 1979.

Foreign Relations of the United States, 1969–1976, Vols. 1–35, US Government Printing Office, 2003–2014.

Frankel, Max. *The Times of My Life and My Life with* The Times. New York: Random House, 1999.

Gardner, Lloyd C. *Pay Any Price: Lyndon Johnson and the Wars for Vietnam*. Chicago: Ivan R. Dee, 1995.

Gellman, Irwin F. *The Contender: Richard Nixon, The Congress Years, 1946–1952*. New York: Free Press, 1999.

Gentry, Curt. *J. Edgar Hoover: The Man and the Secrets*. New York: W. W. Norton & Company, 1991.

Geyer, David C., ed. *Foreign Relations of the United States, 1969–1976, Volume XL, Germany and Berlin, 1969–1972*. Washington: US Government Printing Office, 2007.

———. *Foreign Relations of the United States, Volume XIII, Soviet Union, October 1970–October 1971*. Washington: US Government Printing Office, 2011.

———, Nina D. Howland and Kent Sieg, eds. *Foreign Relations of the United States, 1969–1976, Volume XIV, Soviet Union, October 1971–May 1972*. Washington: US Government Printing Office, 2006.

Goldman, David and Erin Mahan, eds. *Foreign Relations of the United States, Volume VII, Vietnam, July 1970–January 1972*. Washington: US Government Printing Office, 2010.

Gray, L. Patrick, III, and Ed Gray. *In Nixon's Web: A Year in the Crosshairs of Watergate*. New York: Henry Holt, 2008.

Grose, Peter. *Gentleman Spy: The Life of Allen Dulles*. Boston: Houghton Mifflin, 1994.

Haig, Alexander M. Jr., and Charles McCarry. *Inner Circles: How America Changed the World: A Memoir*. New York: Warner, 1992.

Halberstam, David. *The Powers That Be*. New York: Knopf, 1979.

———. *The Coldest Winter: America and the Korean War*. New York: Hyperion, 2007.

Haldeman, H. R. *The Haldeman Diaries: Inside the Nixon White House*. New York: G. P. Putnam's Sons, 1994.

Helms, Richard, and William Hood. *A Look Over My Shoulder*. New York: Random House, 2003.

Hersh, Seymour. *The Price of Power: Kissinger in the Nixon White House*. New York: Summit, 1983.

Himmelman, Jeff. *Yours in Truth: A Personal Portrait of Ben Bradlee*. New York: Random House, 2012.

Holland, Max. *Leak: Why Mark Felt Became Deep Throat*. Lawrence, KS: University of Kansas Press, 2012.

Hougan, Jim. *Secret Agenda: Watergate, Deep Throat and the CIA*. New York: Random House, 1984.

Howland, Nina, and Craig Daigle, eds. *Foreign Relations of the United States, 1969–1976, Volume XXV, Arab-Israeli Crisis and War, 1973*. Washington: US Government Printing Office, 2011.

Hughes, Ken. *Chasing Shadows: The Nixon Tapes, the Chennault Affair and the Origins of Watergate*. Charlottesville, Va.: University of Virginia Press, 2014.

Humphrey, David C., ed. *Foreign Relations of the United States, 1969–1976, Volume II, Organization and Management of US Foreign Policy, 1969–1972*. Washington: US Government Printing Office, 2006.

———, and James E. Miller, eds. *Foreign Relations of the United States, 1964–1968, Organization and Management of US Foreign Policy; United Nations*. Washington: US Government Printing Office, 2004.

Isaacson, Walter. *Kissinger: A Biography*. New York: Simon & Schuster, 1992.

Jaworski, Leon. *The Right and the Power: The Prosecution of Watergate*. New York: Reader's Digest, 1976.

Jayakar, Pupul. *Indira Gandhi: An Intimate Biography*. New York: Pantheon, 1988.

Johnson, Thomas. *American Cryptology during the Cold War, 1945–1989; Book IV: Cryptologic Rebirth, 1981–1989*. Center for Cryptologic History, National Security Agency, 1999.

Johnson, U. Alexis, with J. O. McAllister. *The Right Hand of Power*. Englewood Cliffs, NJ: Prentice-Hall, 1984.

Karnow, Stanley. *Vietnam: A History*. New York: Viking: 1983.

Keefer, Edward C., and Carolyn Yee, eds. *Foreign Relations of the United States, 1969–1976, Volume VI, Vietnam, January 1969–July 1970*. Washington: US Government Printing Office, 2006.

Kissinger, Henry A. *White House Years*. Boston: Little, Brown, 1979.

———. *Years of Upheaval*, Boston: Little, Brown, 1982.

———. *Years of Renewal*. New York: Simon & Schuster, 1999.

———. *Diplomacy*. New York: Simon & Schuster, 1994.

Krepinevich, Andrew, and Barry Watts. *The Last Warrior: Andrew Marshall and the Shaping of Modern American Defense Strategy*. New York: Basic, 2014.

Krogh, Egil, with Matthew Krogh. *Integrity: Good People, Bad Choices and Life Lessons from the White House*. New York: PublicAffairs, 2007.

Kutler, Stanley I. *The Wars of Watergate: The Last Crisis of Richard Nixon*. New York: Knopf, 1990.

———. *Abuse of Power*, New York: Free Press, 1997.

Lawler, Daniel J., and Erin Mahan, eds. *Foreign Relations of the United States, 1969–1976, Volume XIX, Part 1, Korea, 1969–1972*. Washington: US Government Printing Office, 2010.

———, ed. *Foreign Relations of the United States, 1969–1976, Volume XX, Southeast Asia, 1969–1972*. Washington: US Government Printing Office, 2006.

Lenzner, Terry. *The Investigator: Fifty Years of Uncovering the Truth*. New York: Blue Rider Press, 2013.

Liddy, G. Gordon. *Will: The Autobiography of G. Gordon Liddy*. New York: St. Martin's, 1980.

Lukas, J. Anthony. *Nightmare: The Underside of the Nixon Years*. New York: Viking, 1976.

Maas, Peter. *Manhunt: The Incredible Pursuit of a CIA Agent Turned Terrorist*. New York: Random House, 1986.

MacMillan, Margaret. *Nixon and Mao: The Week That Changed the World*. New York: Random House, 2007.

Mahan, Erin R., ed. *Foreign Relations of the United States, 1969–1976, Volume XII, Soviet Union, January 1969–October 1970*. Washington: US Government Printing Office, 2006.

———, ed. *Foreign Relations of the United States, 1969–1972, Volume XXXII, SALT I, 1969–1972*. Washington: US Government Printing Office, 2010.

———, ed. *Foreign Relations of the United States, 1969–1976, Volume XXXIII, SALT II, 1972–1980*. Washington: US Government Printing Office, 2013.

McElveen, James, and James Siekmeier, eds. *Foreign Relations of the United States, 1969–1976, Volume XXI, Chile, 1969–1973*. Washington: US Government Printing Office, 2014.

Menges, Constantine. *Inside the National Security Council: The True Story of the Making and Unmaking of Reagan's Foreign Policy*. New York: Simon & Schuster, 1988.

Merrill, William H. *Watergate Prosecutor*. East Lansing, MI: Michigan State University Press, 2008.

Miller, James E., and Laurie Van Hook, eds. *Foreign Relations of the United States, 1969–1976, Volume XLI, Western Europe; NATO, 1969–1972*. Washington: US Government Printing Office, 2012.

Mitchell, Greg. *The Campaign of the Century: Upton Sinclair's Race for Governor of California and the Birth of Media Politics*. New York: Random House, 1992.

———. *Tricky Dick and the Pink Lady: Richard Nixon vs. Helen Gahagan Douglas—Sexual Politics and the Red Scare, 1950*. New York: Random House, 1998.

Morris, Roger. *Uncertain Greatness: Henry Kissinger & American Foreign Policy*. New York: Harper & Row, 1977.

———. *Haig: The General's Progress*. Chicago: Playboy Press, 1982.

———. *Richard Milhous Nixon: The Rise of an American Politician*. New York: Henry Holt, 1990.

Newhouse, John. *Cold Dawn: The Story of SALT*. Washington: Pergamon-Brassey's, 1989.

Nixon, Richard. *RN: The Memoirs of Richard Nixon*. New York: Grosset & Dunlap, 1978,

Novak, Robert. *The Prince of Darkness: 50 Years Reporting in Washington*. New York: Crown, 2007.

Perry, Mark. *Four Stars: The Inside Story of the Forty-Year Battle Between the Joint Chiefs of Staff and America's Civilian Leaders*. Boston: Houghton Mifflin, 1989.

Phillips, Steven E., ed. *Foreign Relations of the United States, Volume XVII, China, 1969–1972*. Washington: US Government Printing Office, 2006.

Poole, Walter. *The Joint Chiefs of Staff and National Policy, 1969–1972*. Washington: Office of the Chairman of the Joint Chiefs of Staff, 2013.

Powers, Richard Gid. *Secrecy and Power: The Life of J. Edgar Hoover*. New York: Free Press, 1987.

Powers, Thomas. *The Man Who Kept the Secrets: Richard Helms and the CIA*. New York: Knopf, 1979.

Prados, John. *Keepers of the Keys: The National Security Council from Truman to Bush*. New York: Morros, 1991.

Qaimmaqami, Linda W., and Adam M. Howard, *Foreign Relations of the United States, 1969–1976, Volume XXIV, Middle East Region and Arabian Peninsula, 1969–1972; Jordan, September 1970*. Washington: US Government Printing Office, 2008.

Rhodes, Richard. *Arsenals of Folly: The Making of the Nuclear Arms Race*. New York: Knopf, 2007.

Riebling, Mark. *Wedge: The Secret War Between the FBI and CIA*. New York: Knopf, 1994.

Rodriguez, Felix, and John Weisman. *Shadow Warrior: The CIA Hero of a Hundred Unknown Battles*. New York: Simon & Schuster, 1989.

Rosen, James. *The Strong Man: The Life of John N. Mitchell*. Garden City, NY: Doubleday, 2008.

Selvage, Douglas E., and Melissa Jane Taylor, eds. *Foreign Relations of the United States, 1969–1972, Volume XV, Soviet Union, June 1972–August 1974*. Washington: US Government Printing Office, 2011.

Shawcross, William. *Sideshow: Kissinger, Nixon and the Destruction of Cambodia*. New York: Simon & Schuster, 1979.

Sheehan, Neil. *A Bright Shining Lie: John Paul Vann and America in Vietnam*. New York: Random House, 1988.

Shepard, Alicia. *Woodward and Bernstein: Life in the Shadow of Watergate*. Hoboken, NJ: John Wiley & Sons, 2007.

Short, Philip. *Mao: A Life*. New York: Henry Holt, 1999.

———. *Pol Pot: Anatomy of a Nightmare*. New York: Henry Holt, 2004.

Sirica, John J. *To Set the Record Straight: The Break-in, the Tapes, the Conspirators, the Pardon*. New York: W. W. Norton & Co., 1979.

Smith, Louis J. *Foreign Relations of the United States, 1969–1976, Volume XI, South Asia Crisis, 1971*. Washington: US Government Printing Office, 2005.

Snepp, Frank. *Decent Interval: An Insider's Account of Saigon's Indecent End Told by the CIA's Chief Strategy Analyst in Vietnam*. New York: Random House, 1978.

Snider, L. Britt. *The Agency and the Hill: CIA's Relationship with Congress, 1946–2004*. Washington: Center for the Study of Intelligence, 2008.

Sorley, Lewis. *Thunderbolt: From the Battle of the Bulge to Vietnam and Beyond: General Creighton Abrams and the Army of His Times*. Herndon, VA: Brassey's, 1992.

Stanford, Phil. *White House Call Girl: The Real Watergate Story*. Port Townsend, WA: Feral House, 2013.

Stone, Roger, with Mike Colapietro. *Nixon's Secrets: The Rise, Fall, and Untold Truth about the President, Watergate, and the Pardon*. New York: Skyhorse, 2014.

Strober, Gerald, and Deborah Hart Strober. *Nixon: An Oral History of His Presidency*. New York: HarperCollins, 1994.

Sullivan, William C., with Bill Brown. *The Bureau: My Thirty Years in Hoover's FBI*. New York: W. W. Norton & Co., 1979.

Talbott, Strobe. *The Master of the Game: Paul Nitze and the Nuclear Peace*. New York: Knopf, 1988.

Tanenhaus, Sam. *Whittaker Chambers: A Biography*. New York: Random House, 1997.

Thomas, Evan. *The Man to See: The Life of Edward Bennett Williams*. New York: Simon & Shuster, 1992.

Ungar, Sanford. *FBI: An Uncensored Look Behind the Walls*. Boston: Little, Brown, 1976.

Van Atta, Dale. *With Honor: Melvin Laird in War, Peace, and Politics*. Madison: University of Wisconsin Press, 2008.

Walters, Vernon A. *Silent Missions*. Garden City, NY, Doubleday, 1978.

Webb, William J. *The Joint Chiefs of Staff and the War in Vietnam 1969–1970*. Washington: Office of the Chairman of the Joint Chiefs of Staff, 2002.

———, and Walter Poole. *The Joint Chiefs of Staff and the War in Vietnam 1971–1973*. Washington: Office of the Chairman of the Joint Chiefs of Staff, 2007.

Weiner, Tim. *Legacy of Ashes: The History of the CIA*. New York: Random House, 2007.

———. *Enemies: A History of the FBI*. New York: Random House, 2012.

Weinstein, Allen. *Perjury: The Hiss-Chambers Case*. New York: Random House, 1978.

Woodward, Bob. *Bush at War*. New York, Simon & Schuster, 2002.

———. *The Commanders*. New York: Simon & Schuster, 1991.

———. *Plan of Attack*. New York: Simon & Schuster, 2004.

———. *State of Denial*. New York: Simon & Schuster, 2006.

———. *The Secret Man: The Story of Watergate's Deep Throat*. New York: Simon & Schuster, 2005.

———. *Veil*. New York: Simon & Schuster, 1987.

Woodward, Bob, and Carl Bernstein. *All the President's Men*. New York: Simon & Schuster, 1974.

———. *The Final Days*. New York: Simon & Schuster, 1976.

Worley, D. Robert. *Orchestrating the Instruments of Power: A Critical Examination of the US National Security System*. Raleigh, NC: Lulu Press, 2012.

Zumwalt, Elmo R., Jr., *On Watch: A Memoir*. New York: Quadrangle, 1976.

ARTICLES

Armour, Lawrence A. "Unraveling the Watergate Grab-Bag," *Wall Street Journal*, June 10, 1974.

Associated Press. "New Book Insists That Watergate's Deep Throat Is Reporters' Invention," *St. Louis Post-Dispatch*, September 27, 1998.

"A Telltale Tape Deepens Nixon's Dilemma," *Time*, January 22, 1974.

Barringer, Felicity. "An Author Questions the Existence of Deep Throat, Watergate's Man in the Shadows," *New York Times*, September 21, 1998.

Barry, James A. "Managing Covert Political Action," *Orbis: A Journal of World Affairs*, Summer 1993.

Best, Richard A., Jr. "The National Security Council: An Organizational Assessment," Congressional Research Service, December 28, 2011.

Burr, William, and Jeffrey Kimball. "Nixon's Nuclear Ploy," *Bulletin of the Atomic Scientists* 59, no. 1 (January–February 2003).

Churcher, Sharon, and Barry Wigmore. "All the President's Con Men?" *Daily Mail*, June 12, 2005.

Coulter, Ann. "Deep Throat's Best-Kept Secret: He Didn't Really Exist," *San Gabriel Valley Tribune*, June 13, 2005.

"Dirty, but Surely Beyond Tricks," *Time*, October 15, 1973.

Ferguson, Andrew. "Watergate-Gate," *Commentary*, April 2012.

"Fight over the Future of the FBI, The," *Time*, March 26, 1973.

Gerth, Jeff. "Richard M. Nixon and Organized Crime," *Penthouse*, July 1974.

Goldberg, Jonah. "Please Reveal All the Reporters' Moles," *Kansas City Star*, February 24, 2005.

Greenberg, David. "Throat Clearing," *Slate*, June 1, 2005.

Hersh, Seymour M. "The Pardon," *The Atlantic*, August 1983.

Hougan, Jim. "The McCord File," *Harper's*, January 1980.

Kraft, Joseph. "Untangling the Wiretap Puzzle," *San Francisco Chronicle*, June 29, 1974.

Lardner Jr., George. "Krogh Secrecy Ordered, Attorney Says," *Washington Post*, November 14, 1973.

Logan, Cedric. "The FISA Wall and Federal Investigations," *New York University Journal of Law & Liberty*, 2009.

McGowan, Richard J. "Watergate Revisited," *The Barnes Review*, March/April 2003.

Minzesheimer, Bob. "25 Years of Chasing Deep Throat," *USA TODAY*, June 24, 1999.

Noah, Timothy. "John Dean Says Deep Throat Was Not a G-Man," *Slate*, June 17, 2002.

———. "Yes, Virginia, There Is a Deep Throat," *Slate*, May 8, 2002.

O'Connor, John D. "I'm the Guy They Called Deep Throat," *Vanity Fair*, July 2005.

"Questions About Gray," *Time*, March 5, 1973.

Sagan, Scott D., and Jeremi Suri. "The Madman Nuclear Alert: Secrecy, Signaling and Safety in October 1969," *International Security* 27, no. 4.

Schwartz, Jerry. "Decades Pass, but Watergate Scandal's Deep Throat Remains a Deep Secret," Associated Press, May 6, 2002.

"Secret Files of J. Edgar Hoover, The," *US News and World Report*, December 19, 1983.

Sorley, Lewis. "The Real Afghan Lessons from Vietnam," *Wall Street Journal*, October 11, 2009.

Stayton, Richard. "Fade In," *Written By*, April/May 2011.

"*Tavoulareas v. Piro*: An Extensive Exercise in Judgment," *The George Washington Law Review*, May 1988.

Thimmesch, Nick. "The Iron Mentor of the Pentagon," *Washington Post*, March 2, 1975.

Thompson, Bob. "The Hersh Alternative," *Washington Post*, January 28, 2001.

Van Riper, Frank. "FBI and Political Spying," *New York Daily News*, October 13, 1973.

"Watergate Three, The," *Time*, May 7, 1973.

Willon, Phil, and Michael Fechter. "Watergate: The Untold Story," *Tampa Tribune*, January 19, 1997.

Woodward, Bob. "Ex-CIA Aide, 3 Cuban Exiles Focus of Letelier Inquiry," *Washington Post*, April 12, 1977.

———. "CIA Director Fires 2 Mid-Level Employees," *Washington Post*, April 27, 1977.

GOVERNMENT DOCUMENTS

CIA visitor logs, Vernon Walters, 1972–1976.
White House telephone logs, John Dean, 1971–1973.

LEGAL DOCUMENTS

Phillip Mackin Bailley v. The Inmate Committee, Western District of Washington, 1999.
Maureen K. Dean and John W. Dean v. St. Martin's Press, et al., US District Court, District of Columbia, 1992, Michael Douglas Caddy deposition, March 29, 1994.
United States of America v. John Doe, US District Court, District of Columbia, 1974, Richard Nixon grand jury testimony, June 23, 1975.
United States v. Felt, Gray, Miller.
United States v. Krogh, motion for discovery, October 31, 1973.
United States v. G. Gordon Liddy, US District Court, District of Columbia, transcript of interview with Al Baldwin.
United States v. Edwin Paul Wilson, Southern District of Texas, opinion on conviction, October 27, 2003.

INTERVIEWS, ORAL HISTORIES, AND TRANSCRIPTS

Association for Diplomatic Studies and Training
John Holdridge, Richard Kennedy, Winston Lord, Peter Rodman, Harold Saunders, William Watts

Author Interviews
Joseph Califano, Beverly Gage, Walter Pincus, Richard Gid Powers

Colodny Collection
Alexander Butterfield, John Dean, John Ehrlichman, Michael Getler, H. R. Haldeman, Seymour Hersh, Neille Russell, Donald Stewart, Dan Thomasson, Bob Woodward, Ronald Ziegler

Johnson Library
Cartha "Deke" DeLoach

Nixon Library
Joseph Califano, Alexander Haig, H. R. Haldeman, Tom Charles Huston, Egil Krogh, John Lehman, Elliot Richardson, William Ruckelshaus, James Schlesinger

Society of Former Special Agents of the FBI
Cartha "Deke" DeLoach

Other Sources
Bernstein, Carl, and Bob Woodward, Meet the Press, NBC, August 8, 1999.
Mitchell, John, interview with Stanley Kutler, February 9, 1988.

REPORTS

Best, Richard A. Jr., *The National Security Council: An Organizational Assessment*, Congressional Research Service, December 28, 2011.
Chile: Implications of the Letelier Case. Central Intelligence Agency, May 1978.
Chinese Cultural Revolution, The, National Intelligence Estimate, 13-7-67, US Intelligence Board, May 25, 1967.

Chinese Reactions to Certain Courses of Action in Indochina, Special National Intelligence Estimate 13-10-70, US Intelligence Board, June 11, 1970.

Clandestine Introduction of Nuclear Weapons into the US, The, National Intelligence Estimate 4-70, US Intelligence Board, July 7, 1970.

Communist China and Asia, Special National Intelligence Estimate, US Intelligence Board, March 6, 1969.

Communist China's Military Policy and Its General Purpose and Air Defense Forces, National Intelligence Estimate 13-3-67, US Intelligence Board, April 6, 1967.

Cronin, John. *The Problem of American Communism in 1945; Facts and Recommendations.*

Final Report of the Select Committee to Study Governmental Operations with Respect to Intelligence Activities, US Senate, Book I, Foreign and Military Intelligence, 1976.

Final Report of the Select Committee to Study Governmental Operations with Respect to Intelligence Activities, US Senate, Book II, Intelligence Activities and the Rights of Americans, 1976.

Final Report of the Select Committee to Study Governmental Operations with Respect to Intelligence Activities, US Senate, Book III, Supplementary Detailed Staff Reports on Intelligence Activities and the Rights of Americans, 1976.

Final Report of the Select Committee to Study Governmental Operations with Respect to Intelligence Activities, US Senate, Book IV, Supplementary Detailed Staff Reports on Foreign and Military Intelligence, 1976.

Final Report of the Select Committee to Study Governmental Operations with Respect to Intelligence Activities, US Senate, Book V, The Investigation of the Assassination of President John F. Kennedy: Performance of the Intelligence Agencies, 1976.

Final Report of the Select Committee to Study Governmental Operations with Respect to Intelligence Activities, US Senate, Book VI, Supplementary Reports on Intelligence Activities, 1976.

Kraemer, Fritz G. A. "US Propaganda: What It Can and Can't Be," *Readings in Counter-Guerrilla Operations, 1961.*

North Korean Intentions and Capabilities with Respect to South Korea, Special National Intelligence Estimate 14.2-67, US Intelligence Board, September 21, 1967.

Official History of the Bay of Pigs Operation, Volume I, Air Operations, March 1960–April 1961, Central Intelligence Agency, September 1979.

Official History of the Bay of Pigs Operation, Volume II, Participation in the Conduct of Foreign Policy, Central Intelligence Agency, October 1979.

Official History of the Bay of Pigs Operation, Volume III, Evolution of CIA's Anti-Castro Policies, 1959–January 1961, December 1979.

Outlook for Cambodia, The, Special National Intelligence Estimate 57-70, US Intelligence Board, August 6, 1970.

Outlook for Chile under Allende, The, Special National Intelligence Estimate 94-71, US Intelligence Board, August 4, 1971.

Outlook from Hanoi: Factors Affecting North Vietnam's Policy in the War in Vietnam, The, Special National Intelligence Estimate, 14.3-70, US Intelligence Board, February 5, 1970.

Potential for Revolution in Latin America, The, National Intelligence Estimate 80/90-68, US Intelligence Board, March 28, 1968.

Security Conditions in Five Countries of the Western Pacific Area, Special National Intelligence Estimate, 40/50-66, US Intelligence Board, October 13, 1966.

Short Term Political Prospects in Panama, Special National Intelligence Estimate, 84-65, US Intelligence Board, December 21, 1965.

Short-Term Prospect for Cambodia, The, Special National Intelligence Estimate 57-73, US Intelligence Board, May 24, 1973.

Soviet Approach to Summit II, The, National Intelligence Estimate 11-9-73, US Intelligence Board, June 1, 1973.

Soviet Capabilities for Strategic Attack, National Intelligence Estimate, 11-8-66, US Intelligence Board, October 20, 1966.

Soviet Capabilities for Strategic Attack, National Intelligence Estimate, 11-8-67, US Intelligence Board, October 26, 1967.

Soviet Economic Problems and Prospects, National Intelligence Estimate 11-5-67, US Intelligence Board, May 25, 1967.

Soviet Forces for Intercontinental Attack, National Intelligence Estimate, 11-8-70, US Intelligence Board, November 24, 1970.

Soviet Forces for Intercontinental Attack, National Intelligence Estimate, 11-8-71, US Intelligence Board, October 21, 1971.

Soviet Nuclear Programs, National Intelligence Estimate, 11-2A-69, US Intelligence Board, July 3, 1969.

Soviet Space Program, The, National Intelligence Estimate 11-1-69, US Intelligence Board, March 26, 1970.

Soviet Strategic Attack Forces, National Intelligence Estimate, 11-8-68, US Intelligence Board, June 23, 1969.

Soviet Strategic Attack Forces, National Intelligence Estimate, 11-9-69, US Intelligence Board, September 9, 1969.

Soviet Strategic Defenses, National Intelligence Estimate, 11-3-69, US Intelligence Board, October 2, 1969.

"Unauthorized Disclosure of Classified Defense Information Appearing in the Jack Anderson Columns in *The Washington Post* dated December 14 and December 16, 1971," Young report.

USSR and China, The, National Intelligence Estimate 11/13-69, US Intelligence Board, August 12, 1969.

USSR and the Egyptian-Israeli Confrontation, The, Special National Intelligence Estimate 30-70, US Intelligence Board, May 14, 1970.

Index

About the Author

Ray Locker is the Washington enterprise editor of *USA Today*. Before joining *USA Today*, he was an editor, reporter, and columnist for the Associated Press, *Los Angeles Times*, *Tampa Tribune*, and *Montgomery* (Alabama) *Advertiser*. He and his family live in North Bethesda, Maryland.